RSM Tenon Financial Management Limited
Personal Financial Planning Manual 2010/11

RSM Tenon Financial Management Limited

Personal Financial Planning Manual

2010/11

Twenty-sixth edition

Editor **John White** ACII, Chartered Insurance Practitioner

RSM Tenon Financial Management Limited

Bloomsbury Professional

Bloomsbury Professional Ltd, Maxwelton House, 41–43 Boltro Road, Haywards Heath, West Sussex, RH16 1BJ

© RSM Tenon Financial Management Limited 2010

A CIP Catalogue record for this book is available from the British Library.

ISBN: 978 1 84766 521 8

Typeset by Phoenix Photosetting, Chatham, Kent
Printed and bound in Great Britain by CPI Antony Rowe, Chippenham, Wilts

Preface

Welcome to the 26th edition of the RSM Tenon Financial Management Limited Personal Financial Planning Manual designed to help both practitioners and individuals who want to maximise their wealth in the most tax efficient manner possible and plan for the most secure future over varying lifecycles. The manual is designed to help you get some of the basics right with useful updates on ensuring a thorough and robust financial planning process and the essential inclusion of tax planning.

Although the manual will be of interest and benefit to you it should not replace the value of time out with a trusted private client adviser who will ensure you have a planned strategy to meet your financial aspirations in the short- and long-term future.

We are all busy individuals running our businesses, families, portfolios, estates or just enjoying our life, there are so many aspects of the personal financial advice and tax planning that are forgotten about and this manual concentrates on giving an up-to-date view of the areas that are important to individuals at whatever stage of life they are at.

Updates in this year's edition cover have had to be reviewed twice due to the change in government and the budget amendments our new leaders have made. It is interesting times with a coalition government that is new to most of us however they still have the same global problems to deal with. These will require continued high tax rates and reducing state benefits as well as increasing the burden of pension provision for the future on the individuals. Early planning now could save us all some financial hardship in the future.

We can all take advantage of the new ISA limits and those paid over £100,000 need to be very careful with the advice they take as the wrong type of investment or the amount can affect their tax payments with the new rules relating to pension planning. General reading of the tax section to review opportunities to minimise the ever increasing tax burden will be your most valuable time spent this year.

This financial year 2010/11 continues to challenge us all as financial planning in a still depressed economic climate is always difficult. Striking a balance between debt reduction and investing for the future is incredibly difficult. We have still not hit the positive growth cycle in the economy that I hoped would be with us by now when writing this last year so prudence in planning for the future remains key.

The Manual

The purpose of this manual continues to be to provide financial advisers with a source of reference and as a starting point to establish key concepts.

A summary of the principal features is provided at the beginning of each section, followed by further details, cross references and statutory references.

As in previous years we would welcome feedback from readers of the manual in respect of the content and the layout.

The sequence of this manual is as follows:

The introductory section contains sections on the Regulatory Framework and Planning. The planning section provides a consideration of the financial planning process and gives a broad review of some of the initial considerations an adviser is likely to have to take into account when considering a client's situation and needs.

Part 1, Insurance considers the various types of insurance contracts, including those which might be used to provide protection for individuals in the event of either their death or if they become ill. Insurance products, the primary intent of which are savings and investment, are within Part 3 which deals with investments.

Part 2, Retirement Planning outlines the pension arrangements which are likely to be appropriate for the majority of individuals. The Introduction and Planning sections at the beginning and end of Part 2 provide useful overviews, with details of specific schemes in the intervening sections.

Part 3, Investments provides an outline of the more widely-encountered types of investment arrangements currently available within the UK, including insurance based savings and investment plans.

Part 4, Tax Planning has detailed sections on Income Tax, Capital Gains Tax and Inheritance Tax.

Part 5, The Life Cycle seeks to lead the adviser through the key matters faced by most individuals in different stages of their lives.

The Advisory Team

Thanks are made to both the financial management and the tax team within RSM Tenon.

Special thanks for their contribution to:

RSM Tenon Financial Management Limited

Amy Matson, Andrew Bucklow, Caroline Bodkin, Chris Wise, Dawn Johnson, Iain Newton, Ian Gibson, Malcolm Washburn, Peter O'Sullivan, Sarah Hore and Vinodh Josh.

RSM Tenon tax department

Sharon Omer-Kaye, Graham Wainwright, Nick Waterhouse-Brown, Lucia Fellino and Stephanie Churchill.

The editor and contributors cannot be held responsible for any loss resulting from anything in this manual in any circumstances.

The law is as stated at July 2010.

JOHN WHITE ACII, Chartered Insurance Practitioner

RSM Tenon Financial Management Limited Contact Details

BASINGSTOKE

Clifton House
Bunnian Place
Basingstoke
Hampshire
RG21 7JE

Tel: 01256 370370
Fax: 01256 370380

BIRMINGHAM

Charterhouse
Legge Street
Birmingham
B4 7EU

Tel: 0121 3333100
Fax: 0121 3591848

BRISTOL

Howard House
Queens Avenue
Clifton
Bristol
BS8 1QT

Tel: 0117 925 9255
Fax: 0117 980 6900

CHORLEY

Sumner House
St Thomas's Road
Chorley
Lancashire
PR7 1HP

Tel: 01257 518000
Fax: 01257 518001

GLASGOW

2–4 Blythswood Square
Glasgow
G2 4AD

Tel: 0141 272 8000
Fax: 0141 272 8001

GLASGOW

Spectrum Building
7th Floor
55 Blythswood Street
Glasgow
G2 7AT

Tel: 0141 2853300
Fax: 0870 1973268

HARROGATE

The Hamlet
Hornbeam Park
Harrogate
HG2 8RE

Tel: 01423 859459
Fax: 01423 859460

LEEDS

2 Wellington Place
Leeds
LS1 4AP

Tel: 0113 244 5451
Fax: 0113 242 6308

LONDON (Chiltern Street)

66 Chiltern Street
London
W1U 4JT

Tel: 020 7535 1400
Fax: 020 7535 1401

LONDON (Moorfields)

45 Moorfields
London
EC2Y 9AE

Tel: 0207 920 3200
Fax: 0207 920 3201

MANCHESTER
York House
York Street
Manchester
M2 3BB

Tel: 0161 200 6080
Fax: 0161 200 9047

MILTON KEYNES

Cedar House
Breckland
Linford Wood
Milton Keynes
MK14 6EX

Tel: 01908 577 450
Fax: 01908 577 451

NOTTINGHAM

The Poynt
45 Wollaton Street
Nottingham
NG1 5FW

Tel: 0115 948 9400
Fax: 0115 948 9401

STOKE

5 Ridge House
Ridge House Drive, Festival Park
Stoke on Trent
ST1 5SJ

Tel: 01782 262121
Fax: 01782 287246

SUNDERLAND

RSM Tenon House
Ferryboat Lane
Sunderland
SR5 3JN

Tel: 0191 511 5000
Fax: 0191 511 5001

TELFORD

3 Hollinswood Court
Stafford Park 1
Telford
TF3 3DE

Tel: 01952 290244
Fax: 01952 290006

WINDSOR

Amberley Place
107– 111 Peascod Street
Windsor
SL4 1TE

Tel: 01753 754400
Fax: 01753 754401

Contents

How to Use the Manual

The manual is split into five main *parts*:
   Insurance
   Retirement Planning
   Investments
   Tax Planning
   The Life Cycle
Each part commences with a list of the *contents* and an *introduction* to the subject matter of that part. Each introduction is specific to that part, thus the introduction to:

- Insurance, sets out the main planning areas to consider both for individuals and businesses.
- Retirement Planning, outlines the main types of retirement provision and planning opportunities for various events.
- Investments, deals with the major considerations in planning a portfolio.
- Tax Planning, explains the key provisions of income tax, capital gains tax and inheritance tax and the strategies to consider.
- The Life Cycle, considers some of the changes in circumstances that a family might face from the cradle to the grave.

There then follow the various planning concepts and ideas, each one being dealt with as a separate *section*. Where possible, each section keeps to a set format. Most sections commence with a *box* containing brief details of the key features of that section. Further, more *detailed information* follows the box. A typical section appears as follows:

Description	A brief description of the topic being covered
Ages	The minimum and maximum age requirement (if any)
Suitable for	The most suitable type of individual
Advantages and Disadvantages	Short notes on the advantages or benefits and disadvantages or problems in taking the action described
Charges	Brief details of possible costs
Investment limits	The minimum and maximum sums which are allowed by the plan or which are commercially sensible

FURTHER DETAILS

Commercial Aspects

This amplifies the brief details and description and adds further information.

Taxation Aspects

Contains the taxation treatment of that particular plan. The rules are usually technical and professional advice is normally advisable before embarking upon a particular course of action.

CROSS REFERENCES

These refer to other sections which may be helpful in considering the alternatives.

At the end of the parts on insurance, retirement planning and investments, a brief glossary of many of the main terms used within those fields has been included.

Planning

Each individual's circumstances are unique and any financial plan should be tailored to reflect a person's individual needs.

The purpose of this part of the manual is to outline the process of personal financial planning and to show how the plan then needs to evolve to take into account an individual's changing circumstances.

The remainder of the manual is devoted to specific areas of personal financial planning.

PERSONAL FINANCIAL PLANNING: ITS MEANING AND PURPOSE

One definition of personal financial planning is:

'the establishment and development of a comprehensive financial plan that is tailored to an individual's needs and which maximises and protects financial resources, and is adapted to meet that individual's changing circumstances during the various stages of his or her life.'

THE PERSONAL FINANCIAL PLANNING PROCESS

In order to ensure that a financial plan will meet an individual's needs and requirements, it is important to have a systematic planning process.

It is generally accepted that the following stages are involved:
(a) assembling the information;
(b) establishing and agreeing financial objectives, intentions and attitude to risk;
(c) processing and analysing the information;
(d) constructing a comprehensive plan with recommendations;
(e) implementing the recommendations and the plan;
(f) reviewing and updating the plan.

(a) Assembling the Information

The information required will obviously vary from person to person. An individual with substantial wealth who is married with children will have considerably more data than an individual who is single and has only just started their career.

The 'fact find' is an important tool in ensuring that all the necessary information is obtained and an example of the form is provided on p xxv.

(b) Establishing and Agreeing Financial Objectives

In order to prepare a comprehensive personal financial plan, it is not sufficient to look only at an individual's current situation or at one aspect in isolation. It is the responsibility of the adviser to assist an individual in establishing realistic financial objectives which are measurable in terms of amount and in terms of potential attainment as well as the priority given to each.

It is very important at this stage to establish an individual's future intentions, goals and ideals, marital status, number of dependants and business prospects, etc.

It is also important to ascertain an individual's attitude to making investments in terms of risk, time frames, and ethical considerations etc.

(c)   Processing and Analysing the Information

Having obtained all the necessary information and having discussed an individual's objectives with him/her, it is likely to be appropriate to prepare:

1   A statement of the individual's current financial position, setting out what the individual owns, what is owed and therefore what his/her net worth is, ie assets less liabilities.

2   A cash flow statement setting out the individual's regular income and outflows and confirming whether there is surplus income to invest or a need to supplement income out of assets etc.

(d)   Constructing a Comprehensive Plan with Recommendations

Based on the individual's stated financial objectives, the adviser will then consider whether existing assets need to be re-ordered and decide which investment products are appropriate to meet the individual's needs.

The plan will then be written up and presented to the individual. The content of the plan is likely to include the following.

Current Financial Position

The individual's assets, liabilities, liquidity, future inheritances etc will be set out in a series of schedules and will include the statement of current financial position and the cash flow statement referred to above. This is intended to provide the individual with an overview of his/her current situation.

The individual's tax position will also need to be fully taken into account as part of the planning process.

Recommendations

The plan will summarise the recommendations and the actions which the individual needs to take to meet his/her financial goals and objectives. He/she will therefore have a concise summary of what actions are needed before reading the other parts of the plan in detail.

Some personal financial advisers set out their recommendations at the end but this is a matter of personal preference.

In addition, where regulated financial products are being recommended, the plan will explain why the adviser has concluded that the transaction is considered to be 'suitable'.

Disability and Death

The individual's situation and that of his/her family will be considered and appropriate recommendations made according to their perceived needs.

Retirement Provisions

The plan will set out what provision has been made to date and what shortfall has been identified based on the individual's stated objectives. The plan will then set out the course of action required to make good the gap in future income needs from the date of anticipated retirement.

Investment Strategy

This section of the plan will concentrate on the individual's existing investments, and show how these might be re-ordered to provide the required level of capital growth/income, based on the level of risk, time frame and ethical considerations that the individual may have as well as his tax position.

Estate Planning

Based on the individual's existing assets, the current IHT liabilities can be calculated and recommendations put forward in terms of mitigating IHT in appropriate ways, having regard to the individual's preferences and objectives.

Other Areas

An individual is likely to have personal borrowings, the principal one of which will be a mortgage on his/her house. It may be appropriate to put forward recommendations in terms of how the existing borrowings can be restructured to improve their efficiency. The individual may also have school fee commitments in which case the plan will outline the extent of the individual's need to provide for these over and above the provision already made to date (if any) and put forward recommendations in terms of meeting the shortfall.

Illustrations and Quotations

Where these are enclosed, they must comply with the relevant regulatory requirements. In particular, aside from providing key features documents etc, clear explanations of the purpose of each investment should be provided.

Appendices

If the plan is complex, it may well be appropriate to have the various appendices at the end although this is very much a matter of preference and some personal financial advisers may find it more appropriate to have the appendices at the end of each section of the plan.

(e)   Implementing the Recommendations and the Plan

Once the adviser and individual have discussed the plan and have the adviser's recommendations, the appropriate steps need to be taken to implement them. Among other things these will include the following.

The Completion and Processing of Insurance, Pension and Investment Product Applications and Proposals

Most advisers assist individuals in completing proposals and applications. It is important to ensure that all the relevant information and details are provided and for this reason, it is good practice for the adviser to give the individual a photocopy of the forms concerned.

The applications for life insurance, permanent health insurance and critical illness will need to be medically underwritten as will any life insurance taken out in conjunction with pension arrangements or waiver of premium benefits etc. The adviser's administrative colleagues will be responsible for ensuring that these procedures are efficiently carried out and that the individual's wishes relating to the location for medical examinations etc are duly observed.

In addition, where financial evidence is required to support proposals, for example in the area of key person assurance, the adviser will need to co-ordinate the preparation of the required information before it is submitted to underwriters.

The adviser will also need to co-ordinate the preparation of trust documentation and oversee the process of negotiating with the Pensions Schemes Office as and where this is required.

Once issued, the policy documentation should be carefully checked to ensure that it is technically and factually correct before it is despatched to the individual.

Documenting the Arrangements

It is important that all the relevant information advice and considerations leading to that advice are properly documented. In particular, the client should receive a proper summary so that it can be used as a source of reference in the future.

(f)   Reviewing and Updating the Plan

All plans need to be reviewed and updated. How regularly this is done will depend on the individual's differing needs and requirements and what is specifically agreed. Usually, it is necessary to review circumstances at least every two years and probably annually.

The reviews will take into account any changes in circumstances, for example a change of job, a new addition to the family, inheritances as well as changes required as a result of legislation, in particular taxation.

The review process provides an adviser with a regular opportunity to renew and build on the relationship with the individual and is likely to be a source of further business.

Regulatory Framework

FINANCIAL SERVICES AND MARKETS ACT 2000

The Financial Services and Markets Act 2000 (FSMA) was enacted on 14 June 2000. The FSMA provides the framework within which a single regulator for the financial services industry, the Financial Services Authority (FSA), will operate. It equips the FSA with a full range of statutory powers and creates the Financial Services and Markets Tribunal. The Act also establishes the framework for single ombudsman and compensation schemes to provide further protection for consumers. The FSA took on full responsibility as a single regulator from 1 December 2001. The FSMA provides, amongst other things, for:

- the constitution and accountability of the FSA;
- the definition of the scope of regulated activities;
- the control of financial promotion;
- powers of the FSA to authorise, regulate, investigate and discipline authorised persons;
- the recognition of investment exchanges and clearing houses;
- arrangements for the approval of controllers and the performance of regulated activities;
- the provision of financial services provided by members of the professions;
- regulation and marketing of collective investment schemes;
- certain criminal offences;
- powers to impose penalties for market abuse; and
- the transfer to the FSA of registration functions in respect of building societies, friendly societies, industrial and provident societies and certain other mutual societies.

Businesses authorised and regulated under the Act include:

- banks;
- building societies;
- insurance companies;
- friendly societies;
- credit unions;
- Lloyd's;
- investment and pensions advisers;
- stockbrokers;
- professional firms offering certain types of investment services;
- fund managers;
- derivatives traders;
- mortgage lenders;
- mortgage advisers;
- general insurance advisers.

The regulation of financial services has, historically, been the responsibility of a range of different bodies:

- the Securities and Investment Board (SIB);

- the Self-Regulating Organisations (SROs), most recently: the Personal Investment Authority (PIA), the Investment Management Regulatory Organisation (IMRO) and the Securities and Futures Authority (SFA);
- the former Supervision and Surveillance Branch of the Bank of England;
- the Building Societies Commission (BSC);
- the Insurance Directorate of the Treasury;
- the Friendly Societies Commission (FSC);
- the Registry of Friendly Societies.

These functions are now carried out by the FSA as the single regulator. The Government announced proposals to introduce legislation to reform the regulation of financial services in May 1997. Subsequently, steps were taken to transfer responsibility for regulation to the FSA when this was established on 27 October 1997 as the successor to the SIB. This enabled the FSA to bring together the staff of the predecessor regulators at its offices in Canary Wharf and to organise itself in a way that reflects the future regulatory arrangements.

Certain functions under the Banking Act 1987 were transferred by the Bank of England Act 1998. In other cases, the FSA entered into contracts with the relevant bodies to perform regulatory functions on their behalf pending Royal Assent and implementation of the provisions of the Act. For example, the Treasury contracted with the FSA to perform certain functions under the Insurance Companies Act 1982. The FSA also took on the function of UK competent authority for listing quoted companies from the Stock Exchange on 1 May 2000.

The Act broadly continues the regime for recognised investment exchanges and clearing houses under the Financial Services Act 1986, although FSA powers under the Act are wider than those under the predecessor legislation.

The FSA regulates the Lloyd's insurance market, and has powers of direction over the Council of Lloyd's, although the latter will retain its responsibilities under Lloyd's Acts for the superintendence and governance of the Society of Lloyd's.

The recognised professional bodies regime under the FSA 1986 has ceased to operate. Professional firms (such as solicitors, accountants and actuaries) carrying on mainstream regulated activities are authorised and regulated directly by the FSA. However, some categories of professional firm benefit from an exclusion from the scope of regulation under the Act, subject to arm's-length oversight by, and certain powers of, the FSA. The Act does not affect the professional bodies' wider powers to regulate the professional activities of members of their respective professions.

The Act has coordinated and modernised financial regulatory arrangements established under a number of different enactments:

- Credit Unions Act 1979;
- Insurance Companies Act 1982;
- Financial Services Act 1986;
- Building Societies Act 1986;
- Banking Act 1987;
- Friendly Societies Act 1992.

Those enactments were generally supplemented by secondary legislation or rules. When the Act came into force, the powers conferred by the Act were used to repeal, or substantially repeal, the relevant parts of that legislation and the rules and regulations made under it. Other enactments which were also repealed, or substantially repealed, include the Policyholders

Protection Acts 1975–97; Industrial Assurance Acts 1923–48; and the Insurance Brokers Registration Act 1977.

The Act also provided for the transfer to the FSA and the Treasury of the remaining functions, including functions relating to the registration of mutual societies, of the Building Societies Commission, the Friendly Societies Commission and the Registry of Friendly Societies.

In summary, the FSA regulates and authorises:
- all financial businesses;
- unit trusts and OEICs.

It recognises and supervises:
- investment exchanges;
- clearing houses.

FSA Approach

The FSMA gave the FSA four statutory objectives:
- maintaining market confidence;
- promoting public understanding of the financial system;
- protecting consumers;
- reducing the potential for financial crime.

To meet these four objectives the FSA:
- focus on the financial position of firms and their conduct of business;
- improve the information and advice available to customers and promoting improvements in financial literacy;
- develop risk management measures to protect consumers;
- focus on money laundering, fraud and dishonesty and criminal market misconduct.

When the FSA were preparing for their new powers, which they received on 1 December 2001, their activities included:
- the development of a single handbook detailing the requirements for regulated people;
- grandfathering to ensure a smooth transition for firms regulated under the current regime;
- developing an integrated risk assessment framework to analyse risks arising from any source;
- establishing a new organisational structure;
- preparation of indicators for performance measurement;
- piloted thematic regulation on –
  - the impact of low inflation;
  - after point of sale treatment of customers;
  - money laundering;
  - e-commerce.

Under the FSMA the FSA has powers to investigate matters including:
- regulatory concerns about authorised firms and individuals employed by them;
- suspected misleading statements and practices under s 397 of the FSMA;
- suspected contraventions of the general prohibitions under s 19 of the FSMA and related offences; and
- suspected offences under various other provisions of the FSMA.

The FSA's powers of information gathering and investigation are set out in Part XI of the FSMA.

The FSA's powers to take enforcement action include power to:
- discipline authorised firms under Part XIV of the FSMA and approved persons under s 66 of the same Act;
- prohibit an individual from being employed in connection with a regulated activity, under s 56 of the 2000 Act.

Core Statements of Principle

The core principles which the FSA require regulated firms to observe are:

Integrity

1   A firm must conduct its business with integrity.

Skill, Care and Diligence

2   A firm must conduct its business with due skill, care and diligence.

Management and Control

3   A firm must take reasonable care to organise and control its affairs responsibly and effectively, with adequate risk management systems.

Financial Prudence

4   A firm must maintain adequate financial resources.

Market Conduct

5   A firm must observe proper standards of market conduct.

Customers' Interests

6   A firm must pay due regard to the interests of its customers and treat them fairly.

Communications with Clients

7   A firm must pay due regard to the information needs of its clients, and communicate information to them in a way which is clear, fair and not misleading.

Conflicts of Interest

8   A firm must manage conflicts of interest fairly, both between itself and its customers and between a customer and another client.

Customers: Relationships of Trust

9   A firm must take reasonable care to ensure the suitability of its advice and discretionary decisions for any customer who is entitled to rely upon its judgement.

Clients' Assets

10 A firm must arrange adequate protection for clients' assets when it is responsible for them.

Relations with Regulators

11 A firm must deal with its regulators in an open and cooperative way, and must disclose to the FSA appropriately anything relating to the firm of which the FSA would reasonably expect notice.

Activities covered under the Regulated Activities Order and the Financial Services and Markets Act 2000

Part II of the Regulated Activities Order details the activities that can be undertaken related to all specified investments or to a particular specified investment or only to designated investments.

The regulated activities described, in general terms, are as follows:

- accepting deposits;
- effecting or carrying out contracts of insurance;
- establishing, operating or winding up a collective investment scheme, acting as trustee or depository of such a scheme or acting as sole director of an investment company with variable capital (or agreeing to do any of these things);
- buying, selling, subscribing for or underwriting designated investments as principal or agent (or agreeing to undertake any of these activities);
- agreeing or making arrangements:
  (i)   for another person (whether as principal or agent) to buy, sell, subscribe to or underwrite a particular designated investment; or
  (ii) for persons to participate (either as principal or agent) with a view to buying, selling, subscribing to or underwriting designated investments;
- safeguarding and administering, or arranging for the safeguarding and administration of, assets belonging to someone else where those assets:
  (i)   consist of or include designated investments; or
  (ii) where the arrangements under which they are safeguarded and administered have at any time been held out as ones under which such designated investments would be safeguarded and administered (or agreeing to safeguard and administer assets in these circumstances or agreeing to arrange to do so);
- sending, on behalf of someone else, dematerialised instructions relating to securities by means of either a relevant system in respect of which an operator is approved under the Uncertified Securities Regulations 1995 or a computer-based system established by the Bank of England and the London Stock Exchange;
- managing, on a discretionary basis, assets which belong to someone else and which consist of or include designated investments, or managing assets, on a discretionary basis, where the arrangements for their management are such that those assets may consist of or include designated investments;
- giving advice or agreeing to give advice to:
  (i)   investors or potential investors;
  (ii) agents for investors or potential investors;
  on the merit of:
  (a)   buying, selling, subscribing to or underwriting a designated investment;

(b) exercising any right conferred by an investment to acquire, dispose, underwrite or convert an investment;

- advising an underwriting member of Lloyd's on membership, continuation or withdrawal from a syndicate;
- managing the underwriting capacity of a Lloyd's syndicate as a managing agent;
- establishing, operating or winding up a stakeholder pension scheme;
- provider of funeral plan contracts;
- lender or administrator of regulated mortgages contracts;
- general insurance.

Activities not covered by the Financial Services and Markets Act 2000

- Bank and building society current and interest bearing accounts (covered by the Banking Act 1987 and Building Societies Act 1986);
- National Savings Bank accounts;
- other loans for the purchase of goods and services (Consumer Credit Act 1974));
- physical dealings in commodities, and futures dealings for commercial purposes;
- land and buildings;
- 'alternative' investments (eg stamps, antiques, works of art);
- investing one's own money;
- transactions between companies in the same group;
- employee share schemes;
- buying and selling private company shares (if the shares carry 50% or more of the voting rights);
- activities of trustees and personal representatives not holding themselves out as offering investment services;
- advice necessarily given in the course of a profession or non-investment business (this is meant to cover things like advice given by an accountant or solicitor on, say, purely tax or legal aspects of an investment. To recommend particular investments would bring the activity within the scope of the Act);
- advice in newspapers, journals and magazines where the principal purpose is not to lead people to invest in a particular investment;
- most buy to let mortgages.

Treating Customers Fairly (TCF)

Expanding on principle 6 of the FSA's core principles, the Treating Customers Fairly initiative has become central to the delivery of the FSA's retail regulatory agenda.

The retail regulatory agenda aims to ensure an efficient and effective market and thereby help consumers achieve a fair deal. Through work on TCF, the intention of the FSA is to deliver improved outcomes for retail consumers.

Because of the wide range of activities and business models carried out by authorised firms, it is not possible to prescribe TCF in a way that applies to everyone. Firms must therefore determine for themselves what fairness means in the context of the size, structure and nature of their business and respond to the initiative accordingly.

Conduct of Business (COBS) Regime

The FSA handbook sets out requirements for conducting investment business. Some of the main principles of this regime are as follows.

Compliance

There is a requirement that all firms appoint a compliance officer to oversee the compliance procedures and to ensure that the rules are being adhered to. The compliance procedures of a company are, in the main, monitored internally by the compliance officer, although the FSA may arrange a visit from one of their own inspectors from time to time.

Know your Client

Advisers are required to demonstrate that the recommendations made are based on a client's own individual circumstances. Therefore, reasonable steps have to be taken to obtain sufficient information from the client before any advice is given. This takes the form of a detailed fact find, an example of which can be found following at p xxix.

Suitability

All advisers have to demonstrate that any recommendations made are suitable for the particular client based on their circumstances. No product can be sold to a client if it cannot be demonstrated that it is suitable. Furthermore, if the adviser is tied or multi-tied and the product provider/s they represent do not market a suitable contract, then no transaction can take place. Independent financial advisers have an additional requirement to demonstrate that they are recommending a suitable product provider to ensure that a client's needs are fully satisfied.

Disclosure of Information

There is a requirement that before any advice is given and a business transaction is entered into, an adviser must provide the client with information about the firm, the adviser's status and the obligations and responsibilities under which the advice is given. The adviser also has a duty to disclose details of the charges and their effect on the performance of an investment, together with clear information on the remuneration the adviser will receive for the sale of a contract.

MiFID

The Markets in Financial Instruments Directive (MiFID) is a major part of the European Union's Financial Services Action Plan.

The Directive sets the initial authorisation conditions and ongoing regulatory requirements for investment firms, Regulated Markets and Multilateral Trading Facilities. It is designed to foster competition and a level-playing field, and to ensure appropriate levels of protection for investors and consumers of investment services across Europe.

Member States were required to finalise legislation and rules to give effect to the MiFID provisions by 31 January 2007. Firms needed to comply with these by 1 November 2007. In the UK, this required amendments to the Financial Services and Markets Act (FSMA), and to the rules of the FSA.

The approach taken by the FSA was to implement the Directive in a pragmatic and proportionate way; meeting the requirements of MiFID in a way that made sense for UK markets, consistent with their statutory objectives and principles of good regulation;

FSA rules will generally be based on copied-out directive text (known as 'intelligent copy-out') to avoid placing any unintended additional obligation on firms. Any future national measures that go beyond directive requirements will be proposed only when justified in their own right and where consistent with directive provisions.

Reforming the Conduct of Business Regime

The Conduct of Business regime has changed – and grown – considerably since it was introduced in 2001, reflecting changes in both the financial markets and the regulatory environment. These changes have made the FSA handbook increasingly difficult for users to navigate and understand – and therefore comply with. The FSA also recognised that some rules had become ineffective or disproportionate in correcting the market failures for which they were introduced.

The FSA therefore announced in 2006 that they would take the opportunity provided by the substantial overhaul of the conduct of business regime required to implement MiFID to review the structure and content of the FSA handbook. To coincide with the implementation of MiFID, the new COB regime (known as COBS) took effect from 1 November 2007.

Depolarisation

Up until 30 November 2004, firms that advised on package products were either independent financial advisers, able to give advice on investments across the whole market, or tied agents offering investments from a single provider or from another member of their marketing group. From 1 December 2004, these rules were partially swept away and firms had the additional option of setting up multi-tied arrangements with a limited range of product providers. This was seen as a halfway house between being independent and being a tied agent. As at 1 June 2005, the transitional period ended and firms had to comply with additional disclosure requirements that were previously optional.

A consequence of these rules is that if a firm wants to describe itself as 'independent' it needs to offer advice across the whole market and give the customer the option to pay for advice by fee only, although there is the option to charge a combination of fee and commission. Those firms that do not offer the fee-only option and advise across the whole market are unable to include the word 'independent' in their name and this will put the investor on notice that such advisers offer a more limited range of products from a limited number of companies than an Independent Financial Adviser firm.

Any firm selling and advising on investments in packaged products to private customers must provide them with specified information. Using the FSA designed Key Facts 'about our services and costs' disclosure document template at the start of the sales advice process or on initial enquiry would address this requirement. The compulsory requirement to use the Key Facts documentation was withdrawn on the implementation of the MiFID and some firms reverted back to using a 'Terms of Business' letter to provide this information. The Key Facts document entitled 'about our services and costs' contains information about the firm and informs the customers whether they are being offered products from the whole of the market place, as with an IFA, or products from a limited number of companies – the multi-tied agent – or from a single company or marketing group of companies – like the old tied agent. The document also indicates to the customer the basis of the advice being provided in that the firm offers a full advice service, will make a recommendation of a product by the use of questions or provide a limited advice service.

In addition it provides information on how the client will be charged with examples of what the client can expect to pay depending on the product, also offering alternative options of payment for advice by fee, the payment for advice by commission, or by a combination of fees and commission.

The format of this document provides the details that give information to the potential client/investor to make a comparison between different companies and to compare a firm's charge for advice. This is to encourage investors to compare the products and services so that they can make a more informed decision as to which adviser to choose.

The 'about our services and costs' document became 'guidance' in the FSA Rules from 31 August 2009. Using the template provided by FSA would ensure that certain regulatory disclosure rules would be complied with. The use of the document is not compulsory but the disclosure requirements must be given in another medium if the FSA template is not used.

Retail Distribution Review

In June 2006, as part of their retail market strategy, FSA launched the Retail Distribution Review (RDR) to address their observations since regulation began in 1988. FSA state that this is in response to insufficient consumer trust and confidence in the products and services supplied by the market. They decided to go beyond treating the symptoms and sought to address the root causes to complement their aim to improve consumer capability, ensure fair outcomes for consumers and prepare the market for the future. FSA spent two and a half years seeking input from a wide range of industry practitioners, consumer representatives and other stakeholders to get their views on the issues to be addressed and to identify potential solutions.

There are three measures that FSA regard as most fundamental to delivering the market outcomes that they set out to achieve and which they believe will improve the interactions between consumers and the industry. These are to:

- improve the clarity for consumers of the characteristics of different service types and the distinctions between them;
- raise professional standards; and
- reduce the conflicts of interest inherent in remuneration practices and improve transparency of the cost of all advisory services.

The FSA is consulting on these changes during the period to 31 December 2012.

Financial Planning Questionnaire

Client Name:

Correspondence
address:

Telephone:　Home

　　　　　　Work

　　　　　　Mobile

E-mail Address:

Completed By:

Date Completed:

This questionnaire is deliberately comprehensive and we encourage you to take the time to complete it, since only by having a full picture of your personal and financial circumstances can we be certain that our recommendations to you are appropriate.

If you prefer not to answer a question please strike through the box, write "Do not wish to disclose" and initial the section. If unable to answer a question, please insert a question mark.

In some cases it will not be possible to enter all relevant information on the questionnaire. Please give additional details on the notes page at the end, or on separate schedules and attach any relevant supporting documentation.

1　Personal details

	Self	Spouse/Partner
Full Name		
Date of Birth		
Nationality		
Marital Status		
Occupation		
Tax District and Ref No (if known)		
National Insurance Number		

2 Medical details

	Self	Spouse/Partner
Height	_____	_____
Weight	_____	_____
Smoker? *(within last 12 months)*	_____	_____
How is your general health?	_____	_____

3 Other advisers

	Self	Spouse/Partner
Solicitor	_____	_____
Stockbroker	_____	_____
Banker	_____	_____
Accountant	_____	_____
Other advisers	_____	_____

4 Family details

	Names	Date of Birth/ Age	Notes: i.e. Married, Employed, Financially dependent
Details of children, step-children, grandchildren or other dependants	_____	_____	_____
	_____	_____	_____
	_____	_____	_____
	_____	_____	_____

5 Employment details

	Self	Spouse/Partner
Occupation Employed/Self-employed/Duties	_____	_____
Employer/Business name and address	_____	_____
	_____	_____

	Self	Spouse/Partner
Year of joining service	_____	_____
Anticipated retirement age	_____	_____
Previous employment details	_____	_____
Please provide company names and dates	_____	_____
Notes on the above	_____	_____
Are you expecting any changes in your circumstances?	_____	_____
	_____	_____
	_____	_____

6   Income details

		Self	Spouse/Partner
Income	Basic annual salary *(gross)* or self-employed income	_____	_____
	Bonus/Commission/ Overtime	_____	_____
	Benefits in kind	_____	_____
	Dividend *(from private co)*	_____	_____
	Investments	_____	_____
	Rental	_____	_____
	Private Pension	_____	_____
	State Pension	_____	_____
	Company Pension	_____	_____
	Other	_____	_____
	Total Gross Income	£ _____	£ _____

	Self	Spouse/Partner
Tax rate	_____ %	_____ %

Tax reference

Tax District

National Insurance Number

Notes on the above

6.1 Outgoings

	Self	Joint	Spouse/Partner
Mortgage on main residence			
Type of mortgage			
Name of lender			
Amount outstanding	£	£	£
Approximate value of property	£	£	£
Redemption date	£	£	£
Pension premiums	£	£	£
Monthly repayments *(including life insurance premiums)*	£	£	£
Other outgoings/ loans-approximate monthly outlay	£	£	£
Future liabilities *(approximate monthly outlay)*	£	£	£
Total	£	£	£
Disposable Monthly Income	£	£	£

Expenditure

7 Assets (current market value)

	Self(£)	Joint(£)	Spouse/Partner(£)
Home *(main residence)*			
Contents/effects/car			

Investment Property _____ _____ _____

Stocks & Shares*
Unit and Investment
Trusts* *(including
PEPs and ISAs)* _____ _____ _____

Insurance Bonds*

Building Society Deposits*
(including Cash ISAs) _____ _____ _____

Bank Accounts* _____ _____ _____

National Savings* _____ _____ _____

Share Options (specify) _____ _____ _____

Other Assets (specify) _____ _____ _____

* please attach schedule or valuation

Do you regularly use your capital gains tax allowance?   Y   N

	Y	N
Self	◯	◯
Spouse/Partner	◯	◯

If you are a beneficiary of a trust, please provide full details at the back of this questionnaire.

8   Life insurance policies

Life Assured	Company and policy number	Type of Policy (endowment, term, whole of life)	Sum Assured £	Maturity Date	Premium paid
_____	_____	_____	_____	_____	£ ____ pa/pm
_____	_____	_____	_____	_____	£ ____ pa/pm
_____	_____	_____	_____	_____	£ ____ pa/pm
_____	_____	_____	_____	_____	£ ____ pa/pm
_____	_____	_____	_____	_____	£ ____ pa/pm

8.1 Other insurances (e.g. Private Health Cover, Personal Accident)

	Self	Spouse/Partner
Cover	_____	_____
Income Deferred	_____	_____
Replacement Period	_____	_____
Expiry Date	_____	_____

9   Regular savings

Self or Spouse/ Partner	Type	Fund	Commencement Date	Monthly/ Annual Amount	Present Value
_____	_____	_____	_____	£ _____	£ _____
_____	_____	_____	_____	£ _____	£ _____
_____	_____	_____	_____	£ _____	£ _____
_____	_____	_____	_____	£ _____	£ _____
_____	_____	_____	_____	£ _____	£ _____
_____	_____	_____	_____	£ _____	£ _____

10 Pensions

Occupational Pensions

Please attach all relevant pension scheme booklets and the most recent annual statement

Current Scheme	Self	Spouse/Partner
Name of Scheme	_____	_____
Type – Executive Pension Plan	○ (please tick)	○ (please tick)
– Final salary	○	○
– Money Purchase	○	○
– Group Personal Plan	○	○
– Small Self Administered Scheme	○	○
Date entered employment	_____	_____

Date joined Scheme   _____   _____

Contracted in or out?   _____   _____

Lump sum death benefit   _____   _____

Normal retirement age   _____   _____

Additional Voluntary
Contributions
    – Through Company
      Scheme?
    – Free Standing?   _____   _____

Do you have deferred/
preserved pensions from
a previous employment? If
so, what is the approximate
value   _____   _____

Company/previous
employer(s) name(s)   _____   _____

Personal Pensions and Retirement Annuity Policies
* (If insufficient space, please use notes page at back of the booklet and attach the most
  recent statements/documentation)

Insurance Company (PPP or RAP)	Fund	Date of first premium paid	Regular/ Single premiums	Amount of premium	Selected retirement age
Self					
_____	_____	_____	_____	£ _____	_____
_____	_____	_____	_____	£ _____	_____
_____	_____	_____	_____	£ _____	_____
Spouse/Partner					
_____	_____	_____	_____	£ _____	_____
_____	_____	_____	_____	£ _____	_____
_____	_____	_____	_____	£ _____	_____

	Self	Spouse/Partner
At what age would you like to retire?	_____	_____
What income do you plan to achieve at retirement?	_____	_____

11 Wills (please give main provisions and supply copies if possible)

Self   Spouse/Partner

_____   _____

_____   _____

_____   _____

_____   _____

_____   _____

_____   _____

12 Planning priorities

Please rank your requirements/objectives by numbering the following:
Starting with 1 for the most important.

	Self	Spouse/Partner
Provision for retirement		
Capital protection		
Maximising income		
Inheritance tax planning		
Family – on serious security illness		
– on death		
Mitigation of tax liabilities		
Future business purposes		
Investment for children		
Planning for school fees/ higher education		
Other – please specify		
Notes (on above)		

Are you expecting any
changes in your
circumstances?

_____

_____

_____

_____

13 Adviser summary of client needs

This section is completed by your adviser and identifies those areas of financial planning which he/she considers need to be addressed based on the information provided.

Pensions   Has a need been identified?   Yes ○   No ○

Does the client agree with the need(s)   Yes ○   No ○

Describe the need(s)

_____

_____

Investment   Has a need been identified?   Yes ○   No ○

Does the client agree with the need(s)   Yes ○   No ○

Describe the need(s)

_____

_____

Protection   Has a need been identified?   Yes ○   No ○

Does the client agree with the need(s)   Yes ○   No ○

Describe the need(s) in respect of Death, Critical Illness, PHI etc.

_____

_____

Other   Has a need been identified?   Yes ○   No ○

Does the client agree with the need(s)   Yes ○   No ○

Describe the need(s), Inheritance Tax Planning, Long Term Care, Wills, Emergency Fund etc.

_____

_____

_____

_____

14 Investor attitude to risk

It is important that we fully understand your attitude to investment risk. This will help us provide you with suitable recommendations that are tailored to meet your specific needs and objectives. To assist you, we have devised five investment risk categories and these are shown below. Please study each category carefully then tick the one box which most closely describes your views. There is space at the end to expand your response, should you feel that some modification or further comment will help us to better understand your requirements. An example of this may be where your attitude to risk is different for separate aspects of financial planning, e.g. you may be medium risk for pension planning, but low risk for medium term savings.

Definition of investment periods – **short term** (less than 5 years) – **medium term** (5 to 10 years) – **long term** (over 10 years).

Rating	**Low Risk**
1	I am cautious and dislike risk, preferring security of capital and predictable investments. I accept that this may result in lower rates of return being achieved, and that the real buying power of my money may not keep pace with inflation, particularly over the medium to longer term. I also accept that interest returns from deposit based investments may move up or down, sometimes quite suddenly, and therefore be no security as to the levels of income arising.

Self ◯   Partner/Spouse ◯

2   Below average risk

I am prudent in my outlook. Although mainly attracted to the security of lower risk investments, I am willing to accept a limited exposure to equity investments (stocks and shares) and/or property markets. I would accept a limited degree of fluctuation in the value of my capital, in exchange for the potential of improved medium to longer term returns. My aim is to at least maintain the real buying power of my money, as compared to inflation, over the medium to longer term.

Self ◯   Partner/Spouse ◯

3   Medium risk

I regard myself as a balanced investor. Part of my portfolio should contain investments which provide security of capital with some provision for earlier access during the investment period. For medium to longer term investments, I accept that a medium risk approach would require a significant proportion of my funds to be placed in equity based investments (stocks and shares). I am therefore prepared to accept some fluctuation in the value of my capital, in return for the potential of improved medium to longer term rewards. My aim is to improve the real buying power of my money, as compared to inflation, over the medium to longer term.

Self ◯   Partner/Spouse ◯

4   Above average risk

I am prepared to accept a higher than average degree of risk in my portfolio, in the hope of achieving well above average longer term returns. I accept that this strategy requires a high degree of exposure to equity investments (stocks and shares) and/or property markets, and I understand the performance of such investments may be volatile, particularly over the shorter term. Also that such equity based investments may need to be more widely spread geographically, and there may therefore be increased exposure to currency markets and political risks. My aim is to significantly improve the real buying power of my money, as compared to inflation, over my selected investment term.

Self ◯   Partner/Spouse ◯

5   **High risk**

I am willing to accept a high level of risk in relation to my portfolio. I realise that such strategy involves investment in specialist funds and products whose performance may be highly volatile, and where a more unusual geographical exposure of investments may be appropriate. Such products may in addition give rise to high risk exposure in currency markets, and/or political risks. I also appreciate that certain high risk investments may not easily be realisable, as there may not be a ready market for the sale of such investments at the required time, and that it may be difficult or impractical to obtain reliable data for valuing such investments. My aim is to substantially improve the real buying power of my money, as compared to inflation, over my selected term, and I fully accept that my invested capital would be substantially at risk accordingly.

Self ○   Partner/Spouse ○

	Self		Partner/Spouse	
	Yes	No	Yes	No
Do you wish to consider ethical investments?	○	○	○	○

15 Risk assessment

	Low 1	Low/med 2	Med 3	Med/high 4	High 5
Pensions	○	○	○	○	○
Investments & savings	○	○	○	○	○

Self

Signed: _____   Date: _____

Name: _____

Spouse/Partner

Signed: _____   Date: _____

Name: _____

16 Additional notes

Date: _____

To whom it may concern:

Please accept this letter as my/our authority to release to XXXXXXXXXX any information which they may request in respect of my/our pensions and investment arrangements, as they are acting with my full knowledge.

Yours faithfully

Signed: _____   Spouse/Partner: _____

Name: _____   Name: _____

Date: _____

To whom it may concern:

I appoint XXXXXXXXXX as my/our Independent Financial Advisers with immediate effect. Please give them any information they require and act on their instructions. I understand that they are regulated by the FSA and are therefore entitled to ongoing commission.

Yours faithfully

Signed: _____   Spouse/Partner: _____

Name: _____   Name: _____

Tax Rates

TAX RATES

Personal taxation

Income Tax 2010/11

Taxable income £	Saving Income	
	Dividends %	Other %
£1 – £2,440	10	10
£2,441 to £37,400	10	20
£37,401 to £150,000	32.5	40
Over £150,000	42.5	50

Taxable Income £	Other Income %
£1 – £37,400	20
£37,401 to £150,000	40
Over £150,000	50

Notes

1   Taxable income is after personal allowances and allowable charges. For 20010/11 the allowances are:

	£
Each individual – below 65	6,475
Each individual – aged[2] 65–74	9,490
Each individual – aged[2] 75 or over	9,640
Additional allowance for married couples	
Each individual – born after 6 April 1935	nil
Each individual – born after 6 April 1935 & aged 75 & over, maximum amount	6,965
Each individual – born after 6 April 1935 & aged 75 & over, minimum amount	2,670
Age[3] – income limit	22,900

2   The personal allowances and tax rate band thresholds change from 6 April of each year. For age allowance individual or spouse must be 65 or 75 or over at any time in the year of allowance.

3   For marriages before 5 December 2005 the allowance is given to the husband initially and the wife can elect to split the allowance or both can elect to utilise any excess efficiently. Only available where one spouse is aged 65 or over on 6 April 2000. For marriages on or after 5 December 2005 the allowance is given to whichever partner has the higher income. Restricted to 10% subject to minimum married couples allowance of £2,670.

4   Single age allowance reduced by £1 for every £2 income exceeds limit but not so as to reduce the allowance below the normal individual allowance.

5   Personal allowance is reduced by £1 for every £2 for adjusted net income which exceeds £100,000. The personal allowance can be reduced to nil.

6   Dividends are grossed up by a tax credit equal to one-ninth of the cash amount, ie dividend received of £90 is grossed up by £10 to reach taxable dividend of £100. The grossed up dividend is deemed to be the highest part of the income, followed by other savings income, then all non-savings income such as earnings.

  The tax credit is offset against the tax liability on the dividend to reduce the liability to nil for basic rate taxpayers, or to a rate of 22.5% for 32.5% taxpayers and 32.5% for 42.5% tax payers.

  The tax credit is not recoverable even if the taxpayer's rate falls below 10%.

  Non-UK dividends must be grossed up by the tax credit and foreign tax credit relief may be available.

7   Discretionary, Accumulation and Maintenance Trusts are taxed at 42.5% on the grossed-up dividend income. The first £1,000 of income is however taxed at the lower 10% rate for dividends or 20% rate for other investment income.

8   Relief given at 20% up to a maximum of £500,000 invested in the Enterprise Investment Scheme and relief given at 30% up to a maximum of £200,000 invested in Venture Capital Trusts.

9   Individual Savings Accounts (ISAs) – interest, dividends or capital gains within the ISA are not taxable. Qualifying individuals are aged 18 or over.

	Annual Maximum £
Maximum	10,200
Made up of:	
Cash	5,100
Stocks and shares	balance to 5,100

  Individuals age 16–17 can invest an annual maximum of £5,100 in a cash ISA.

10 The State Pension is taxable income.

Capital Gains Tax 2010/11

	£
Annual exemptions	
Individual	10,100
Personal representatives (maximum 3 years)	10,100
Trust (subject to restriction)	5,050
Chattels exemption	6,000

Taper relief

Abolished for disposals after 6 April 2008.

Entrepreneurs' relief

Entrepreneurs' relief took effect from 6 April 2008.

The relief will be available in respect of:

Gains made on the disposal of all or part of a business, or

Gains made on disposals of assets following the cessation of a business;

By certain individuals who were involved in running the business.

The relief operates such that capital gains up to a capped amount are subject to an effective rate of tax of 10%. Any gain above this capped amount is charged at the flat rate of tax in force at that time.

The capped amount also represents a lifetime allowance therefore not a capped amount per disposal but for lifetime disposals post 6 April 2008.

Disposals in the period 6 April 2010 to 22 June 2010 up to £2million of lifetime gains could qualify for entrepreneurs' relief. Any capital gain on a disposal in this period that did not qualify for this relief would be subject to a 18% capital gains tax rate.

For disposals in the period 23 June 2010 to 5 April 2011 the capped amount was increased so that £5 million of lifetime gains could qualify for entrepreneurs' relief. Any capital gain on a disposal in this period that did not qualify for this relief would be subject to a 28% capital gains tax rate.

There is a minimum qualifying period of ownership of one year.

Indexation allowance

Abolished for individuals, trustees and personal representatives for disposals after 6 April 2008. It continues for companies.

Capital Gains Tax Deferral

Capital gains may be deferred into an Enterprise Investment Scheme. Deferral into Venture Capital Trusts ceased for shares issued after 5 April 2004.

Rate of tax	6 April 2010 to 22 June 2011	23 June 2010 to 5 April 2011
Individual	18%	18 or 28%
Discretionary trust	18%	28%
Accumulation and maintenance trust	18%	28%
Trusts with life tenant (other than settlor or spouse)	18%	28%
Personal representatives	18%	28%

Inheritance Tax 2010/11

Rates and thresholds

Chargeable values	%
325,000	Nil
Excess	40 on death
	20 on chargeable lifetime transfers

Ready reckoner

Chargeable values	Cumulative tax on death
400,000	30,000
750,000	170,000
1,500,000	470,000
3,000,000	1,070,000

(a) Where death occurs within seven years of a chargeable lifetime transfer, the death rate applies with a credit for any tax already paid.

(b) Potentially exempt transfers are not charged to tax unless death occurs within seven years of the transfer. Where death does occur within that period the potentially exempt transfer is aggregated with chargeable transfers in the previous seven years and then charged.

(c) Business Property Relief 50% or 100%.
Agricultural Property Relief 50% or 100%.

(d) Exemptions:

Annual	£3,000
Small gifts	£250
Gifts in consideration of Marriage:	
parent	£5,000
grandparent	£2,500
other	£1,000
Gifts to charity	
Normal expenditure out of surplus income	
Transfers between spouses	

Gift by UK domiciled spouse to non-UK domiciled spouse, exemption limited to £55,000.

(f) Legislation now allows the transfer of unused nil-rate band on the death of one spouse or civil partner to the surviving spouse or civil partner on their death provided they die after 8 October 2007.

BUSINESS TAXATION

Corporation Tax

Year to 31 March 2011			
Profits	*Rate*	*Tax*	*Marginal*
£	%	£	*Relief Fraction*
300,000	21	3,000	—
1,200,000	29.75	357,000	7/400
1,500,000		420,000	

Excess at 28%

Profits above are as adjusted for tax purposes. The rate of tax will be affected if there are associated companies.

Capital Allowances

Annual Investment allowance – relief on £100,000	100%
Plant and machinery	
Writing down allowance on reducing balance	20%
Long life assets and Integral features	
Writing down allowance on reducing balance	10%
Research and development	100%
Expensive cars purchased pre April 2009 (max £3,000)	20%
Car purchased from April 2009 with CO_2 emissions > 160g/km	10%
Car purchased from April 2009 with CO_2 emissions <160 g/km	20%
Cars with low CO_2 emissions (<110g/km)	100%
Energy Saving and water efficient plant as defined	100%
Industrial and agricultural buildings and hotels	
Writing down allowance on cost	1%

Value Added Tax 2010/11

Standard rate from 4 January 2011	20%
Standard rate from 1 January 2010 to 3 January 2011	17.5%
Reduced Rate	5%
Registration limits:	
Taxable turnover (annual)	£70,000
Deregistration limit:	
Taxable turnover in next 12 months below	£68,000
Annual accounting limit	
Taxable turnover (annual)	£1,350,000
Cash accounting limit	
Taxable turnover (annual)	£1,350,000

National Insurance 2010/11

Class 1 (Employees and Employers)

Earnings threshold – employee		£110 per week
– employer		£110 per week
Upper earnings limit – employee	£844 per week	
– employer		No limit

	Earnings	Standard	Contracted Out
Employees –	First £0–£110	0%	0%
–	£110.01–£770	11%	9.4%
	£770.01–£844	11%	11%
–	Over £844	1%	1%
Employer –	£0–£110	0%	0%
–	£110.01–£770	12.8%	9.1%
	(11.4% COMP)		
–	over £770	12.8%	12.8%

Class 1A (Employers)

Payable on most benefits in kind	12.8%
provided to employee earning	
£8,500 p.a., and directors	

Class 2 (Self-Employed)

Flat rate per week	£2.40
Annual earnings exception limit	£5,075

Class 3 (Voluntary)

Flat rate per week	£12.05
Annual	£626.60

Class 4 (Self-Employed)

Rate on profits between £5,715 and £43,875	8.0%
Rate on profits above £43,875	1.0%

BENEFITS IN KIND

Use of Company Car

Scale rate based on carbon dioxide emissions and list price:
   15% on list price of cars emitting up to 130g/km

increased by 1% per 5g/km over the 130g/km limit capped at 35% of list price

3% supplement on diesel cars (subject to 35% cap)

Use of Company Car without an official CO_2 emission rate

Cars with a cylinder capacity of	Registered on or after 1 January 1998	Registered before 1 January 1998
Up to 1,400 cc	15%	15%
1,401 cc – 2,000 cc	25%	22%
2,001 cc or more	35%	32%

Fuel Benefit

Scale rate based on carbon dioxide emission:

£2,700 if emissions less than 130g/km

increased by £180 per additional 5g/km

greater than or equal to 230g/km maximum benefit is £6,300

Diesel supplements added up to maximum of £6,300

Use of Company Van

Van benefit	£3,000
Van fuel benefit	£550

Both figures are nil if the restricted private use conditions are met.

Cheap Loans (non qualifying)

up to £5,000	No taxable benefit
greater than £5,000	Benefit = loan × official rate of interest (currently 4.00%)

Benefits not subject to tax and NIC

Examples are:

Mobile phones supplied by employer, restricted to one phone per employee from 6 April 2006

Relocation costs up to £8,000

Certain childcare for children under 18

Approved Mileage Allowance Rates

For business journeys using own transport.

	First *10,000 miles*	*Additional* *Miles*
Cars and vans	40p	25p
Motor cycles	24p	24p
Bicycles	20p	20p

STAMP DUTY LAND TAX

On Residential Property (from 1 January 2010)

Not exceeding £125,000 (£150,000 for disadvantaged areas)	Nil
£125,001 – £250,000 (£150,000 – £250,000 for disadvantaged areas)	1%
£250,001 – £500,000	3%
£500,001 or more	4%
£1,000,000 or more (effective from 6 April 2011)	5%

First time buyers can claim relief for SDLT on transactions up to £250,000 between 25 March 2010 and 25 March 2012.

On Non-residential Property (from 1 January 2010)

Not exceeding £150,000	Nil
£150,001 – £250,000	1%
£250,001 – £500,000	3%
£500,001 or more	4%
£1,000,000 or more (effective from 6 April 2011)	5%

STAMP DUTY

On Shares

Stamp duty reserve tax	0.5%

TAX CREDITS

Working Tax Credit	*Maximum Annual Rate* £
Basic element	1,920
Second adult and Lone Parent elements	1,890
30-hour element	790
Disability element	2,570
Severe disability element	
50 plus return to work payment	
– 16–30 hours	1,320
– 30+ hours	1,965
Childcare element	*Maximum Weekly Rate*
– maximum eligible cost (2 or more children)	300
– maximum eligible cost (1 child)	175
– percent of eligible costs covered	80%

Child Tax Credit	*Maximum Annual Rate* £
Family element	545
Family element – where child under the age of one	1,090
Child and young person element	2,300
Disability element	5,015
Severe disability element	6,110

Common Features	*Annual Rate* £
First income threshold (taper start point)	6,420
First withdrawal taper rate	39%
Second income threshold (taper start point)	50,000
Second withdrawal taper rate	6.67%
First threshold for Child Tax Credit only	16,190

Pension Credit	*Weekly Rate* £
Standard minimum guaranteed income age 60 and over	
– single	132.60
– couple	202.40
Savings credit if age 65 and over and savings held	
– single	up to 20.52
– couple	up to 27.09
Savings credit only available if income is not greater than	
– single	
– couple	270.00

Child Tax Credit is available to those with children and a joint income of up to £58,175 a year (£66,350 if there is a child under one year old)

Working Tax Credit is available to those with joint income of less than £16,190 (or more if there are children)

Charitable Giving

Gift Aid relief is available to individuals and companies without limit for gifts of money to charities.

Gift Aid payments can be tax relieved in the previous tax year if a claim is made by a higher rate taxpayer.

An individual can nominate a charity to receive their tax repayment via their tax return from 2003/04.

Relief is also available for gifts of property, shares and securities to charities.

Interest on Tax and NIC (current rates)

	Paid Late	*Repayment*
Income Tax, CGT and NIC	3%	0.5%
Inheritance Tax	3%	0.5%
Corporation Tax (CTSA)	3%[1]	0.5%[2]
Corporation Tax (Instalments)	1.5%[1]	0.5%[2]

[1] Tax deductible
[2] Chargeable to tax

Abbreviations

ADLs	Activities of daily living
AEI	Average earnings index
AIM	Alternative Investment Market
APPS	Appropriate personal pension scheme
AVC	Additional voluntary contribution
BES	Business expansion scheme
CA 1985	Companies Act 1985
CAA 2001	Capital Allowances Act 2001
CD	Certificate of deposit
CGT	Capital gains tax
CIMP	Contracted-in money purchase plan
CIRTA	Convertible, increasable, renewable term assurance
COMPS	Contracted-out money purchase schemes
CPI	Consumer Price Index
CSOP	Company share option plan
DTA	Double tax agreement
DWP	Department of Work and Pensions
EBT	Employee benefit trust
EIS	Enterprise Investment Scheme
EPP	Executive Pension Plan
ESC	Inland Revenue Extra-Statutory Concession
ESOP	Employee Share ownership plan
EZPT	Enterprise Zone Property Trust
FA	Finance Act (eg FA 1989 – Finance Act 1989)
FIFO	First in first out
FSA	Financial Services Authority
FSMA	Financial Services and Markets Act 2000
FSA 1986	Financial Services Act 1986
FSAVC	Free standing additional voluntary contribution
FTSE 100	Financial Times Stock Exchange 100 share index
FURBS	Funded unapproved retirement benefit scheme
GMP	Guaranteed minimum pension
HMRC	Her Majesty's Revenue & Customs
ICTA 1988	Income and Corporation Taxes Act 1988
IDB	Inter-dealer broker
IHT	Inheritance tax
IHTA 1984	Inheritance Tax Act 1984
IMRO	Investment Managers Regulatory Organisation
IRPR	Inland Revenue press release
IR SPSS	Inland Revenue Savings, Pensions, Share Schemes
ISA	Individual Savings Account
ITA 2007	Income Tax Act 2007
ITEPA 2003	Income Tax (Earnings and Pensions) Act 2003
ITTOIA 2005	Income Tax (Trading and Other Income) Act 2005
LAPR	Life assurance premium relief
LAUTRO	Life Assurance and Unit Trust Regulatory Organisation
LEAP	Livestock exclusion annual premium
LIFFE	London International Financial Futures Exchange
LPI	Limited Price Indexation

LTC	Long Term Care
MAPA	Member agents' pooling arrangement
MFR	Minimum Funding Requirement (Pensions Act 1995)
MiFID	Markets in Financial Instruments Directive
MVA	Market valuation adjustment
MWPA	Married Womens' Property Act 1882
NAE	National Average Earnings
NAPF	National Association of Pension Funds
NRD	Normal retirement date
NRE	Net relevant earnings
OEIC	Open ended investment company
OMO	Open market option
OPAS	Occupational Pensions Advisory Service
OPB	Occupational Pensions Board (now part of OPRA)
OPRA	Occupational Pensions Regulatory Authority
PA 1995	Pensions Act 1995
para	paragraph
PAYE	Pay As You Earn
PCLS	Pension commencement lump sum
PEP	Personal Equity Plan
PET	Potentially exempt transfer
PHI	Permanent Health Insurance
PIA	Personal Investment Authority
PIBS	Permanent interest bearing shares
PMI	Private medical insurance
PPB	Personal Portfolio Bond
PPCC	Personal pensions contribution certificate
PPS	Personal pension scheme
PRAS	Pension relief at source
PSO	Pension Schemes Office of the Inland Revenue (now part of IR SPSS)
QROPS	Qualifying Recognised Overseas Pension Scheme
QUEST	Qualifying employee share ownership trust
RAP	Retirement annuity policy
RPB	Recognised Professional Body
RPI	Retail Prices Index
s	section
S2P	State Second Pension
SAYE	Save As You Earn
Sch	Schedule
SDLT	Stamp Duty Land Tax
SEAQ	Stock exchange automated quotations
SERPS	State Earnings Related Pension Scheme
SFA	The Securities and Futures Association
SHEP	Second-hand endowment assurance policy
SIB	Securities and Investment Board
SIPP	Self-invested Personal Pension Scheme
SP	Inland Revenue Statement of Practice
SRO	Self-Regulatory Organisation
SSA 1990	Social Security Act 1990
SSAS	Small Self-administered Pension Scheme
SSCBA	Social Security Contributions and Benefits Act 1992
TCA 2002	Tax Credits Act 2002
TCGA 1992	Taxation of Chargeable Gains Act 1992
TESSA	Tax Exempt Special Savings Account
TMA 1970	Taxes Management Act 1970

UCITS	Undertaking for collective investments in transferable securities
UURBS	Unfunded Unapproved Retirement Benefit Scheme
VAT	Value Added Tax
VATA 1983	Value Added Tax Act 1983
VCT	Venture Capital Trust
WGS	Woodland grant scheme

Part 1   Insurance

1.1 Introduction

Insurance has an important dual role to play in financial planning, both as a means of providing financial protection and as an investment. Premiums can be paid by way of regular savings or as a lump sum. However, the charging structure and taxation system of life companies make it necessary for any potential investors to look closely at their after-tax return and to compare this with other non-insurance investments.

The introduction of full disclosure of commissions for regulated policies from 1 January 1995, together with the requirement for life insurance companies to demonstrate the effects on investment performance of their own charges, ensured that prospective investors had fairly clear information as to the costs that they will incur when taking out a policy.

The different uses of life assurance may be summarised as follows:
1   to provide protection;
2   to both fund and mitigate inheritance tax liability;
3   as a regular savings medium (refer to investment section);
4   as a lump sum investment (refer to investment section);
5   to provide a tax-efficient income (refer to investment section).

Protection

For those who wish to make financial provision for dependants or protect a business, there will always be a need for insurance to provide the required level of protection. The most commonly used life assurance policies for protection purposes are term assurance, of which there are numerous types, and whole of life.

Life insurance policy premiums have fallen in recent years by up to 40% with some life offices. This is primarily due to actuarial re-basing of underwriting procedures in lieu of statistical information showing that the AIDS crisis has not escalated to the extent the actuaries at first feared. The rate in the fall in premiums has lessened over the last couple of years.

At present the term products are proving statistically to be more popular since whole of life plans have not had as much product development by the life offices. A few years ago, term plans were simply based on life cover but the introduction of multiple benefits such as critical illness, death benefit, and other 'add-ons' with the one term policy have prompted increased popularity.

Permanent health insurance provides a continuing income in the event of prolonged incapacity, while critical illness policies provide a lump sum if an insured individual suffers a condition covered by the policy.

Long-term health care insurance provides a planned way to pay for some, or all, of the costs of long-term care that may be required by individuals who are unable to look after themselves, due to deteriorating health or old age. Some of these policies are available purely on an insurance basis and some are linked to investment, possibly offshore.

Family income policies provide a regular monthly or quarterly income for the deceased's dependants. The term 'family income' is, in a way, a misnomer as the policy is written to provide a capital sum, payable by instalments, for a selected period thus avoiding liability to income tax.

Finally, endowment policies bridge the gap between investment and protection, providing both a guaranteed sum assured on death and a maturity value. Endowments are currently discussed in the press more for their lack of targeted performance than their usefulness and are, consequently, rather less popular than, say, five years ago.

Inheritance Tax Funding and Mitigation

Life assurance has an important role to play in IHT planning, although much thought needs to be given to strategy and the use of some fairly sophisticated packaged products.

There are two main uses of life policies in relation to IHT planning:
1   funding for the tax; and
2   making lifetime gifts to utilise lifetime exemptions.

On death, a tax-free fund is placed in the beneficiary's hands, with which the inheritance tax liability can be settled. Commonly, whole of life policies are used for this purpose.

Various life offices also offer more sophisticated schemes, which in some cases enable a donor to make a potentially exempt transfer yet retain an income of sorts without falling foul of the gift with reservation rules.

Frequently, a form of decreasing term assurance, commonly referred to as gift *inter vivos* cover, again with benefits written in trust, is matched with potentially exempt transfers to cover any tax liability that would fall due if the donor were to die within seven years of making a gift.

However, the elderly may feel that they will not survive seven years from making a gift and for medium-sized estates tapering reliefs are of little use. They may look to the use of annuities to fund life policies to provide for the tax.

When using life insurance policies within certain types of trusts, it must be noted that the Finance Act 2006 introduced changes that affect the IHT planning surrounding these type of policies. These changes were introduced in the Finance Act 2006 and include chargeable lifetime transfers, periodic and exit charges. Refer to Part 4 for further details.

The Finance Act 2006 can be found at: http://www.opsi.gov.uk.

Conclusions

Insurance does still form a foundation for effective personal financial planning and should be regarded as a priority. It is important that time is spent ensuring that the correct insurance arrangements are put in place. As far as investment is concerned, the system of taxing life assurance policies can still provide competitive advantages.

1.2 Term Assurance

LEVEL TERM

Description	A life assurance policy established for a set number of years, where the sum assured is paid only if death occurs during the policy term.
Suitable for	Low cost provision for repayment, on death before a specific date, of loans or other specific liabilities or as personal protection for the family of a breadwinner.
Advantages	1 A cheap form of life assurance in relation to the sum assured.
Disadvantages	1 The policy has no surrender or encashment value during or at the end of the term. 2 Medical evidence may be required and the cost of cover may be expensive or unavailable for those in poor health. 3 Further medical evidence will be required if cover is still needed at the end of the initial term, and poor health may prevent this. 4 If the premium is unpaid, the policy will lapse at the expiry of the 'days of grace'.

INCREASING TERM ASSURANCE

Description	A term assurance policy under which the cover increases at regular intervals either at a pre-determined rate or in line with the Retail Prices Index (RPI).
Suitable for	Individuals who expect their life assurance needs to increase perhaps due to the addition of children to the family or the effects of inflation.
Advantages	1 The increasing capital sum may reduce the need to take out additional life cover later in life when the cost would be greater.
Disadvantages	1 The policy has no value on surrender, or at the end of the term. 2 Further medical evidence will be required if cover is still needed at the end of the initial term, and poor health may prevent this.

DECREASING TERM ASSURANCE/MORTGAGE PROTECTION

Description	A term assurance policy under which the sum assured decreases annually or at other intervals by a specified amount.
Suitable for	Providing for repayment of a mortgage should death of the mortgagor occur before the loan has been repaid.
	Providing a fund to pay additional IHT should the donor die within seven years of making a potentially exempt or chargeable lifetime transfer, often known as Gift Protection Assurance where the sum assured stays constant for the first three years and then decreases by 20% each year for the remaining four years.
	Providing for a reducing commitment (eg to fund school fees), which will terminate in a number of years should death of a breadwinner occur in the period. Ideally written in trust.
Advantages	1 An inexpensive form of life assurance.
Disadvantages	1 The policy has no value on surrender or at the end of the policy term.
	2 For IHT the possibility of tapering relief and the need to take other relevant transfers of the donor into account may make it difficult to estimate the policy proceeds required to fund the tax. Level term assurance may be more appropriate where the lifetime gift is within the nil rate band as taper relief would not reduce the IHT on the gift and decreasing term assurance will not provide sufficient cover in such a case.

CONVERTIBLE TERM ASSURANCE

Description	A level term assurance with an option to convert at any time during the term, to a whole of life or endowment assurance, without further evidence of health. With some policies the conversion option can be for a term or further convertible term assurance.
Suitable for	A young person with a current need for term assurance and a likelihood of a need for a substantive policy in the future.
Advantages	1 A cheap form of life assurance until the conversion is effected.
	2 The policy offers flexibility and can be converted at any stage within the original policy term without further charge or medical evidence.

Disadvantages	1	As the policy is converted at rates applicable to the age of the life assured at the date of conversion (which are not usually guaranteed) and not at the rates effective for the age of the life assured when the policy was originally effected, the premiums may be substantially higher, particularly with an older life assured, after conversion.
	2	Medical evidence is required at the outset and the cost of cover may be expensive or unavailable for those in poor health.

FAMILY INCOME BENEFIT POLICIES

Description	Term assurance to provide on death within a specified period, regular monthly or quarterly income to the deceased's dependants.	
Suitable for	Married persons who will require income to make up for the loss of the deceased partner's income or to cover additional recurring costs of single parent families.	
Advantages	1	The regular payments are treated as capital and are tax free.
	2	Premiums are low as this is a form of decreasing term assurance.
	3	Cover can be on an increasing basis.
Disadvantages	1	No surrender or encashment value.
	2	Medical evidence may be required.
	3	On intestacy the life tenants may lose the benefit of the payments to the reversionary interests.

FURTHER DETAILS

A number of insurance companies provide term assurance policies combining several of the options described above (typically including those to convert and increase) with the option to renew the policy for a further period.

Term assurance policies with variable, as opposed to fixed, rates are now commonplace, as are preferential premium rates for those in certain occupations/professions. In addition, critical illness may be added to these types of plans.

CROSS REFERENCES

Whole Life Assurance   **1.3**
Key Person Assurance   **1.10**
Partnership Assurance   **1.11**
IHT – The Charge to Tax   **4.15**
IHT – Potentially Exempt Transfers   **4.17**

1.3 Whole Life Assurance

Description	A permanent contract to pay a fixed sum on the death of the life assured.
Ages	Minimum 16, maximum 89.
Suitable for	All individuals requiring to provide a sum on death, especially as part of IHT planning.
Advantages	1 The sum assured on death is free from income tax, CGT and, if written under appropriate trust, IHT.
	2 Premiums can cease at a specified age, for example 65, thereby reducing the financial burden on retirement, though the cost of such 'limited premium' policies will, naturally, be higher than equivalent policies where the premiums are payable throughout life.
	3 Can be linked to provide other benefits such as Critical Illness and Business Protection.
Disadvantages	1 The underlying growth of the policy will be subject to income tax and CGT within the life company's funds.
	2 There is a potential charge to higher rate tax on surrenders of the policy in part or whole.
	3 The sum assured may become inadequate in times of inflation.
	4 Premiums are more expensive the older the life to be assured and for those in ill health or who follow hazardous pursuits – in some cases cover is not available when it is needed the most.
	5 Medical evidence is required.
	6 In some cases premiums can be subject to substantial increases on review dates if the life office does not achieve a certain rate of investment return.
Premium limits	Minimum premium approximately £5 per month or £50.00 per annum – no maximum.
Charges	If unit-linked policies are effected – there may be initial fund charges of up to 5% and an annual management charge of approximately 1% of the fund value.
	For non-unit-linked policies there is usually a fixed monthly policy charge of approximately £3.00 to £3.50.

FURTHER DETAILS

Commercial Aspects

The following whole life policies are currently available.

(a) With-profits, Without-profits and Low Cost

With-profits, without-profits and low cost policies are described in detail in Section 3.23, *Endowment Assurance*.

(b) Unit-linked (flexible) Policies

Unit-linked policies can combine life cover with a savings element and there is more flexibility as the policyholder can vary the life assurance and savings element as his circumstances dictate. This type of policy is often termed 'variable' or 'flexible'.

With these policies, for a given level of premium, the life assured can choose the level of life cover required, between maximum and minimum levels. The initial level of cover is maintained until the first policy review which is usually after ten years. If the fund has performed as well as anticipated, it should be possible to continue the policy at the same level of life cover for a further period, normally five years, without any increase in premium, or further evidence of health. Thereafter the policy will usually be reviewed every five years until the age of 70 and thereafter annually.

If the level of life cover selected at the outset is high, and/or the funds have not performed as well as expected or if mortality experience has been worse than expected, it may be necessary to increase the premium for the succeeding period, or to accept a lower level of cover for the same premium.

Other alternatives are available. A surrender value may be taken or life cover may be continued at the existing level for a number of years until the invested funds are exhausted, ie the policy will have become self-funding for a period. The policyholder also has options to vary the level of life cover and the investment element at the time of review.

The number of options available on periodic review dates and the guarantee of insurability may make these policies attractive in certain circumstances and certainly give the policyholder maximum flexibility in their life assurance arrangements. Some of these policies, particularly those having the widest range of options, are 'non-qualifying' policies and are therefore liable to a higher rate income tax charge in certain circumstances.

General

Whole life policies can be written on a joint-life, first-death or last survivor basis. Joint-life policies are generally cheaper than single life policies. If payment is due on the first death of one of the joint lives, it will be termed joint-life first-death; if payment is due on the second death of the joint lives, it will be termed last survivor.

It is possible to insure another person's life but only if there is sufficient insurable interest. The sum assured is paid to the owner of the policy on the death of the life assured. In the case of husband and wife each spouse is deemed to have an unlimited insurable interest in the other's life.

The premiums for whole life policies will be lower, the younger and healthier the life assured. Female lives are underwritten at lower rates than male lives because of their increased longevity.

Uses of Whole Life Policies

1   Financial provision for dependants on the death of the life assured.
2   Provision of funds for IHT purposes – see *IHT Insurance* (Section 4.30).
3   Provision of funds on death to repay loans or discharge other liabilities.
4   Other uses: Section 1.10, *Key Person Assurance*, Section 1.11, *Partnership Assurance*.

Taxation Aspects

A charge to higher rate tax arises if the policy is surrendered in part or in whole within the first ten years (see Section 1.13). Cashing of bonuses is treated as part surrender of the policy.

Upon the death of the life assured, the policy proceeds should be tax-free if the policy is qualifying.

CROSS REFERENCES

Key Person Assurance   **1.10**
Partnership Assurance   **1.11**
Life Assurance Taxation   **1.13**
IHT – Insurance   **4.30**

1.4 Critical Illness Insurance

Description	An insurance policy which pays out the sum assured upon the diagnosis of certain specified illnesses (eg heart attack, stroke, cancer or permanent total disablement etc). Critical illness cover can be obtained as a standalone benefit or as an optional benefit within a whole life policy, endowment or term assurance policy. It is usually cheaper to obtain life cover including critical illness cover than standalone critical illness cover, due to the larger number of providers and, therefore, a more competitive market. Plans are available for both individual and group schemes.
Suitable for	Individuals, their dependants, the self-employed and employers wishing to protect their employees against specified illnesses.
Ages	16–74.

Advantages

1 The policy will pay the sum assured on the diagnosis of specified illnesses when the benefit may be most needed. The lump sum can be used in any way the beneficiary wishes.
2 The policy can be used to complement existing life cover.
3 Policies can be corporate or individually owned.
4 The proceeds are normally tax free.
5 Cover is available against a wide range of critical illnesses.
6 Some policies now offer 'buyback' cover – which provides continued cover for core conditions after you have made a critical illness claim.
7 Many policies include 'children's cover' within their benefits which provides an element of critical illness cover for children between the ages of 30 days and up to 18 years.

Disadvantages

1 Premiums vary dramatically, but cover can be quite costly due to the likelihood of a claim being made.
2 Policy benefits and the conditions covered can vary considerably from insurer to insurer, making comparison difficult.
3 Non-qualifying policies are potentially subject to higher rate(s) of income tax.
4 Underwriting is usually quite stringent due to the level of risk taken on by the insurer, and existing conditions are likely to be excluded from cover.
5 The level of claims paid can vary dramatically from provider to provider and this should be taken into account when deciding on the most suitable policy.

Premiums	Generally, minimum premiums of £5–£10 per month, no maximum.
Charges	Charges vary from provider to provider and depend on the policy type.

FURTHER DETAILS

Commercial Aspects

Critical illness policies meet a need not covered by most other types of insurance. They should be considered separately to life assurance and not as a substitute for it. Critical illness policies provide a lump sum when an individual suffers a serious and usually life threatening illness. Critical illness policies are used in both individual and corporate situations.

It should be noted that the types and definitions of illness currently covered vary quite widely between different insurers, as does claims payment history, and care is needed in selecting the most appropriate policy to meet an individual's needs.

Critical Illness v Income Protection Insurance

Critical illness pays out a lump sum on diagnosis whereas Income Protection Insurance (formerly permanent health insurance (PHI) pays a replacement income whilst the individual is unable to work due to ill health. In this respect, the two are quite distinct and both have an equally important role in full financial planning.

CROSS REFERENCES

Key Person Assurance   **1.10**
Partnership Assurance   **1.11**

1.5 Income Protection Insurance

Description	A policy which pays out regular sums of money to the insured upon the insured becoming unable to work through sickness or accident. Payment is made on completion of a pre-agreed deferred period (between one day and one year) and payment continues until the insured returns to work, the policy termination age (generally normally retirement age) or death. Key person income protection (formerly known as PHI) is set out in Section 1.10, *Key Person Assurance*.
Suitable for	All individuals who are employed or self-employed and individuals with dependants who will have ongoing financial commitments in the event of long-term ill-health. Additionally, these policies are suitable for employers wishing to protect themselves against the cost of key person disability, or relieve themselves of the responsibility of continuing to pay the salaries of employees generally, in the event of long-term ill-health.
Ages	Minimum 16; maximum 65.
Advantages	1 Provision of an income whilst unable to work. 2 If the policy is effected personally, no income tax arises on payments under the policy. 3 If a company effects the policy, payments to the employee may be deducted as a business expense. 4 Under a guaranteed policy, once the insurer accepts the risks, they cannot withdraw the cover (unless the premiums are not met or full medical disclosure was not made at application stage), even if the insured's health declines. 5 Many providers include rehabilitation or proportionate benefit, allowing the claimant to return to work on a part-time basis or to a different occupation whilst continuing to receive a reduced payment from the provider. 6 Benefits and premiums can be indexed, ensuring that they keep track with inflation. 7 Some insurers have links with medical insurance groups and can provide private medical insurance, or other benefits, at a discount.
Disadvantages	1 Premiums can vary dramatically and cover for a reasonable income may seem quite costly due to the likelihood of a claim being made.

2   Medical evidence is required by the life company and cover may be more expensive or even unavailable for those in poor health or in 'high risk' occupations.

3   If a company effects the policy, payments under the policy in the first instance are treated as a trading receipt (but offset by payment of benefit as salary under PAYE).

4   There are limits on the amount of cover available – often with no more than 60% of income being available under an individual policy and 75% under a company policy.

5   For the most part, Income Protection is a term policy and has no cash in value at any time, although a small number of providers do offer policies with an investment element.

6   Terms and types of policy can vary dramatically and care should be taken to ensure that the most appropriate policy is chosen in each situation.

Investment limits   Minimum premium approximately £10 per month.

Charges   Charges vary from policy to policy but are incorporated within the regular premiums.

FURTHER DETAILS

Commercial Aspects

Income Protection Insurance (also known as permanent health insurance) is a form of insurance which guarantees payment of regular income for a stated period, or up to a stated age, in the event of accident or illness causing loss of earnings.

There is a limit to the amount of cover which is available under these contracts. Many insurance companies have a maximum benefit limit of between 50% and 75% of the policyholder's earnings. Some providers allow for state incapacity benefits within their maximum, whilst others make payments less any state incapacity benefit received.

Most policies have the facility for the income benefits to increase at a set rate of up to 5% per annum or in line with the RPI without further evidence of health.

All contracts have a deferral period before benefits are paid (generally ranging between four weeks and 52 weeks) which can be chosen by the policyholder. The longer the period of deferral the lower the premium.

Preferential premium rates apply to certain occupations/professions.

Taxation Aspects

Individual Effecting the Policy

No tax relief is available on the premiums paid. The benefits payable on individual income protection insurance policies are exempt from tax.

Group schemes for unincorporated businesses achieve a saving in premiums as against individual arrangements, but proprietors may expect to be assessed to income tax on their share of the premium paid. The premiums in respect of the proprietors/partners would not normally be allowed for tax purposes.

Companies Effecting the Policy for Employees

Premiums would normally be a deductible expense for corporation tax purposes, although in each case the position should be checked with the local inspector of taxes before effecting the policy. The premiums paid for any member of a company with a proprietorial interest in the employer's business are unlikely to be deductible, unless the shareholding is insignificant.

On making a claim the benefits would be paid to the employer and received by him as a taxable trading receipt. When the employer pays the same to the disabled employee, the payments are treated as salary and thus treated as a business expense. No tax is therefore effectively paid by the employer on the benefit.

In the employee's hands, the benefits are received as earnings and taxed as such under the PAYE and National Insurance procedures.

CROSS REFERENCES

Key Person Assurance **1.10**
Partnership Assurance **1.11**
Critical Illness Insurance **1.4**

1.6 Private Medical Insurance

Description	PMI is designed to provide cover for medical expenses incurred during acute illness or injury. PMI must not be seen as a complete substitute for the NHS. The purchase of PMI provides peace of mind in the knowledge that medical treatment can be obtained promptly for an eligible condition. The purchase of PMI does not mean that a superior treatment is being obtained outside the NHS. It can be arranged for either individuals or groups.
Suitable for	Individuals, their dependants, the self-employed and employers wishing to provide cover for their employees.
Start-up criteria	For the purpose of entry to a PMI policy, there is no minimum age but there is usually, a maximum entry age which can vary.
Advantages	1 Provision for cost of private medical treatment.
	2 Policies cover treatment in a private hospital or in private rooms within National Health Service (NHS) hospitals.
	3 Discounts are available for membership of group schemes (whether premiums are paid by the employer or not).
	4 A cash payment to the policyholder (normally payable when a policyholder or member stays in a non-fee paying NHS hospital). (This benefit may not be included when the policy provides tax relief.)
Disadvantages	1 PMI is designed to work in tandem with the NHS. It therefore follows that there are certain exclusions common to most policies. These are usually: chronic conditions, AIDS, alcoholism, drug and substance abuse/self-inflicted injury, cosmetic treatment, out-patient drugs and dressings, dentistry (other than specified oro-surgical procedures), certain pre-existing conditions existing before the policy commences, routine pregnancy/sterilisation, infertility, termination of pregnancy, war risks, kidney dialysis, surgical or mobility aids, spectacles, contact lenses and hearing aids. This list is not exhaustive and exclusions on policies should be checked carefully before policy inception. However, cover may be provided after an initial moratorium period of say, two years for certain types of cover if there is no recurrence of a previous medical condition although this depends on which form of underwriting has been chosen. FMU is the assessment and agreement

of an insurance risk. The process involves the disclosure of medical history which enables the Insurer to assess the risk. Once the assessment is complete, the member is notified of any special terms (eg exclusions) and given the opportunity to agree these terms. These excluded conditions are, usually, permanent throughout the life of a policy although the member can request that an excluded condition be considered for removal by the Underwriters.

2   Cash limits on treatment depend on the policy chosen. Some policies are full refund with no overall annual maximum. Budget or Low Cost schemes are designed to cover private in-patient hospital treatment. Out-patient treatment is usually restricted to being related to in-patient treatment. Budget or Low Cost schemes only provide out-patient consultations, tests and physiotherapy where it is connected to a permissible claim for in-patient or day-case treatment. There is also a restriction of the choice of hospitals or restriction of cover for specific medical conditions only.

3   Premiums can increase substantially with age.

4   Employees provided with cover by their employers will be subject to tax on the premiums as a benefit-in-kind if they are earning over £8,500 per annum.

5   Insurance Premium Tax is levied at 5%.

| **Contribution limits** | Variable. |
| **Charges** | Variable depending on the type of policy. |

FURTHER DETAILS

Commercial Aspects

Private medical insurance (PMI) is similar in some respects to income protection insurance but covers the cost of medical treatment rather than providing a replacement income.

In order to obtain treatment under a PMI policy, it is normally a requirement that the referral is made by an individual's General Practitioner to a specialist.

Cover is normally available on a banded/scale basis which reflects the differing costs of rooms in private hospitals and private rooms in NHS hospitals around the UK. Premium costs vary accordingly.

The industry has established a simple benchmarking system. The new format has been welcomed and providers have agreed to add a benchmarking table to their literature. This will enable both the adviser and the customer to compare products more easily.

Taxation Aspects

Where employers can contribute to group PMI schemes, the premiums are normally deductible as an expense for corporation tax purposes.

Employees earning more than £8,500 will be subject to income tax on the amount of the premiums deemed to apply to them as a benefit-in-kind.

PMI benefits are tax-free (even where benefits include a lump sum cash payment).

1.7   Long-term Care Insurance

Description	Regular or single premium insurance policies which are used to provide the necessary funding to cover the cost of long-term care. Benefits may be paid directly to the claimant or to a recognised provider of care for the elderly or chronically infirm once the insured is unable to perform a specified number of activities of daily living (ADLs), and sometimes after a specified deferred period. Some policies are based on the same structure as unit linked, flexible whole life policies and some are pure insurance contracts.
Suitable for	Individuals who need immediate care or who wish to ensure that they will receive adequate and independent care in old age or because of chronic illness or severe disability.
Age at entry	Typically 50–75 for prefunded contracts and 60 to 100 for immediate care contracts although contracts do vary.
Advantages	1 The benefit can pay for nursing home care or for care at home, including 24-hour nursing.
	2 There is no tax liability if payments are made from the insurer direct to the care provider.
	3 Policies can be funded on either a lump sum or regular premium basis and benefits can be indexed to help them keep track with rising costs.
	4 Contracts are available to provide immediate cover for people who are chronically sick, disabled or in need of care.
	5 The regular payments received can often be higher than those available from an annuity.
	6 Some contracts are structured as investments, with the fund being returned, or a pre-agreed death benefit, being paid if no claim is made during the lifetime of the policyholder.
Disadvantages	1 There are currently relatively very few providers of long-term care contracts and the cover provided by each is not always directly comparable.
	2 No tax relief is currently available on premiums for the elderly.
	3 The policies tend to provide cover for long-term care only and, as such, may not necessarily cover acute conditions such as hip replacement or other major surgery.
	4 There are potential implications on tax and even reductions in certain state benefits if the benefits are paid directly to the claimant.

Cost	Minimum premium generally £50 per month or £1,000 single premium for pre-funded products with immediate care contributions dependent on the income required.
Charges	Dependent upon the contract.

FURTHER DETAILS

Commercial Aspects

A number of insurers have withdrawn from the pre-funded long-term care market despite predictions that demand for this cover will increase due to the ageing population.

In turn, the demand for immediate need care payment plans is increasing, as is the cost of care, resulting in an increase in premiums for this type of cover.

In order to be able to claim benefits, the insured individual must usually be incapable of performing two or three out of what is usually a total of six activities of daily living (ADLs), such as bathing, dressing and feeding oneself, benefits are payable either immediately or after a specified deferred period.

Taxation

HMRC has confirmed that no tax charge will be levied on the insured when proceeds of policies are paid directly from the insurer to the care provider.

State Provision

From April 2005 the State will meet the full cost of care where a person's whole assets are less than the lower limit set out below and proportionate costs where assets are valued between the lower and upper limit—

	Lower	*Upper*
England	14,250	23,250
Wales	22,000	22,000
Scotland	14,000	22,750
Northern Ireland	14,000	23,000

CROSS REFERENCES

Pre-Retirement   **5.7**
Retirement   **5.8**

1.8   Purchased Life Annuities

Description	A lump sum investment with a life company which provides a tax-efficient guaranteed income for a fixed period or the remainder of the policy holder's lifetime.
Ages	No limit, but the investment return is greater the older the annuitant. Unless temporary life annuities are effected, annuities as an investment should not generally be considered for males and females below the ages of 70 and 75 respectively.
Suitable for	All taxpayers who require a fixed income from capital in a tax-efficient form, guaranteed for a specified period or the life of the annuitant.
Advantages	1 Annuity payments are treated as part taxed income and part untaxed return of capital.
	2 If the annuitant is not a taxpayer, payments can be made gross of income tax.
	3 Payments are guaranteed.
	4 There are a number of companies which now offer PLAs on an impaired life basis.
Disadvantages	1 It is usually not possible for the purchaser to surrender the annuity once purchased.
	2 Payments in real terms decrease with inflation, unless the annuity is escalating or unit-linked, and may affect eligibility for means-tested social security benefits, council tax benefit and age allowance.
	3 The income element of annuity payments is subject to a 20% tax charge and higher rates of income tax where the annuitant is a higher rate taxpayer. In most instances the 20% tax will be deducted at source by the life company.
	4 Unless a capital protected annuity is purchased, the 'unused' capital will not be returned on death.
	5 Capital protection not available in certain circumstances.
	6 The prevailing annuity rates at the time of purchase could drastically affect the level of income provided.
Investment limits	Minimum investment approximately £5,000. No maximum.
Charges	Policy charge of approximately £5–£15 per annum which depends upon the frequency of the annuity instalments and not the level of annuity purchased.
	Charges are usually taken into account when calculating the annuity payment.

FURTHER DETAILS

Commercial Aspects

(1) Life Annuities

Annuities can be recommended for elderly investors for part of their capital if they wish to increase their spendable income in a reasonably tax-efficient way and do not mind reducing the estate they will leave on death.

Contracts can be written on joint-life, first-death or last survivor basis. On death, no capital is returned unless a capital protected annuity is effected which guarantees that if death occurs before a total, equal to the cost of the annuity, has been paid, the balance will be returned to the deceased's estate. However, most companies will offer a guarantee that the annuity payments will be made for a specific period even if the annuitant dies within that period.

The rate of return on an annuity is dependent upon the age of the investor, the type of the annuity chosen and the prevailing interest rates at the time of purchase. Annuity payments can be annual, half-yearly, quarterly or monthly, either in arrears or in advance.

An escalating annuity can provide an income which increases by typically a fixed amount per year, for example 3 or 5% up to a maximum of 8%. The selection of an escalating income will reduce the level of initial income. It is also possible to purchase unit-linked annuities, although it should be noted that if investment performance deteriorates, there is only a small guaranteed return offered.

It is now possible to obtain a PLA on an impaired life basis, with higher rates available for smokers, overweight people and those in poor health.

(2) Temporary Annuities

These are similar to life annuities but are payable only for a predetermined number of years. The age of the annuitant with these contracts plays a much smaller part in fixing the rate of return and temporary annuities are therefore available for use by individuals of all ages as a means of funding regular outgoings for a specified period.

Uses of Purchased Life Annuities

1   Provision of a tax-efficient income, particularly for the elderly (see Section 1.9, *Home Income Plans*).
2   IHT planning – purchase of an annuity without guarantee can be an effective method of reducing an annuitant's estate for IHT purposes. The IHT savings must, however, be weighed against the loss of capital to the policyholder's heirs.
3   A means of funding regular outgoings such as life assurance premiums.
4   In conjunction with a capital investment to provide guaranteed income and return of initial capital outlay.

Taxation Aspects

Purchased Life Annuities are often suitable for higher rate taxpayers since HMRC regard a proportion of such annuity payments as a return of capital which is not liable to tax. The capital element is greater for annuitants of advanced years and is fixed at the outset.

The income element is subject to a 20% tax rate and higher rate where appropriate.

The 20% tax charge is deducted by the life company before payment of the annuity instalment is made to the policyholder and this satisfies the basic rate tax liability. It is, however, possible for non-taxpayers to have annuity payments made gross of tax.

A higher rate taxpayer will be liable to pay an additional 20% income tax on the income element of the annuity.

CROSS REFERENCES

Home Income Plans   **1.9**
IHT – Insurance   **4.30**
The Young   **5.2**
Retirement   **5.8**

1.9   Home Income Plans

Description	Equity is released through a Lifetime Mortgage or a Home Reversion Plan and is automatically invested into an annuity that is built into the plan, to generate an income for life. A cash lump sum may be available in addition to an income, but the amount may be restricted. A life company or building society provides a loan of up to 80% of the property value of which at least 90% must be invested in a purchased life annuity with the remaining 10% available as cash.
Ages	Usually minimum 65+ for home reversion plans although some will go as low as 55 for a lifetime mortgage – for married couples eligibility is based on the youngest age.
Suitable for	Owner-occupiers of flats and houses who need to increase their spendable income.
Advantages	1 Facility for the aged to increase spendable income.
	2 Annuity payments are regarded as part capital and part income. The capital portion is not taxable.
	3 A lifetime annuity guarantees that the income will be paid for as long as you live.
	4 Interest rate on the mortgage is fixed for life with some schemes.
	5 Investor can take part of the mortgage for their own use.
	6 Basic rate tax on these plans is charged at the savings rate.
Disadvantages	1 Annuity payments can affect eligibility for means-tested social security benefits, council tax benefit and age allowance.
	2 Rate of interest on the annuity payments is fixed for life with some schemes.
	3 The investor is tied to the investment in an annuity unless the property is sold.
	4 Inflation will erode the value of the annuity.
	5 Received 'bad press' some years ago when in some cases investment returns failed to match mortgage interest rates.
	6 Early repayment penalties can be extremely high.
Investment limits	Minimum property value approximately £40,000. The mortgage is usually limited to 80% of the valuation.
Charges	Charges are wide and varied including administration fees, arrangement fees, legal and surveyors' fees as well as professional advice fees.

FURTHER DETAILS

Commercial Aspects

These plans enable the elderly to 'unlock' capital tied up in their home, providing them with a tax-efficient income for the rest of their lives. This method of obtaining an income from capital should, however, only be used when other sources of capital have been exhausted.

The money borrowed is repaid from the proceeds of the sale of the property upon the death of the home owner or when they move into long-term care. Some companies offer a limited degree of capital protection if death should occur in the early years of the scheme. There is the facility in some schemes to increase the loan once the scheme has been in force for a number of years, by way of a 'top up' mortgage.

The annuity can be written on a joint-lives, last-survivor basis with the benefit that annuity payments will be paid for the duration of the survivor's life. It is possible to take a mortgage, on an interest only basis, direct from a building society and purchase the annuity from the life company offering the best rate at the time.

A large number of elderly people entered into Home Income Plans in the 1980s only to find that interest rates soon moved against them. There were many horror stories where the actual mortgage interest payable moved ahead of the investment return leaving some elderly people having to make net payments rather than receive a net income. The problem was compounded by falling property prices.

However, the plans are beginning to gain in popularity once more due to support from Help the Aged for schemes such as Safe Home Income Plans (SHIPs). Furthermore, schemes can now be tailored to meet individual circumstances.

Taxation Aspects

Income tax relief for interest on loans taken out after 8 March 1999 is no longer available.

For loans taken out prior to 9 March 1999, irrespective of whether the borrower is a taxpayer or not, basic rate tax relief is available on the interest on loans up to £30,000, provided all of the following conditions are satisfied:

1   the loan was made as part of a scheme under which not less than nine-tenths of the proceeds are used to purchase an annuity on either the borrower's life or the joint lives of the borrower and spouse on a last survivor basis;
2   that at the time the loan was made the persons to whom it was made or each of the annuitants had attained the age of 65 years;
3   the loan was secured on land in the UK or Eire and the person to whom it was made or one of the annuitants owns an estate or interest in that land;
4   the person to whom it was made or each of the annuitants uses the land on which the loan is secured as his only or main residence at the time the interest is paid;
5   where the property was the main residence prior to 9 March 1999 and ceases to be so used, on moving to, say, a nursing home;
6   where a replacement loan is taken out to repay a pre-9 March 1999 loan.

The annuity payment is treated as part return of capital which is not regarded as taxable income and part income which is. Any outstanding loans on the death of the mortgagor should reduce the estate for IHT purposes.

The companies marketing these schemes make two deductions before making the annuity payments, the net loan interest and basic rate tax on the annuity payment. Higher rate taxpayers must pay any further tax due; non-taxpayers can arrange for the annuity payments to be paid gross of basic rate tax.

Purchase Schemes – Home Reversion

There are schemes available where a share of the property is 'sold' at a substantial discount to the company offering the scheme. The main disadvantage with these schemes is that the future appreciation of the property share that is sold is in the hands of the company to the total exclusion of the investor's heirs whereas with the 'mortgage schemes' the investor retains full control of a 'growing asset'. The main advantage of this option is that the amount of the property sold is pre-defined at outset and is not subject to interest charges. This means the home owner knows exactly what will be left in their possession and what ultimately will be inheritable. In addition further reversions may be possible if additional cash is required.

CROSS REFERENCES

Purchased Life Annuities   **1.8**
Retirement   **5.8**

1.10 Key Person Assurance

Description	Assurance cover effected by a company on the life of a 'key employee' whose death, incapacity or enforced retirement would affect the profitability of the company. The benefits are paid to the company on the occurrence of the insured event.
Age of key person	Minimum 18, maximum 75.
Suitable for	Companies, partnerships.
Advantages	1 Benefits are payable to the company in order to fund the replacement of a key person and compensate the company for any loss of profits which may ensue from his death, incapacity or forced retirement.
	2 Premiums paid may be allowable as a deduction against corporation tax (but see below).
	3 The policy proceeds may be free of corporation tax in the hands of the company (but see below).
Disadvantages	1 Generally, if the premiums are allowable as a deduction in computing corporation tax liability, the policy proceeds will be taxed as a trading receipt in the hands of the company.
	2 There is no return of premiums at the end of the term nor any surrender value under term assurance policies.

FURTHER DETAILS

Commercial Aspects

Many companies will have certain directors and/or other employees who are vital to the profitability of the company. This is because they may have a specialised knowledge or skill, be in control of a research project, or be a salesman with important personal contacts.

The death, incapacity or retirement of such a key person may severely affect the profitability of a company and therefore, in order to compensate for the financial strain resulting from such an event, a company may effect a key person assurance on the life of the individual concerned, with the company receiving the sum assured or other benefits on his death, incapacity or retirement.

To cover death and retirement, the policy could be one of whole life, endowment or term assurance. In most cases, however, it will be pure life protection cover that will be required, ie without an investment element, which means that term assurance may well be the most suitable and often provides the cheapest option. In most cases cost will be a very relevant factor to a business. Term assurance will therefore be particularly appropriate where the term of the policy is fixed or where cover for a fixed short-term period is required. Where longer term protection is needed, and particularly where it is important to ensure future insurability, then a flexible whole of life plan on a maximum cover basis may well be more suitable. The advantage of a whole life policy is that it will exist throughout the key person's service and probably obtain a surrender value which could be taken by the company at a later stage or assigned to the key person in recognition of services for him to use for his own purposes, for example family protection or IHT mitigation. An endowment policy will produce a lump sum at maturity or earlier death and would be suitable where the key person had a fixed retirement date as the policy could be timed to mature at that date. A term assurance policy would only produce a sum on death within the term specified.

There is no definitive formula for determining the appropriate level of cover. The objective should be to replace the loss of profit to the business over the period that it will take to find a replacement. The tax treatment of the premiums paid and proceeds received varies with the type of policy effected and this could be a substantial factor in the type of policy chosen for key person purposes, irrespective of the additional benefits a particular policy may offer.

Key Person Income Protection Insurance

If a key person is absent from work for a prolonged period as a result of sickness or accident, the profitability of the business can suffer. Key person income protection insurance can be effected to offset such disruption. The principal features of this form of cover are:

1   the term is usually for a period of between five and ten years;
2   benefits will usually be paid for a maximum of either two or five years;
3   the minimum deferral period is four weeks, but usually 13 or 26 week deferred periods are chosen (arranged, typically, to coincide with the point at which it is expected that profits will begin to suffer);
4   calculation of the appropriate amount of benefit will take into account the need for a contribution towards any loss of profits as well as payment for a temporary replacement, but it will also be borne in mind that the key person may be able to act in an advisory capacity, even while physically incapacitated, and may also be able to resume his duties in due course.

Key Person Critical Illness Insurance

It is now also becoming increasingly common to insure key individuals so that if they suffer a life threatening illness covered by the policy, the employer will secure a lump sum.

The policy may be 'free standing' or a 'bolt-on' to a whole-of-life policy or term assurance policy.

Taxation Aspects

Allowance of Premiums Paid

Premium payments under whole life or endowment policies are treated as capital payments as they produce a capital asset in the form of the surrender value. They are disallowable in the employer's taxation computation.

Term assurance does not have a surrender value and is therefore outside the criteria above. To qualify as a deduction as a trading expense, however, term assurance must satisfy the following.

1   It must be taken out wholly and exclusively for the purposes of the trade, for example to compensate an expected loss of profits on the key person's death.

2   The policy should be for a short period, preferably not more than five years and certainly less than ten years, as beyond that time it is difficult to quantify loss of profits in what may be very different trading conditions. A five-year renewable policy is usually acceptable as a 'short term' policy (subject to confirmation from HMRC, as outlined below).

3   Where the key person is a director holding more than say, 5% of the shares, it will be necessary to show that the intention is a trading one and is not for proprietorship reasons. This may be difficult for family owned companies.

4   There should be an employer/employee relationship.

Provided the above conditions are met the term assurance premiums should qualify for relief.

Taxation of Policy Proceeds

If the term assurance meets the criteria above and is an allowable deduction, any proceeds from the policy will be taxed as a trading receipt. The non-claiming of such premiums as allowable will not in itself prevent the proceeds being taxed as a trading receipt (but see below).

It may be possible, however, to arrange for the sum assured to be paid out to the company in tranches to secure maximum benefit from the small companies' rate of corporation tax.

The proceeds of term assurance which does not meet the trading criteria, together with all whole life and endowment policy proceeds, will generally not be taxed as a trading receipt of the company, as they relate to capital. No capital gains will arise on the proceeds unless the policyholder acquired the policy for money or money's worth from another person.

The tax treatment of policies of life assurance effected by companies with regard to both premiums and policy proceeds is judged by HMRC on the merits of each case. It is therefore prudent for the company to inform HMRC as to the purpose of the policy, in order that the tax position with regard to premiums paid and the eventual receipt of the policy proceeds can be established in advance.

In many cases, it will be preferable to avoid having the policy proceeds treated as a trading receipt as the loss of corporation tax relief on the premiums will be small compared with the potential tax on the policy proceeds. For this situation to apply potentially, it will be necessary to have HMRC's confirmation that the premiums are disallowable as a trading expense.

Any life policy taken out by a company which gives rise to a surrender value will be taxed as a non-qualifying policy and any excess of surrender value over premiums paid will be liable to corporation tax.

Inheritance Tax and Key Person Policies

The payment of the sum assured to the company will not be liable to IHT. If, however, the key person is a major shareholder, a large inflow of cash into the company could inflate the value of his shareholding within his estate and therefore (if the shareholding does not qualify for Business Property Relief) the potential IHT liability on that estate. In these circumstances, it may be possible to arrange for the policy proceeds to be paid by instalments, thereby minimising any possible increase in the value of those shares.

Taxation of Key Person Income Protection Insurance

Premiums are usually allowable as a deductible expense, provided the cover is short-term and the benefits are payable to the employer to cover loss of profits due to the loss of the key person's services. The premiums may be disallowed if the key person is a proprietor or a principal shareholder in the business.

It is probable that the benefits would be taxed as income of the company irrespective of whether or not the premiums are allowable. Where the premiums for the cover are paid wholly by the firm, the benefits received by the firm will be treated as a trading receipt but if they are then paid out to the sick employee and/or as remuneration to any replacement employee the normal rules as to deductibility will apply. Where the employee has contributed to the premiums, any benefits received under the policy and passed on to the employee, to the extent of the employee's contributions, will also be exempt from tax (ITTOIA 2005 s 743).

Taxation of Key Person Critical Illness Policies

Premiums are allowable as a deductible expense in similar circumstances to any key person life assurance policy and claim proceeds similarly treated.

CROSS REFERENCES

Term Assurance   **1.2**
Whole Life Assurance   **1.3**
Critical Illness Insurance   **1.4**
Income Protection Insurance   **1.5**
Partnership Assurance   **1.11**

1.11   Partnership Assurance

Description	A means of providing funds to the continuing members of a partnership to enable them to purchase a deceased or retiring partner's share of the business. Also included are other recommended assurances for incapacity and retirement.
Suitable for	Individual partners or groups of partners.
Advantages	1 Funds are provided in a tax-efficient form. 2 There may be IHT advantages. 3 Prevents cash difficulty in the partnership on death, incapacity or retirement.
Disadvantages	1 Premiums are not treated as a business expense if the partnership effects the policy. 2 Differences in partners' states of health and ages can cause inequity in funding premiums. 3 Changes in partnership circumstances could adversely affect the situation.

FURTHER DETAILS

Generally

A retiring partner looks to the other partners to purchase his share from him when he retires. The cash produced can then be used to provide a pension in retirement. Similarly, on death, the partner would expect the sale of his share to provide for his widow and dependants after his death.

If the partnership share is valuable, particularly if goodwill is valued, the continuing partners may not be able to finance the purchase. This would quite often cause severe financial and practical problems to the partnership, the partners and the retiring partner or the deceased partner's dependants.

Partnership assurance provides the following benefits:

1   it helps reduce or remove the need for continuing partners to borrow funds, liquidate assets or reduce profits/savings in order to provide the money to buy the other partner's share;
2   it helps avoid other less attractive solutions, eg looking for a new partner to provide the funds to buy the other partner's share;
3   it helps ensure a fair, commercial price is provided for the partner's share.

Objectives

The main objectives of partnership assurance are:

1   to put cash in the hands of the continuing partners to enable them to purchase a fellow partner's share in the event of death, illness or retirement;

2   to share the cost of any assurance fairly between the partners;
3   to minimise any liability to CGT and IHT on the proceeds or premiums paid;
4   to be sufficiently flexible to cope easily with incoming and outgoing partners.

On Death

There are various ways of structuring the assurance to achieve most of the above objectives and two suggestions are as follows:

1   Each partner effects a policy on his own life in trust for the benefit of surviving partners, but on early retirement leaving the policy proceeds for the benefit of his spouse.
  - (a)   Differences in partners' ages and states of health could cause inequity in the premiums paid by each partner on which there could be an exposure to IHT. This could be minimised by, for example, adjustment to the profit shares or the use of flexible unit-linked whole-of-life policies.
  - (b)   On the death of a partner his interest in each of the surviving partners' trust policies would terminate and the value of those interests, if any, would form part of his estate for IHT purposes.
  - (c)   New partners can easily be introduced if specific partners are not named under the trust policies. The incoming partner would effect appropriate assurance on his own life in trust for his partners.
2   Each partner effects a policy on a 'life of another basis' in respect of each of his partners.
  - (a)   The value, if any, of policies on the other lives would form part of the deceased partner's estate for IHT.
  - (b)   The young partners would have to pay higher premiums on the lives of the senior partners.
  - (c)   This method does, however, become cumbersome when more than, say, four partners are involved, and is therefore restricted to small partnerships.

The best type of policy for the purchase of a deceased partner's share on death is term assurance. Such policies are much cheaper than whole life policies and have no surrender values.

However, individuals will no longer have the right to pensions tax relief on the cost of new personal life insurance policies under both personal and occupational schemes.

This will apply to all personal contributions made to an occupational scheme on or after 1 August 2007 in respect of personal term assurance policies, unless the insurer received a PTA application before 29 March 2007 and the policy was taken out as part of the pension scheme before 1 August 2007.

For personal pension policies it will apply to all contributions made on or after 6 April 2007 unless the insurer received a PTA application before 14 December 2006 and the policy came into force before 6 April 2007.

Where an individual continues to be eligible for relief on such contributions where he met the above criteria he will cease to be entitled to relief if the policy to which the contribution relates is varied outside its original terms so as to increase the sum assured or lengthen the term of the insurance. However, if there is an option under the policy which is then exercised this will not affect the relief due.

The above change will not affect the position regarding PTA where this is secured by employer contributions, and such contributions will continue to be eligible for tax relief.

On Incapacity

If the partnership is concerned about meeting the need to find funds if a partner is incapacitated leading to a need to either reduce his involvement or to retire, then critical illness cover may well be appropriate.

This cover may either be added to existing whole life or term assurance policies or, alternatively, free standing critical illness cover can be arranged.

Key person permanent health insurance may also on occasions be appropriate where the profitability of the business will suffer in the event of the prolonged absence of a partner as a result of sickness or accident (see Section 1.10, *Key Person Assurance*).

On Retirement

If the retirement date is fixed then each of the younger partners could effect a policy on his own life timed to mature at the time of the older partners' retirement. Term assurance is not suitable and an endowment policy on a with-profits or unit-linked basis may be appropriate. A whole life policy could be used and surrendered at the date of retirement but some loss of benefits will be encountered. If cost is an important factor a 'low cost' whole life policy may be used. This combines the use of decreasing term assurance and conventional whole life policies. The policy remains the property of the partner if he leaves the partnership.

If the retirement date is not fixed, then an Individual Savings Account or an open-ended unit-linked endowment will allow the flexibility of encashment when necessary. A more radical suggestion to deal with the problems on retirement and also on death is set out below.

Formal Arrangements for Dealing with Disposal/Acquisition of Partner's Share

The arrangement for the disposal and acquisition of a partner's share should be regulated formally.

Automatic Accrual Method   A large part of the value of a senior partner's share in a partnership will consist of goodwill. If this goodwill can be ignored and left in the partnership then the cash required to purchase a retiring partner's share is much lower. A simple clause is all that is required to be inserted in the partnership deed to record this and the goodwill thereafter belongs to the partnership as a whole rather than the individual partners. The points to note are as follows.

1   No IHT should be chargeable on giving up the goodwill as normally the loss would be mutual as between the partners and not intended to confer any gratuitous benefit[1].
2   The permanent capital of the firm is built up.
3   New partners do not find the cost of contributing capital as onerous as before.
4   Partners effectively giving up goodwill, for which they paid originally, may be compensated by either:

    (a)   an annuity charged on future profits of the partnership to run from retirement; or

    (b)   additional drawings to fund a life policy to replace the capital forgone; or

    (c)   additional drawings to fund retirement annuity and/or personal pension premiums to provide a pension in retirement.

5   Any residual capital remaining to be bought out can be funded by an endowment policy as outlined above under 'On Retirement'.

Double Option Agreements   In order to ensure that a deceased or retiring partner's share is purchased by the surviving or continuing partners, all the partners should enter into a 'double option' agreement which permits the outgoing partner or the executors of a deceased partner the option of selling the interest to the continuing/surviving partners and the continuing/ surviving partners the option of purchasing the same. HMRC do not treat such an agreement as a 'binding contract for sale' and, therefore, IHT business property relief should not be affected.

Such options will be expressed to be exercisable within a specified period (usually a number of months). Providing the necessary notice is served by one party within the specified period, the exercise of the option will bring about the sale. Commercial considerations generally compel the exercise of the options.

If critical illness cover is effected, then a single option agreement may also be appropriate. This allows the critically ill partner to sell their interest but does not give the other partners an option to insist they sell.

Taxation Aspects

Disposal/Purchase of Partner's Share Following Death

Capital Gains Tax   The double option agreement normally specifies that the price to be paid for the shares is the open market value.

Generally, the assets being purchased will have been revalued on the death of the partner so that, unless there has been a significant increase in value between the date of death and date of purchase, there should be no significant CGT consequences.

Normally, life assurance policies are exempt from CGT except where a person subsequently acquires an interest in the policy for consideration in money or money's worth. For this reason, it is important to write the life assurance policy under trust from inception for the benefit of co-partners before the life assurance company assumes risk. Where a policy is written under trust after such a date, there could be CGT implications.

Inheritance Tax   A double option agreement is evidence that the arrangement is of a commercial nature and, therefore, should not jeopardise any eligibility for IHT business property relief.

However, it is good practice that, as part of the partnership share purchase agreement, an undertaking is completed stating that the policy proceeds are to form part of a commercial transaction.

Payment of the policy premiums to a policy written under trust for selected beneficiaries will normally represent actual or potentially exempt transfers of value for IHT purposes. But, as part of a current partnership share purchase arrangement, it is likely that an absence of gratuitous benefit can be shown. Where no gift is intended, but the payment is obligatory, no liability will arise.

If there is any element of gratuitous intent, it is likely that the payment could fall within the payer's annual and/or normal expenditure out of income exemption.

Careful consideration needs to be given to the IHT implications where either:

1 a new trust is declared or brought to an end; or
2 the power of appointment in a flexible trust is to be exercised to change the beneficial interest under that trust.

Income Tax The proceeds from a qualifying life policy will not incur a personal liability to income tax. Where a non-qualifying life assurance policy is effected, a liability to higher rate income tax may arise on any 'profit' from the policy if at the time of death (or surrender of the policy) the policyholder is or, by including any profit on the policy, becomes a higher rate taxpayer.

The profit represents the difference between the premiums paid and the surrender value immediately prior to death.

Disposal/Purchase of Shares on Critical Illness

Capital Gains Tax Where the agreement provides for the sale/purchase of shares or other assets in the event of critical illness and that the purchase is to be made at market value, then the normal valuation procedures will take place and, to the extent that there is a difference between the indexed acquisition price and the price paid on disposal, there will be a CGT liability.

It is also popular for option agreements to specify that in the event of a sale following critical illness, the purchase price is determined by reference to either a fixed price or a fixed formula, as opposed to market value, eg a proportion of a multiple of profits.

The grant of a non-market value option will be a disposal for CGT purposes. Provided the option is granted on commercial terms, it is unlikely that HMRC will seek to impose a charge to CGT.

Provided all the partners enter into the agreement on similar terms, then the commerciality test is likely to be satisfied.

For IHT, similar reasons are likely to mean that the grant of the option would not be regarded as intending to confer any gratuitous benefit and that it was made on arm's-length terms.

Inheritance Tax Where a critically-ill partner's option enables him to sell his share in excess of the market value of his share at the date of disposal, this is unlikely to have any adverse IHT implications.

The purchaser of shares in circumstances where the price is in excess of the market value should not be treated as making transfers of value at the time that the option is exercised, provided that the whole arrangement is commercial with no gratuitous intent.

Where the purchase price is less than market value, it may be argued that the disposer has made a transfer of value. However, provided the arrangement can be shown to be commercial, there should be no necessity to substitute market value in circumstances where fixed price arrangements are being used.

Pre-Owned Assets Tax (POAT)

Business trusts which have included the settlor as a potential beneficiary are within the scope of the recently introduced tax charge on pre-owned assets. This income tax charge was introduced with effect from 6 April 2005. Although essentially aimed at arrangements to avoid the inheritance tax 'gift with reservation' rules, the charge can also impact on business assurance trusts.

To avoid the impact of POAT for a business trust, the settlor should be excluded as a potential beneficiary from the trust.

Other Insurance Investments

Permanent Health Insurance (see Section 1.5) and Personal Pensions (see Section 2.3) should also be considered.

CROSS REFERENCES

Term Assurance   **1.2**
Whole Life Assurance   **1.3**
Critical Illness Insurance   **1.4**
Income Protection Insurance   **1.5**
Personal Pensions   **2.4**
IHT – The Charge to Tax   **4.15**
IHT – Business Property Relief   **4.19**

1.12 Share Purchase Assurance

Description	A means of providing funds either to the continuing shareholders or to the company itself to enable the shareholders or the company to purchase the shares of a deceased/ incapacitated/ retiring shareholder.
Suitable for	Co-shareholders in private companies, especially shareholding directors in family companies.
Advantages	1 Enables remaining shareholders to maintain control over the business.
	2 Provides funds to the remaining shareholders to enable them to purchase the shares from the deceased/ incapacitated/ retired shareholder or their estate, or provides funds to the company to enable it to purchase the shares.
	3 Safeguards the standards of living of incapacitated shareholders or deceased shareholders' dependants.
	4 May assist a deceased shareholder's estate to fund an IHT liability.
	5 Ensures that shares remain with the shareholders who actively participate in the company.
	6 Purchase by the company may be treated as capital gains.
Disadvantages	1 Shareholders need to fund the premiums out of their taxed income.
	2 Differences in shareholders' states of health and ages can cause inequity in funding premiums (although this can be overcome by the drawing up of an appropriate agreement).

(Please note that reference in the table above and the text below to 'shareholders' relates to both director shareholders and non-director shareholders. Where retirement and incapacity are referred to, this would only apply to director shareholders, whilst death is relevant to both).

FURTHER DETAILS

Generally

The shares of major shareholders in private companies frequently pass directly to their spouses on death. The surviving spouse may not wish to take an active role in the company and could be forced or decide to sell the shares to an outsider to the detriment of the remaining shareholders and possibly the company itself.

Even if the surviving spouse or other beneficiary were to take an interest in the company, he or she might lack the necessary skills to make a useful contribution. Fragmentation of the shareholding, where the shares are left to a number of beneficiaries, could also be undesirable, not least by altering the balance of control.

A large part of the problem can be avoided by early planning, particularly by the use of appropriate trust vehicles as set out in Sections 4.10, 4.11, 4.12, 4.13, 4.14 and 4.15. However, the problem can be reduced by arranging the necessary finance to buy the shares on the death, incapacity or retirement of a shareholder and life assurance can be arranged to ensure that funds are available for the purchase. There are two distinct methods and these are set out below.

Shareholder Share Purchase

The shareholders within a specified period (usually a number of months) enter into mutual agreements (known as 'double option' or 'cross option' agreements) which would be exercised on the death/incapacity/retirement of a shareholder. The options would provide that the continuing shareholders could require the retiring/incapacitated shareholder/the executors of the deceased shareholder to sell the shares to them and the retiring/incapacitated shareholder/executors could require that the continuing shareholders buy the shares.

Where the objective is to purchase shares on the death of a shareholder, term assurance may be appropriate and could contain options to increase, renew or convert the policy. In certain cases a whole life policy may be more appropriate but this will result in higher premiums. Either low-cost or unit-linked policies could be used. Where a purchase of shares is desired in the event of a shareholder's disability leading to a need to either reduce his involvement in the business or retire, then critical illness cover may well be appropriate. Single option agreements are generally used in the case of critical illness cover which would be exercised by the critically ill shareholder. Where the purchase of shares is on the retirement of a shareholder, term assurance is not appropriate and a unit-linked or with-profits endowment policy may be best. Each shareholder would effect a policy on his or her own life in trust for the other shareholders.

A form of 'flexible' trust would normally be used to ensure that the proceeds of a policy on the life of a shareholder would be paid to the remaining shareholders but that changes in shareholders could also be catered for. On the shareholder's death the survivors would receive funds to enable them to purchase the deceased's shares. Where the shareholders' ages are very different and/or there are loadings for additional health risks the premium costs may be disproportionate and the shareholders may wish to make cash adjustments for this.

Company Share Purchase

Companies are allowed to purchase their own shares which are then treated as cancelled. Thus the shares of a deceased, incapacitated or retired shareholder may be purchased by the company and the shareholder or executors would receive cash for the shares. A number of formal procedural steps need to take place before the shares can be purchased, for example, checking the company's powers in the articles of association, passing a formal resolution etc. In addition, the company must either have distributable profits or the purchase must be made out of a fresh issue of shares for that purpose. The purchase of the shares may be funded by the use of life assurance policies. An assurance policy is taken out on the life of the shareholder but set up so that in the event of a claim the sum assured will be paid to the company. The sum assured would equal the value of the shares held by the shareholder. It must be remembered that all shareholders would need to be insured for the respective value of their shareholding.

Taxation Aspects

Shareholder Purchase

The double option/cross option agreement ensures that business property relief for IHT purposes is available on death. If a buy and sell agreement is used, business property relief will be lost. No IHT should arise on the premiums payable as they will either not be chargeable as not being gifts or will fall within normal exemptions or be potentially exempt.

The premiums are not allowed as a deduction for tax purposes unless they are paid as part of a personal pension plan (see the reference to personal pension plans in section 1.11 *Partnership Assurance*). Provided a qualifying policy is used there should be no tax liability in respect of the policy proceeds.

Company Purchase

The premiums paid will not be allowed for corporation tax and the policy proceeds should not be taxed as a receipt. Any chargeable gain arising on the policy, ie the excess of the surrender value over premiums previously paid, will form part of the company's income and be liable to corporation tax. (See *The Taxation of Company-Owned Life Assurance Policies*, 1.13.)

The payment by the company will be a distribution for tax purposes and will require distributable profits in the company. The shareholder will receive the distribution net of tax and will be assessed to higher rate tax on the grossed-up receipt.

Alternatively, permission may be sought from HMRC to have the distribution treated as a capital distribution. To qualify for this the company must be unquoted, the purchase must be for trading purposes, the shareholder must be UK resident and have held the shares for five years.

The trading purpose is satisfied if the purchase is to enable an IHT liability to be settled or where on retirement the shareholding is substantially reduced. Where clearance is given the cash paid is not treated as a distribution. The receipt is treated as capital in the shareholder's hands and on death is not taxable and on retirement is subject to CGT.

Where EIS relief has been claimed by any shareholder a purchase of any shares may negate the relief.

CROSS REFERENCES

Term Assurance **1.2**
Whole Life Assurance **1.3**
Critical Illness Insurance **1.4**
Key person Assurance **1.10**
Estate Planning **4.14**
IHT – Business Property Relief **4.19**

1.13 Life Assurance Taxation

INTRODUCTION

There are currently two elements to the taxation of life assurance policies. First, the deduction of tax from the policyholder's 'premium fund' held by the life office. Secondly, the taxation of the individual in respect of premiums paid and the subsequent return from the policy, whether by way of partial surrender, total encashment, maturity or death. These are dealt with in the following paragraphs.

THE LIFE FUND

The income and gains of a life fund come mainly from the following sources.
1   Dividends from companies resident in the UK. Such dividends are called franked investment income and the life fund will not have to pay any further tax on these dividends.
2   Dividends from foreign companies, fixed interest stocks, gilts, interest and similar income. Tax at 20% is payable by the life fund on the excess of this income over expenses, although the expenses incurred in acquiring life assurance business are relieved over seven years rather than being allowed in the year they are incurred.
3   Gains on government securities (gilts) and corporate bonds are free of CGT but the interest element of the gain is taxed as income.
4   Unrealised gains/losses of circulating capital are taxable as well as realised gains on shares, property and other assets at 20%. Indexation allowance is available but there is no annual exemption. The allowance is not available on circulating capital.

THE POLICYHOLDER

Qualifying and Non-Qualifying Policies

For tax purposes, policies are treated as either qualifying for favourable tax treatment with regard to premiums paid and policy proceeds, or non-qualifying, the latter of which do not obtain such favourable tax treatment.

The 'qualification rules' are complex and vary with the class of policy effected and no attempt is made to explain those rules in detail here. It will always be made clear by the life company to any policyholder whether or not the actual policy effected 'qualifies' or not. As a general rule qualifying policies would include whole life, term assurance and endowments with terms of ten or more years. Non-qualifying policies would include single premium bonds, and some unit-linked whole-of-life policies.

Life Assurance Premium Relief (LAPR)

LAPR is available only on premiums paid to a qualifying life policy and will be given only if the policy is on the life of the policyholder or spouse or civil partner, the premium is actually paid by them and the payer is resident in the UK.

LAPR is not available on policies taken out after 13 March 1984. If a pre-14 March 1984 policy is varied after 13 March 1984, so as to increase the policy benefits or to extend the term of the insurance, LAPR will no longer be available on that policy. Variation includes the exercise of an option, for example, on convertible term assurance. It would also include converting a without-profits policy to with-profits or whole life to endowment.

LAPR is given by the policyholder's withholding 12½% from the gross premium. The total amount of gross premiums eligible for relief is the higher of £1,500 per tax year and one-sixth of the policyholder's total taxable income.

With the application of independent taxation a limit of £1,500 or one-sixth of personal taxable income is available to each spouse.

After separation, each party to the marriage is entitled to their own £1,500 or one-sixth limit. Policies taken out on the life of the other before divorce will qualify for relief within those limits after divorce.

Clawback of Premium Relief

Provisions were introduced in the Finance Act 1975 to recover all or part of the tax relief allowed on qualifying policies on the occurrence of specific events, as the Revenue became concerned that a number of qualifying policies were being effected with the deliberate intention of being surrendered in the first few years. The profit gained on such policies was not as a direct result of the investment of the premium by the insurance company, but rather from the tax relief obtained by the policyholder.

Separate provisions were made for clawback of premium relief within four years of taking out the insurance ('short-term' clawback) and after a few years ('long-term' clawback). Since LAPR was abolished on any new policies taken out after 13 March 1984, the events upon which clawback will now apply are:
(a) surrender or part surrender of the policy;
(b) the encashment of any bonuses credited to the policy;
(c) policy loans at a non-commercial rate of interest.

Clawback will apply only if one or more of these events have happened at any time previously; no clawback will occur if there has been no previous clawback event.

Taxation of Gains on Policies

Gains or profits made on all non-qualifying life policies and, in certain circumstances, qualifying life policies are subject to higher rate income tax. Such gains are often called chargeable gains but they have no connection with CGT. The various chargeable events are as follows.
1   Death of the life assured.
2   Maturity or surrender in whole of the policy rights.
3   Part surrenders including certain policy loans at non-commercial rates of interest.
4   Assignment of the policy for money or money's worth. Assignments of part and transfer of a share in the rights under the policy are included. Assignment or transfers of interests as a gift are excluded.

In respect of qualifying life policies no chargeable event can occur in any of the above situations after the shorter of ten years or three-quarters of the policy-paying term has elapsed, unless the policy becomes paid-up within that period. If death or maturity occurs within that time, a chargeable event does not arise unless the policy has been converted into a paid-up policy.

Where a chargeable event occurs, chargeable gains arise in the following events under all life policies, whether qualifying or not.

(a) On death, if the surrender value immediately prior to death, plus any earlier benefits received, exceeds the premiums paid plus the total taxable gains on previous chargeable events.

(b) On maturity or the surrender in whole of the rights conferred by the policy, if the amount paid out plus any earlier benefits received (eg 5% annual withdrawals from a single premium bond) exceeds the premiums paid plus the total taxable gains on the previous chargeable events.

(c) On the occurrence of certain part surrenders that exceed the 5% per annum cumulative withdrawal allowance, the gain is the amount of that excess.

(d) On assignment, if the consideration plus any earlier benefits received exceeds the premiums paid plus the total taxable gains on the previous chargeable events.

These rules apply to policies taken out after 13 March 1975. For policies taken out or varied between 20 March 1968 and 13 March 1975 different rules apply.

Partial Surrenders (the 5% Rule)

This rule allows annual 5% 'tax-free' withdrawals from a single premium bond. The year is calculated from the date of the policy. Each year the policyholder may withdraw 5% of the single premium. If the 5% allowances of earlier years have not been used up they are carried forward for cumulative use in succeeding years. At the end of each policy year the amounts withdrawn in that year are compared with cumulative allowances to date. If the amounts withdrawn exceed the allowances a chargeable event occurs and the excess will be subject to tax.

On termination of the policy these withdrawals are brought into account in calculating any chargeable sum on termination, as set out in point (b) in the preceding section.

It is usually preferable to have a series of single premium bonds to allow complete surrender rather than one large policy out of which partial surrenders are made. These rules only apply to policies taken out after 13 March 1975.

Top-slicing Relief

Where a chargeable gain has arisen, a basic rate taxpayer will not suffer tax on the chargeable gain unless the size of the gain places him within the higher rate band or affects his eligibility to full age allowance, if appropriate. A higher rate taxpayer paying 40% tax will suffer a tax charge at a rate of 20%. A higher rate taxpayer paying 50% tax will suffer a tax charge of 30%. In each case this is equivalent to the difference between the higher rate of income tax in the year 2010/11 of either 40% or 50% and the 20% deemed to have already been paid by the product provider on life funds.

To prevent an excessive tax charge on a chargeable gain, top-slicing relief may be claimed and operates as follows.

1 The chargeable gain is divided by the number of complete years the policy has been in force in order to calculate the 'slice'.
2 The slice is then added to the policyholder's other income for the year in which the event occurred.
3 The difference between the deemed rate of tax and the higher rate of income tax is charged on the slice as if it were the highest part of the taxpayer's income.
4 Note: in rare instances, it is possible that the slice could push the investor into the position where part of the slice fell in 40% tax and part in 50% tax or exceptionally in the case of very large investments where part fell into basic rate tax, part in 40% tax and the very top slice in 50% tax.
5 The resultant amount of tax is then multiplied by the number of years in 1 above to give the amount assessed.

It follows that the claim will be of benefit only where the chargeable gain places the taxpayer within the higher rate tax band.

Note: Top Slicing Relief does not apply to determine qualification for age related income tax allowances. The whole of the gain is taken into consideration to determine if the age allowance income limit has been exceeded.

Offshore Portfolio Bonds

Again these have been very popular in recent years as a vehicle for CGT deferral and in some cases income tax deferral.

For a UK-based investor paying higher rate taxes and regularly using their CGT exemption, the Offshore Portfolio Bond allows unlimited trading free of CGT, since the assets within the bond structure are owned by an offshore insurance company and not the investor. Furthermore, if collective investments are used, rather than individual stocks and shares, ICTA 1988 s 739 does not apply and the income within the bond can accumulate free of income tax (other than withholding or imputed taxes suffered on dividends received by the bond).

Even if individual stocks and shares are used the impact of s 739 can be minimised by following an investment strategy based on low income/high capital growth.

Anti-avoidance legislation has discouraged the holding of personal assets in personalised bonds taken out after 16 March 1998 as a 15% assumed gain will be assessed annually on a cumulative basis, making these arrangements most unattractive. See *Offshore Bonds*, Section 3.16 for exclusions and transitional reliefs. Personalised bonds are still marketed, however, primarily holdings are only in collective investments such as OEICs, unit trusts and life funds so as not to suffer this onerous legislation.

The Taxation of Company-Owned Life Assurance Policies

With effect for accounting periods ending on or after 1 April 2008, the taxation of gains on life assurance policies are taxed as loan relationships (which is outside the scope of this book).

Before April 2008, the gains on life assurance policies owned by companies, taken out after 14 March 1989 (or policies before this date which were subsequently varied) were taxed very similar to the above chargeable event rules.

CROSS REFERENCES

Personal Pensions   **2.4**
Unit-linked Single Premium (Investment) Bonds   **3.14**
Offshore bonds   **3.16**

1.14 Glossary of Insurance Terminology

LIFE ASSURANCE POLICIES

Child's deferred assurance This is an endowment assurance, on the life of a child, which can be taken as cash at maturity or may be converted to a full endowment or possibly whole life assurance. These policies enable parents to provide their child with the potential for a lump sum at a pre-set age (often 18 to 25) or to continue life cover without any further medical declaration.

Contingent survivorship assurance The sum assured is paid out in the event that one named person predeceases another named person. For example; in the event that a son wishes to provide funds for his widowed mother if he should predecease her. If he outlives his mother the contract ends without return.

Convertible temporary/term assurance Initially a term assurance policy where the sum assured is paid on the death of the life/lives assured during the term of the contract. However, the policy includes an option to convert to a whole life or endowment policy with an equivalent sum assured at any time during the contract term (usually up to a maximum age of 60) without further medical evidence. This type of policy can be suitable for a young person or couple with limited means who require immediate cover with the option to convert to a savings contract or whole life policy at a later date.

Critical illness An illness, specified in an insurance policy, on the diagnosis of which the sum assured (including profits, where applicable) will be paid out assuming the life assured survives the appropriate survival period.

Decreasing term assurance The sum assured reduces by a specified amount each year the policy is in force – used mainly as a mortgage protection policy where a loan is decreasing annually.

Endowment assurance The policy proceeds are payable on survival to a specified date or earlier death – used mainly as a savings contract in order to build a capital sum, or as an alternative to repaying a mortgage on a capital and interest (repayment) basis.

Endowment – low cost (with profits) A combination of an endowment assurance and decreasing term assurance. Developed for mortgage requirements. The endowment policy has a sum assured less than the outstanding capital but, with the addition of the maturity value should, in theory, be sufficient to repay the loan. The decreasing term assurance provides repayment of any shortfall outstanding on death prior to maturity. In recent years considerable problems have arisen as policies have failed to achieve anticipated maturity values.

Endowment – non-profit   The sum assured is payable on survival to a specified date or an earlier death without the addition of profits.

Endowment – pure   The policy proceeds are payable on survival to a specified date but with no return on death – rarely used except for group pension and tax mitigation schemes.

Endowment – with-profits   The full sum assured together with accrued bonuses is payable at maturity or on an earlier death.

Family income benefits policy   This is a decreasing term assurance contract with benefits being payable if death should occur during contract term. Premiums and benefits can be level or increasing and the benefits are generally paid to the beneficiary(ies) as a regular tax-free income until the end of the policy term.

High income bonds   Derivative based high income investments. Some bonds include capital protection whilst in other cases return of capital is linked to the performance of stock market indices.

Income protection insurance   A contract which, after an agreed deferment period, will provide a regular, tax-free income up until a selected retirement age in the event of the life assured becoming unable to work due to ill-health. Benefits and premiums can be level or increasing and contracts and benefits vary greatly. Because the benefits are paid tax free, most providers limit cover to no more than 50–65% of earnings.

Issue risk policy   An assurance to cover a reversioner in a settlement or other person who will suffer loss by the birth of a child or children, eg to the life tenant of a settlement.

Key person assurance   The insurance by a company on the life of a key employee whose death or disability could affect profits. The policy can be one of term assurance, whole of life, endowment, personal accident, critical illness or permanent health insurance.

Long-term care insurance   An insurance contract which is aimed at helping to cover the cost of immediate long-term care needs or potential future costs.

Maximum investment plan   A unit-linked policy with the minimum sum assured necessary to obtain 'qualifying status' – the majority of the premiums being used for investment in unit-linked funds.

Personal Portfolio Bond   The benefits under the life assurance policy are linked to assets which are personal to the bondholder rather than the usual unit-linked investments of the insurer.

Renewable term assurance   The sum assured is paid on death only if this occurs within the specified term of the policy. At the end of the term (depending on the age of the life assured), the policyholder has the option to renew the policy for a further term of years.

SHIPs   SHIP (Safe Home Income Plans). The UK equity release industry body which was launched in 1991 and aims to protect the interests of the consumer within the UK equity release market.

Single premium bonds   Non-qualifying life policies which have nominal life cover and maximum investment (after charges) of the capital sum paid. Used as an investment medium and also used extensively in capital conversion schemes and in inheritance tax arrangements.

Temporary/term assurance   The sum assured is paid on death of the life (lives) assured only if it occurs within the specified term of the policy. A term assurance policy provides low-cost cover for a fixed term.

Whole life assurance   The sum assured is paid on the death of the life (lives) assured whenever it occurs. It can be used to provide a capital sum on death to meet Inheritance Tax liabilities or funds for partnership or key person purposes. Little or no investment element unless with-profits or unit-linked.

ANNUITIES

Capital protected   An annuity which guarantees that if death occurs before an amount equal to the purchase proceeds of the annuity has been paid, the balance will be returned to the deceased's estate.

Certain   An annuity for a specified number of years irrespective of the duration of the annuitant's life – can be used to fund school fees.

Compulsory purchase/open market option   An annuity which is purchased with an individual's pension funds at their chosen retirement age or age 75. The income is taxed as earned income.

Deferred   An annuity for life commencing at an agreed date in the future – used extensively for school fees and pension provision.

Equity-linked   The underlying value of the annuity is divided into a number of units in an equity fund and the annuitant is permitted to withdraw a fixed number of units each year during the remainder of his life – used in order to mitigate the effects of inflation.

Escalating   Annuity payments increase each year in order to mitigate the effects of inflation.

Guaranteed   An annuity which will continue for a stated number of years

Immediate   Annuity payments commence on the purchase of the contract and continue throughout life – used for pension provision or to provide an assured with a tax-efficient income for life where this need overrides the requirement to preserve capital.

Impaired life annuity   An annuity where higher rates are paid for individuals with lower life expectancy such as smokers or individuals in poor health.

Joint life annuity   An annuity on the life of one person which continues on his/her death – often at a reduced rate – in the name of his/her spouse.

Lifestyle annuity   An annuity which takes into account the individual's occupation, wealth, diet, exercise levels and even postcode. Those deemed by the insurer to have a shorter life expectancy as a result of the above factors may be offered higher rates.

Overlap   Overlap is the name given to a situation which can occur with a joint life annuity. Say, for example, that a person takes out an annuity which pays an income which continues in the name of his spouse after his death but at a reduced rate of 50%. Normally the reduction would occur immediately on his death. However, if the annuity has a guarantee period of say five years and death occurs after just two years, then if the annuity was bought 'with overlap' the full annuity would be payable for the remaining three years of the initial guarantee period along with the reduced annuity of 50%. At the end of the initial five-year period, the full annuity would cease but the reduced annuity of 50% would continue for the rest of the spouse's life.

Proportion   Where an annuity payment is made in arrear rather than in advance, should the annuitant die, the annuity will normally cease immediately and no further payments are made (unless there is an unexpired guarantee period) .Where the annuity was bought 'with proportion' a proportionate payment up to the date of death is made. For an annuity paid annually in arrear this can make a substantial difference should death occur just before the next annuity instalment is due.

Purchased life annuity   An annuity granted for consideration in money or money's worth by an insurance company in the ordinary course of business of granting annuities on human life. Such contracts are treated for tax purposes as consisting of a capital portion which is not regarded as taxable income and an interest portion which is. The capital portion varies with the age of the prospective annuitant.

Retirement annuity   A plan for the purpose of pension provision for the self-employed or those in non-pensionable employment prior to the introduction of personal pension plans. The resulting pension payments are treated as earned income for tax purposes. Tax relief is, however, available on the premiums paid.

Reversionary   An annuity for life, which commences on the death of a named individual – useful where, for example, a husband may wish to make provision for his wife on his death.

Temporary   An annuity where payments cease at the end of either a fixed term, or on the prior death of the annuitant, whichever occurs first – often used as an investment to fund premiums on a 'qualifying' life or endowment policy.

With-profits annuity   An annuity which will vary according to the with-profits bonus rate declared by the life company.

TERMINOLOGY

Bonus   See *With-profits*

Clawback   Where a qualifying policy effected before 14 March 1984 and attracting life assurance premium relief is surrendered in whole or in part, HMRC may reclaim some of the relief given in respect of the premiums paid.

Cooling-off period   A person who agrees to take out a policy of life assurance is allowed at least 14 days from his signature on the proposal form during which to change his mind and avoid the contract.

Insurable interest   In order for an assurance policy to be a valid contract in law, the proposer of the policy must have an insurable interest in the life to be assured. In effect the relationship must be one of financial loss to the proposer should the life assured die. A person is deemed to have an insurable interest in their own life and that of their spouse. The principle of insurable interest is, however, now commonly waived by many life companies.

Life assurance premium relief   The tax relief available on premiums payable to life policies taken out before 14 March 1984 and not varied since that date (currently 12.5%). The relief is deducted by the policyholder and the net premium is paid over to the life company. The relief is, however, limited to premiums which do not exceed the greater of one-sixth of the policyholder's income or £1,500. Each person has an individual limit of £1,500 or one-sixth of their personal taxable income.

Paid-up policy   Where premium payment is stopped during a contract term, the policy may be made paid-up. The policy will then remain in force for the original term, but the sum assured under the policy will be reduced to a level which reflects the total of the premiums actually paid.

Profits   See *With-profits*

Qualifying policies   In order for a policy to avoid a tax charge on the policy proceeds it must comply with certain complex qualification rules relating to the length of the contract, the benefits provided therefrom, the level and frequency of premiums permissible and the life to be assured. Life assurance premium relief is available on pre-14 March 1984 qualifying policies.

Surrender value   The amount payable to the policyholder on early termination of a policy which has an investment element included within it. As a general rule, in the first two years of an endowment policy and the first three years of a whole life policy, there is unlikely to be any significant surrender value. The position is somewhat better with unit-linked policies in a time of favourable investment market conditions.

Unit-linked   Contracts which are unit-linked produce returns which are determined by reference to the value of insurance company investment funds, unit trusts or other property. These types of policy cannot guarantee a final return as this will fluctuate with the performance of the investment market, but must guarantee a small minimum sum assured if qualifying status for the contract is to be obtained.

With-profits   The initial sum assured is increased by the regular addition of 'profits' or 'bonuses' which are paid to with-profits policyholders following the valuation of the life fund by the life assurance company's appointed actuary. He will calculate the available surplus after determining the assets and liabilities of the fund and after putting part of the surplus into reserves. Reversionary bonuses are usually declared annually and tend to reflect realised gains within the life fund. Once added, they form part of the emerging policy proceeds, and are guaranteed. In addition, many companies pay a terminal bonus when the policy matures (and in some cases an early surrender) which tends to reflect market conditions and unrealised gains within the life fund. Terminal bonuses can fluctuate and are therefore not accurately quantifiable until shortly before the maturity of the policy or until surrender. Considerable concern has been expressed at the underperformance and lack of transparency of with-profit funds.

Part 2   Retirement Planning

2.1 Introduction

The provision of an adequate income in retirement is the cornerstone of personal financial planning as it:
- ensures that an individual's pre-retirement standard of living is maintained;
- enables IHT planning to be undertaken as post-retirement income has been secured.

HMRC registered pension schemes:
- are a practical consideration, whether they are for employees (including directors) of companies or businesses with approved pension schemes, or in employments carrying no pension rights, or self-employed, or non-earners;
- are highly efficient in terms of the treatment of the contributions, investment income and capital gains accruing to the fund and the eventual pension entitlement subject to certain limits:
  - subject to certain limits, pension contributions are fully deductible from income for corporation tax and income tax purposes;
  - income and gains arising in the funds are not liable to income tax or CGT (tax credits on dividends are no longer repayable);
  - part of the pension entitlement can be commuted for a tax-free lump sum on retirement;
  - the pension when drawn is taxed as earnings;
  - lump sum benefits paid on death before retirement can usually be paid free of IHT;
- can offer the opportunity for loan finance to be raised against the accruing pension fund.

HMRC impose certain conditions which must be met in order for schemes to be registered pension schemes. This is now the responsibility of Inland Revenue Savings, Pensions, Share Schemes (IRSPSS), a business stream at HMRC having previously been the responsibility of the Pension Schemes Office (PSO) of the Inland Revenue.

THE KEY CONCEPTS

Prior to the introduction of the legislation contained within the Finance Acts of 2004 and 2005, there were eight, separate tax regimes under which schemes were required to operate. The pension simplification legislation aimed to overhaul the system and replace it with one 'simplified' regime, full details of which can be found in Section 2.2. In practice however, where schemes' existing rules fall *within* the remit of the new legislation they are not obliged to amend them to allow members to take advantage of the new opportunities. Owing to the administrative issues and the costs involved it is likely that many legacy schemes will continue to operate as they have previously. It is therefore important to understand the base from which all types of schemes have been derived.

Types of Pension Scheme

There are two basic types of pension scheme:
1   occupational pension schemes; and
2   personal pension schemes (PPSs).

However, on 6 April 2001 the defined contribution tax regime (DC regime) came into being. This regime brought together the tax regime for personal pensions, stakeholder pensions and money purchase occupational schemes that choose to opt into the regime.

An overview of the two types and the DC regime are given below.

Occupational Pension Schemes

These are often also referred to as employer sponsored pension schemes or company pension schemes.

They may be defined benefit schemes which promise a specific pension at retirement – for example 1/80th or 1/60th of final salary for each year of service, or money purchase schemes where the contributions are specified but not the benefits.

Defined Benefit Schemes

These are characterised by a promise to provide a certain level of benefit on retirement or death calculated according to a pre-determined formula.

They are often final salary schemes where the determinants of what an employee receives from a scheme at normal retirement date (NRD) are his or her length of service, the amount of final remuneration, at or near retirement, and HMRC rules regarding the maximum that can be paid out by way of either pension or tax-free lump sum (see below). The key is the promise given by the scheme (in effect the employer) to pay a fixed percentage of final remuneration up to a maximum of two-thirds after 20 or more years' service. Following on from pension simplification, all individuals are restricted in benefits at retirement by the Lifetime Allowance (£1,800,000 for 2010/11) and for defined benefit schemes the notional value of the benefits to be tested against this limit are calculated using a factor of 20:1 (ie every £1,000 of pension benefit is valued at £20,000), plus any additional lump sum entitlements.

Occasionally they will be average salary schemes (sometimes called career average schemes) where the pension is based on the average of salary over the period of membership (rather than salary towards the end of the period as under final salary schemes). Normally the average allows for the revaluation of salary for earlier years.

Employees may or may not be required to contribute.

Money Purchase Schemes

These are established on the basis that the employer determines what they are prepared to spend by way of contributions. These are usually expressed as a percentage of employees' salaries though contributions can alternatively be based on monetary amounts which vary between employees. The contributions are usually invested with a life insurance company or sometimes where large amounts are involved with independent investment managers. At the scheme's normal retirement date, each employee has a 'pot' available to provide benefits.

This 'pot' may be taken via secured pension in the form of a scheme pension or lifetime annuity, unsecured pension in the form of pension fund withdrawal or short-term annuity, or if aged over 77 (see Section 2.2), alternatively secured pension. As with defined benefit schemes, the benefits payable are subject to the lifetime allowance, with the value of the fund being the amount tested against the limit.

As in the case of defined benefit schemes, employees may or may not be required to contribute.

Differences

The fundamental difference between the two types of scheme is that the defined benefit scheme undertakes to pay out a pension calculated according to a pre-determined formula and therefore has an open-ended financial commitment which is underwritten by the employer. This contrasts with a money purchase scheme where the employee effectively bears the investment and mortality risks and the size of the pension will depend on the rate at which the contributions grow once invested and the cost of buying the pension. The employer's commitment is merely to make the periodic contributions promised.

Basic Principles and Tax Incentives

Occupational pension schemes are generally governed by trust law and trustees need to ensure that the HMRC rules are applied so that pension monies cannot be diverted for improper purposes. Neither can a charge be taken over pension fund monies by way of security for loans. Some occupational pension schemes, particularly in the public sector, are established by statute and governed by regulations thereunder.

Contributions can be invested in a variety of ways depending on the size of the scheme. Small schemes, particularly those with fewer than 100 members, are likely to invest in funds managed by insurance companies or operate as insured schemes. Larger schemes – typically with more than 250 employees – may invest in managed funds offered by either insurance companies or other investment houses (either investing the money via an in-house investment department or alternatively employing external fund managers) and operate as self-administered schemes.

Providing an occupational pension scheme is a 'registered pension scheme' it will enjoy a range of significant tax privileges. These can be summarised as freedom from income tax, corporation tax and CGT on income and capital gains which arise from the investment of contributions in the fund. Pension funds can no longer reclaim tax credits on UK dividends. All funded registered pension schemes which hold UK equities are affected by this change.

Subject, in the case of high earners*, to the changes introduced by the April 2009 budget outlined in Section 2.2, employees are able to claim tax relief on their contributions at their marginal rate of tax providing they do not exceed 100% of gross earnings, ie including taxable benefits as opposed to just basic salary. Employers can claim their contributions as a corporation tax expense.

At retirement a proportion of the fund can be taken as a pension commencement lump sum or tax-free cash up to 25% of the value of the fund or notional fund in the case of defined benefit schemes and the balance of the fund is then used provide an income which is taxed as earned income under Pay As You Earn (PAYE).

* People earning over £130,000.

Revenue Limits and Legislative Changes

The concept of HMRC maximum benefits that existed for occupational pension schemes prior to 6 April 2006 has now vanished.

All schemes are now subject to the Lifetime Allowance which has now reached £1.8m for 2010/11 and will remain at this level until it is reviewed in 2016/17. Any benefits in excess of the lifetime allowance will be subject to the following recovery charge:

* 25% if taken as income; and
* 55% if taken as a lump sum.

These charges are significant and it is certainly worth individuals undertaking appropriate levels of planning in order to structure their retirement benefits in such a way as to avoid them. Care should be taken where individuals had already reached the lifetime allowance at 5 April 2006 as it was possible to protect such benefits from the recovery charge provided this was done prior to April 2009. However, the provisions in the Finance Acts 2004 and 2005 that relate to this area are amongst some of the most complex and independent professional advice should be sought.

Pension Commencement Lump Sum (Tax-free Cash)

All schemes are now able to provide up to 25% of the fund value or notional fund value in the case of defined benefit schemes. There will be some individuals with historic entitlements in excess of this. These entitlements will be retained within the related scheme, however care should be taken if considering transferring benefits to an alternative arrangement as these entitlements could be lost. Again, professional and independent advice should be sought.

Personal Pension Schemes (PPSs)

Before 1 July 1988, the self-employed and employees not in an employers' occupational pension scheme could only make pension provision by establishing one or more retirement annuity policies. Concern had been building through the 1980s about some of the unfairness of the occupational pension scheme arrangements, particularly given the more volatile workforce with people changing jobs more frequently.

As part of this process, personal pension schemes were introduced on 1 July 1988 and replaced retirement annuity policies from that date.

Although retirement annuity policies could not be taken out after that date, those with existing policies can continue to make contributions and also increase them subject to the provisions of the policies concerned.

The special treatment and continuance of retirement annuity policies are dealt with in the *Personal Pensions* section.

The Defined Contribution Regime

Prior to the advent of the Simplified Regime, stakeholder pension schemes, together with personal pension schemes and occupational pension schemes that opted into the defined contribution regime all came under the umbrella of the defined contribution regime (DC regime).

This distinction has now gone and all pension schemes fall under the remit of the single, simplified regime.

Concurrency

Pre-6 April 2006 and prior to 6 April 2001, members of occupational pension schemes were not permitted to contribute to a personal pension scheme in respect of the same source of earnings.

From 6 April 2001, members of occupational pension schemes could contribute to a DC regime scheme subject to certain restrictions, however under the simplified regime we have been introduced to the concept of 'full concurrency'. This means that individuals can now contribute to as many registered pension schemes as they like with tax relief limited to the greater of 100% of UK earnings or £3,600 subject to an overall annual allowance of £255,000 (2010/11), and in the case of high earners to the measures introduced in the April 2009 budget and outlined in Section 2.2. Employers can make unlimited tax relieved contributions regardless of the member's salary, however any contributions in excess of the annual allowance will result in a tax charge of 40% on the employee.

Eligibility

The Finance Act of 2004 has introduced the concept of a relevant UK individual for the purposes of entitlement to tax relief on personal contributions. An individual can be considered a relevant UK individual under the following circumstances:

● where they have relevant UK earnings, chargeable to income tax for that tax year. Relevant earnings are defined as employment income, Sch D income from a trade profession or vocation, and patent income under ICTA 1988; or
● where the individual has been resident in the UK at some time during the tax year; or
● where the individual was resident in the UK both:
    – at some time during the five tax years immediately before the year of the contribution (subject to £3,600 maximum); and
    – at the time when the individual became a member of the pension scheme; or
● where the individual or their spouse has earnings for the tax year from overseas crown employment.

Contributions Paid Net of Basic Rate Tax

With effect from 6 April 2001, self-employed policyholders pay their personal pension contributions net of basic rate tax rather than gross. This means that self-employed individuals are treated identically to employed individuals, with their pension provider claiming back the tax relief from HMRC.

Any claim for higher-rate tax relief will continue to be made via their local tax inspector or self assessment.

Contributions to retirement annuity contracts continue to be paid gross, although subject to the provider making the necessary alterations to its systems, it is now possible for retirement annuity contributions to be paid net of basic rate tax. The cost to providers of doing so is likely to prove prohibitive.

Life Assurance

The 2007 budget effectively removed the facility whereby contributions to provide life assurance within the pension regime were tax relieved. In a statement issued after the budget HMRC confirmed that for all applications submitted by 13 December 2006, insurers had until 31 July 2007 to process the business and the tax relief would apply. This 31 July 2007 deadline also applied to term assurance applications associated with existing personal pensions in force prior to 13 December 2006 where applications were submitted before 12 April 2007. For any other circumstances there is now no longer the option to provide pension term assurance in this way; however existing arrangements will continue unaffected.

Waiver of Premium Benefit

From 6 April 2001, individuals will no longer be able to provide themselves with waiver of premium benefit under a new DC regime policy.

Should individuals require waiver of premium benefit, a separate contract would need to be effected to provide the necessary benefits.

The premiums paid by the individual to the separate policy will not qualify for tax relief.

Policies started prior to 6 April 2001 and retirement annuity contracts can continue to provide waiver of premium benefit.

Carry Forward and Carry Back

There is now no option for carry forward or carry back under personal pension schemes or retirement annuity policies.

Personal Pension Schemes – Variations

Stakeholder Pensions

Although the introduction of personal pension schemes made the provision of pensions more flexible and widely available there were still some concerns. These included the need for there to be some earnings to be able to participate in personal pension schemes, the lack of awareness amongst employees particularly where the employer had not made pension provision for the employees and also some concern about the charging structures of the personal pension schemes.

As a result of this, stakeholder pensions were introduced with effect from 6 April 2001. The Government merged the stakeholder regime and personal pension regime into a 'new defined contribution regime' which encompassed money purchase occupational schemes which opted into the regime but excluded retirement annuity policies. Following the pension simplification legislation, all schemes now operate under a single regime, however many of the features of the defined contribution regime are still relevant.

The regime allowed annual contributions without reference to earnings up to a gross contribution level of £3,600 per annum. This still applies. However after that, individuals can now contribute up to 100% of earnings if greater.

Stakeholder schemes must meet various standards including a maximum charge of 1.5% of the fund per annum within the first ten years and 1% thereafter without any other charges under the stakeholder scheme being allowed. Stakeholder pensions have been available from April 2001 and employers had until October 2001 to offer access to their employees. For new employees they have to be offered access within three months of starting service. There is no obligation for the employer to contribute.

The employer had to designate a stakeholder scheme by 8 October 2001 but this did not extend to recommending one. This requirement has now been removed under the Pensions Act 2008.

All relevant details on stakeholder pensions are included in the section within this part of the Manual.

Group Personal Pensions

Employers have adapted the personal pension scheme regime to provide pension provision for their employees. A group personal pension is a series of individual personal pension plans of employees grouped together for administrative convenience.

The employer has normally decided that using a group personal pension arrangement is more appropriate than an occupational pension scheme.

The individual policies belong to the employees but there is normally one provider and communication and administration is much simplified. In addition the employer can make its own contributions to the policies with the minimum of fuss.

If membership of a group personal pension scheme is offered then employers can be exempt from the stakeholder pension requirements. To be exempt the employer must contribute at least 3% of basic pay, allow entry within three months of joining and the scheme must not in general apply exit penalties. The employer can insist that the employee pays a matching 3% contribution. The employer may not make membership of a group personal pension scheme compulsory.

Self Invested Pension Plans

Many individuals and particularly higher earning self-employed individuals or partners in partnerships are increasingly using the self invested pension plan. The self invested pension plan is set up with an appropriate provider. It is funded by transfers from suitable retirement annuity policies, personal pension policies, or transfers from other registered pension schemes. It can also be funded from periodic contributions in the same way as a personal pension. The individual appoints investment advisers to invest into a wide range of investments or could, if so minded, direct that the funds be invested in certain types of commercial property with appropriate borrowings to facilitate this.

This arrangement often allows such individuals the ability to properly review their portfolio of policies and ensure that the investment is structured as best can be to provide the appropriate retirement pension.

NEST

As can be seen from Section 2.3 State Pensions, the Pensions Act 2008 also ratified the introduction of Personal Accounts with effect from 1 October 2012. This has since been renamed National Savings Employment Trust (NEST).These will be introduced over a four-year period and the new duties will apply to the largest employers first with some of the smallest not being affected until 2016.They will effectively be personal pensions, run on an occupational basis and administered by employers.

All employees will be automatically enrolled into a personal account as long as they are aged between 22 and the state pension age; they earn more than the Primary Threshold (£5,720 per annum in 2010/11) and their employer does not already offer a pension scheme with benefits equal to or greater than a personal account.

There are likely to be several investment funds to choose from (including environmental and ethical options), as well as a default fund for those not wanting to make a choice. Once an individual has begun a personal account, it will stay with them throughout their career, regardless of when they change employers. Transfers in or out will not be allowed and refunds of employee contributions will only be available under limited circumstances.

The aim will be to accrue a fund which will provide an income in retirement. As with traditional money purchase pensions the policyholder will not be able to access the funds before age 55 when there will also be an option to take 25% of the fund as tax-free cash. The only option for providing income is to buy a lifetime annuity from an insurance company.

As far as contributions are concerned, these have been set at 4% of qualifying band earnings for employees, 3% for employers, with the Government contributing an extra 1% itself via basic rate tax relief. Qualifying band earnings will be between £5,035 and £33,500 initially and will be increased in line with National Average Earnings each year. This 8% minimum contribution will be phased in over a three-year period (for example in 2012, employers will only have to pay in 1%).

The Government is naturally keen to maximise the benefits to members, and the stated long-term aim is for an annual management charge of 0.3% to be the only charge against a member's fund. However, at least in the early years of NEST it is proposed that there will also be a 2% initial charge taken from every contribution paid to the scheme.

Following the last election, the coalition Government has announced an independent review of auto enrolment which was to be concluded by 30 September 2010.

Pension Fund Withdrawal (Income Drawdown)

Pension Fund Withdrawal allows a more flexible way of drawing benefits from personal pension schemes and money purchase occupational schemes than annuity purchase.

It avoids the need to purchase an annuity on retirement and allows the income to be drawn on a flexible basis. Income drawdown is likely to be best for those with a fund in excess of £100,000 who are prepared to accept some risk in retirement.

2.2 Pensions Simplification and Finance Acts of 2004 and 2005

The Finance Acts 2004 and 2005 have resulted in the most far-reaching and comprehensive overhaul of the tax treatment of UK pension schemes since 1921. This reform is commonly referred to as 'Pensions Simplification'. There were previously eight taxation regimes applicable within the UK pension system but these have now been replaced with one universal regime. This regime has applied to all types of tax approved (or 'registered') pension schemes since 6 April 2006 ('A Day').

There is no doubt that for individuals commencing pension provision for the first time after 6 April 2006 the rules will be far simpler and far more transparent. However, for those individuals with existing provision as at 6 April 2006, the desire of the pensions industry to ensure that individuals are not disadvantaged has made things far from simple for many. The need for analysis of these individuals' current arrangements and subsequent advice has been, and continues to be paramount. Furthermore, this has been compounded by the subsequent amendments following pensions simplification which have been or are intended to be introduced and which, where relevant, are covered in this section.

Which Schemes have been Affected?

All UK-approved and unapproved schemes have been affected. This means all stakeholder, group personal pensions, occupational defined contribution (DC) and defined benefit (DB) schemes, public schemes established under statute and unapproved arrangements known as 'FURBS' and 'UURBS'. The new legislation took effect from April 2006.

Tax Relief on Contributions under Registered Schemes

Members are now able to contribute to any number of registered pension arrangements at the same time. Annual tax relief on personal contributions will be given on the higher of £3,600 and 100% of UK earnings subject to an annual allowance, currently £255,000 per annum in 2010. The Government has announced that the allowance will remain at this level for the tax years 2011/12 to 2015/16 inclusive. The allowance for future years will be set by the Treasury, but cannot be reduced.

In addition, following the April 2009 budget, the Government announced its intention to restrict the availability of higher rate tax relief on contributions to Registered Pensions Schemes with effect from 6 April 2011 for people with a gross taxable income of £150,000 or more. Relief will be tapered away so that for those earning £180,000 and over it is worth 20%, the same as to a basic rate taxpayer. The Pre-Budget Report in December 2009 subsequently extended these measures to people with relevant income over £130,000.

The Government was concerned that individuals likely to be affected by the change in 2011 would pay substantial pension contributions before then and it therefore introduced what it referred to as 'anti-forestalling legislation' in the Finance Act 2009. This anti-forestalling legislation applies to pension contributions/pension accrual from 22 April 2009 to 5 April 2011 (ie until the main legislation takes effect in April 2011). The anti-forestalling legislation restricts higher rate tax relief on pension contributions for individuals on incomes of £130,000 (£150,000 prior to December 2009) or higher that are in excess of their normal pattern prior to the new regime coming into effect.

This was achieved by introducing a special annual allowance which set an upper limit of £20,000 on the amount of non-regular pension savings for which full tax relief at rates above basic rate can be given that applies from 22 April 2009 and an associated tax charge which is collected via an individual's self-assessment tax return.

Pre-22 April payments are not subject to the special annual allowance charge but do not provide protection for future payments unless the existing payments were paid on a regular basis. A pattern of single payments does not provide protection even where the pattern can be easily demonstrated.

Regular payments that were paid at least quarterly prior to 22 April are known as Protected Pension Input Amounts and provide protection against the special annual allowance charge for future regular payments up to the level that was previously being paid. Originally, in order to qualify these regular payments had to continue to be paid to the same scheme but this was subsequently amended provided the new arrangement replaced the old one on broadly the same basis.

Whilst the anti-forestalling regime currently in place is unaffected, the new coalition Government has announced that the restrictions on tax relief for high earners from 6 April 2011 will not go ahead in their present form. Instead they are considering reducing the annual allowance to a level that raises at least the same amount of revenue and feel that a figure of £30,000 to £45,000 will achieve this.

There is no limit on employer contributions, but amounts over the annual allowance per employee (or value inflows* in the case of DB schemes) are deemed to be a benefit in kind on that individual with a fixed tax liability of 40%.

*Derived by multiplying the increase in accrued entitlement over the year by a factor of ten.

Employer contributions also generally attract relief from corporation tax as business expenses although relief may be spread over a number of tax years (see below). Further to this, an employer's contribution to a registered pension scheme will be allowable for tax relief purposes if it satisfies the 'wholly and exclusively' criteria for the purposes of the trade test, as set out in CTA 2009 s 74 and s 34 of the Income Tax (Trading and Other Income) Act 2005. The final decision as to whether or not the contribution meets the 'wholly and exclusively' criteria will rest with the local inspector of taxes. However HMRC have issued some guidance in this area, confirming that employer contributions will be allowable unless there is a non-trade purpose. The focus has now shifted away from the pension contribution in isolation and over to the individual's total remuneration package. HMRC have indicated that in the case of controlling directors the remuneration package is likely to be a commercial decision and therefore unlikely to be challenged. Care should still be taken however in cases where pension contributions are high in relation to salary as the local inspectors may have grounds to challenge.

Care should also be taken in cases of family members or other connected persons where their total remunerative package could be deemed by HMRC to be non-commensurate with their duties. This is likely to be of particular significance in cases where there is no unconnected employee with a comparable benefits package. In such cases, not only may HMRC rule the total remuneration to be disallowed but further it may be deemed to be part of the proprietor's benefits and as such taxable on the director.

Tax Relief – Employers

The tax relief obtained by employers may need to be spread over a number of years, depending on the amount of contribution paid. This becomes relevant where:

- the contribution is more than 210% of the previous chargeable period (usually the company's accounting period) contribution; and
- the relevant excess contributions (RECs) are £500,000 or more. RECs are defined as the excess over 110% of the amount paid in the previous chargeable period.

The timescale over which the contribution is spread varies depending on the amount of the RECs.

Standard Lifetime Allowance (SLA)

Since 6 April 2006 the maximum tax privileged amount that anyone can have invested across their pension plans when they choose to take their benefits is known as the Standard Lifetime Allowance and is £1.8m for 2010/11 (in the case of DB schemes this will equate to the deemed capital value* of accrued rights). This has been capped at this level for the tax years 2011/12 to 2015/16 inclusive. The allowance for future years will be set by the Treasury, but cannot be reduced.

*Deemed capital value is derived in most cases by multiplying the accrued pension entitlement by a factor of 20.

Pensions that were in payment at A-Day must be multiplied by a factor of 25 for the purposes of valuation against the SLA. This is only relevant where additional pension benefits are being accrued and/or will be brought into payment, now known as crystallisation.

'Recovery' tax charges apply upon crystallisation, to funds accumulated above the SLA as follows:

- 25% where excess funds are taken in income form; and
- 55% where excess funds are taken as a lump sum.

There are ways to protect the value of pre A-Day pension benefits above this limit from the tax charge (see transitional protections below).

Valuing benefits for the purposes of testing against the SLA can be a complicated process particularly where a number of arrangements are in place.

Pension credits acquired from a divorce settlement prior to A-Day may be registered with HMRC within three years of A-Day, in which case the individual's personal lifetime allowance (PLA, see below) will be increased to take account of the pension credit.

Where an individual transfers benefits from a registered pension scheme to a recognised overseas scheme after A-Day, a test will be required against the SLA (or PLA, see below). Any excess funds would be subject to a recovery charge.

Tax-free Cash Entitlements

Individuals accumulating pension savings for the first time after A-Day will have a maximum tax-free cash entitlement of 25% of the 'pension value'. In the case of money purchase schemes this would normally equate to 25% of the fund value. Under DB schemes current typical commutation factors will result in tax-free cash entitlements being below 25% of the deemed pension value. It is up to trustees and employers to decide if they wish to alter their scheme design to facilitate this higher entitlement albeit at the expense of a lower annual pension figure.

It is now permissible to take 25% of protected rights funds and 25% of Additional Voluntary Contribution and Free-Standing Additional Voluntary Contribution funds as tax-free cash subject to the appropriate amendments being made to the scheme rules.

Many individuals, in particular those with existing accrued occupational pension rights, will have tax-free cash entitlements as at A-Day of greater than 25% of the pension fund or value (in the case of DB schemes). These entitlements are automatically protected (and indexed in line with increases in the SLA), however care should be taken as the protection will normally be specific to the arrangement in which the funds were held at A-Day (unless a transfer post A-Day is a result of a scheme wind-up or bulk transfer post A-Day) and the tax-free cash sum must normally all be taken at one time leaving no unvested benefits under the arrangement.

In addition to the protection detailed above individuals may also be entitled to a further 25% entitlement on any funds deemed to be attributable to post A-Day contributions.

Where an individual registered for enhanced protection or primary protection (see below) the protections afforded to tax-free cash entitlements may be subject to different, more complex provisions. These are outlined below.

Transitional Protections

For members that had accumulated savings at or around the lifetime allowance at A-day, two differing forms of protection from the recovery charge could be applied for. These are **'Primary Protection'** and **'Enhanced Protection'**. Formal registration for either or both of these protections must have been made by 5 April 2009.

Primary Protection

This was only available to individuals who as at 6 April 2006 had accrued funds/pension entitlements in excess of the SLA at the time of £1.5m. Under this option, the pre A-Day fund value becomes the individual's personal lifetime allowance (PLA) and is then indexed in line with the increase in the SLA up to the date benefits are crystallised. Funds up to this indexed amount will be protected from the recovery charge.

The pension fund/accrued pension at 6 April 2006 must be tested against previous HMRC maximum limits prior to registering for protection.

Tax-free cash (TFC) entitlements at A-Day under this option are protected as follows:

A-Day		*Crystallisation*
TFC up to 25% and up to £375k (25% SLA)	=	lower of 25% of SLA and 25% of fund
TFC more than 25% and more than £375k	=	TFC at A-day revalued in line with increases in the SLA
TFC up to 25% and more than £375k	=	TFC at A-day revalued in line with increases in the SLA

Enhanced Protection

This was only available to individuals who have opted out of active membership of their schemes and who do not participate in any 'registered' pension arrangements after A-Day. For such individuals all benefits payable after A-Day will normally be exempt from the recovery charge. As well as individuals with accrued funds/pension valuations over the SLA this option was also available to those with lower valuations.

Under enhanced protection individuals with DC funds will enjoy the benefit of full post A-Day fund growth. Pensions under DB schemes will normally be based on pre A-Day pensionable service and accrual rates but, if scheme rules allow, may be based on final pensionable salary when benefits are first taken. Final pensionable salary will, however, be subject to certain HMRC limits, depending upon which of the previous regimes applied.

If final pensionable pay is instead taken as at A-Day the resultant deferred pension can be increased in line with the greater of RPI, 5% or such other rate as may be prescribed by HMRC.

The pension fund/accrued pension at A-Day must be tested against HMRC maximums under the previous regimes, and any excess surrendered, prior to registering the protections.

TFC entitlements at A-Day under this option will be protected as follows:

A-Day		*Crystallisation*
TFC up to 25% and up to £375k	=	lower of 25% of SLA and 25% of fund
TFC more than 25% and up to £375k	=	TFC at A-day in line with increases in the SLA
TFC up to 25% and more than £375k	=	% of fund at A-Day applied to fund
TFC more than 25% and more than £375k	=	% of fund at A-Day applied to fund

Subject to the fund value/pension value being greater than the SLA (£1.5m) at A-Day it was possible for an individual to register for both primary protection and enhanced protection. It would then be possible to opt out of enhanced protection and resume contributions whilst still benefiting from Primary Protection.

Registering for Protection

Unvested pre A-Day rights had to be registered within three years of A-Day in order to gain protection from the recovery charge.

Rights to TFC sums in excess of 25% of the SLA should only have been registered if protection from the recovery charge was being sought for the related pension rights.

Individuals had to register on HMRC's registration form, which captured all of the information required.

Once registered, HMRC issued a certificate to the individual. The onus was on the individual to gather the necessary details for registration and he/she had to provide the scheme administrator with a copy of the certificate. Where benefits were vested in tranches, an individual had to keep records of the percentage of his PLA used and notify the scheme administrator of the remaining entitlement at subsequent crystallisations.

Retirement Age

- Post 6 April 2010 it will only be possible to take benefits between the ages of 55 and 75. This will apply to all schemes.
- Individuals who were members of personal pension schemes and retirement annuity contracts at 6 April 2006, and who had a right to retire earlier under the 'special occupation' provisions have this right protected, subject to a reduced lifetime allowance applying.
- Concessionary terms also apply to deferred or current members of occupational pension schemes. If they are contractually allowed to take benefits from age 50 they will still be able to, as long as the contractual provision was in place before 10 December 2003, remains in place until 5 April 2006 and the member takes their full benefits.
- Another important change is that members are now able to take pension benefits and continue in employment, potentially still accruing benefits (scheme rules permitting). This allows members to 'wind down' their employment from age 55.
- It is still possible to retire early on the grounds of ill health, subject to satisfactory medical evidence.

Authorised Benefits

New forms of taking retirement benefits have now come into effect, although some only apply to DC schemes and only then if scheme trustees have facilitated them. These are:

Secured Income

Scheme pensions Such pensions can be paid either out of the scheme's own resources or be secured with insurance companies; they cannot however decrease in payment to the member, except in very limited circumstances. A guaranteed period of up to ten years' 'value protection' may be applied to the scheme pension.

Lifetime annuities Secured via insurance companies and can be investment linked. These can be guaranteed for up to ten years or incorporate 'value protection'. Value protection is only available on death before age 75 and takes the form of a refund equal to the initial capital value less the instalments paid, less tax at 35%.

Alternatively secured pension (from age 75 only) – ASP This option provides an alternative to individuals who have reached the age of 75 and do not wish to purchase an annuity. In practice it is similar to income drawdown (see below) but the income limits that apply are different:

- minimum – 55% of the amount established from tables published by the Government Actuary's Department; and
- maximum – 90% of the amount established from tables published by the Government Actuary's Department.

On death, the value of the plan must be used to provide income for the individual's spouse or dependants. If none exist the funds can pass to a registered charity as a lump sum. The 2007 budget amended the treatment of ASP funds on death and effectively removed the facility whereby a lump sum could be transferred to another member of the same scheme. Any such transfer will now be treated as an unauthorised payment and will attract a tax charge of 70% and may then also be subject to inheritance tax. In practice it is unlikely that the situation will arise as any such payment may lead to the scheme being deregistered and providers will be unwilling to accept the associated consequences. Prior to April 2007 pensions could be guaranteed for the first 10 years but this provision has now been removed following the Finance Act 2007.

Anyone who has an alternatively secured pension can opt for a scheme pension or lifetime annuity at any time.

Unsecured Income

Pension Fund Withdrawal (Income Drawdown) Under this option the member draws down an income directly from the fund. The minimum income level under this option will be £0 (subject to DWP requirements) and the maximum will be based on 120% of the amount established, according to the member's age and sex, from tables published by the Government Actuary's Department. Any level of income can be selected between these limits but must be reviewed on a five-yearly basis.

Where an individual taking unsecured income switches to secured income it is only possible to add a guarantee period to the extent that income has been in payment for less than ten years.

When a member who commenced income drawdown after 6 April 2006 subsequently buys an annuity, a scheme pension or reaches age 75 and subsequently opts for ASP, a further test against the SLA or PLA must be undertaken. Any excess funds will be subject to a recovery charge.

There are advantages associated with utilising this facility including death benefits, income tax efficiency and investment control, however the disadvantages of utilising this option must also be appreciated, in particular any income is not guaranteed and is dependent upon investment returns.

Short term annuities This option allows the member to purchase an annuity or series of annuities with all or part of their fund. The annuity cannot be payable for more than five years or to age 75, if earlier. It can however, be set up with dependant's pension or payments can continue until the end of a guaranteed period in the event of the annuitant's death.

Both of the options outlined above are available until the age of 75. At this time, the individual must secure a scheme pension, lifetime annuity or alternatively secured pension. However, the coalition Government announced in the June 2010 Budget that the requirement to buy an annuity at age 75 will be removed from 6 April 2011. The exact details are subject to consultation but an annuity or alternatively secured pension will not be required until age 77. Anyone reaching age 75 between 22 June 2010 and 6 April 2011 will in effect be able to go into unsecured pension rather than alternatively secured pension which would obviously take them past 6 April 2011 when the new rules will apply. Death benefits, including the associated tax charge of 35%, will be as for unsecured pensions. Anyone who reached age 75 prior to 22 June 2010 who is already in alternatively secured pension is unaffected.

Death Benefits

Death before Vesting

Lump sum: There is no limit on the lump sum death benefit that can be paid before taking benefits. The amount up to the SLA or the members' own PLA where protection has been registered will be payable tax-free. Any excess lump sum will be subject to a 55% recovery charge, payment of which will be the responsibility of the recipient of the lump sum.

Dependants' pensions: Dependants' pensions may be provided without limit, in addition to or instead of a lump sum. However, there can be no guaranteed period and no provision for value protection.

The definition of 'dependant' will broadly follow current rules, ie spouse and children under 23 will automatically qualify and unmarried couples where financial interdependency exists. The Civil Partnership Act has ensured same-sex couples who have registered their relationship under the terms of the Act are treated equally to opposite-sex married couples.

Death after Vesting

The benefits payable in the event of a member's death after vesting depend on whether the pension is unsecured (ie income drawdown, short term annuities) or secured (ie a scheme pension, lifetime annuity or ASP).

Unsecured: If a member dies during drawdown before age 77 the benefits payable to his/her dependants are either:

- a lump sum equal to the remaining fund value less a 35% tax charge, or
- dependants' pensions, which can be drawn from the fund until the dependant's 77th birthday in line with the unsecured pension rules detailed above.

If a member is taking income by means of a short-term annuity then, in the event of death, and, assuming funds have been fully vested, the balance of the fund will be treated in the same way as would the residual funds in a drawdown arrangement, ie full refund less 35% tax. No lump sum is payable from the short-term annuity.

Secured:

- the remaining instalments under a guarantee period;
- if value protection was taken, a lump sum equal to the initial purchase price less instalments paid less a 35% tax charge;
- dependants' pensions (secured under scheme, via annuity, unsecured income or ASP after age 75);

- if a member draws his or her pension under ASP and dies after age 75, leaving no dependants, the remaining fund can be left to a registered charity as a lump sum. Following the budget 2007 there is now effectively no option for the transfer of wealth between members. Any lump sum benefit paid to the estate would be treated as an unauthorised payment and subject to tax charges of 70% tax and potentially also subject to IHT. In practice it is unlikely that this will occur as any such payment could lead to the scheme being deregistered.

Lump sum death benefits payable under all registered pension funds will normally be free of IHT. However, there are exceptions, for example, it is likely that cascading pension wealth on death under ASP will, in some circumstances, trigger an IHT charge as outlined above.

Employer Financed Retirement Benefit Schemes (EFRBS)

These were previously known as unapproved pension arrangements (FURBS and UURBS). Changes in taxation rules have made FURBS far less attractive, meaning remuneration and reward structures for senior executives may need to be revisited.

Benefits in respect of contributions made to a FURBS (funded unapproved retirement benefit scheme) before A-Day may still be paid as a TFC sum on death or retirement after A-Day. Unapproved benefits accrued after A-Day are taxable on the member and, if National Insurance is to be avoided only 25% may be taken as a cash lump sum.

If contributions are made into an existing FURBS after A-Day the lump sum that emerges is apportioned between the pre A-Day (tax free) and post A-Day (taxable) elements.

Post A-Day investments in the fund are taxed at the rates applicable to trusts generally, so the previous preferential tax status has been lost.

After A-Day, the exemption from IHT has been removed from FURBS funds arising from contributions made after this date. However, the IHT exemption is still available to lump sum death benefits from FURBS arising from pre A-Day contributions.

There was an opportunity to roll an UURBS (unfunded unapproved retirement benefit scheme) into a registered scheme during the three months following A-Day, without the 'contribution' being counted against the Annual Allowance.

Pensions and Divorce

The process for dealing with pension funds on divorce involves the issue of a pension sharing order by the courts. This details the amounts of debit and credit, where the scheme member has a pension debit and the ex-spouse has a pension credit of equal value, which will effectively reduce the value of the member's benefits.

Members of occupational schemes will find that previously, the pension debit counted towards their HMRC maximum benefits, while pension credits did not count towards that of the ex-spouse. Post-pension simplification, a pension credit will count against the lifetime allowance of the ex-spouse, whereas pension debits will not count towards the lifetime allowance test.

Where pension sharing orders were effected prior to A-Day, anyone with a pension credit can apply for an enhancement to their lifetime allowance to offset it. Any pension debit from a sharing order effected pre A-Day can be ignored, although it does need to be taken account of when calculating maximum benefits at 5 April 2006 for the purposes of applying for transitional protection.

Permitted Scheme Investments

There is now only one set of rules governing the allowable investments in all pension schemes. This will be of particular interest to members of Small Self Administered Schemes (SSAS) or Self Invested Personal Pension Schemes (SIPP) where differing rules previously applied. It is now possible to invest in a far wider range of investments. However there are still certain important restrictions and clients with SSAS or SIPP schemes should be aware that the new rules may not facilitate certain transactions that the previous rules did. Transitional protections should allow investments held before A-Day to still be held.

Trustee Borrowings

Trustees can borrow money as long as it is used to benefit the scheme. Usually this is to make investments such as:
- property purchase;
- loan back to the employer; and
- purchase shares.

All schemes are now able to borrow up to 50% of the net value of the scheme's fund.

Property Purchase via Pension Schemes

All pension schemes are permitted to invest in the following types of property:
- commercial property;
- hotels, guesthouses and nursing homes;
- riding stables, golf courses, forestry, woodlands and agricultural land;
- non-income producing land; and
- overseas, commercial property.

Residential Property

It had been proposed that SIPPs would receive immediate tax relief for investments in residential property. A proposal that had been widely described as a tax break for the rich, who could use a SIPP to buy a second home or items such as fine wine.

In what was described by the press as a 'Treasury U-turn', however, the Chancellor announced in his pre-budget report (PBR) on 5 December 2005 that the purchase of residential property by a SIPP or SSAS, or indeed the purchase of virtually any esoteric asset, will be treated as an unauthorised member payment. This will attract a 40% tax charge (based on the purchase cost) on the scheme member and in most cases a further 15% tax charge on both the member and the scheme.

Indirect investment in taxable property via genuinely diverse commercial vehicles will not be subject to the tax charges on taxable property.

However, the legislation will prevent pension schemes sheltering such taxable property within a separate investment vehicle, for example a private unit trust or unquoted company.

In simple terms, if the pension scheme owns an interest investment vehicle then for these purposes, unless one of the following exemptions applies, the pension scheme is treated as owning the assets of that vehicle.

There are three specific exemptions where indirect investment into taxable property will not trigger the aforementioned tax charges. These are indirect investment by a registered pension scheme in taxable property via:
1   REITS (Real Estate Investment Trusts);
2   other kinds of vehicle; and
3   trading concern.

Loans

The facility whereby the pension schemes loan money back to the employer is a good way of using the pension scheme to raise finance for the company and also to generate investment returns for the scheme. This is an option that was previously only available to SSASs and is now, subject to scheme rules, available to all pension schemes. The scheme can lend up to 50% of the market value of the scheme's assets.

If a loan was granted before A-Day, and the terms are subsequently revised after A-Day, the whole loan would become subject to the post A-Day rules.

Stocks and Shares

The regulations of 6 April 2006 allowed for up to 5% of the assets of a registered pension scheme to be held in shares of the sponsoring employer, or up to 20% of the assets where there is more than one sponsoring employer. The Finance Act 2006 however imposed retrospective restrictions in the form of the taxable property rules which are summarised below.

Shareholdings in Trading Companies

A pension scheme will be treated as having invested in taxable property if it buys shares in a trading company:
- that is controlled by the pension scheme and/or associated or connected parties,

or
- which scheme members or connected parties are controlling directors of,

or
- which a company that scheme members or connected parties are controlling directors of holds an interest in (either directly or indirectly), and
- which holds any individual item of tangible moveable property worth more than £6,000 or used personally by a scheme member or connected party.

Tangible moveable property means any asset that can be touched and moved. As this includes assets such as machinery, computer equipment, vehicles and furniture, this rule effectively means that most SIPP or SSAS investments in the shares of a connected company will fall foul of the taxable property rules.

Shareholdings in Non-trading Companies

If a pension scheme buys shares in a non-trading company, for example, an investment company such as an OEIC or REIT, it will be treated as having invested in taxable property if:

- the pension scheme and connected parties own 10% or more of the company (or its voting or income rights), or
- it is a close company, or
- it holds animals for sporting purposes (either directly or indirectly), or
- it does not hold:
  - assets worth at least £1m, or
  - at least three residential properties (or, even if it does, any single directly-held taxable property asset is worth more than 40% of the company's total assets).

The tax penalties that apply on investment into taxable property are significant:

- an unauthorised member payment tax charge of 40% of the property value;
- a scheme sanction charge of 15% of the value of the property payable by the scheme;
- if the cost of the property is more than 25% of the value of the fund a further unauthorised payment charge of 15% of the property value payable by the member;
- a possibility that the scheme is deregistered with a further 40% charge payable by the scheme.

Owing to the complexity of the provisions outlined above and the potential tax consequences, it is unlikely that in practice any providers will permit investment into taxable property.

Connected Transactions

The 'connected person' rules have disappeared but any pension asset used by a member or associate of a member on non-commercial terms will result in an 'unauthorised payments charge' being applied. All transactions must take place at fair market value, otherwise unauthorised payments charges will result.

Personal Chattels

Investment into personal chattels such as those listed below is not permitted:

- antiques;
- films;
- fine wines;
- gemstones and jewellery;
- gold bullion;
- oriental rugs;
- rare books;
- stamps;
- vintage cars and yachts; and
- works of art.

Value Stripping Investments

Investment into assets that are designed to remove value from tax-privileged funds will be discouraged:

- All investments must be acquired, disposed of or leased on commercial terms.
- The use of investments and changes to investments that allow for value to be taken out of the scheme assets will be discouraged by the imposition of hefty tax charges.
- The use of annuities that provide that certain payments can be made directly or indirectly on the death of members will be prevented.
- All loans to third parties must be on normal commercial terms.

Personal Use of Assets

Any use of assets by a member or an associate of a member on non-arm's length terms (ie a commercial rent is not paid) will give rise to a tax charge on the member – an 'unauthorised payments charge'. This will be fixed at 40% of the deemed value of the unauthorised payment received by the member. This deemed value is based on the existing rules around benefits in kind.

An unauthorised payments surcharge of 15% will be levied where the value on the unauthorised payments made exceeds 25% of the scheme's asset value in a 12-month period.

Where such unauthorised payments are instead made to the employer under an employer-sponsored arrangement these charges will similarly be imposed on the employer.

Other Tax Charges

A scheme sanction charge may be imposed on the scheme administrator where in any tax year a 'scheme chargeable payment' is made to a member. This is at a maximum rate of 40%.

A scheme de-registration charge of 40% of asset value would be levied on the scheme administrator where a registered scheme becomes de-registered.

Areas of Advice

Depending on an individual's circumstances there are potentially numerous areas that individuals need to give careful consideration to post A-Day. Some of these are listed below but this list is by no means exhaustive and advice should be sought in all instances:

- What was the value of the individual's pension arrangement(s) at A-Day?
- What is the tax free cash entitlement in relation to the scheme's and if higher, HMRC rules?
- Is the standard lifetime allowance likely to be breached?
- If protection is appropriate which type is most beneficial?
- Is there a potential trade-off between maximising TFC payments from the scheme(s) and protecting the funds from recovery tax charges?
- Given new investment rules could new strategies be put in place involving pension scheme purchase as opposed to company or individual purchase?
- Should a strategy be employed which aims to address a number of these issues if relevant or should the focus be on one particular aspect?
- If the new limits introduced are likely to impact, then notwithstanding any protections that are appropriate, are there more tax efficient ways in

which to be remunerated after 6 April 2006 rather than via continuing employer pension contributions?

STATUTORY AND OTHER REFERENCES

Finance Act 2004
Finance Act 2005
Budget 2007
HMRC BIM47106
Finance Act 2007
Finance Act 2008
Pensions Act 2007
Pensions Act 2008
Budget 2009
Budget 2010

2.3 State Pensions

Description	Provision of retirement benefits by the State consisting of two parts: the basic component (the flat-rate 'old age' pension), and the additional component.
Ages	State pension age 65: women born before April 1955 have a state pension age lower than age 65 on a sliding scale with the earliest possible state pension age of 60 for women born before April 1950.
Advantages	1 Defined benefit.
	2 Inflation-proofed before and after retirement.
	3 Partially earnings related, partially independent of the level of earnings.
	4 Individual completion of a BR19 form will give an indication of all State pension benefits earned to date.
Disadvantages	1 Earnings in excess of the upper earnings limit (upper accrual limit from April 2009) are excluded from the additional component.
	2 There is no right to commute part of the pension for a tax-free lump sum; nor is there a death-in-service lump sum.
	3 No retirement pension is paid before state pension age.
	4 No tax relief on personal contributions.
	5 Increases in pension after retirement linked to Retail Prices Index (RPI) not National Average Earnings (NAE). Therefore benefits will gradually become worth less compared with earnings (although the Pensions Act 2007 has since restored the link to NAE for the basic State pension from 2012).
	6 The self-employed do not qualify for the additional component.

FURTHER DETAILS

State Retirement Pensions

The State retirement pension comprises the basic component and the additional component. The basic component is not earnings related and is determined by an individual's National Insurance record. The additional component is earnings related and would include any pension under the former Graduated Scheme, the former State Earnings Related Pension Scheme (SERPS) and the current State Second Pension (S2P). State retirement pensions are payable from State pension age.

The Basic Component

To be eligible for the basic component (basic State pension) an individual requires 10 or 11 qualifying years. This provides the minimum basic State pension (25% of the maximum amount). To achieve the maximum amount of basic State pension (£97.65 per week for a single person, £156.15 per week for a married couple in 2010/11 requires qualifying years for about 90% of the individual's working lifetime. Qualifying years are those tax years in which an individual has paid a requisite level of National Insurance contributions, through employment or self-employment, or has been given credits, or has paid voluntary National Insurance contributions. The working lifetime is measured from age 16 to State pension age.

An individual may use the National Insurance contribution record of a deceased spouse in order to top up their own entitlement.

The basic component is currently adjusted annually in line with the RPI. However, the coalition Government announced in the June 2010 Budget that from 6 April 2011, the basic state pension will go up by the highest of the increase in earnings, prices or 2.5% (see later).

The Additional Component

Graduated Scheme

The Graduated Scheme existed between April 1961 and April 1975. Employees who paid graduated National Insurance contributions during this period will receive a graduated retirement benefit. The amount depends on the number of units of graduated contributions which were paid and their value when the benefit is claimed.

State Earnings Related Pension Scheme (SERPS)

SERPS was introduced from April 1978 and replaced the Graduated Scheme. SERPS provided an earnings-related pension on the slice of earnings which fell between the Lower Earnings Limit and the Upper Earnings Limit ('band earnings'). Originally SERPS offered a pension of 25% of the average of revalued band earnings over the best 20 years, with revaluation based on NAE. This was modified in 1988 to average revalued band earnings over the working lifetime from 6 April 1978, and the percentage is being reduced progressively from 25% to 20% for band earnings after 1987/88. This affects individuals who reach State pension age in 1999/2000 or later and will be fully effective from 2009/10.

The SERPS pension for a person who is widowed is also being reduced from 100% of the deceased's SERPS pension to 50%. This is being phased in over an eight-year period from October 2002.

The SERPS pension is adjusted annually in payment in line with the RPI.

State Second Pension (S2P)

S2P was introduced from April 2002 and replaced SERPS. It is being introduced in two stages and will initially be an earnings-related scheme along the lines of SERPS. Later it is intended that S2P would be a flat-rate pension.

S2P provides a pension on the same slice of earnings as SERPS but introduces three bands for those earnings. The first band is between the Lower Earnings Limit (£5,044 in 2010/11) and the Lower Earnings Threshold (£14,100 in 2010/11); the second from the Lower Earnings Threshold to the Secondary Earnings Threshold (£32,200 in 2010/11); and the third from the Higher Earnings Threshold to the Upper Earnings Limit (£43,375 in 2010/11).

Rather than accruing benefits at a 20% rate as under SERPS, the first band of earnings has an accrual of 40%, the second an accrual of 10% and the third an accrual of 20%. Further, individuals with earnings in the first band whose earnings are below the Lower Earnings Threshold will have benefits calculated as if their earnings were at the Lower Earnings Threshold. Individuals with *no* earnings who are carers may also be treated as having earnings at the Lower Earnings Threshold for the purpose of S2P if they satisfy certain conditions.

S2P is adjusted annually in payment in line with the RPI.

With effect from April 2009, the Upper Earnings Limit was replaced by the Upper Accrual Point for the calculation of both S2P and contracted out rebates. It is fixed at £40,040 (the 2008/09 level of the Upper Earnings Limit).

A knock on effect of this change is that, since April 2009, earnings between the Upper Accrual Point and the Upper Earnings Limit have been subject to the full contracted-in rate of national insurance contributions (NI) even though they do not qualify for state pension entitlement.

Similarly NI reductions or rebates in respect of individuals contracted out private pensions (including contracted out salary related pension schemes) are now only based on earnings up to the Upper Accrual Point.

Contracting Out

It is possible to contract out of S2P/SERPS through membership of a suitable alternative pension scheme. Contracting out can be on either a salary-related basis or on a money-purchase basis. Normally a salary-related basis would be chosen by defined benefit schemes, whilst a money-purchase basis would be used by money-purchase occupational pension schemes, personal pension and stakeholder schemes.

A scheme that was contracting out on a salary-related basis had to provide a Guaranteed Minimum Pension (GMP) prior to April 1997 in respect of the period of contracted out service since April 1978. From April 1997 a scheme contracts out on a salary-related basis by meeting a quality test on benefits.

The State calculates the SERPS component as if the individual were not contracted out. It then makes a Contracted Out Deduction on account of the individual being contracted out. Accordingly a small element of SERPS may be payable even if an individual were contracted out. However, from April 1997 no top up element was provided under SERPS.

A scheme contracting out on a money-purchase basis has to provide protected rights. These are built up from the investment of National Insurance rebates and must be used to secure benefits in a prescribed form.

The position on National Insurance depends on the method of contracting out and differs between occupational pension schemes and other schemes. Where a scheme is contracted out on a salary-related basis, both the employer and the employees pay lower National Insurance contributions. In 2003/04 those contributions were lowered by 3.5% and 1.6% of band earnings respectively. However, the scheme must provide a minimum quantum of benefit which is reflected in the employer's ordinary contributions to the scheme and any member contributions required.

Where an occupational pension scheme is contracted out on a money purchase basis, both the employer and the employees pay lower National Insurance contributions to the State. In 2003/04 those contributions were lowered by 1.0% and 1.6% of band earnings respectively. However, the reduction in National Insurance which is paid to the State must instead be paid to the scheme. In addition, the scheme is eligible for payments which bring the total up to an age-related scale varying from 2.6% of band earnings to 10.5% of band earnings, but the additional payments are made after the tax year-end.

Other schemes which are contracted out on a money purchase basis (for example personal pensions) receive age-related payments direct from the State after the tax year-end. These range from 4.2% of band earnings to 10.5% of band earnings, with the employee's share being 1.6% of band earnings. Employers and employees pay full rate National Insurance contributions.

Under S2P, an individual earning between the Lower Earnings Limit and Lower Earnings Threshold would be given an S2P top-up as if they had earnings at the Lower Earnings Threshold. Those earning between the Lower and Upper Earnings Thresholds will also receive an S2P top-up based on the difference between S2P and the benefit on which the National Insurance rebate is based. There are no top-ups for those earning over the Higher Earnings Threshold.

Contracting out through defined contribution schemes (i.e. money purchase, personal pension and stakeholder arrangements) is to be abolished from 6 April 2012. Anyone contracted out of a defined contribution scheme at that time will automatically be contracted back into the State Second Pension.

The State Pension Credit

Guarantee Credit

- provides a minimum level of income for people aged over 60;
- provides guaranteed income of at least £132.60 (single pensioner) and £202.40 (married couple) – 2010/11; and
- is means tested.

Savings Credit

Payable from age 65, it is given at 60p per £1 of income above the basic State pension up to the guarantee credit ceiling and then withdrawn at 40p per £1 of income thereafter.

State Pension Age

State pension age will be equalised progressively from April 2010. Formerly, State pension age was 65 for men and 60 for women. The new State pension age will be 65 and this will affect all women born after April 1955.

Equalisation will be phased in progressively over ten years. Women born after April 1950 and before April 1955 will have a State pension age of between 60 and 65.

The Pensions Act 2004 introduced a new choice for people who put off claiming their State pension and made important changes to the existing rules from 6 April 2005.

At State pension age, people will be able to:

- stop working and claim their State pension; or
- claim State pension but carry on working (full-time or part-time); or
- put off claiming State pension (whether they are working or not).

The new rules will normally give people extra State pension for the time they put off claiming and a new choice of how to take the extra money, either as:

- extra State pension – worked out at 1% for every five weeks they put off claiming (this is equivalent to 10.4% extra for every year they put off, compared to 7.5% extra before 6 April 2005). They must put off claiming their State pension for at least five weeks to get extra State pension compared to seven weeks prior to 6 April 2005; or
- taxable lump sum – based on the State pension they would have received in the period they have put off claiming, plus interest added each week and compounded. The interest added each week will be equivalent to an annual interest rate 2% above the Bank of England's base rate. They also get their weekly state pension when they claim it, paid at the normal rate. State pension must be delayed for at least 12 months to benefit from the lump sum choice. The lump sum is taxable at the individual's prevailing marginal rate in the tax year of claiming it.

The existing maximum time limit of five years for earning extra State pension has been removed, it can now be put off indefinitely. The maximum backdating period increases from three months to 12 months by 5 April 2006.

Taxation Aspects

Employers   Contributions to both the State and contracted-out schemes are deductible for corporation tax purposes.

Employees   Contributions to the State scheme are not deductible for income tax purposes whereas contributions to company pension schemes and personal pension schemes are deductible. All benefits are treated as earned income for tax purposes.

The self-employed   National Insurance contributions cannot be deducted for income tax relief.

Proposed Changes to the State Pension

On 25 May 2006, the Government published its Pension White Paper: 'Security in Retirement: towards a new pension system'. On 28 November 2006, following consultation on the White Paper, the Government published the Pensions Bill to legislate for long-term pension reform. The proposed changes will not take effect immediately but will be implemented over a period from 2010 to 2044. The main proposals are summarised below.

State Pension Reforms

- Basic State Pension to be linked to National Average Earnings from 2012 at the earliest.
- State Second Pension to be flat rate by 2030.
- Qualifying requirements for Basic State Pension and State Second Pension reduced, including reduction in number of years required to qualify for Basic State Pension to 30.
- Savings credit frozen to reduce means testing which is widely seen as a deterrent to pension saving.
- State pension age to rise as follows:
  - From 65–66 in 2024
  - From 66–67 in 2034
  - From 67–68 in 2044
- Final salary contracted out occupational schemes will have the right to convert GMP rights to an ordinary scheme pension, which would be calculated under the scheme's own rules. Any conversion will be subject to certain safeguards to protect the members' interests.

Personal Account System

From 2012, the White Paper also suggests a Personal Account System with the following main features:
- Employer contributions of 3% of band earnings.
- Employee contributions of 4% of band earnings (+ 1% tax relief).
- Auto enrolment for employees.
- From a date yet to be stipulated by the Secretary of State (but expected to be April 2012) contracting out will cease for money purchase arrangements and contracting out certificates will be cancelled automatically.

The Pensions Acts of 2007 and 2008 which became law in July 2007 and November 2008 have since confirmed all of the above changes.

Further Proposed Changes

Following the June 2010 Budget, the coalition Government have announced that they intend to accelerate the increase in the State Pension age to 66 and a review will be launched shortly. This review is expected to be conducted quickly as the changes need to be implemented fairly.

There were no suggestions of the timescales for this within the Budget documentation, but the Coalition Agreement suggested that the date State Pension age would start to increase to 66 would not be sooner than 2016 for men and 2020 for women.

In addition, the Chancellor confirmed that the promised consultation on the removal of the statutory retirement age of 65 will take place shortly. The Government's aim is to phase it out from April 2011.

This change will allow employees of all ages to continue working as long as they are able to meet the demands of their job, thereby removing an obvious anomaly in the UK's anti-age discrimination law. The consultation is likely to focus on the practical implications of the change for employment terms and pension provision.

CROSS REFERENCES

2.4   Personal Pensions

Description	Personal pensions are available to individuals in receipt of net relevant earnings (NRE), after deductions of allowable expenses. However, it is possible to contribute up to £3,600 pa into a Personal Pension without the need for NREs.
Age	Retirement Benefits are available from age 55 and must be crystallised by age 75. The minimum age increased from age 50 to 55 on 06 April 2010.
Suitable for	The self-employed/employees who are not in an occupational pension scheme, employees who are in an occupational pension scheme and wish to make additional provision or non-earners.

Advantages

1. Premiums paid rank for income tax relief at the contributor's highest marginal tax rate for the relevant year, although restrictions apply for high earners.
2. Individuals can contribute up to the higher of 100% of salary or £3,600.
3. The invested funds are free of most taxes (NB pension funds can no longer reclaim tax credits on dividend income).
4. Ability to take up to 25% of fund at crystallisation as a tax free pension commencement lump sum.
5. Pension provision can be made for widows/widowers and dependants.
6. Death benefits can be written under trust to avoid IHT exposure.
7. Retirement date can be flexible and actual retirement is not required in order to take pension benefits.
8. The policy is the property of the individual.
9. Borrowings may be advanced against accumulated fund or the projected lump sum benefits at retirement.

Disadvantages

1. The amount of premiums payable for qualified tax relief is limited by earnings, excess contributions are taxed accordingly.
2. Assets of the fund are not normally available for use in a self-employed's business.

Investment limits	Minimum investment varies depending on the provider but can be as little as £20 per month. The maximum investment is dependent upon earnings and the annual allowance.
Charges	In the past single premium policies had lower charges than regular premium policies; the latter tended to have heavier charges in the early years to pay for the costs of setting up and commissions (if payable). New policies (post April 2001) tend to have a single charge based on the value of the fund accrued.

FURTHER DETAILS

Investment Options

Legislative Background

On 1 July 1988 personal pension schemes replaced retirement annuity policies (RAPs). However, existing RAP contracts may continue and, in addition, many existing RAPs incorporate the option to increase the premiums without the need to effect a new policy. Some RAPs contain guaranteed annuity rates.

Investment Simplification

Following the Finance Acts 2004/05 it is now possible for all registered pension schemes to invest in a wider range of assets. This includes Personal Pension plans and Retirement Annuity contracts. However in reality most providers will continue to offer the investment options shown below, allowing individuals to opt for a Self Invested Personal Pension (SIPP) if they want to take advantage of the full range of permitted investments.

With-profits

This has historically been the most popular class of contract, providing a fund and/or pension benefits at retirement resulting from the addition of bonuses at intervals according to the level of contributions payable.

Bonuses are of two types: the reversionary bonus, usually declared annually, which once added forms part of the emerging policy benefits; and the terminal/maturity bonus, added only when the pension becomes payable. Reversionary bonuses generally have regard to the long-term investment performance of the fund, and past bonus declarations are only an indication of future levels. Terminal bonuses have regard to the surplus earned in the fund over the life of the policy and (sometimes) to market conditions at retirement, and should not be relied upon when projecting future fund values.

With profit funds can be subject to a Market Value Reduction (MVR) if the policy-holder decides to switch funds, transfer the benefits or take the benefits before Normal Retirement Date.

Annuity rates on retirement date can make a significant difference to the amount of pension provided and can vary sharply over a short period. Some RAPs contain guaranteed annuity rates which can be valuable at a time of low interest rates.

The benefit on death before retirement can vary considerably between policies – from no return at all (although this is now usually a feature of older style policies) to the return of the accumulated fund – some life offices offer a choice. Since every benefit costs money, the lower the death benefit, the higher will be the pension benefits (other things being equal). Most providers now only offer a return of the accumulated fund. Those which have given return of premium will usually allow the policy to be altered to return of fund.

Unit-linked

Units in one or more selected funds are purchased as each premium is paid, usually at the offer price. The unit value – published daily or weekly in certain newspapers – is based on the market value of the underlying securities, properties and cash balances in the fund. The value of the policy on retirement is the bid value of the units: there is rarely a minimum guaranteed value; sometimes there is a guaranteed minimum annuity rate. Unit-linked policies therefore carry a greater risk than with-profits policies although the potential investment growth can be greater.

Some policies offer an option under which the pension continues to be linked to the units after retirement, which may provide the possibility of the pension keeping pace with inflation, but with a corresponding risk.

It is now common for pension providers to offer policyholders links to externally managed funds meaning that they are not limited to the life assurance company's own funds. Individuals should be aware that in return for what is perceived to be a greater degree of investment management, a higher annual management charge is often levied for utilising these funds.

Taxation

Tax Relief

In order to obtain tax relief on premiums in excess of £3,600 pa an individual must have relevant earnings from self-employment, either alone or in partnership; remuneration from an office (eg director) or employment.

'Relevant earnings' excludes anything which arises from the acquisition, right to or disposal of own company incentive scheme shares and anything in respect of which tax is chargeable as an ex gratia or compensation payment.

Qualifying Premium Limits for Personal Pensions

The maximum contribution made by the individual that will qualify for income tax relief is the greater of 100% of UK earnings and £3,600.00 (gross).

The maximum contribution made by the employer that will qualify for tax relief is equal to the annual allowance in force at the time of the payment (£255,000 for 2010/11). Any payments in excess of the annual allowance will result in a 40% tax charge on the employee.

On 22 April 2009 the Chancellor announced during his budget that from 6 April 2011 tax relief will be limited to 20% for individuals with an annual income of £150,000 or more. Tax relief will be tapered between 50% and 20% for income between £150,000 and £180,000. This was subsequently extended from December 2010 to individuals with relevant income over £130,000. Between these dates the anti-forestalling legislation as outlined in Section 2.2 has been introduced.

Again, as mentioned in Section 2.2, this has subsequently been superseded by the announcement in the budget of June 2010 from the new coalition Government that these restrictions in their present form will no longer go ahead from 6 April 2011. The anti-forestalling regime currently in force is unaffected.

The Payment of Premiums

With effect from 6 April 2001, both self-employed individuals and employees pay personal pension scheme premiums net of basic rate income tax. Higher rate income tax relief needs to be claimed separately through self-assessment.

Personal Pension Term Assurance

The Finance Bill 2007 removed the facility whereby life assurance could be provided alongside a Personal Pension with tax relieved contributions.

Excess Premiums

Premiums over and above the limits as set out by HMRC can be made, however they will not qualify for tax relief.

Carry-forward and Carry-back

There is now no option to carry premiums forward or back.

Retirement Annuity Policies (RAPs)

Retirement annuity policies are no longer available but existing RAP contracts may continue and premiums may be paid into them. Although in theory retirement annuities will fall into the same, simplified regime as Personal Pensions, in practice it is unlikely that many providers will amend their scheme rules and systems to allow policyholders to take advantage of the changes. As a result of this, the old rules on which these policies are based continue to be relevant.

Contribution Limits

Many retirement annuity policies will still operate maximum contribution limits of 17.5% of relevant earnings for an individual under the age of 51 rising to 27.5% for individuals between the ages of 61 and 74. These contributions are not subject to an earnings cap. Where providers allow it, individuals can contribute up to the greater of £3,600 and 100% of UK earnings.

Taxation

The tax regime in respect of retirement annuity policies and personal pension schemes is similar to that relating to occupational pension schemes in that there is no income tax, corporation tax or CGT on the income or gains arising from the funds into which retirement annuity policies and personal pension scheme contributions are invested. However, pension funds are no longer able to reclaim tax credits on UK dividend income.

Contributions to retirement annuity policies continue to be paid gross, with a reclaim of tax relief through the Inspector of Taxes, however where providers' systems allow it, contributions can be paid net of basic rate tax relief following the Finance Acts of 2004 and 2005.

Employers may claim tax relief on personal pension scheme contributions which they pay. Such contributions are aggregated for the purposes of the maximum statutory limits with employees' contributions.

Retirement Age

Retirement annuity policies could previously only provide for retirement on or after the age of 60 unless the individual is in a special occupation.

However, prior to 6 April 2010 it was possible for members to draw benefits from age 50 but this has now increased to age 55. Benefits may be taken earlier if the policyholder:

1   becomes incapable through ill-health of carrying on his or her occupation;
2   has an occupation in which the retirement age is customarily before the age of 50, eg professional footballers.

Contracting-out

Appropriate personal pension schemes effected by employees on or after 1 July 1988 may be used to contract-out of SERPS/S2P. The employer continues to pay the normal full National Insurance contributions and the Department of Work and Pensions (DWP) computes the rebate entitlement based on earnings and pays the rebate in arrears to the personal pension scheme. The Pensions Act 2007 made provision for the abolition of contracting out via personal pensions with effect from a date to be decided (but probably April 2012) which has now subsequently been confirmed.

Retirement annuity policies cannot be adapted to contract out of SERPS/S2P.

Where an individual is already paying the maximum contribution as a percentage of his total earnings towards retirement annuity policies, he may take out further personal pension schemes up to the new increased limits.

Retirement Annuity Policies and Personal Pension Schemes – Planning Points

The self-employed and employees in non-pensionable employment are both subject to the same retirement annuity policy and personal pension scheme limits. However, whilst an employee may have the option to join an occupational pension scheme, as opposed to paying retirement annuity policy or personal pension scheme contributions, the self-employed who wish to make pension provision must use either retirement annuity policies or personal pension schemes to do so, if they wish to obtain the tax benefits which are available.

It is important for individuals (whether or not they are self-employed or employees in non-pensionable employment) to take careful account of the options open to them, if they have both retirement annuity policies and personal pension schemes.

Individuals have a reasonable spread of existing retirement annuity policies which provide for either increases in the regular contributions or further single contributions to be paid and the policies are with life assurance companies with a history of good investment performance, then they may wish to continue with these policies, rather than to effect personal pension schemes.

With the advent of full concurrency individuals can now contribute to both Personal Pensions and Retirement Annuity Contracts at the same time, subject to the contribution limits as set out in previous sections.

Some RAPs contain guaranteed annuity rates or other features which might also warrant consideration.

Personal Pension Schemes

Recent pensions legislation has made pension planning considerably more complex and expert advice is required. The planning section (Section 2.12, *Pension Planning and Practicalities*) sets out some of the main considerations in more detail.

SIPPs and GPPs

A self-invested personal pension (SIPP) is a personal pension in which the various pension policies are brought together in a SIPP and the policyholder can be involved in the investment policy of the SIPP. Further details are set out in 2.5 *Self-Invested Personal Pensions*.

Employers wishing to provide benefits whilst at the same time keeping administration to a minimum may choose to set up a group personal pension scheme (GPP). A GPP is a series of individual policies grouped together for administrative convenience and they are the property of the employee policy holders and are subject to each employee's contribution limit. Further details are set out in 2.6 *Group Personal Pensions Schemes*.

CROSS REFERENCES

Partnership Assurance   **1.11**
Self-Invested Personal Pensions   **2.5**
Group Personal Pensions Schemes   **2.6**
Stakeholder Pensions Schemes   **2.7**
Pension Planning and Practicalities   **2.12**

STATUTORY REFERENCES

Finance Act 2004
Finance Act 2005
Pensions Act 2007

2.5 Self-Invested Personal Pensions

Description	A SIPP is a personal pension which gives you greater choice and control over where an individual can invest pension monies. A SIPP allows investment in a wide range of funds and other investments – even individual stocks and commercial property.
Suitable for	High net worth, financially sophisticated individuals requiring the ability to specify the assets in which they invest for retirement, particularly partners in the professions.
Advantages	1 Enable the consolidation of existing pension arrangements in one wrapper. 2 Income can be drawn from the fund whilst still working (from age 55). 3 Whilst drawing income from a SIPP, the rest of the fund remains invested, rather than being used to buy an annuity. 4 As with a PPP, SIPPs provide the flexibility of income drawdown, phased retirement and deferred annuity purchase. 5 The costs of running a SIPP are transparent.
Disadvantages	1 Costs for low premiums can be expensive.

FURTHER DETAILS

SIPPs were introduced in 1989 and have since become increasingly popular amongst high net worth, financially sophisticated individuals. The number of such policies is increasing rapidly and providers report that the main reason that these have been taken up is the desire by holders to consolidate their existing pension arrangements within one wrapper and to take advantage of the broader scope of the permitted investments and the greater control and flexibility that goes with them, especially following pension simplification. Any provider must be authorised under the Banking Act 1988. Additionally from 6 April 2007 SIPP operators must also be authorised and regulated by the Financial Services Authority.

Permitted Investments

In the form of SIPPs, personal pension scheme providers can give members a wider degree of investment choice, including the ability to have a specified say in which assets should be held and when they should be bought or sold. In January 2001, the Inland Revenue issued the Personal Pension Schemes (Restriction on Discretion to Approve) (Permitted Investments) Regulations 2001. These came into force on 6 April 2001 and set out specific details on permitted investments.

Permissible investments are:
- stocks and shares listed on any recognised stock exchange;
- futures and options traded through a relevant exchange;
- authorised unit trusts, investment trusts and OEICs;
- UK-based tax-exempt unauthorised unit trusts;
- FSA regulated unit trusts resident outside the UK;
- investment policies or unit-linked funds of EU insurance companies;
- commercial property;
- land including development land, farmland and forestry;
- deposit accounts;
- traded endowment policies.

There are specific controls on investments which must be complied with if the SIPP is to be recognised as a registered pension scheme. In particular, HMRC prohibits the following categories of investment:
- residential property and associated land;
- personal chattels, capable of private use.
- However, the Finance Acts 2004 and 2005 have relaxed the rules to allow the following:
- loans to connected parties, ie scheme members, relatives, partnerships in which they are partners and companies which they control;
- unquoted company shares.

Property Purchase

It is possible for the SIPP to invest in the following types of property:
- commercial property;
- hotels, guesthouses and nursing homes;
- riding stables, golf courses, forestry, woodlands and agricultural land;
- non-income producing land;
- overseas, commercial property.

The property may be bought outright from the funds in the SIPP, or the SIPP may borrow to purchase the property. HMRC restricts the amount that the trustees may borrow to 50% of the net asset value of the scheme. This limit includes any existing borrowing and the amount needed for any VAT, Stamp Duty Land Tax or other expenses relating to the purchase. Schemes that have borrowed to purchase property under the pre-simplification rules are not required to restructure their borrowings to bring them into line with the new legislation. The loan is made to the trustees, who also make the loan repayments out of the rental income and are legal owners of the property.

There are considerable tax advantages if an SIPP is used to invest in property. For example, there is no income tax payable on the rent received, no CGT on profits from the sale of the property and the rent that the company pays is tax deductible.

Partners in partnerships are able to combine policies to create a larger fund to enable, for example, the purchase of new partnership premises.

It is worth noting that whilst certain investments may be permissible under the HMRC rules, it does not mean that all SIPP providers will allow the investment in their plan. A number of mainstream providers, for example, will not allow overseas commercial property in their plans.

Loans and Borrowing

A SIPP may also make loans to unconnected third parties, but not the members. All loans have to be on a commercial basis at a rate determined from time to time and fully secured. Additionally the SIPP trustees must ensure that the nature of loan is prudent and a suitable action for a SIPP to take.

A SIPP may also borrow for legitimate investment purposes, outside of property purchase, to further the aims of the scheme. The maximum amount that can be borrowed is limited to 50% of the scheme's net assets at that time. Any new borrowing has to take into account existing borrowing in the 50% total.

Prohibited Investments

Most types of conventional investments are freely permitted, but there are some restrictions designed solely to prevent abuse.

Any SIPP holding prohibited assets directly or indirectly will have all tax advantages removed which will broadly mean that it is at least no more advantageous to hold such assets in a pension scheme than it is to hold them personally.

Prohibited assets include direct or indirect investment in residential property and certain other assets such as fine wines, classic cars and art and antiques.

If a SIPP directly or indirectly purchases a prohibited asset the purchase will be subject to an 'unauthorised member payments charge'. This will recoup all tax relief given on the amounts used to purchase the asset. This means that:

- the member will be subject to an income tax charge at 40% on the value of the prohibited asset;
- the scheme administrator will become liable to the scheme sanction charge, which will usually be a net amount of 15% of the value of the asset;
- if the set limits are exceeded the cost of the asset may also be subject to the unauthorised payments surcharge, which is a further charge on the scheme member of 15% of the value of the asset; and
- if the value of the prohibited asset exceeds 25% of the value of the pension schemes assets, the scheme may be de-registered which would lead to a tax charge on the scheme administrator on the value of the scheme assets at the rate of 40%.

An important point to note is that by using a SIPP wrapper an investor is not tied to the product of one pension provider but is free to choose the most suitable investment medium for circumstances between now and the date that the member draws pension benefits down.

Connected Party Transactions

A SIPP can also enter into an investment transaction with someone connected to the SIPP member. Such transactions must be carried out on an arm's-length basis which means that a SIPP can buy, sell or lease a property from or to the member, their family or their business provided the transaction takes place at market value.

Retirement Options

SIPPs have the same retirement options as personal pension plans. Thus, in retirement:

- part of the fund could remain invested to provide growth and income;
- part could be commuted to a tax-free lump sum and the remaining fund, ie three times that amount, would then need to be used to purchase an annuity;
- part could be commuted to a tax-free lump sum and the remaining amount could go into an unsecured pension (income drawdown) to provide flexible retirement benefits;
- after age 75 there is the option to continue to draw from the fund using an alternatively secured pension, meaning that there is now no requirement to purchase an annuity should the individual not wish to do so.

Death Benefits

The death benefits provided by a SIPP are the same as those provided by personal pension plans. Any lump sum death benefit must be paid within two years of the member's death.

If death occurs prior to the member's retirement, the following options exist:

- the full value of the fund can be returned to the beneficiaries, provided it derived from personal pension plans;
- the spouse can opt to purchase an annuity, use an unsecured pension, or, if aged 75 or over, an alternatively secured pension.

If death occurs after retirement, when benefits are being taken, the following options exist:

- if income is being drawn via an unsecured pension, the value of the fund passes to the spouse or dependants and is subject to a 35% tax charge;
- the surviving spouse can purchase an annuity;
- the surviving spouse can elect to continue drawing an income through an unsecured pension (or alternatively secured pension if aged 75 or over) or secured pension in the form of a lifetime annuity or scheme pension;
- if income is being drawn via an alternatively secured pension and there are dependants the funds must be used to provide a dependants' pension in the form of an unsecured pension, alternatively secured pension or secured pension in the form of a lifetime annuity or scheme pension;
- if income is being drawn via an alternatively secured pension and there are no dependants there is effectively only one option available following changes in the rules from April 2007.

The charity lump sum death benefit – member can nominate a registered charity to receive some or the entire remaining ASP fund.

Prior to April 2007 there was the option to transfer the remaining ASP funds to a member or member of other arrangements within the same registered scheme (the transfer lump sum death benefit). This option was withdrawn from 6 April 2007 and means if these benefits were paid they would be subject to an authorised payment tax charge as well as being assessed for inheritance. This could result in an up to 82% tax charge.

If death occurs after retirement and either if an annuity has been purchased or if in receipt of a scheme pension, various options will exist, but will depend on which kind of annuity was purchased or the scheme rules, for example whether there is a guarantee period or a widow's pension.

State Second Pension

The Department for Work and Pensions (DWP) has introduced changes in the Personal and Occupational Pension Schemes (appropriate Schemes) Protected Rights Amendments 2008.

New government rules came into effect on 1 October 2008 and announced that if an individual has built up a protected rights fund through contracting out of the State Second Pension – S2P (formally known as SERPS), they will let investors wishing to take control of their investments hold Protected Rights funds in SIPPs. Previously the only option is to accrue benefits in a traditional style personal pension plan.

It must be noted that SIPPs cannot accept 'minimum contributions' from HMRC to enable an individual to remain contracted out of the State Second Pension on an ongoing basis. Additionally, one area of protected rights the DWP does not plan to change is the requirement for individuals to purchase a 50 per cent pension to a spouse or registered civil partner.

CROSS REFERENCES

Partnership Assurance   **1.11**
Pensions Simplification and Finance Acts 2004 and 2005   **2.2**
Pension Planning and Practicalities   **2.12**
Investment Property   **3.18**
Married with Older Children   **5.6**
Pre-Retirement   **5.7**

2.6 Group Personal Pensions Schemes

Description	Series of individual personal pension plans, usually of employees, grouped together for administrative convenience.
Age	Maximum 75.
Suitable for	Employees who are not in an occupational pension scheme.
Advantages	1 Premiums paid qualify for income tax relief at the contributor's highest marginal tax rate for the relevant year, although restrictions apply for high earners.
	2 The invested funds are free of most taxes (pension funds can no longer reclaim tax credits on dividend income).
	3 Possibility of taking part of the accumulated fund on retirement as a tax-free lump sum.
	4 Pension provision can be made for widows/ widowers and dependants.
	5 Death benefits can be written under trust to avoid IHT exposure.
	6 Retirement date can be flexible and actual retirement is not required in order to take pension benefits.
	7 The policy is the property of the individual.
	8 Borrowings may be advanced against accumulated fund or the projected lump sum benefits at retirement.
Disadvantages	1 The amount of member premiums eligible for income tax relief is restricted to 100% of UK earnings.
Investment limits	Minimum investment for single premium is usually £500–£1,000; regular premiums from £30 per month or £300 per year.
Charges	Group schemes tend to have lower charges than individual personal pension plans.

FURTHER DETAILS

Grouped Personal Pension Schemes

Personal pension schemes are covered in detail in Section 2.4. Employers wishing to provide benefits whilst at the same time keeping administration to a minimum may choose to set up grouped personal pension schemes.

A grouped personal pension scheme (GPP) is in effect a series of individual policies grouped together for administrative convenience and they are subject to the personal pension scheme limits.

These schemes have become increasingly popular for those employers not wishing to undertake substantial administration. It also allows employers to avoid most of the requirements of the Pensions Act 1995.

The New Defined Contribution Regime

The Government has merged the stakeholder regime and personal pension regime into the 'defined contribution regime'.

From October 2001 all employers with more than four employees, aged 18 or over and earning above the national insurance lower earnings limit must offer their employees access to a designated stakeholder scheme. Employers can be exempt if membership to a GPP is offered. To be so exempt the employer must contribute at least 3% of basic pay, offer GPP membership within three months of joining (except to those under 18 years of age) and allow payroll deductions for employee premiums. The GPP must not apply exit penalties.

Taxation

Contributions by the employee are allowed for income tax up to 100% of UK earnings. Employer's contributions are usually allowed for corporation tax. By contributing directly into the GPP the employer can save National Insurance, as would the employee.

The combined contributions of employer and employee can exceed 100% of earnings but should not exceed the annual allowance (£255,000 for 2010/11) except in the year that retirement benefits are taken, when contributions are unlimited.

CROSS REFERENCES

Personal Pensions   **2.4**
Stakeholder Pension Schemes   **2.7**
Pension Planning and Practicalities   **2.12**

2.7   Stakeholder Pension Schemes

Description	Provision of retirement benefits commencing at ages 50 (55 from April 2010) to 75 by payment of single or regular premiums.
Age	Maximum 75.
Suitable for	Self-employed, employees or unemployed.
Advantages	1 Premiums paid rank for income tax relief at the highest rate paid for the relevant year, although restrictions apply for high earners. 2 The invested funds are free of most taxes. 3 Possibility of taking part of the accumulated fund on retirement as a tax-free lump sum. 4 Pension provision can be made for widows/widowers and dependants. 5 Death benefits can be written into the contract. 6 Retirement date can be flexible and actual retirement is not required.
Disadvantages	1 The amount of premiums payable is unlimited, but with limits on the amount eligible for tax relief (overpaid premiums are refunded). 2 Assets of the fund are not normally available for use in a self-employed business. 3 Waiver of premium benefit cannot be included within the policy. 4 Less choice of investment funds when compared with personal pensions.
Investment limits	Minimum investment is £20.
Charges	Maximum of 1.5% pa for the first ten years reducing to 1% pa thereafter of the value of the fund. No other charges can be made from the fund.

FURTHER DETAILS

Legislative Background

The Government outlined its proposals for stakeholder pensions in the Green Paper *Partnership in Pensions*, in December 1998. The basic legislative framework for stakeholder pension schemes was subsequently set out in the Welfare Reform and Pensions Act 1999 (the 1999 Act).

Defined Contribution Regime

The Government merged the stakeholder regime and personal pension regime and it is now referred to as the 'defined contribution regime'. The following comments apply to all plans which come under this new regime (personal pensions, stakeholder pensions and money purchase occupational schemes which opt into this regime).

- Contributions of up to £3,600 pa are allowed without reference to earnings. Contributions in excess of this level are permitted in accordance with the current HMRC limits.
- To contribute to a stakeholder pension, a person must be resident in the UK or an employee abroad on Crown duties (or the spouse of such an employee).
- All member contributions are paid net of basic rate tax, even for self-employed members and members with no earnings.
- Carry-forward and carry-back of unused relief was abolished from April 2005.
- Waiver of premium is not allowed as a benefit for new plans after April 2001. A separate contract to insure contributions against non-payment will be permitted, but no tax relief will be given on the premiums for this contract. Some contracts will provide cover for non-payment due to a period of unemployment.
- There is no limit on the amount of life cover that can be taken out, although any payment on death (including the return of pension funds) in excess of the personal lifetime allowance will be subject to a tax charge of up to 55%. Contributions to life cover will come within the annual allowance.

Scheme Governance

The Government is particularly keen to ensure it provides as much protection as possible for scheme members and announced the following:
- Schemes can be established under trust or via a contract with an FSA-authorised scheme manager.
- Stakeholder schemes must be registered with the Pensions Regulator.
- The marketing of stakeholder pensions to prospective members will be regulated by the FSA.
- All schemes must offer a default investment option.

Minimum Standards

Stakeholder pensions must meet various standard requirements. These are as follows:
- The maximum charge for stakeholder will be 1.5% pa for the first ten years reducing to 1% pa of the value of the fund thereafter.
- No other charges will be allowed under the stakeholder scheme.
- Advice, and other services, cannot be paid for from the fund unless these can be included within the maximum charge. They can, however, be paid for under a separate contract.
- With-profits funds can be offered as an investment option, but no extra charge can be made and the fund should be ring-fenced to ensure that all money goes to the members.
- The minimum contribution, regular and single, to stakeholder is £20. There is no minimum frequency or payment term.
- An annual statement should be issued to show contributions, investment performance and charges.

Employee Access

The Government announced the following measures to ensure that as many employees as possible will have access to stakeholder pensions:

- Stakeholder pensions have been available since April 2001, and employers had until October 2001 to comply with the regulations on offering access.
- Employers with less than five employees are exempt from having to provide access to a designated stakeholder pension.
- If an employer has an occupational pension scheme then this will also exempt the employer as long as employees can join within 12 months of starting work. Membership can be closed to employees under 18 years of age or within five years of retirement.
- Employers can also be exempt if membership of a GPP is offered. The employer must contribute at least 3% of basic pay, offer GPP membership within three months of joining (except to those under 18 years of age) and allow payroll deduction for employee premiums. The GPP must not apply any 'exit penalties'.
- If an employer is not exempt from offering a stakeholder scheme then employees should be offered access to a stakeholder scheme within three months of starting service.
- If an employee is making personal contributions into a stakeholder scheme by payroll deduction, the employee must be allowed to alter these payments every six months.
- Employees earning below the National Insurance Lower Earnings Limit do not have to be offered access to the designated stakeholder scheme or GPP.

Designating a Scheme

In designating a stakeholder scheme an employer must do the following:

- designate a stakeholder scheme (but not recommend one) from the register held by the Pensions Regulator;
- consult with the relevant employees on the choice of nominated scheme;
- provide information to employees on the stakeholder scheme (the name and address of the scheme and a telephone contact number are the minimum);
- operate a payroll deduction facility through which employees' contributions are deducted from pay and remitted to the stakeholder scheme;
- check periodically thereafter that the stakeholder scheme continues to be on the pensions regulator register.

Concurrency

Prior to 6 April 2001, members of occupational pension schemes were not permitted to contribute to a personal pension scheme in respect of the same source of earnings.

However, with effect from 6 April 2006, members of occupational schemes can contribute to any registered pension scheme. The maximum contribution to a registered pension scheme on which income tax relief is given is restricted to 100% of UK earnings.

PENSIONS ACT 2008

The Pensions Act 2008 has put into law the reforms to the private pension system which will see the introduction of National Employment Savings Trusts (NEST) from 2012. The National Employment Savings Trust is likely to replace Stakeholder arrangements. It is planned that all eligible workers, who are not already in a good quality workplace scheme, will be automatically enrolled into either their employers' pension scheme or the new NEST pensions.

CROSS REFERENCES

Introduction to Pensions   **2.1**
Personal Pensions   **2.4**
Group Personal Pension Schemes   **2.6**
Tax Rates (for NI limits)   xlv

2.8 Occupational Pensions

Description	Often referred to as company pension schemes although also available for employees of partnerships and sole traders.
	Provision of retirement (and other) benefits consisting of a pension in retirement with the option to commute part for a lump sum; also a pension to a widow and dependants on death and lump sum benefits if death occurs before retirement. Dependants' pensions cannot, in total, exceed what the member's pension would have been.
Suitable for	Employees likely to remain with the employer for a reasonable period.
Advantages	1 Company contributions are allowed as a deduction for corporation tax.
	2 Employees' contributions are allowed as a deduction in calculating income tax on earnings.
	3 Pension funds are free of most income taxes but cannot reclaim tax credits on UK dividend income.
	4 There is the option to exchange part of the pension on retirement for a tax-free lump sum.
	5 Pension provision can be made for widows or widowers and dependants.
	6 A lump sum payment can be provided on death-in-service.
Disadvantages	1 Assets of the fund are not available for use in the business unless the scheme is self-administered.
	2 An employee who leaves before normal retirement date may suffer a substantial reduction in his or her potential pension benefits.
	3 Pension scheme Trust Deed and Rules can place restrictions on the maximum benefits accrued in different circumstances and the form in which benefits may be paid (i.e. lump sum or pension).
Contribution limits	No minimum contribution, although uneconomic for group schemes investing below £2,000–£3,000 per annum. Tax relief on employee contributions up to annual allowance. Allowance is 100% (subject to a maximum of £255,000 in 2010/11) or £3,600, whichever greater. No limit on employer contributions but amounts over the annual allowance per employee will be deemed to be a benefit in kind. Please be aware that tax relief may be restrictedor some higher earning individuals. Full details are shown in Section 2.2. As stated

> fthe regulations regarding these restrictions
> have recently been repealed and at the time
> of writing we are awaiting confirmation of the
> replacement regulations. The consultation period
> concerning these ended on 27 August 2010 and
> the Government are expected to confirm their
> intentions by the end of September 2010.

FURTHER DETAILS

Types of Scheme

Schemes can vary both as to the basis of providing benefits and as to their funding. In the private sector, these are typically established under trust and are run by trustees appointed for this purpose. In the public sector, these are typically established by statute and governed by regulations, and are run by a government department or other administering body appointed for this purpose. There are many choices of design of scheme available and some of the main types are summarised below:

Defined Benefit (often referred to as Final Salary)

This is a common type of scheme for medium-sized to larger employers. Pension benefits are typically determined by the employee's length of pensionable service and their pensionable remuneration, either during that service or often towards the end of that service.

Combinations of poor investment performance and increasing longevity have shown that funding these schemes can represent a heavy open-ended commitment to employers. But they can provide a considerable degree of security to employees who spend their whole working lives in one scheme with one employer (unless the scheme is wound up with a deficit). However, early leavers may be at a significant disadvantage.

The Pensions Act 1995, accounting standards and poor investment performance over recent years, have combined to make defined benefit schemes unattractive to many medium-sized and larger employers in the private sector. Many schemes are being closed to new, if not all members, with pension provision for new recruits offered through a money purchase scheme.

Defined Contribution (often referred to as Money Purchase)

Employers providing benefits under this type of scheme do so on the basis of undertaking to contribute a percentage of each employee's salary or alternatively, a specific monetary amount, but without any promises as to the benefits which would be payable at retirement. From the employer's perspective, the cost of providing pension benefits is controlled. At retirement the employee receives benefits based on the accumulated fund built up. Economic conditions at retirement may impact on the cost of purchasing pension benefits. Under these schemes the investment and annuity risk is carried by the employees. Money purchase schemes will tend to favour younger employees where the set amount has a longer investment term in which to grow and employees may change jobs several times during their career.

The complexity of running an occupational pension scheme is such that many money purchase pension schemes are now established by way of group personal pensions or group stakeholder pensions.

Contracting-out

Section 2.3, *State Pensions* explains contracting-out and the operation of the State Second Pension (S2P).

Employments which count for pension benefits on retirement under an occupational pension scheme may be contracted out of S2P. Employers may choose which employments will be contracted-out, but then all employees in the relevant employments are automatically contracted-out if they are members of the contracted out occupational pension scheme. Similarly, if an employee is in an employment which is not contracted-out, then the employee cannot be contracted-out under the occupational pension scheme, i.e. it is not an individual's decision except insofar as it is their decision whether or not to join the scheme.

Contracting-out may be on a salary-related or on a money-purchase basis. Defined benefit schemes that are contracted-out are normally contracted out on a salary-related basis whilst defined contribution schemes are normally contracted out on a money-purchase basis. Where the scheme is contracted out on a Trust basis, employers and employees pay lower National Insurance contributions. Where an individual within a Contract based scheme wants to contract-out , the employer and employee pay the full rate of National Insurance contributions. Payment is made to the scheme in the form of rebates by the DWP on behalf of the employer and employee.

Contracted-out Money Purchase Schemes (COMPS)

This type of scheme is a product of the Social Security Act 1986 which made it possible for money purchase schemes to contract out. COMPS are funded by rebates from National Insurance contributions arising from contracting-out, as well as whatever additional contributions the employer and employees make.

COMPS have made it easier for companies to contract-out without having to give specific undertakings to provide a minimum quantum of benefit as in the case of contracting-out on a salary-related basis (see Section 2.3). However, whilst the advantage of such schemes is that there is no open-ended commitment, as in the case of schemes contracted-out on a salary-related basis, the administration for a smaller employer should not be underestimated in terms of operating two sets of National Insurance contribution tables.

COMPS schemes are eligible for age-related rebates, part of which is paid directly to the scheme by the employer and the employee on a flat basis, with the DWP paying the balance of the age-related rebate after the end of the tax year. However, the level of such rebates is either the same or lower than that available to appropriate personal pensions. This disadvantage, however, needs to be weighed against the timing difference of investment of the National Insurance rebates. A part of the rebate for COMPS is paid following the end of the pay month with the balance to the age-related rebate paid by the DWP following the end of the relevant tax year. By contrast, personal pension schemes receive the whole of their rebates from the DWP following the end of the relevant tax year.

Appropriate personal pensions have, in practice, proved much more popular than COMPS. With much less administration involved, and slightly higher rebates available, many employers have been content to establish group appropriate personal pensions for their staff. Many insurers have moved away from the COMPS market in favour of group appropriate personal pensions.

Individual Arrangements

Employers often decide to provide benefits for certain employees via individual arrangements rather than by including them as members of a group scheme or alternatively decide to use individual arrangements to supplement group scheme benefits.

These are covered in more detail in Section 2.9, *Executive Pension Schemes*.

Benefit Restrictions – 17 March 1987 to 6 April 2006

Employees joining an employer's pension scheme on or after 17 March 1987 were subject to the following restrictions for pre-6 April 2006 service.

Maximum Benefits – Pre-6 April 2006

- The maximum rate at which pensions may accrue is restricted to 1/30th of final remuneration for each year of service therefore resulting in a minimum of 20 years' service being required to provide a maximum pension of 2/3rds of final remuneration as opposed to only ten, hitherto.
- The rate at which tax-free cash sum benefits at retirement can be built up is restricted to 3/80ths of final earnings for each year of service and with a faster build up of tax-free cash allowed only where pension benefits build up at a similar rate.
- A maximum monetary limit was introduced on the maximum tax-free cash at retirement. This maximum limit of £150,000 was based on a maximum salary of £100,000. The maximum salary was increased for the first time since introduced to £105,600 with effect from 6/4/2005.

Earnings Cap – Pre-6 April 2006

Employees joining pension schemes on or after 1 June 1989 or new schemes set up on or after 14 March 1989 could only be provided with approved pension benefits based on a maximum earnings 'ceiling' or 'cap' of, initially, £60,000. This figure was increased by the RPI since its introduction in 1989, and was £105,600 in 2005/06. This in turn means that the maximum tax-free cash sum was £158,400 and the maximum approvable pension was £70,400 per annum.

The maximum 2/3rd final remuneration pension could have been provided on retirement between the ages of 50 and 75, after 20 years' service with an employer (subject to the prevailing earnings cap).

The maximum tax-free cash sum was the greater of 3/80th of final salary for each year of service up to 40 years or 2.25 times the amount of pension before commutation. (Again, this was subject to the prevailing earnings cap.)

To help the pensions industry with the transition into the new pensions tax regime, and in particular those schemes whose rules still restrict benefits by reference to the earnings cap, HM Revenue & Customs (HMRC) agreed to publish details of a notional earnings cap setting out what the earnings cap would have been had it still been in existence, each year until 2011. The notional earnings cap for 2010/11 is £123,600.

Lifetime Allowance – Post-6 April 2006

From 6 April 2006 the maximum amount that anyone can have invested across all of their pension plans when they choose to take their benefits was £1.5m (2006/07). The life-time allowance for the tax year 2010/11 is £1.8m.

For defined benefit schemes, the capital value is derived by multiplying the accrued pension by a factor of 20. Pensions in payment are multiplied by a factor of 25.

Benefits in excess of the lifetime allowance at crystallisation will be subject to tax charges.

Transitional protection is available for those members with benefits at or near the Lifetime Allowance at 6 April 2006. See Section 2.2, *Pension Simplification and Finance Acts 2004 and 2005.*

Minimum Funding Requirement

The Minimum Funding Requirement was replaced by the Statutory Funding Framework in September 2005. Employers no longer have to fund their scheme to a 'one size fits all' set level. Instead, scheme trustees are able to decide on a Strategy for Funding for the scheme's liabilities and correcting any deficits.

The trustees' responsibilities include the preparation and maintenance of the Statement of Funding Principles and setting out their policy of meeting the Statutory Funding objective. This must be agreed with the employer.

Trustees must obtain an actuarial valuation at least once every three years and draw up a schedule of contributions showing the rate of contributions to be paid by the employer and member in order to meet the statutory funding framework. The schedule must be certified by a scheme actuary, who must be satisfied this meets with the statement of investment principle.

When the SFF is not met, trustees must put in place a recovery plan which has been agreed with the employer. The recovery plan must set out the steps to be taken to meet the SFF and the timeframe for doing so.

Annual Increases in Pension

Pensions from defined benefit schemes which accrue from 6 April 1997 will be subject to annual increases in line with the increase in the RPI (subject to a maximum of 5%). These increases are known as Limited Price Indexation (LPI). From 6 April 2006, the increase in RPI may be capped at 2.5%.

Defined benefit schemes are required to have a periodic actuarial valuation. If this reveals a surplus, then it may be possible to refund part or this entire surplus less tax to the employer. A refund would, however, not be possible for a scheme until such time as LPI was provided on pensions which accrued prior to 6 April 1997 (in excess of any Guaranteed Minimum Pensions).

Excessive Surplus

At the time of a periodic actuarial valuation, an actuarial certificate is required to confirm whether the scheme has an excessive surplus based on the results of a prescribed valuation. The purpose is to prevent schemes from carrying forward excessive amounts of surplus in a tax-advantaged environment. Carrying forward an excessive surplus can cause a scheme to lose part of its tax exemptions.

A scheme may put forward proposals to eliminate an excessive surplus, including benefit improvements, a contributions reduction (for up to five years) or a refund to the employer. A refund to the employer could only be considered if the scheme provides LPI on pensions which accrued prior to 6 April 1997 (in excess of any Guaranteed Minimum Pensions). Any refund to the employer would be taxable.

Scheme Membership

Sexual Equality – Barber v Guardian Royal Exchange and Subsequent Court Cases

The European Court of Justice Judgment on 17 May 1990 in *Barber v Guardian Royal Exchange* confirmed that Art 119 of the Treaty of Rome, which:

- requires men and women to receive equal pay for equal work; and
- defines pay for this purpose as the ordinary basic or minimum wage or salary and any other consideration, whether in cash or kind, which the worker receives;

does apply to benefits from company pension schemes.

As a consequence of the UK's membership of the EC, Art 119 of the Treaty of Rome has direct applicability to the UK and overrides any UK legislation which may be inconsistent with it.

The *Barber* judgment specifically concerned the entitlement to redundancy benefit and, having considered Mr Barber's claim, the court decided that he was entitled to benefit equal to a woman in the same situation.

It is generally accepted that the judgment effectively outlaws sex discrimination in pension scheme arrangements but, unfortunately, the European Court of Justice confusingly stated that its rulings did not apply prior to the date of the judgment, 17 May 1990, except where legal proceedings had already been initiated.

This led to considerable debate as to what this actually meant and a number of alternative interpretations were put forward, including:

- it applied to the whole of any pension payment which commences to be paid after 17 May 1990;
- it applied to all pension payments paid after 17 May 1990, whenever they started; or
- it only applied to any pension entitlement earned after 17 May 1990.

Clarification was sought during the months immediately following the judgment and the National Association of Pension Funds (NAPF) obtained an opinion from Counsel during the late summer that the ruling only applied to any pension entitlement earned after 17 May 1990.

The *Coloroll* case, among others, was sent to the European Court of Justice to clarify the *Barber* judgment.

Equal Treatment

Any scheme rule which discriminates between the sexes will be interpreted to give the more favourable treatment to both sexes.

Beginning with *Barber v Guardian Royal Exchange* and through to *Coloroll* and *Smith v Avdel Systems*, the law on the equality of pension benefits between males and females has been a vexed subject. Most of the issues are now clear. Occupational pension schemes have had to provide equality of pension provision between males and females since May 1990. If a scheme did not have equal retirement ages in 1990, the effective retirement age from 1990 was that which was the more favourable to the individual. For men and women in similar employment, the employee could retire at the lower of the male and female retirement ages on an unreduced pension; or the employee could choose to remain in employment and accrue further benefits until the higher of the male and female retirement ages. *Coloroll* and *Smith v Avdel Systems* established that subsequently a pension scheme could change its retirement age and, as long as that change did not give rise to any new inequality, that this could stand for the future.

It has been conclusively established that occupational pension schemes must give equal access to benefits and equal benefits. Employers who have not amended their schemes will have automatically adopted the most favourable retirement age, but could change that for future service.

Judgment in the case of *Foster Wheeler v Hanley and Others* given on 28 November 2008 regarding application of an early retirement rule, has demonstrated that Defined Benefit Schemes would be well advised to seek legal advice in order to revisit their actions on closing the Barber Window.

Changes to Contracted-out Money Purchase Schemes

Because of the *Barber v Guardian Royal Exchange* case, a late change was made to SSA 1990 legislation to enable the benefits arising from protected rights to be paid at any time between the ages of 60 and 65 to both men and women.

Access for Part-Timers

It was always thought that the equal access requirements set out in the Social Security Pensions Act 1975 were sufficient to ensure compliance with the Treaty of Rome, Art 119. However, in *Bilka-Kaufhaus* (1986) the European Court found that employees could not be excluded from an occupational pension scheme on the grounds of being a part-time worker if that exclusion amounts to indirect discrimination.

The *Vroege* case brought this matter to the fore and it means that part-timers can demand to be admitted into a pension scheme they were previously excluded from as long as they are willing to pay their share (if any) of the pension contributions. The *Preston* case established that admission to the scheme can be backdated to 1976. However, claims need to be lodged within six months of leaving service.

The implications for occupational pension schemes clearly vary, but employers who employ a lot of part-time workers could face a very large increase in costs, both to backdate benefits and in employing part-time workers in the future.

Age Discrimination

The UK implemented the EC Council Directive 2000/78/EC establishing a framework for equal treatment in employment and occupation. The regulations came into force for all purposes except pensions on 1 October 2006. Further consultations were laid before Parliament on 10 November 2006 and came into force on 1 December 2006. These further consultations referred to pensions.

The Age Regulations state that no employer may directly or indirectly treat one employee less favourably than another on account of age unless the treatment is 'a proportionate means of achieving a legitimate aim' or age is 'a genuine determining occupational requirement'.

Pension schemes are affected by this legislation by some degree but there are certain exemptions as pensions are inherently age discriminatory and the Government recognises that many age-related rules and practices are necessary for the proper operation of pension schemes especially Final Salary Schemes. For those rules that are not specifically exempted, employers must consider whether they can justify their ongoing use.

Voluntary Scheme Membership

Employees are no longer compelled either to join or remain members of an employer-sponsored occupational pension scheme from 6 April 1988. If they opt out they are not obliged to effect any other pension arrangements and if they do, the employer is not obliged to contribute, nor is the employer obliged to readmit an employee who has opted out.

The Pensions Act 2008 Act introduced compulsory pension provision which means from 2012, employers will need to automatically enrol most of their staff in a pension scheme and pay a contribution.

Administration

Register of Pension Schemes

All company pension schemes with more than one member are required to register with the pension scheme registry, which is maintained by the Pensions Regulator, which replaced OPRA on 6 April 2005.

The pensions registry provides a tracing service to help individuals track down the whereabouts of past pension rights. Schemes are therefore required to notify the registry of relevant changes, such as change of name or change of employer.

The registry is financed by an annual levy on company pension schemes which is collected every three years.

The Pensions Advisory Service (TPAS)

TPAS is a voluntary body which provides free advice and assistance to members of the public on occupational pensions and personal pensions.

Members of the public can approach TPAS directly or via their local Citizens Advice Bureau.

TPAS does not provide financial or investment advice or advice on State benefits.

Its primary role is in handling the more minor problems which members of the public have not been able to resolve with their pension schemes or pension providers. More serious problems may be referred to the Pensions Ombudsman.

Independent Trustee on Insolvency

If the employer to a trust-based occupational pension scheme becomes insolvent, then at least one trustee must be appointed who is independent of the employer.

It is the obligation of administrators, receivers and liquidators to appoint independent trustees if the scheme is one covered by the scope of SSA 1990.

Liability on Employer on Winding-up of Pension Scheme

When winding up a defined benefit scheme in deficit the shortfall is a debt due from the employer to the scheme's trustees and the trustees are able to pursue the employer for this. However, the debt is not a preferential one and the trustees will be treated equally with other non-preferential creditors. Even if full recovery is made of the debt, this does not mean that members' benefits are fully secure. The extent to which benefits are secure depends upon the cost of securing those benefits, usually with insurance companies.

The Pension Protection Fund (PPF)

The PPF became operational on 6 April 2005. It will pay compensation to members of eligible defined benefit pension schemes when there is a qualifying insolvency event in relation to the employer and where there are insufficient assets in the pension scheme to cover PPF levels of compensation.

PPF compensation payments will be funded partly by the assets from schemes for which the PPF has assumed responsibility and partly by an annual levy raised on eligible pension schemes.

Disclosure of Information

It is compulsory to disclose certain information to members and recognised trade unions. This includes actuarial information (if applicable) as well as accounting information and the scheme's legal documentation. Member specific information must be provided in certain instances (eg a benefit statement on leaving service), but in other instances information need only be provided on request.

There must also be produced an annual report from the trustees, to include an investment report, audited accounts, actuarial statement (if applicable) and various certificates or schedules.

The Pensions Regulator

The Pensions Regulator replaced OPRA in April 2005 and is the new regulatory body for work-based pension schemes in the UK. The new regulator has a defined set of statutory objectives, has wider powers to investigate schemes and take action where necessary. They take a proactive, risk-focused approach to regulation and provide practical support for the regulated community.

Compensation and Levy

A compensation scheme has been established to protect against fraud or theft in the event of insolvency of the sponsoring employer. The scheme is funded by a levy on occupational pension schemes.

Trustees

Trustees are responsible for setting an investment strategy after taking suitable advice although they are allowed to delegate the day-to-day investment decisions to a manager. Trustees are required to keep minutes of their meetings and are responsible for the appointment of scheme auditors. One-third of the trustees had to be nominated by the members by 31 October 2007.

Whistle Blowing

Where a scheme is required to appoint an actuary or an auditor under Pensions Act 1995, that scheme actuary or scheme auditor has a statutory duty to inform the Pensions Regulator immediately of any irregularity in the conduct of the scheme by either the trustees or employer. Others may inform the Pensions Regulator but the obligation to do so only falls on the scheme auditor and scheme actuary.

In a recent statement, the Pensions Regulator focused on the risk of unacceptable behaviour associated with pension schemes which is perhaps more likely to occur during these extremely difficult times. The importance of good governance is highlighted and a warning against fraud and dishonesty includes reference to raising the awareness amongst scheme members of the risks of trust-busting/pension liberation activities.

In addition to its own focus on identifiable areas of risk, the Regulator also obtains significant information to help fulfil regulatory responsibilities through whistle-blowing reports. The duty to whistle-blow imposes a reporting requirement on certain individuals involved in the running of pension schemes including trustees, managers and persons involved in administering the scheme. Such persons are obliged to report materially significant breaches of the law relating to the administration of pension schemes to the Regulator. The Code of Practice on 'Reporting Breaches of the Law' is available on the Regulator's website and provides detailed advice for individuals falling within the scope of the whistle-blowing legislation. Anyone who does have potential whistle-blowing duties is also expected by the Regulator to have an understanding of these duties and to be familiar with the Code of Practice.

The Pensions Act 2004 provides that the duty to report a breach of the law to the Regulator overrides any duty of confidentiality that the person making the report may have and it is not, therefore, deemed to be a breach of confidentiality if someone decides to report a breach.

Refunds of Surplus

The surplus provisions may require schemes to make refunds to employers or otherwise face a partial loss of tax exemptions. Any refunds require the consent of the trustees and that members are notified. The Social Security Act 1990 laid down that a surplus could only be paid to employers if Limited

Price Indexation is added to past and future service pensions so the first use of any surplus will be to augment members' benefits in this way.

This provision will inevitably lead to a negotiation between the trustees and the employer about how any surplus is to be used, but the Act makes it clear that the employer must consent, which prevents trustees requiring Limited Pension Increases to be given for past service. The employer may still use contribution holidays, as agreed in the contribution schedule, to control surplus.

The surplus provisions mean that all occupational pension schemes are required to submit valuations to HMRC on a prescribed valuation basis every three years. If a scheme's assets exceed its liabilities by more than 5% on the prescribed basis, the scheme will have to take steps to reduce the surplus to less than 5% in one or more of the following ways:

- by increasing the scheme benefits (within HMRC limits);
- by reducing or suspending contributions from the employer and/or employees for up to five years; or
- by a refund of surplus to the employer subject to a 35% tax charge (PSI 20.6.6 published 31/7/2002) which may not be offset against other profits.

The remedial action must be taken within five years (or within 15 years from the scheme's date of commencement if longer). Tax penalties apply for a scheme with an excess surplus if it takes insufficient action to reduce it to below 5%. These will apply retrospectively to the effective date of the valuation which identified the excessive surplus.

Schemes with less than 12 members and insured schemes where the policies are contribution related, i.e. money purchase schemes, are exempt from the surplus rules.

Priorities on Winding-up

Pensions Act 1995 prescribes a statutory order of priorities for final salary schemes which are wound up. However, this has subsequently been replaced by amending regulations (SI 2004/1140) which promote non-pensioners' non-contracted-out accrued rights above pension increases and combining them with contracted-out rights for priority purposes.

One of the effects of these changes is that trustees are able to obtain a statutory discharge of their obligations on winding-up through other transfers of benefit such as to other occupational schemes or personal pension plans.

Taxation

Employers' ordinary annual contributions will normally be allowed as a deduction from profits chargeable to tax in the year paid providing the scheme is a registered scheme, receives exempt approval and does not provide benefits in excess of HMRC limits. 'Ordinary Annual Contribution' has no statutory definition, but in general it is accepted that there must be uniformity in the basis for the amount of contributions from year to year, eg a fixed percentage of payroll. There is no minimum number of years for which a rate of contribution needs to be paid to qualify as Ordinary Annual Contributions, but as a rule of thumb that rate should continue for no less than three consecutive years. Employer contributions need to meet the normal trading deduction requirement of being wholly and exclusively for the purpose of the trade. There was no equivalent requirement for employer contributions to approved schemes prior to 6 April 2006.

There may be occasions when the employer wishes to make contributions over and above its ordinary annual contributions to an occupational pension scheme. For example, this may be in order to augment benefits, to provide benefits for back service, or if there is an actuarial deficiency. These additional contributions are known as special contributions.

Special contributions enable employers to increase the amounts they pay into the pension scheme, within the limits of funding requirements where relevant, opportunities can be created for contributions to be stepped up in years of high profitability, or if profits are likely to suffer tax at high marginal rates.

The tax relief for large employer pension contributions may be subject to rules that require the tax deductions to be spread over a period of up to four years.

Spreading of tax deductions is only required where there is a substantial increase in the level of employer deductions. The current year contributions need to exceed 210% of those in the previous year. Some specific contributions to occupational schemes are ignored for this purpose.

Where spreading is required, it applies only to part of the contributions. This part, the relevant excess contributions (RECs) is the current year's contributions, again with some specific exceptions for occupational scheme contributions, less 110% of those in the previous period.

Where the RECs are less than £500,000, no spreading is required. For RECs over £0.5m the RECs amount is for tax purposes spread equally over periods of up to the next three years as summarised:

- £0.5m to £1.0m   Current plus next year
- £1.0m to £2.0m   Current plus next two years
- £2.0m or more   Current plus next three years

Employees' contributions are allowed as a deduction from earnings in computing the income tax liability under former Sch E although the tax relief will be limited to 100% of the individual's total remuneration (up to a maximum of £255,000 in 2010/11) or £3,600, whichever is greater. This is subject to the restrictions for high earners outlined under Section 2.2 and the proposed changes to these outlined under Table B of this section.

The impact of National Insurance makes it cheaper for the employer to pay pension contributions for higher paid employees than to increase their remuneration by the same amount.

CROSS REFERENCES

2.9 Executive Pension Schemes

Description	Usually known as EPPs they provide retirement/ death-in-service benefits, either separately or in addition to those under an occupational pension scheme.
Suitable for	Directors and senior executives as an alternative to, or in addition to, a group scheme.
Advantages	1 All the advantages of occupational pension schemes generally. 2 Increased benefits for a selected employee or group of employees. 3 Absorbing otherwise taxable profits. 4 Easily coupled to loan packages. 5 Immune from the claims of company creditors. 6 Privacy – the benefits being provided can be kept confidential from main scheme members.
Disadvantages	1 Possible restrictions on maximum benefits and form in which benefits may be paid (ie lump sum or pension). 2 Other disadvantages as for occupational pension schemes generally.
Investment limits	Minimum investment by the employing company can be as low as £500 for single member schemes. Maximum investment for employers and employees are the same as for occupational/personal pension schemes generally.

FURTHER DETAILS

Commercial Aspects

Executive pension plans have been a highly effective way of increasing the remuneration package of employees, particularly shareholder directors. They are also a way of providing funds enabling directors to retire, leaving the next generation of managers in control without imposing undue financial strains on the company, and ensuring that the future financial well-being of the retired directors is not dependent upon the future performance of the company.

Changes in legislation have reduced the attractions of executive pension plans. The restrictions preventing all of the fund being taken in tax-free cash and the 20-year service requirement for maximum benefit, introduced in 1987, reduced their flexibility, particularly for short-term employees and high earners. Additionally, the earnings cap introduced in the Finance Act 1989 which applied to all new schemes set up on or after 14 March 1989, and to new scheme members joining on or after 1 June 1989, had further limited their tax planning possibilities. Pension simplification has brought EPPs into line with personal pension schemes.

Controlling Directors

A controlling director is a person who is within ten years of retirement who has been a director and either alone or with associates has or could have had control over the ordinary share capital of the company.

Taxation Aspects

The employer's contributions will normally be allowed as a deduction from profits chargeable to tax in the year the contribution is paid provided that they are incurred wholly and exclusively for the purpose of the employer's trade or profession. Contributions by employees are allowed as a deduction from earnings up to 100% thereof in computing the tax liability under former Schedule E. This is subject to an upper limit of £255,000 (20010/11). This is subject to the restrictions for high earners outlined under Section 2.2 and the proposed changes to these outlined under Table B of Section 2.8

CROSS REFERENCES

2.10 Small Self-Administered Schemes

Description	These are approved occupational pension schemes which must have fewer than 12 members and the assets may be invested in a range of assets with effective control by the company.
Suitable for	Directors/senior management.
Advantages	1 Members can effectively control investment policy, including: (a) creating a hybrid scheme (part-insured and part-invested); (b) lending on commercial terms up to 50% of the fund to the employer; (c) investing in commercial property which may be leased to the company at a commercial rent. 2 Advantageous corporate tax planning opportunities. 3 Provision of pension allows IHT planning to be undertaken.
Disadvantages	1 Self-administration may absorb company management time. 2 Professional costs of establishing the scheme (about £2,000–£3,000); and costs of running the scheme: investment advice, administering payment of benefits, and provision of a pensioner trustee (about £500–£1,250 per annum). 3 Absence of security offered by an insurance company and risk of loss through bad investment management.
Investment limits	No minimum investment stipulated but with wholly self-administered schemes the annual contributions required are approximately £10,000–£15,000 to be viable. Maximum investment for employers and employees are the same as for occupational/personal pension schemes generally.

FURTHER DETAILS

Commercial Aspects

A Small Self-Administered Scheme (SSAS) is a self-administered pension scheme with fewer than 12 members. It is usually set up by controlling directors of family companies who either wish to have personal control over the scheme investments or wish to link their pension scheme investments with assets which relate to their business.

These schemes have become an integral part of tax planning for many companies to the extent that the principal purpose, that of the provision of retirement benefits, has become obscure because of the tax planning opportunities available. It is important, nevertheless, to bear in mind that these schemes are subject to the same HMRC limits in terms of maximum benefits.

Mixed and Hybrid Schemes

SSASs may be invested on a fully-insured basis (ie with an insurance company), non-insured (ie invested directly or in other collective investments) or hybrid (ie part of the funds invested with an insurance company).

A limited number of insurance companies offer schemes with standard documentation and provide the independent trustee and administrative facilities at a standard charge. A percentage of the funds may have to be invested in life insurance company funds but the trustees are allowed control over the investment of the balance. One of the advantages is that the costs of such schemes are normally lower than for wholly self-administered schemes. The disadvantage is that in many instances 'front end' charges, principally commission, will be taken out of the insured portion unless commission is waived and reinvested.

The mixed or hybrid scheme may appear attractive to the smaller company because of its cost advantages and because the life insurance company undertakes the normal administration which would otherwise fall on the trustees. Post 5 April 2006, many insurers have relinquished their roles as scheme administrators so a careful cost/benefit risk analysis should be undertaken before making any decisions.

Loans

The trustees of a SSAS are not permitted to lend money (either directly or indirectly) to a scheme member or to a person connected with a scheme member.

A loan to the employer (or any associated company) will be permitted only if it satisfies the following requirements:

- It is utilised for the purposes of the borrower's business, i.e. the money must be used to benefit the borrower's trade.
- The loan cannot be granted for more than five years (with a possible extension of three years).
- It is at a commercial rate of interest.
- It is evidenced by an agreement in writing, which includes provisions to the effect that the loan will be repaid immediately if the borrower breaches any of the conditions of the agreement, ceases to carry on business, becomes insolvent or if the loan is required to pay benefits under the scheme.
- It is fully secured against tangible assets.

The aggregate of any loans must not exceed 50% of the market value of all the scheme's net assets (including any transfer values received from other schemes).

HMRC require pension schemes trustees to act in the best interests of scheme members and, in particular, may withdraw approval of a scheme where:

- a loan is made solely to keep an ailing business afloat;
- a loan is made to an employer who is technically insolvent;

- the scheme trustees fail to take all legal steps open to them to enforce the repayment of a loan to an employer in the circumstances described at point 4 above.

As a rule, loans should not be made to the employer (or any associated company) unless the trustees would be prepared to lend the same amount on the same terms to an unconnected party of comparable standing.

Although the regulations do not preclude an outstanding loan from being rolled over into a fresh loan, HMRC will not agree to a loan being rolled over after that date without it being subject to the conditions set out above.

The roll-over of unpaid interest into a new loan will not be permitted.

Connected Transactions

Any pension asset used by a member or associate of a member on non-commercial terms will result in a tax charge.

Borrowing

The amount which the trustees of a SSAS may borrow is restricted to the aggregate of:
- 50% of the scheme's net assets at borrowing date; and
- any borrowing in place before 6 April 2006 can be kept in place even if this is more than 50%.

The borrowed money must be used to benefit the scheme.

Permitted Investments

There is now only one set of rules governing the allowable investments in all pension schemes. However there are still certain important restrictions and clients with SSAS schemes should be aware that the new rules may not facilitate previous allowable transactions.. Transitional protections should allow investments held before A-Day to still be held. The following table shows typical allowable and prohibited investments:

Allowable Investments	**Prohibited Investments**
Commercial Property	**Residential Property**
Land	Unsecured loans to the principal employer
Shares in unquoted companies	Antiques
Secured loans to the principal or participating employer(s)	Rare books, furniture, rugs
Secured or unsecured loans to unconnected parties	
Quoted equities on the London and recognised worldwide stock exchanges	Fine wines
Gilts, bonds and fixed interest stocks	Works of art
Investment trusts	Vintage cars
Open Ended Investment Companies	Yachts/moorings
Insured pension funds	Jewellery and gem stones
Bank and building society deposits	
Offshore managed funds	Loans to member trustees or their families
Futures and options	Plant and machinery
Copyrights	
Gold bullion	

Property purchase

All pension schemes are permitted to invest in the following types of property:
- commercial property;
- hotels, guesthouses and nursing homes;
- riding stables, golf courses, forestry, woodlands and agricultural land;
- non-income producing land;
- overseas, commercial property.

Taxable Property

The purchase of residential property by a SSAS, or virtually any esoteric asset (detailed as prohibited in the table above), will be treated as an unauthorised member payment. This will attract a 40% tax charge (based on the purchase cost) on the scheme member and in most cases a further 15% tax charge on both the member and the scheme.

Indirect investment in taxable property via genuinely diverse commercial vehicles will not be subject to the tax charges on taxable property. However, the legislation will prevent pension schemes sheltering such taxable property within a separate investment vehicle, eg a private unit trust or unquoted company.

In simple terms, if the pension scheme owns an interest in an investment vehicle for these purposes, unless one of the following exemptions applies, the pension scheme is treated as owning the assets of that vehicle.

There are specific exemptions where indirect investment into taxable property will not trigger the aforementioned tax charges. One specific example for investing into residential property to avoid this charge would be the use of a REITS (Retail Estate Investment Trusts).

Regulatory Issues

Schemes with less than 12 members and where all decisions are made unanimously or have an independent trustee, are exempt from the trustees' knowledge and understanding requirements of the Pensions Act 2004 and the member nominated trustee requirements. If every member of the scheme is a trustee, the scheme will also be exempt from the internal disputes.

Information to HMRC

The administrator of the scheme has to provide HMRC with specified information and documents within 90 days after any of the following transactions:
- any purchase or sale of property or land;
- any loans by the pension scheme to the employer (or to any associated company);
- any purchase or sale of shares in the employer (or any associated company) or an unlisted company;
- any borrowing of money; or
- the purchase, sale or lease from or to the employer (or any associated company) of any asset other than land, property or shares.

One SSAS per Company

Pre A-Day, in April 2006, a company used to be able to operate only one small self-administered pension scheme. As small self administered schemes are classed as registered pension schemes the pension simplification legislation effectively relaxed this restriction.

Transitional Provisions

As a transitional measure, investments made before 15 July 1991 (including loans) which do not comply with the regulations may be retained provided they were acceptable under previous Inland Revenue practice. Such investments may be disposed of by the trustees in due course to whomever they wish (including scheme members and their relatives) provided that the disposal is on an arm's-length basis at full market value.

Investment Restrictions

The maximum proportion of a self-administered pension scheme's assets which can be invested in shares of the sponsoring employer is restricted to 5% of the scheme's assets.

Shares can also be bought in more than one sponsoring employer as long as the total holdings are less than 20% and shares in any one sponsoring employer are less than 5%.

Taxation Aspects

The maximum benefits permissible under approved pension schemes set up before 14 March 1989 were so widely drawn that it was frequently possible for the company to make very substantial contributions in respect of those members drawing large remuneration. This coupled with the flexibility in amount and timing of contributions year by year, enabled the company to use a SSAS as a tax planning vehicle, possibly keeping profits chargeable to corporation tax within the small companies' rate, avoiding the marginal and full rates.

The structure of an SSAS was considerably less attractive and less flexible for new schemes set up on or after 14 March 1989 and for members joining existing schemes on or after 1 June 1989. The effects of the earnings cap being linked to the RPI as opposed to the AEI severely reduced the attractions of this type of scheme for post-31 May 1989 members.

Following the changes to the pension regime at A-Day, the tax-planning benefits of this type of arrangement are much less attractive.

CROSS REFERENCES

2.11 Unapproved and Alternative Schemes

Description	A means of maximising provision for retirement particularly where the maximum benefit limits restricts normal provision.
Suitable for	High earners.
Ages	Normal maximum 75 years.
Advantages	1 Corporation tax relief on funded scheme contributions.
	2 Tax free lump sum of all benefits on retirement (accrued pre-6 April 2006).
Disadvantages	1 Investment risk.
	2 Benefits accrued post-6 April 2006 are taxed on member.
	3 Accounting disclosure required.
	4 Investments taxed at trust rate.
Charges	Variable; tailored schemes may be costly to set up.

FURTHER DETAILS

Unapproved ('Top up') Pension Schemes

These were introduced in order to provide employers with means of providing whatever level of retirement benefits they wish to for their employees over and above the benefits which may be provided from an exempt approved pension scheme which is limited to the maximum funding rate.

Members of personal pension schemes, as well as members of approved occupation pension schemes, may also be able to be members of unapproved schemes. It may also be used as an alternative to approved pension provision.

New tax rules for unapproved arrangements introduced on 6 April 2006 make these types of arrangements much less attractive.

Employer Financed Retirement Benefit Schemes (EFRBS)

From April 2006, unapproved schemes, previously known as FURBS and UURBS are known as ERFBS. Under this type of scheme the employer pays a sum into a trust; the assets are invested and are paid to the employee on retirement or are used to provide retirement benefits on retirement. The trust may invest in any type of investment permitted by the scheme.

Benefits accrued before 6 April 2006 may be paid as a tax-free cash sum on death or retirement. Benefits accrued after this date will be taxable on the member and, if National Insurance is to be avoided; only 25% may be taken as a cash lump sum.

Post-6 April 2006 investments in the fund will be taxed at the rates applicable to trusts.

IHT will be due on death benefits from funds accrued from contributions paid after 6 April 2006.

Alternative Investments

Individuals can rely on other forms of non-pension investments to provide retirement benefits.

ISAs

Income and gains from ISAs are exempt from tax. Although there is no tax relief on the initial investment, the ISA can be cashed without tax charge.

Collectives

Collectives such as Unit Trusts and Open Ended Investment Companies are exempt from CGT on gains within the collectives. Any gains made by an individual will initially be set against their £10,100 CGT annual exemption, the balance of the gain exceeding the annual exemption being taxed at a flat rate of 18%.

Offshore Funds

Non-distributor roll-up funds are gross investment funds and maximise the gains to investors. Tax is charged when the fund is sold. If this can be structured in a year of non-residence or when the individual is a basic rate taxpayer, the tax charge will be minimised. The five-year non-residence rule does not apply to such gains as they are charged to income tax and not CGT.

CROSS REFERENCES

Pension Simplification and Finance Acts of 2004 and 2005   **2.2**
Self-Invested Personal Pensions   **2.5**
Pension Planning and Practicalities   **2.12**
Investment Trusts   **3.7**
Unit Trusts and OEICs   **3.8**
Offshore Funds   **3.10**
Individual Savings Accounts (ISAs)   **3.27**

2.12 Pension Planning and Practicalities

Description	Seeking to maximise the pension provisions by identifying the most appropriate scheme for the individual, considering a scheme and also, whilst in the scheme, planning life changes on employment, retirement, divorce and death.
Suitable for	All persons.
Advantages	1 Early investment magnifies the potential return.
	2 Choice of scheme and provider can make significant differences to the return.
	3 Flexibility in the plans allows for life changes.
Disadvantages	1 Pensions are complex and experienced independent advice can be expensive but valuable and worth it in the long run.
	2 Younger lives may not see the need to provide early.
Investment limits	As laid down by statute and once a year's reliefs have gone it is more difficult to compensate for them.
Charges	The Government are seeking to minimise charges on universal schemes to provide access to all; expert advice can be expensive to meet regulatory requirements.

FURTHER DETAILS

Pensions are an increasingly complex technical area and the difficulties faced by employees (and employers) in deciding which route is best have increased substantially. This section is set out as follows:

- Which type of pension scheme?
- Planning, whilst in a scheme
- Leaving an employer
- Options upon retirement
- Divorce

WHICH TYPE OF PENSION SCHEME?

Many of the distinctions between different types of pension scheme have vanished following the introduction of the new legislation contained within the Finance Acts 2004 and 2005, however, in practice many individuals will still hold historical arrangements where the rules of the scheme have not been altered to reflect changes. Indeed in some cases it is unlikely that the governing scheme rules will ever be amended.

The *self-employed*, for example, are still only able to effect personal pension schemes (including stakeholder schemes) and therefore the decisions they need to take are concerned with the type of personal pension arrangement and the provider most suited to their needs. Careful consideration should also be given to the way in which they wish to see their contributions invested.

For *employees*, the choice might not be nearly as straightforward, as they may have to decide between effecting their own private pension scheme (or stakeholder scheme) and joining a pension scheme that is sponsored by their employer, if there is one, and they are eligible to join it now or in the future.

The following paragraphs set out some of the questions that an employee should seek answers to and some of the considerations that he or she should take into account before making any decision.

On joining a company, an employee should ascertain:

- whether or not the employer offers a pension scheme for employees into which the employer contributes and, if so, would he or she be eligible to join either now or in the future;
- what ancillary benefits such as death-in-service pensions and life assurance benefits, and income replacement benefits he or she may be entitled to, and whether these depend upon his or her membership of an employer-sponsored pension scheme;
- if there is an employer-sponsored pension scheme, and an employee chooses to either not join it or to opt out of it, whether the employer would be prepared to contribute to a personal pension scheme (or stakeholder scheme) and, if so, at what rate and on what basis. (An employer may offer additional salary, instead of a contribution, so the employee can make his or her own pension arrangements. Employees (and employers) need to bear in mind that the payment of additional salary incurs National Insurance for both employee and employer);
- if the employer does not offer an employer-sponsored pension scheme, he or she should ask for details of the employer's stakeholder scheme. (An employer must offer its employees access to a designated stakeholder scheme if there are more than four employees and it does not offer an employer-sponsored pension scheme.)

There are several factors for the employee to consider:

- if his or her employer does not offer an employer-sponsored pension scheme, then the choice is simpler. It is between joining the employer's stakeholder scheme (which the employer must make available if it has more than four employees) or effecting his or her own personal pension (or stakeholder) scheme, at the same time ensuring that he or she has sufficient life assurance protection and benefits to replace his or her income in the event of prolonged incapacity;
- if his or her employer offers an employer-sponsored pension scheme, and is unwilling to contribute to any other scheme, then he or she should probably join that scheme in order to benefit from an employer's contribution. Where the scheme is an occupational pension scheme it may be necessary for him or her to remain with the employer for a reasonable period of time (say in excess of two years) in order to benefit from the employer's contribution (such schemes might typically only provide for a refund of the employee's contributions on leaving within two years). Where the scheme is a personal pension (including

a grouped personal pension or stakeholder pension) the employer's contributions become part of his or her fund under the scheme as soon as they are paid;

- if an employee effects a personal pension (including a grouped personal pension or stakeholder pension), then he or she may be able to continue to contribute to it if he or she leaves his or her employer. It is not possible to continue to contribute to an occupational pension scheme once the employee has left his or her employer;

- if his or her employer offers an employer-sponsored pension scheme, but is willing to contribute to another scheme instead if he or she chooses not to join the employer-sponsored scheme or, to opt out of it, then a careful comparison of the advantages and disadvantages needs to be undertaken. This comparison can be very complex, depending on the type of employer-sponsored pension scheme. It can be all the more important for employees who have continued rights under an employer's occupational pension scheme as a result of the changes contained in FA 1989 which introduced the earnings cap (linked to the RPI) in relation to approved pension schemes. Account should also be taken of any continuing rights following on from the Pension Simplification legislation contained within the Finance Acts 2004 and 2005, for example tax-free cash entitlements in excess of 25% of the fund. The comparison also needs to take account of the effect (if any) of such action on the provision or continued provision of ancillary benefits, such as death-in-service pensions and life assurance benefits, and income replacement benefits;

- pre-simplification the scope for funding pensions differed between occupational pension schemes and personal pension schemes (including grouped personal pensions and stakeholder pensions). All pension schemes now fall under one funding regime, however many occupational pension schemes have continued to operate using their old limits and as such may be restricted in terms of the overall level of benefits that they can provide as the overall scope for funding is determined by rates and limits devised in response to previous HMRC maximum benefits;

- many members of occupational schemes may have the opportunity to make additional voluntary contributions (AVCs) under their employer-sponsored pension scheme. These AVC facilities should be considered, but employees also have the choice of effecting their own alternative personal arrangements for such contributions. These alternative arrangements could be a stakeholder pension scheme, a personal pension scheme or a free standing additional voluntary contribution (FSAVC) scheme, depending on what type of employer-sponsored pension scheme is available to them. Indeed, following the pension simplification legislation and the introduction of full concurrency it is possible for employees to contribute to any number of registered pension schemes up to the greater of 100% of UK earnings or £3,600 subject to an overall annual allowance of £255,000 (2010/11)

It is difficult to make generalisations but employees should note that:

- under a final salary scheme the cost of the benefits normally increases with age. For employees who are over, say, the age of 40, the cost to the employer can start to increase quite significantly. The true cost may not, however, be reflected in the employer's contribution rate which is usually expressed as a uniform rate over all the scheme's members and may take into account a surplus (or deficiency) in the scheme. Unless the employer offers to make at least a comparable contribution (to the true cost as recalculated from time to time) to a personal pension (or stakeholder pension) then it might be better to opt for the final salary scheme;

- the position could also be similar for employees under the age of 40, but this is also then dependent upon the expected period that they might remain with the employer. Those intending to stay with their employer for an indefinite period might also be better to opt for the final salary scheme;

- some employees may have greater scope to pay additional voluntary contributions under a personal pension (or stakeholder scheme) than under an occupational pension scheme which is not operating under the new simplified regime (because total employee contributions are still limited to 15% of earnings or of capped earnings). This may be more relevant for higher earners in occupational money purchase schemes of this type which have a low rate of employer contribution;

- this contrasts with personal pensions, stakeholder pensions and occupational pension schemes operating under the new regime, where total tax-relieved contributions can be paid up to the greater of £3,600 or 100% of UK earnings subject to an overall annual allowance;

- HMRC maximum benefits no longer apply to occupational pension schemes, however many schemes will still operate under their old rules which mean that the maximum benefits will effectively still be subject to the pre-simplification limits and will depend, amongst other things, on when the employee joined and left the scheme. Members of both occupational and personal arrangements are now subject to a lifetime allowance (£1.8m for 2010/11) and any benefits in excess of this will be subject to a recovery charge of 55% if taken as a lump sum and 25% if taken as a pension, unless in cases where there is some form of transitional protection;

- each case needs to be separately considered. Weighing up all these alternative factors, and making the right choice is by no means straightforward and professional advice should be taken before decisions are made.

PLANNING WHILST IN A SCHEME

Occupational Pension Schemes

Additional Provision in Excess of that Provided by the Company Scheme

It is likely that the benefits to be provided by an occupational pension scheme in accordance with the scheme rules will be considerably lower than the maximum permitted within the Standard Lifetime Allowance. Consequently, members may feel that they wish to make an additional provision for their retirement. Before the simplification legislation, members of occupational schemes could only do this through in-house AVCs, FSAVCs or contributions to private Stakeholder Pension arrangements (if earnings were not in excess of £30,000). Following the introduction of full concurrency on 6 April 2006 there is now no restriction to the number of registered pension schemes to which an individual can contribute at any one time. The maximum tax-relieved amount that can be contributed across all schemes is the greater of £3,600 or 100% of UK earnings subject to an overall annual allowance set at £255,000 for 2010/11

Additional Voluntary Contributions and Free Standing Additional Voluntary Contributions

Although within the simplified regime it is difficult to see any clear advantage of AVCs and FSAVCs over personal arrangements it is likely that many schemes will still offer these options to employees and as such they may still form an important part of an individual's retirement strategy.

AVCs are additional contributions paid by employees to purchase further benefits. The contributions may (according to the rules of the scheme and wishes of the employee) be placed in the main fund to purchase additional years of service within a final salary arrangement or into a money-purchase fund with a nominated insurance company, or other pension provider, and administered by the trustees.

FSAVCs are additional contributions paid by employees net of basic rate tax to a pension provider of their choice, outside those arranged or managed by the trustees.

Those occupational pension schemes that continue to offer AVC arrangements are now increasingly also offering a choice in terms of how the AVCs may be invested – perhaps providing a choice between a link to a deposit-based fund (for example, with a building society or bank), a with-profits fund of a life insurance company, or unit-linked funds of various descriptions with fund providers.

FSAVCs offer a wider choice but the level of charges needs to be considered and compared to those applicable in respect of AVCs within the main scheme.

Salary Exchange

One way in which both individuals and employers can increase the efficiency of pension contributions is by use of a facility commonly referred to as Salary Exchange Here, an employee, with the agreement of his or her employer, arranges to forego an amount of salary and in return an equivalent pension contribution is made by the employer. Pre-simplification, a common application of this was in cases where the individual was already making personal contributions up to the limit at the time of 15% of total earnings, possibly subject to the earnings cap. With the advent of the simplified regime this is no longer an issue, however many individuals and employers still choose to operate pension arrangements on a salary exchange basis in order to take advantage of the National Insurance savings available, as well as the ability to receive any higher rate tax relief immediately. Where this facility is being used it is important to note that HMRC will not allow a retrospective salary exchange and it is therefore important that the correct documentation is put in place, otherwise the exchange could be viewed as ineffective by HMRC.

Disability

The ability to continue to earn benefits under a scheme depends upon an individual remaining in pensionable service with pensionable earnings. Schemes can provide benefits on ill-health retirement but often an employer will operate a permanent health insurance scheme as a salary continuation arrangement in order that an individual can continue to earn benefits under the scheme. The terms of the insurance can vary, as can the level of cover, but it is possible to insure a level of benefit for the individual as well as payments in respect of pensions and National Insurance contributions.

Funding Pension for Past Service (Back Years)

Often the rate of pension accrual provided by a final salary pension scheme is 1/60 of final salary for each year's service with the company, up to a maximum of 40. Frequently situations arise where the member will not complete 40 years' service as a member of the scheme before normal retirement but has years of service with the company before becoming a member of the scheme. The rules may permit that where service with the company can reach 20 years (ten years if membership commenced before 17 March 1987) by normal retirement date a pension of 40/60 can be provided. This is based on a maximum accrual rate of 1/30 (ie 2/60ths) of final remuneration for each year of service.

The funding requirement to provide for back years of service can be considerable but may be programmed to match companies' circumstances by paying special contributions in years of high profitability, subject to HMRC limits.

Use of Ex Gratia Payments

When an individual is made redundant, he may receive an ex gratia payment from his employer in compensation. The first £30,000 of such payments may be exempt from income tax. Any excess over £30,000 suffers tax at the full rate. It may therefore be advantageous for the individual to arrange with his employer to limit the amount that he receives in cash, particularly if this exceeds £30,000 and to have the balance paid as a 'special contribution' into a pension scheme for his benefit, or applied to the purchase of an approved annuity, thereby avoiding the tax charge on the balance. Care needs to be exercised in order that the special contribution does not overfund the benefits that can be approved, and that the added benefits represent value for money.

Care needs to be taken to ensure that cash payments are not treated as an unapproved pension benefit as they may then become taxable at the member's highest rate of tax. Memorandum 111 of The Social Security (Contributions)(Amendment) Regulations 2009, has confirmed that the payment of any ex gratia payment will be taxed as an unapproved pension benefit unless the circumstances are those of a compulsory redundancy or enforced (as opposed to voluntary) early retirement.

Redundancy payments which form part of a contractual obligation between the employer and employee and which the contract states may be payable as cash are liable to attack by HMRC, which will seek to tax the payment as remuneration of the individual. It is very important that any redundancy package is reviewed to ensure that the £30,000 tax-exempt allowance is available and utilised.

Personal Pension Schemes

Personal pensions are under the control of the employee and the planning is different from that relating to occupational pension schemes. Stakeholder schemes may operate either like personal pensions (or grouped personal pensions) or like occupational pension schemes under trust.

Key actions for all schemes include:
- paying as much as possible as early as possible to maximise the growth;
- catching up on arrears of contributions;
- understanding the differences between unit-linked investments and with-profits investments;
- establishing the position that would apply on disability or ill-health and, where necessary, making arrangements for an income replacement scheme (which may also include a waiver of premium insurance).

A waiver of premium benefit (or pension premium insurance from 6 April 2001) ensures that the policy benefits are not prejudiced in the event of permanent or prolonged ill-health. The benefit will usually be payable after three, six or 12 months' incapacity and will continue up to the selected retirement age. The definition of incapacity should be considered carefully. Even where permanent health insurance cover has been effected, the proceeds are not treated as earned income and thus are not net relevant earnings for premium purposes. This is an important point for the self-employed to bear in mind, although it is possible to pay up to £3,600 pa without net relevant earnings. Many providers have ceased to offer waiver of premium benefit.

Additional actions for personal pensions include:
- examining the impact of charges on setting up policies which reduce the premiums being invested; and
- considering a self-invested pension plan if greater control over the investment discretion is required.

LEAVING AN EMPLOYER

The following options will normally be available to an individual who, on leaving an employer, is a member of an occupational pension scheme. These options are usually set out in what is called a leaving service benefits statement, which must be produced by the scheme within two months of the member leaving service.

Refund of Contributions

If an employee has been in an employer's occupational pension scheme and leaves with less than two years' qualifying service (or where the scheme rules prescribe a shorter period) a refund of personal contributions may be made but the trustees must deduct 20% tax from the payment. If an employee opts to leave an employer's scheme within two years of joining, the employee can forfeit the value of the employer's contributions.

Since 6 April 2006 an employer is also required to offer a transfer value to members with greater than three months' but fewer than two years' qualifying service, as an alternative to a refund of contributions. They may also offer preserved benefits if they choose, however it is unlikely that many employers will do so owing to the administrative burden and associated costs.

Preserved Benefits

On leaving service, benefits are preserved in the occupational pension scheme unless a refund of contributions applies (see above) or the member exercises his or her right to a transfer value in lieu of those preserved benefits.

Preserved benefits under a final salary scheme are generally in the form of a deferred pension payable from normal retirement date. The deferred pension is calculated as the relevant fraction of the employee's pensionable earnings at the time he or she leaves the scheme having regard to his or her service as a member.

Deferred defined benefit pensions must be inflation-proofed. GMP built up between 6 April 1988 and 5 April 1997 must increase in line with RPI capped at 3%. Pensions built up between 6 April 1997 and 5 April 2005 must increase in line with RPI capped at 5% as a minimum. Pensions built up after 5 April 2005 must increase in line with RPI capped at 2.5% as a minimum. Preserved benefits under a money-purchase scheme are generally in the form of members' accounts invested in a range of unitised or with-profit funds. Any investment yield/bonuses that attach to the member's account must accrue at the same rate and be applied towards benefits in the same way as those of a member who remains in pensionable service.

Transfer Payments

A member whose pensionable service terminates on or after 1 January 1986, but more than one year before his normal retirement date, and who is entitled to preserved benefits, acquires a right to a cash equivalent. This is often called their 'transfer value' and it must be used either as:

- a payment which is transferred to another occupational pension scheme to buy additional rights; or
- a single premium to a section 32 buy-out policy. These policies allow individuals to use the transfer value offered by an ex-employer's pension scheme to purchase a policy from a life insurance company or other pension provider; or
- a single premium to a personal pension or stakeholder scheme. These policies also allow individuals to use the transfer value offered by an ex-employer's pension scheme to purchase a policy from a life insurance company or other pension provider.

Whether a transfer is the better option cannot be known in advance. However, by making various assumptions and taking a view as to the likely performance of the underlying investments from the date of investment until the individual's retirement, it is normally possible to make a financial assessment (a transfer value analysis). There may also be non-financial considerations and a full assessment should compare all the options and relate these to the member's personal circumstances.

Consideration should be given to the need to provide for a GMP (if the employment has been contracted-out) under a section 32 policy compared to protected rights under a personal pension scheme, the question of retirement age and, if applicable, what increases in pension are offered by the ex-employer's pension scheme.

Additional factors to take into account as part of the assessment are whether the ex-employer's pension scheme is in surplus or in deficit and whether benefits have been equalised for men and women following the *Barber* judgment. Many schemes still have equality issues in the context of GMPs and the treatment of part-time staff.

Assignment of Executive Pension Plan

If the pension scheme is arranged on an individual basis, eg an executive pension plan, it may be possible to transfer the scheme to the new employer. While such a transfer may leave the accumulated benefits unaltered, fresh HMRC approval must be obtained and service with the new employer will be treated separately from the period of service with the previous employer. This is particularly relevant for employees leaving employers where they were members of schemes either prior to 17 March 1987 or 14 March 1989. The assignment of an individual pension plan may be the best option available for the employee, but the new employer is not obliged to take over the policy.

OPTIONS UPON RETIREMENT

Personal Pensions (and stakeholder pensions and occupational pension schemes operating under the defined contribution regime)

Tax-free Lump Sum

On benefit crystallisation up to 25% of the accumulated fund can be taken as a cash lump sum. Under current tax legislation this lump sum is free of income tax.

The remainder of the accumulated fund must be used to provide a pension, through a secured, unsecured or alternatively secured pension. The pension is taxed as earned income.

Secured Pension

Scheme Pension

A scheme pension is a pension paid to a scheme member by a registered pension scheme, or alternatively on its behalf by an insurance company selected by the scheme administrator. Occupational final salary schemes generally offer scheme pensions. Occupational money purchase schemes can offer a scheme pension but are not required to do so.

Lifetime Annuities

Annuities: Open Market Option

Almost all personal pension providers offer this option, allowing the policyholder to use the fund at retirement to purchase an annuity from the life company that offers the best terms in the market. Most providers do not penalise policyholders on transfer whilst some reward policyholders' loyalty by allowing a bonus if the option is not exercised.

Annuities: The Choice

The policyholder may select from a range of annuities according to his or her requirements. An annuity may be level, increasing or index-linked and payable from monthly to annual intervals. In addition, some life companies offer annuities which are linked to the performance of a with-profits or unit-linked fund.

Annuities: Taxation

Annuities arising from personal pensions are taxed under former Schedule E, the same basis as occupational pension schemes.

The death benefits available from scheme pensions and lifetime annuities will be dependent upon the scheme rules and the terms of the annuity respectively.

Phased Retirement Benefits

While phased retirement (also known as staggered vesting) has always been an option for those with personal pensions schemes, the rules concerning retirement and the timing of benefits have made this option increasingly popular for those with substantial open market option values (generally over £100,000) at retirement.

Phased retirement is the encashment of individual policies of the personal pension scheme gradually throughout retirement up to the age of 77. The tax-free cash that is generated by encashment provides a tax-efficient income and the balance of the funds used to purchase an annuity under the open market option. The remaining policies remain invested in the tax-favourable environment of the personal pension scheme until a further encashment is required. Since the annuities are being purchased at progressively older ages, better annuity rates may be obtained. A further advantage is that the remaining value of the personal pension scheme can be made available to the member's beneficiaries. This provides an IHT shelter for the remaining funds up to the age of 77.

Care needs to be taken with the investment of the personal pension scheme fund to ensure that the capital value does not diminish between encashments. Such arrangements can provide flexibility of income withdrawal well into retirement and, for those with alternative sources of income, can add considerably to the benefit of personal pension schemes over other pension arrangements.

Unsecured Pension

Pension Fund Withdrawal (Income Drawdown)

It is also possible to structure a more flexible way of drawing benefits from those pension schemes that offer the facility through an income drawdown or unsecured pension contract, which is also available for occupational money-purchase pension schemes and buy-out contracts.

The provisions allow the annuitant to draw income from their pension fund without purchasing an annuity up to the age of 77, following the recent coalition Government Budget (previously age 75). The income that can be paid from a drawdown contract is defined by reference to a standard table of annuity rates published by the Government Actuaries Department, which is amended from time to time to reflect changes in long-term interest rates. Income can vary from 0% to 120% of the annuity calculated from the standard table.

On death, after deferment has begun, a distribution of a lump sum from the pension fund would lead to a tax charge of 35% of the value paid. This will not apply if the spouse/dependant continues to make withdrawals or purchase an annuity.

Short-Term Annuity

With a short-term annuity, after drawing the tax-free cash, the majority of the member's pension fund remains invested in their chosen funds, but a portion is used to purchase a temporary annuity which is subject to certain restrictions and cannot be for a term of more than five years and maximum income is calculated in the same way as for pension fund withdrawal.

Alternatively Secured Pension

Once a member has attained age 77 there is the facility to continue drawing from the fund via Alternatively Secured Pension (ASP). The features of ASP are not dissimilar to those of the Unsecured Pension as outlined above, however with ASP income can vary from 55% to 90% of the annuity calculated from the standard Government Actuaries Department tables. It also differs to the Unsecured Pension in that the maximum income limit requires to be reviewed on an annual basis.

On death whilst in ASP, if there are dependants the fund must be used to provide a dependants' pension. If there are no dependants, the remaining fund can be used to pay a charity lump sum death benefit. The member can nominate a registered charity to receive some or all of the remaining ASP fund.

Once in payment no cash lump sum can be withdrawn from the 'drawdown' contract, so any cash lump sums needed must be taken out before the commencement of the income (within the usual limits).

Drawing benefits from the resultant pension fund is likely to be the most effective for annuitants who have a fund of at least £250,000 and who are prepared to accept some investment risk in retirement and who have substantial other assets. The advantage is to allow flexibility in the timing of the purchase of the annuity to avoid having to secure an annuity when rates are very low. They also allow the annuitant to retain control over their pension fund for as long as possible.

Unfortunately the large commissions available on drawdown business have given rise to suggestions that it may become the next mis-selling scandal. Certainly, before advising a client on drawdown, consideration should be given to the following factors:

- identifying the critical yield, ie the return required on the drawdown fund to ensure that the client is no worse off under drawdown than with an annuity;

- future interest rates and hence annuity rates;
- charges – both initial and ongoing;
- equity returns likely on the underlying drawdown fund;
- mortality drag – annuities benefit from a mortality cross subsidy whereas income drawdown funds do not;
- is a with-profits or unit-linked annuity more suitable?

Occupational Pension Schemes

Pension

Under the pre-simplification rules the maximum pension that could be provided was two-thirds of an employee's final remuneration after a period of at least 20 years' service. Under the simplified regime, the maximum available is in fact subject to the Lifetime Allowance (with defined benefit pensions valued at 20:1), ie every £1,000 of pension is valued as £20,000 for the purposes of testing against the Lifetime Allowance. Many schemes operate under their old rules. For this reason, a brief summary of the old rules is given below.

Under the 'old' rules, for those employees with less than 20 years' service, this maximum pension was scaled down by 1/30 for each year. This is based on a maximum accrual rate of 1/30, ie 2/60 of final remuneration for each year of service with a maximum of 20 years' service to count.

Any pension benefits from earlier employment (usually referred to as retained benefits) had to be taken into account in determining the maximum benefits payable.

For employees who joined their employer's pension scheme before 17 March 1987, a different maximum accrual rate may be used which enables two-thirds of final remuneration pension to be payable after only ten years' service.

Although many schemes will still operate using rules devised under the pre-simplification regime, it should be appreciated that post-simplification, all schemes fall under one regime.

Pension Commencement Lump Sum (Tax-free Cash)

A member may opt to take part of his benefits in the form of a lump sum by commuting (exchanging) part of his or her pension benefits (but statutory schemes often provide the lump sum separately from the pension). The lump sum is currently paid free of income tax.

The maximum tax-free cash sum available to any individual is 25% of the notional fund value, however many schemes will still calculate members' lump sums with reference to:

- when he or she became a member of the scheme;
- his or her length of service at the date of retirement; and
- the rules of the scheme.

Such calculations referred to the greater of 3/80 of final remuneration for each year of service (up to a maximum of 40 years) or 2.25 times the amount of the member's pension before commutation, whichever is greater and the maximum tax-free cash sum was limited to the lesser of 1.5 times final remuneration or 1.5 times the prevailing earnings cap, this latter figure being linked to the RPI.

Care should be taken when assessing pension commencement lump sum entitlements as the pre-simplification, occupational basis described above can lead to a figure that is either greater or lesser than the 25% limit. In such cases members should seek independent advice to ensure that any entitlements are maximised and, where appropriate, protected.

Normal Retirement Age

Following legislation contained within the Finance Acts 2004 and 2005, the concept of a normal retirement age has disappeared along with the previous constraints on drawing occupational benefits while still employed by the scheme sponsor. From 6 April 2010 the normal minimum pension age for drawing benefits is 55 for all schemes – both private and occupational.

It is worth noting however, that age 55 (from 6 April 2010) is a **minimum** and schemes can continue to operate an older scheme retirement age should they wish to.

Early and Late Retirement Limits

Early retirement before the age of 55 is not allowed, except in the case of ill-health. For what is deemed as early retirement at any time after age 55 by the scheme, the benefits provided will be subject to the scheme rules and any benefit crystallisation event will give rise to a lifetime allowance test.

DIVORCE

On divorce, pension rights are subject to one of the following:

Earmarking

An arrangement whereby when one party's pension eventually comes into payment, a portion of it will be paid to the other party. Since July 1996, earmarking has been available but has not been extensively used, as it left the pension holder with delaying power, which could deny the divorced spouse the pension share that was intended by the courts. Relatively few earmarked orders were agreed and reliance was placed on taking pension rights into account in the settlement as this produced a more popular clean break between the parties.

Offsetting

An arrangement whereby the pension rights are balanced against another asset, such as the matrimonial home.

Pension Sharing

An arrangement whereby couples split the pension at the time of the divorce to give both parties their own pension pot for the future. The Welfare Reform and Pensions Act 1999 enables pension splitting from 1 December 2000 when divorce settlements are being made.

Under pension splitting or sharing order there would be a reduction in the value of the pension holders' fund, called a pension debit, and a credit in the hands of the former spouse. Occupational pension schemes may create a new category of member covering former spouses so that they become members of the scheme in their own right and with entitlement to the pension credit. With money purchase funds the value of the member's fund would be reduced by the debit. With final salary schemes the credit/debit would need to be revalued to the date of retirement. The basis for determining the amount of pension debit/credit may be the cash equivalent transfer value, or other value agreed by the Court.

Provided a pension was not being paid at the time, the former spouse could transfer the value of the debit to an appropriate pension arrangement. See also the comments in Section 5.6, *Married With Older Children*.

CROSS REFERENCES

2.13 Qualifying Recognised Overseas Pension Schemes (QROPS)

WHAT IS IT?

In April 2006, it was announced that individuals with UK pension rights who have or will become non-resident in the UK for tax purposes, could move their pension benefits out of the UK to a Qualifying Recognised Overseas Pension Scheme (QROPS) with the Revenue's approval. Some of the key requirements for pensions becoming recognised as a QROPS are detailed in s 169 of Finance Act 2004.

The rules of the QROPS should, for the most part, correspond to the rules governing an authorised UK pension scheme. However, a QROPS is generally a more flexible option for individuals who have left or are leaving the UK permanently.

A QROPS is a pension scheme set up outside the UK that:

- Is regulated as a pension scheme in the country in which it was established.
- Must be recognised for tax purposes in the country it is established.

These and other requirements are prescribed under reg 3 of The Pension Schemes (Information Requirements – Qualifying Overseas Pension Schemes, Qualifying Recognised Overseas Pension Schemes and Corresponding Relief) Regulations 2006. The QROPS scheme manager must:

- Have notified HMRC that the scheme is a recognised overseas pension scheme, and have provided evidence of that if required.
- Have informed HMRC of the name of the country or territory in which the scheme is established.
- Have provided any other evidence as required by HMRC.
- Must notify HMRC if the scheme ceases to be a QROPS.
- Have provided HMRC an undertaking to provide information on the payment of benefits to certain scheme members.

WHAT DO THEY SEEK TO ACHIEVE?

The real benefits of a QROPS come into play when the individual has been non-resident in the UK for at least five years and does not intend to return for the foreseeable future. This is because once the individual transfers their UK pension schemes into a QROPS and has not been UK resident in the UK for at least five years, then the overseas QROPS provider no longer has to report any withdrawals or payments to HMRC. The QROPS pension fund becomes subject only to the laws of the relevant jurisdiction. This may mean that:

- Investment choice is in some cases wider than under onshore pensions – and may include the ability to invest in residential property (depending on the Trust rules used to set up the QROPS).
- An increased tax-free cash sum is available – it may be possible to take the whole fund as a lump sum – but this may require a second transfer to an international pension scheme. (However, this may cause HMRC to consider closing the QROPS, as has happened to a Singapore based QROPS.)
- Pension income may be received gross, and so no tax is paid in the QROPS jurisdiction.
- There is no liability to UK inheritance tax (saving up to 82%). Finance Act 2008, Sch 29, ss 18–19.
- Lifetime allowance no longer applies – so there is no limit to the size of funds.

WHO IS IT SUITABLE FOR?

For someone with a UK pension fund, a QROPS can be taken out for non UK residents providing they intend to remain so for the foreseeable future. For those QROPS members who have been resident in the UK at any time in the last five tax years, the scheme must behave as though it were a UK scheme. After five complete tax years, this requirement falls away and additionally, there is no reporting requirement to HMRC.

Benefits cannot be taken until the individual is aged over 50 (or over 55 from 6 April 2010), however benefits may be taken for certain pre A-Day categories of occupation such as footballers. (However, in order to qualify under these rules a 'block transfer' must be affected.)

It would generally be only suitable for larger value pension scheme benefits and the typical transfer value would be in excess of £250,000. Under some circumstances it may be better to leave pension benefits in the UK, if for example Guaranteed Annuity Rates apply to the plan.

There can be issues if the jurisdiction the individual moves to does not interact favourably with QROPS rules. For example, there are clear issues transferring to IRA accounts with US citizens / residents. There may also be certain issues with Australian schemes – and any transfer must be carried out carefully.

However, Guernsey and New Zealand are recognised as jurisdictions with good levels of investor protection and have an established track record of running QROPS successfully.

PLANNING OPPORTUNITIES

While there are a lot of providers QROPS suggesting some quite radical planning opportunities; it is important to note that there are some quite clear guidelines on what HMRC will permit and if a particular QROPS provider ignores the letter, or spirit, of the guidelines then it is not without precedent for HMRC to withdraw the schemes QROPS status resulting in punitive tax charges both on the member and the scheme by way of an unauthorised payments charge. Therefore it is sensible to select QROPS which do not adopt aggressive tax avoidance tactics or market themselves in a way that brings undue attention from HMRC.

MORE FLEXIBLE BENEFITS

The amount of income available from QROPS varies across different providers and jurisdictions but the levels of income that are allowable are at least as good as those available under unsecured pension and generally higher than alternatively secured pension.

Depending on the jurisdiction of the QROPS it may be possible to take pension income which is taxed at a lower rate than a UK pension and possibly at 0%.

As mentioned above it may be possible to take more than 25% or the whole fund as a lump sum – but this may require a second transfer. This may be viewed as too aggressive a strategy by HMRC and so anyone attempting this must tread carefully and it may not be effective if HMRC take a dim view of it.

GREATER INVESTMENT CHOICE

In the first five years the range of allowable investments is similar to those under UK pension rules and so during this period an individual may invest in assets such as, cash accounts, gilts and bonds, shares (equities), unit trusts, investment trusts, OEICs, exchange traded funds, discretionary investment management, commercial property, etc.

However, once the individual has been non-resident for more than five years and the requirement for the QROPS provider to report to HMRC ceases the investment restrictions fall away. Most QROPS providers understand that the QROPS can then invest in virtually any asset, including residential property, which means portfolios of buy-to-let properties can be held. However, some providers will refuse to hold residential property as they believe this is against HMRC guidance. It is important to check the terms of each individual QROPS Pension Trust, as this determines the permitted investments within that particular QROPS.

Alternatively, if the individual opts for a more simplified variant of the QROPS, the Overseas Pensions Scheme or (OPS), which confers no special tax relief benefits, they can transfer residential property or investments in immediately. The advantages of using this sort of vehicle is that it is possible to shelter future income and capital gains from these assets and that they are removed from his estate for the purposes of inheritance tax.

It is possible to invest in land, including islands or parts of islands, under a QROPS, however the QROPS provider may stipulate that the land itself is owned by an underlying company, which is then held by the QROPS. This is to provide a protection to members of the QROPS.

TAX PLANNING ON DEATH

Following the recent emergency Budget (22 June 2010) the Government has announced that it will enter into a consultation period regarding compulsory annuity purchase at age 75. In announcing the consultation the Government also initiated an immediate deferral of any such annuity purchase to age 77. Therefore prior to age 77 any lump sum resulting from UK 'crystallised benefits' would be subject to a 35% charge. Some UK pensions providers will not allow a lump sum after age 77, whereas some will allow a lump sum subject to an 82% tax charge. However, under a QROPS the residual pension fund could be passed to beneficiaries on death without any tax charges, inheritance tax or the 35% charge. Therefore QROPS are attractive to non-UK residents with significant pension funds wishing to pass more of the fund to their beneficiaries/pay less tax. One thing to bear in mind is that UK domiciled individuals would still have to pay 40% of the value of their worldwide assets, including benefits under their QROPS. If they become non-UK domiciled all inheritance can obviously be avoided.

LIFETIME ALLOWANCE PLANNING

A transfer to a QROPS is considered as a 'benefit crystallisation event', and so the pension assets transferred to the QROPS will be compared to the individual's remaining lifetime allowance and the time of transfer. An exception to this rule is where the transfer to a QROPS represents pensions, including unsecured pensions, which were already in payment before April 2006. The value of these benefits is not tested against the lifetime allowance on transfer to a QROPS. However once benefits are within a QROPS the lifetime allowance no longer applies so there is no limit to the size of funds accrued. This enables non- resident individuals to move their pensions overseas whereupon their pension fund can grow in excess of the lifetime allowance – and as a consequence avoid the lifetime allowance charge.

SUGGESTED QROPS

It is important to do thorough due diligence on the jurisdiction of the QROPS provider and rules of the trust under which the QROPS is set up. There is an important balance to strike between the flexibility afforded by the jurisdiction/QROPS rules, the levels of investor protection and how closely the QROPS adheres to the letter and spirit of HMRC rules before and after the five-year period.

Having researched a number of the jurisdictions available Guernsey is currently favoured in most circumstances, as it allows a good deal of flexibility, whilst offering a high level of protection and is not attracting any undue attention from HMRC at the moment. In this jurisdiction, we find that the following QROPS are worth considering: Aurora, Close and Fairbairn.

NOTES

1   Before the transfer is initiated it is important to check that the UK pension scheme provider(s) will allow transfers to QROPS pension schemes.
2   In addition, it is important to check that the proposed QROPS is on the database of allowable QROPS maintained by the HMRC.
3   It is necessary to check investor protection and tax-efficiency of the jurisdiction of the QROPS vehicle.
4   It is important to try to use wherever possible QROPS that do not require an employment contract.
5   Transfers of protected-rights and guaranteed minimum pensions are subject to the same rules as overseas transfers of other pension rights.

6   It is also necessary to check the transparency of charges. Initial charges to set up a QROPS would be a minimum £3,000–£3,500. This would also include typical set-up charges, but may increase depending on complexity, number of schemes transferred and the due diligence required for the specific QROPS jurisdiction transferred to.

7   Transferring to a QROPS is a 'benefit crystallisation event', and so the pension assets transferred to the QROPS will be compared to the individual's remaining lifetime allowance and the time of transfer.

8   It may be possible to undertake in specie transfers to a QROPS – but this will need to be confirmed on a case-by-case basis.

9   QROPS can be used for transfers from a SIPP even if income has been taken.

10 It is possible to have 'authorised payments' within the first five years (ie if the member is over retirement age and not a UK resident), otherwise if income is taken within five years there may be an 'unauthorised payment charge' of 15%.

2.14 Glossary of Pensions Terminology

Accelerated accrual See *Uplifted sixtieths.*

Accrual rate The rate at which pension benefits accrue in relation to years of service, eg an accrual rate of pension equal to 1/60th of final salary for each year of service.

Actuarial assumptions The set of assumptions as to the rates of interest, salary inflation, prices inflation, mortality, used by the actuary in the valuation of liabilities (technical provisions) and the assets of a pension scheme.

Additional component That part of the state pension related to the band of earnings between the lower and upper earnings limits, usually known as SERPS – The State Earnings Related Pension Scheme or S2P – The State Second Pension.

Additional voluntary contributions (AVCs) Contributions to a pension scheme which a member chooses to pay in addition to normal contributions, if any, to secure extra benefits.

Augmentation The increase of benefits over the existing scale of a pension scheme, often for particular employees with short potential service.

Average salary scheme A scheme under which the pension benefit is linked to average salary throughout the period of membership. Now normally revalued annually.

Back service Normally refers to service which preceded the employee becoming a member of the pension scheme. May or may not be pensionable under the scheme.

Band earnings (or middle band earnings) Earnings between the lower and upper earnings limits used in the calculation of the additional component under the state scheme.

Basic component The flat rate element of the state pension. The amount is increased each year, normally in April, in line with the RPI.

Cap See *Earnings cap (abolished with effect from 6 April 2006).*

Ceiling See *Earnings ceiling.*

Commutation Taking a lump sum (within approvable limits) in lieu of all or part of a pension entitlement, normally free of tax, now known as the pension commencement lump sum.

Contracting-out Provisions in the Social Security Pensions Act 1975 and subsequent legislation to enable occupational pension schemes and other types of pension schemes (for example personal pensions) to be contracted-out of the earnings-related part of the state pension scheme.

Controlling director This has two different meanings:

1   A director who (with spouse, minor children and trustees of any settlement made by the director or spouse) controls 20% or more of the voting rights of the company in question. Referred to as a '20% director'. There are no longer restrictions on certain benefits available to such directors.

2   Broadly a director of a company which is controlled by all the directors together and who owns or controls, directly or indirectly, more than 5% of its ordinary shares. Such a director's maximum benefits no longer have to take into account any benefits under earlier retirement annuity policies or personal pension schemes.

Deferred pension   A future pension payable to an early leaver from normal retirement age (see also *Preservation*). Sometimes also used to describe a retirement pension where commencement of payment has been delayed beyond normal retirement age.

Defined benefit scheme   See *Final salary scheme.*

Defined contribution scheme   See *Money purchase scheme.*

Dependant's pension   A pension payable to any person who is financially dependent (such as a wife, husband or minor child) on a scheme member or pensioner, commencing on that member's or pensioner's death or when the main pension ceases to be paid at the end of a minimum guaranteed period.

Deposit administration   A method of funding whereby contributions are deposited with financial institutions, to which interest is added. Funds are withdrawn to provide the benefits as required.

Dynamised remuneration   A permissible adjustment to a member's emoluments for the purpose of computing final remuneration. The emoluments of each year – other than the final year before retirement – in the qualifying base period (say the 12 years up to retirement date), can be increased by a percentage equal to the percentage increase in the RPI from the relevant year to the retirement date (no longer applicable for service after 5 April 2006).

Early leaver   The descriptive name given to members of occupational pension schemes who leave the employer's service other than through retirement, ie upon a change of employer or through redundancy.

Earnings cap   Before the introduction of the new pensions tax regime on 6 April 2006, an 'earnings cap' limited both contributions to, and benefits payable from, tax approved pension schemes. This cap disappeared under the new regime but remains a feature of many pre-existing pension scheme rules as a measure they use to limit increases in benefits payable. To help the pensions industry with the transition into the new pensions tax regime, and in particular those schemes whose rules still restrict benefits by reference to the earnings cap, HM Revenue & Customs (HMRC) agreed to publish details of a notional earnings cap setting out what the earnings cap would have been had it still been in existence, each year until 2011.

The notional earnings cap for 2009/10 will be £123,600.

Earnings ceiling   See *Earnings cap.*

Escalation   Regular increases of pensions in payment, usually by reference to a fixed annual percentage rate or the increase in the RPI during the period under review, whichever is the less.

Executive pension plan   Pension scheme designed for senior executives.

Exempt approved scheme   Under the code of HMRC approval (introduced by FA 1970, as amended by FA 1971 and ICTA 1988), occupational schemes require to be approved by HMRC if they are to qualify for tax relief. If set up under irrevocable trust and meeting the various conditions to qualify, the scheme will be an 'exempt approved' scheme with full tax relief available. With effect from 6 April 2006 such schemes are known as Registered Pension Schemes.

Final pensionable salary/earnings   The amount of earnings on which the pension is calculated in accordance with a pension scheme's rules. In some schemes it will be the average of earnings over a number of years. The definition may include bonus, commission, overtime payments, etc. Post-6 April 2006 there is no limit on the amount of pension benefits that can be taken, but any pension fund in excess of the personal lifetime allowance may suffer a tax charge of up to 55%.

Final salary scheme   A scheme that calculates the amount of pension on pay or salary at or near retirement date and the number of years of membership.

Franking   The practice – now outlawed – by which the required revaluation to be applied to preserved benefits and to guaranteed minimum pension is set off against the totality of pension benefits promised by an employer, instead of being additional (as required by the Health and Social Security Act 1984) to total accrued pension rights at the time the employee leaves the scheme.

Free Standing Additional Voluntary Contributions (FSAVCs)   Additional voluntary contributions made by employees into a money purchase fund of their choice outside those offered by an employer's occupational pension scheme, ie free standing. Only available to members in an occupational pension scheme as an alternative to the scheme's AVC arrangement and subject to the same contribution limits.

Frozen pension   See *Preservation*.

Guaranteed annuity option   The right of a member to have his share of the fund at retirement date applied on specified terms to produce a pension. A valuable right when interest rates are low at retirement date. When they are high more favourable terms are likely to be available in the market than those guaranteed.

Guaranteed minimum pension (GMP)   The minimum pension payable under scheme rules to enable a final salary pension scheme to contract-out under the Social Security Pensions Act 1975. Its purpose was to ensure that a member would be entitled to a benefit at least equal to the additional component which would have accrued to him under the state scheme, had he not been a member of a contracted-out scheme. The GMP thus approximates to the additional component. There are various options open to employers to preserve GMP for early leavers from schemes. GMPs were abolished for contracted-out service from 6 April 1997 when final salary schemes had instead to pass a 'reference test' in order to be contracted-out.

Immediate annuity/pension   An annuity or pension payable from the date of purchase.

Insured scheme   A pension scheme, the benefits of which are secured in the form of insurance policies providing minimum funds or benefits at specified dates with or without profits or on a unit-linked basis.

Lump sum   Normally refers to that part of the retirement benefit which can be taken in a tax-free cash payment (see *Commutation*), known as the pension commencement lump sum with effect from 6 April 2006.

Minimum guaranteed period   The payment of a scheme member's pension may be guaranteed for a minimum period of up to ten years, whether or not the recipient dies during that period. Schemes continue payment for the minimum period or may provide a lump sum, sometimes discounted, in lieu of the outstanding instalments if the original guarantee period did not exceed five years.

Money-purchase scheme   The amount of benefit is determined by the accumulated value of contributions paid by and in respect of the member, and the cost of securing a pension, according to age and sex.

New defined contribution regime   The tax regime covering personal pensions, stakeholder pensions, and money-purchase occupational schemes which opt in from 6 April 2001.

Normal retirement date (NRD)   The date from which members normally retire from the service of the employer. Also the date from which an occupational pension scheme normally first gives a member the right to an unreduced pension (pensions are usually reduced for early payment). It is not necessarily the same date as that on which state benefits are payable ('state pensionable age'). It is no longer necessary to retire to receive pension benefits.

Open market option   Almost all personal pension scheme policies, and certain occupational pension schemes, provide that the fund available at retirement may be used to purchase an immediate pension from a life office other than that with which the pension fund was built up.

Paid-up pension   Pension payable from a future retirement date in respect of which contributions are no longer payable (see *Preservation*).

Past service   Normally refers to pensionable service which a member has already completed under an occupational pension scheme after becoming a member.

Pay as you go scheme   See *Unfunded scheme.*

Pensioneer trustee   An individual or body experienced in pension matters, accepted by HMRC as a pensioneer trustee of small self-administered pension schemes. Pensioneer trustees are no longer needed after 6 April 2006.

Pension sharing or splitting   From 1 December 2000 the ability to share or split pension rights in divorce settlements.

Personal pension scheme   Arrangements which an employee makes with a pension provider instead of belonging to the employer's occupational pension scheme, if any. Available since 1 July 1988 they also replaced retirement annuity policies for the self-employed. Employees have complete portability and transferability of the scheme, the employer can contribute to the scheme if so minded. Employees may use personal pension schemes to contract-out of SERPS/S2P, these schemes being known as appropriate personal pension schemes (APPS).

Portability   The facility to take a pension scheme from one employment to another (see also *Transferability*).

Preservation   The procedure by which the benefit entitlement of an early leaver is not paid out until normal retirement date but preserved within the scheme. The Social Security Act 1973 requires that normally the only benefit to those leaving service with two or more years' qualifying service shall be a preserved benefit or the payment of a transfer value to another scheme. Preserved benefits are variously referred to as deferred benefits, frozen benefits and paid-up benefits.

Defined benefit pensions must be inflation-proofed. GMP built up between 6 April 1988 and 5 April 1997 must increase in line with RPI capped at 3%. Pensions built up between 6 April 1997 and 5 April 2005 must increase in line with RPI capped at 5%. Pensions built up after 5 April 2005 can increase in line with RPI capped at 2.5%.

Protected rights   The rights acquired under pension schemes which contract out of SERPS/S2P on a money-purchase basis under Social Security Act 1986 and subsequent legislation. The rights are separately identified to ensure that the corresponding fund is used to purchase prescribed benefits. Commutation, ie tax-free cash (pension commencement lump sum) is now allowable up to 25% of the value of the fund, the benefits can be taken from age 50 (55 from 2010) and the annuity does not have to increase. However, the requirement to purchase a spouse's pension if the member is married or in a registered civil partnership remains.

Retained benefits   A member's preserved benefits from previous employments which may need to be taken into account when calculating their entitlement to benefits from their current employer's pension scheme.

Reversionary annuity/pension (also called a contingent pension)   An annuity/pension which commences only on the death of another, eg the pension payable to a widow on the death of her retired husband.

Self-administered pension scheme   An occupational pension scheme the assets of which are invested directly on the trustees' behalf by investment managers (as opposed to an insured scheme).

Self-invested personal pension (SIPP)   A personal pension scheme in which the assets are selected by the policyholder (within HMRC guidelines) who may also (again within HMRC guidelines) decide when they should be bought and sold.

Small self-administered pension scheme (SSAS)   An occupational pension scheme with fewer than 12 members where the trustees have freedom (within HMRC guidelines and regulations) to invest the assets as they see fit. It is possible to have hybrid or mixed schemes where part of the fund is self-administered and part insured with a life office.

Stakeholder pensions   Available from 6 April 2001, a type of personal pension scheme which meets prescribed conditions, for example in relation to charges.

State Earnings Related Pension Scheme (SERPS)   The additional earnings-related component of the state pension available from 6 April 1978 to 5 April 2002.

State Second Pension (S2P)   The additional earnings-related component of the state pension available from 6 April 2002.

Superannuation   Another name for a pension.

Surplus   The excess of the value of the assets over the value of the liabilities on the basis of a given set of actuarial assumptions.

Top hat scheme   See *Executive pension plan.*

Top-up schemes   See *Unapproved scheme.*

Transferability   The facility to transfer pension rights from one pension scheme to another on changing employment. (See also *Portability.*)

Transfer payment/value   A payment made by one pension scheme to another, to provide benefits in the receiving scheme in lieu of benefits in the transferring scheme. Where the receiving scheme is a final salary scheme which offers additional years of service in respect of the transfer payment, the years offered will normally fall short of the pensionable service under the transferring scheme.

Unapproved scheme   A scheme set up to provide extra benefits for employees without special tax relief in addition to those provided by an exempt approved pension scheme. (See provisions of FA 1989.) May be funded or unfunded. These schemes are now called employer financed retirement benefits schemes.

Unfunded scheme (Pay as you go scheme)   A scheme under which the benefits are paid from current revenue and no fund is built up in advance to make provision for the payment of future benefits, eg the state scheme.

Uplifted sixtieths/uplifted eightieths   These relate to the additional benefit that can be provided by a pension scheme in respect of years of service with the company including those before the employee became a member of the scheme. For example, a pension of 40/60th could be permitted if the member's total service with the company before normal retirement date will be 20 years or more irrespective of length of membership of the scheme. Similar provisions exist for the amount of pension commutable but only in proportion to pension benefits. Sliding scales could apply to shorter periods of service.

Widow's/widower's option   Most schemes include an option whereby a married person can choose to reduce his pension entitlement in exchange for a pension (not exceeding the level of his remaining pension) payable to the widow/widower (or other dependants) after his death.

Withdrawal option   What the occupational pension scheme rules may offer a member if he leaves service before normal retirement date. Usually the choice is between preserved benefits (see *Preservation*) and a transfer (see *Transfer payment*). In restricted circumstances a refund of an employee's contributions may be offered.

Part 3   Investments

3.1 Introduction

The essence of financial planning is that there should be a plan. The purpose of this introduction is to outline the major considerations in approaching investment planning. The term 'investment' is used here in a wide sense, to include also relevant life assurance and pension plans. Insurance products that are primarily investments are included in this section. These plans will often carry an assurance aspect, but frequently have a significant investment factor. The investment plan will therefore need to cover an individual's or couple's total resources, not just that part available for (say) stock exchange investments.

The major considerations in investment planning fall under the following five headings:

1   personal investment preferences and existing investments;
2   degree of acceptable risk;
3   the purposes of the investment;
4   the time frame;
5   taxation.

Information on these factors and on an individual's personal financial position needs to be gathered together and recorded both for the present and for future planning. This may be done best by employing some form of fact find such as that set out at the appendix to the *Introduction* section of this book.

PERSONAL INVESTMENT PREFERENCES

Investors may well have strongly held views on the types of investment in which they wish to invest. These will frequently result from personal experiences, family background and similar factors, rather than from the clinical analysis of the relative merits of such investments. Ethical and 'green' investments are two of the ways in which such preferences may be expressed. A successful plan can be developed only by taking full account of these preferences and aversions.

Furthermore, before devising an investment plan it is necessary to consider existing investments held. For example, an individual seeking a unit trust type investment may already have considerable exposure to UK equities through, say, a personal pension plan. If looked at in isolation the unit trust investment might well be placed in a UK growth fund, but if the pension plan is considered also, a recommendation to gain exposure overseas might well result. The perfect investment plan will look at all assets and provide for a 'top down' asset allocation starting with currency and moving down to countries, sectors and then individual stocks. Such precision is of course not possible with collective investments, but it is certainly possible to allocate as far down as currency and countries, and leave the chosen fund manager to do the rest.

RISK

One needs to assess an individual's attitude towards risk. The principal risks are related to:
(a) financial factors:
    loss in value, ie market/economic risk,
    change in exchange rates, ie currency risk;
(b) political factors:
    change in tax rates and tax laws,
    exchange control,
    'ethical' considerations;
(c) inflation;
(d) state of health;
(e) systematic factors.

(a) Financial Factors

Any asset which does not have a continuing guaranteed redeemable value, indexed in real terms in the individual's country of residence, carries a financial risk. The risk can usually be reduced by making a spread of investments rather than a single investment and by coupling this to currency hedging where appropriate. Per contra, gearing (ie borrowing to invest more) can increase the risk, hopefully with a corresponding increase in the possibility of gain. The risk of changing interest rates will directly affect fixed interest investors, but will also indirectly affect equity investors.

Investment in the UK by a UK resident does not necessarily avoid the long-term effects of 'exchange rate' risk if sterling is potentially a weak international currency at the time. A spread of investments worldwide is an accepted way of reducing this risk.

Risk is also closely related to the time factor: if there is the strong possibility of a need to realise investments at short notice, the risk of loss is increased.

The smaller the amount of an individual's resources and the greater the proportion of those resources which one's intended investment represents, the more significant the risk factor becomes. It is unlikely that a small investor will have exposure to high-risk investments, such as derivatives, whereas for a wealthy investor such exposure may be relevant.

(b) Political Factors

The political risk requires little further comment: at the top of the scale are tax avoidance schemes and the risk that they will not succeed; but even arrangements which defer a tax liability carry the risk that rates of tax may increase or the legislation may change. The effect – or possible effect – of exchange control regulations (in the UK as well as overseas countries) should not be ignored in relation to overseas investments.

Political stability is a vital factor to consider, especially in terms of the economic performance of the underlying assets in which one invests, and one to which investors should pay particular attention in the case of investments in 'emergent' countries as well as in certain developed economies especially in the Far East and South America (the emerging markets). More recently, the geopolitical aspects have had a profound effect on global economies, and these cannot be ignored when considering investment.

(c) Inflation

The potential impact of inflation on an investment plan should be recognised. In this context, there are now investments which are indexed to price levels, which can eliminate this risk (but not necessarily other financial risks). A well managed investment portfolio should have been constructed having addressed this question. In the UK the Bank of England now has control over interest rates and has inflation targets set by the Treasury.

(d) State of Health

The risk of ill-health is relevant where the investments are of a nature which requires monitoring or management by the investor, where they are aimed at long-term capital appreciation and ill-health increases income needs, or where ill-health can exclude specific investment such as life assurance.

(e) Systematic Factors

One conventional approach to categorising risk is to divide it into systematic and unsystematic factors.

Systematic risk includes all factors influencing markets as a whole, including interest rates, inflation, politics, currency and market risk (the performance of the UK stock market will affect the performance of individual shares and possibly the performance of the US market).

Unsystematic risk is more specific, relating to individual sectors and stocks.

PURPOSE

It is essential to understand the purpose for which the individual is making an investment: is it to satisfy income needs now, or in several years' time on retirement; is it to provide a fund for the surviving spouse or children or both; is it to provide a fund to finance school or university fees; does it represent spare funds set aside for 'a rainy day' or perhaps a fund available for 'fun investment', such as highly speculative investments or purchases with the emphasis on collection rather than investment return?

The purpose will impact on the acceptable degree of risk and on the time frame. Above all, the investor has to decide whether to aim for a capital gain, for income, or a combination of the two. It is frequently the case that a high income is paid at the expense of capital gain. One must look at the income net of inflation and try wherever possible to avoid a diminution of capital.

The purpose may also be slanted towards particular tax considerations, for example:

1   the purchase of efficient investments in terms of estate taxes, ie those which reduce or defer the potential impact of IHT;

2   investment on terms which give a deduction against income, eg venture capital trusts and investment schemes;

3   for UK resident investors there will be an attraction in having capital rather than income receipts. Although the same annual rate applies, the CGT exemption will reduce the effective rate. Normally the income tax personal allowances are absorbed by other income;

4   to take advantage of an overseas domicile or residence situation;

5   to ensure both spouses' personal allowances, lower rate and basic rate
     tax bands are fully utilised for independent taxation.

The purpose may also include life assurance considerations – the
assurance and investment factors need to be looked at separately. To
recognise this, those insurance products which are primarily savings and
investment orientated are now included in this part.

TIME FRAME

This will be governed by purpose, by the individual's age and stage of life.
The longer the time frame, the greater the choice of investments: typically,
a qualifying life policy requires a period of ten years or more; investment
under the enterprise investment scheme requires three years or more (five
years or more for shares acquired before 6 April 2000); dealing costs of
some investments make short period holding time scales impracticable.

As a very general rule, equity investment, whether directly or via unit
trust or investment trust, should not be considered unless there is at least
a five-year time frame. It is essential to allow sufficient time to compensate
for up-front charges and short-term market volatility.

TAXATION

The individual needs to consider the taxation position relating to the
underlying investment itself (eg an authorised unit trust suffers no CGT
on its own investment holdings) and that relating to his own circumstances
(eg will a liability to CGT arise on a sale of those units in that unit trust?).

Any tax liability arising on both the income and capital elements of
the return must be noted, and further, whether this position is likely to
change during the period the investment is to be held either as a result of
a change in personal circumstances (eg on retirement) or of a change in
the tax legislation (eg on a change in government or attitude to perceived
avoidance). Married couples are taxed separately and the tax planning
opportunities this presents must also be examined. Non-taxpayers can
invest in some of the traditional investments without tax being deducted at
source and non-reclaimable.

Next, the tax position must be weighed against the commercial position.
Whilst the two inevitably interact to a greater or lesser extent the decision
should be a commercial one, although tax advantages can turn an average
investment into a good one! On the contrary, the tax advantages often
disguise a high-risk investment.

SUMMARY

A logical and analytical review of the overall picture and specific
opportunities available is required. 'Keep it simple' is frequently one of the
most important maxims plus a healthy disregard for get rich quick promises.
There is always a trade-off between risk and reward. It is crucial to have a
strategy and to have linked that into one's wider financial plan embracing
the adequate provision of a pension and estate planning.

The strategy and plan is not something that remains unchanging but rather, it grows and develops as time passes and one's circumstances change. It needs regular review but not constant tampering. Violent change is seldom required and gradual development is to be preferred.

Professional advisers can help individuals to reach decisions on these factors and to formulate a general investment plan. Within the plan it will normally be for the stockbroker to recommend individual share and stock purchases; for the financial adviser to recommend the policies, annuities and collective investments that meet the client's particular needs; for the land agent to advise in relation to property purchases and so on. The financial adviser, properly authorised and regulated by the FSA, is able to bring together the various elements in a personal financial planning review.

The investments – certainly if they take the form of unit trusts, quoted shares or stock – will need monitoring and the individual will need advice on what and when to sell, as well as buying advice.

An individual's circumstances will change over a period and they should therefore be encouraged to review annually with their advisers the factors built into their investment plan when it was initially designed.

3.2 Government Securities – Index-linked Gilts

Description	Represent UK Government borrowing. The investor receives half-yearly interest, the rate of which is linked to the RPI, plus the nominal value of the stock at the redemption date similarly linked.
Suitable for	Taxpayers (particularly higher rate) and non-taxpayers wishing to protect their capital against inflation and requiring risk-free investment.
Ages	All, but for those under 18, stocks must be held in an adult's name unless purchase is made through the Bank of England Brokerage Services, although stocks so purchased cannot normally be sold until the child reaches seven.
Advantages	1 A secure investment; interest and repayment guaranteed by the Government. 2 Full inflation protection. 3 Interest can be paid gross. 4 No CGT. 5 No stamp duty on purchase and sale.
Disadvantages	1 Interest is liable to income tax at the basic and higher rate. 2 Index-linked securities produce a low level of income. 3 Losses cannot be offset for CGT purposes. 4 If RPI falls, then the interest and capital payments also fall.
Investment limits	Minimum of £1,000; maximum £250,000 for certain gilts, although no more than £25,000 of value of a stock can be purchased through the Bank of England Brokerage Services in any one day.
Charges	Commission payable if purchases or sales made through a bank or broker whilst purchases through the Bank of England Brokerage Services at auction attract no commission.

FURTHER DETAILS

Commercial Aspects

Index-linked securities are similar to fixed-interest gilts, the difference being that the interest payments and the value at redemption are linked to the RPI. The level of income alone is low, although index-linked gilts offer a secure shelter for capital in times of inflation. They are likely to offer a higher (total) real redemption yield than conventional gilts after adjusting for inflation.

To compare index-linked to conventional gilts one has to assume an inflation rate for the holding period. One then calculates the break-even rate of inflation which will produce the same real yield on the index-linked stock as the nominal yield on the conventional gilt, and if one estimates inflation will be above this level, one buys the index-linked stock and vice versa. In addition one needs to consider the after-tax return on both.

Income and Capital

The interest is paid half-yearly.

The payment is calculated by multiplying the coupon (or the capital payment) by:

$$\frac{\text{RPI eight months before interest or final capital payment is due}}{\text{Base RPI of the stock (eight months before its issue)}}$$

The value of interest and capital payments are calculated by comparing the base RPI figure with the RPI figure eight months before each payment is due. The eight-month delay is for administrative and pricing reasons.

Strips

This is where the gilt is split into its separate income elements and the final capital payment (see Section 3.3, *Government Fixed Interest Stock – 'Gilts'*).

Taxation Aspects

For UK private investors the interest is paid gross unless holders elect to be taxed at source. Gilts held at 5 April 1998 require an election for gross interest. Tax on interest received gross in 2007/08 will not be payable until 31 January 2009, subject to the rules on payments on account.

Non-taxpayers can reclaim tax deducted at source. For basic rate taxpayers, where their total income, including savings income, does not exceed the upper limit of the basic rate band, they will only pay tax at 20% on those savings. Where total income exceeds the upper limit of the basic rate band, then for this purpose the gross savings income will be treated as the top slice of income (with dividend income being treated as the highest part of the savings income) and the excess over the threshold will be subject to higher rate tax.

Any gains are exempt from CGT and losses are unrelievable.

CROSS REFERENCES

Government Fixed Interest Stock – 'Gilts' **3.3**
National Savings **3.28**
The Young **5.2**

3.3 Government Fixed Interest Stock – 'Gilts'

Description	Represent UK Government borrowing initially issued at a discount to its redemption value and at a fixed rate (usually) over a known period of years prior to redemption at par.
Suitable for	Taxpayers and non-taxpayers.
Ages	Any, but only if stocks are purchased through the Bank of England Brokerage Services can a child hold stock in own name – but cannot normally sell until seven years of age. Otherwise stock must be held in parents' name until majority.
Advantages	1 Secure investment; interest and repayment are guaranteed by the Government. 2 Capital gains are free of CGT. 3 Interest on stocks can be paid gross. 4 For individuals not ordinarily resident in the UK income arising on certain issues is free from UK income tax. 5 No stamp duty on purchase or sale.
Disadvantages	1 Interest is liable to income tax at the basic and higher rate. 2 If interest rates rise during holding period the capital return may be less than originally paid. 3 Losses cannot be utilised for CGT purposes.
Investment limits	Minimum £1,000; maximum £250,000 for certain gilts, although no more than £25,000 of value of a stock may be purchased through the Bank of England Brokerage Services on any one day.
Charges	Commission payable if purchase or sale made through bank or broker. If purchase made through Bank of England Brokerage Services commission is generally lower.

FURTHER DETAILS

Commercial Aspects

Government stocks are a convenient way for individual investors to provide for known future commitments, eg school fees or CGT commitments if stock is held to maturity.

Stock was issued by the Government for funding purposes and issues have increased through 2009 and into 2010 due to high Government debt levels.

The majority of Government stocks pay a fixed rate of interest over the life of the stock. The interest rate is expressed as an annual percentage rate on £100 nominal stock and this is known as the 'coupon'. The yield on the stock is dependent upon the price of £100 nominal at the time of purchase, for example Treasury 8% 2013 priced at £120.61 per £100 nominal will yield 6.63% until redemption in 2013.

Government stocks also guarantee repayment of the nominal value of the stock on the redemption date. Some dates are fixed, as in the example above; others have a period during which the Government can choose to redeem (for example, 13¾% Treasury Stock 2003–2006) and a small number have no fixed date (for example, War Loan 3½%), the Government being able to redeem at any time.

Normally the Government issues the stock at a discount to its redemption price of £100. As the period prior to redemption decreases, the price of the gilt will rise to reflect this.

Gifts are classified, according to their time to redemption, into shorts, mediums, longs and undated. The financial press and the London Stock Exchange differ in respect of their categorisations. The categories according to the London Stock Exchange are:
- shorts – stocks with less than seven years until redemption;
- mediums – stocks with seven to 15 years before redemption;
- longs – stocks with over 15 years to redemption;
- undated – stocks that have no specified date for redemption.

'Convertibles' are short-dated stocks with an option to switch into a longer maturity date at a series of fixed points, normally half-yearly, during the stocks' lives. The price will normally reflect a premium over 'shorts' and 'longs' and a purchaser would seek the smallest premium with the longest time to the next conversion date so as to maximise any gain if the conventional longs market rises. Disposal or conversion can then take place at a profit.

'Strips' are gilts split into their capital and income elements. Thus a 20-year gilt could be split into 40 half-yearly interest payments and one capital element at redemption. This enables investors to more precisely match their requirements for, say, income over a period. Strippable gilts all have coupon dates that are paid 7 June and 7 December. There is now a structured market for strips.

Taxation Aspects

Interest is subject to income tax and it is taxed as savings income. The interest is paid gross unless holders elect to be taxed at source. Before 6 April 1998, interest on gilts was usually paid net of tax, unless the gilts were purchased through the National Savings Stock Register. Interest on gilts bought before 6 April 1998 will continue to be paid net unless the investor elects for gross payment. Tax on interest received gross in 2007/08 will not be payable until 31 January 2009, subject to the usual payments on account rule. Non-taxpayers can reclaim tax deducted at source. For basic rate taxpayers, where their total income, including savings income, does not exceed the upper limit of the basic rate band, they will only pay tax at 20% on those savings.

Where total income exceeds the upper limit of the basic rate band, then for this purpose the gross savings will be treated as the top slice of income (with dividend income being treated as the highest part of that savings income) and the excess over the threshold will be subject to higher rate tax.

Any gains are exempt from CGT and losses are unrelievable.

Usually taxpayers paying higher rate tax will invest in gilts paying a lower interest rate than those basic rate taxpayers choose. However, much will also depend on the likely capital growth in the gilt prior to maturity. A non-taxpayer would be better off with a high coupon stock, but must take care not to suffer a loss of capital on sale/maturity of the gilt.

Anti-avoidance legislation referred to as the accrued income scheme means it is not possible to convert the income arising on gilts into a tax-free capital gain. Special provisions apply to gilts issued at a 'deep discount'.

CROSS REFERENCES

3.4 Corporate Bonds

Description	Borrowing by companies and UK or foreign national, public or local authorities in a form which is dealt with on the listed and unlisted securities market. The bonds must be 'qualifying corporate bonds', ie denominated in sterling and be fixed interest, non-convertible loans.
Suitable for	Taxpayers and non-taxpayers able to keep their holdings under active review. Useful for matching against future liabilities.
Ages	No limit
Advantages	1 Bonds are CGT free. 2 Higher interest may be obtainable than on UK Government stock. 3 Marketable (although smaller holdings not as marketable as UK Government stock).
Disadvantages	1 Interest is liable to income tax; basic rate tax is deducted at source. 2 No CGT relief for losses on disposal. UK resident holders may be subject to income tax on any accrued interest on sale. 3 Loss may be incurred on sale if interest rates have risen since purchase. 4 Risk higher than on UK Government stock. 5 Market may be narrow.
Investment limits	Minimum purchase about £2,000 to avoid the impact of minimum commission. There is no maximum.
Charges	Brokers' commission rates bid/offer spreads are wide.

FURTHER DETAILS

Corporate bonds are a form of borrowing for companies, nationalised industries and foreign governments. Similar to Government stocks, they pay, over the life of the bond, a fixed rate of interest which is certain and known when the bond is issued. The bonds are traded freely on the Stock Market and are mostly readily marketable, although this may not be the case with lower quality bonds in difficult times. Those sterling denominations issued by foreign governments and nationalised industries are known as 'bulldogs'.

The market price of the bonds (which like Government stocks are usually initially offered at a discount to their redemption price at £100) is determined by the fixed coupon, the number of years to redemption and the level of interest rates generally. Marketability means that the investor has the option of aiming to realise a capital gain by disposing of the bond or holding it for income.

Corporate bonds normally pay higher interest than Government stocks (as they are less secure) and from this viewpoint are attractive for lower basic rate or non-taxpayers.

Types of Bonds

Convertibles

Convertibles are bonds which have the option of converting into the ordinary shares of the issuing company at a predetermined price and time. Interest on the bonds is payable in the normal way until the option is exercised. The option is usually favourable to exercise when the share price is at a premium of say 20% to 25%. At that level the bond tends to follow the share price rather than interest rates but still has the bond features should the share price drop. With some stocks the number of shares receivable diminishes towards the end of the exercise period.

Zero Coupon Bonds

These are known as deep discount bonds and pay little or no interest. They are issued well below par and the return comes at redemption when the guaranteed uplift to the nominal value at the maturity date. Special tax rules (see below) have made these types of bonds less attractive. Such bonds are still attractive, however, for a higher rate taxpayer who expects to be paying lower rate, basic rate or nil rate tax when the bond is redeemed ten, 15 or 20 years from now. An alternative method of income deferral is to use offshore funds – see Section 3.10. In general these bonds require professional management and are also used to speculate on interest rate changes. Consider also Zero Dividend Preference Shares – see Section 3.7, *Investment Trusts*.

Local Authority Bonds

These bonds are issued by local authorities at a guaranteed rate of interest for one year and six days – they are sometimes called 'yearlings'. They are a secure investment depending on the standing of the authority. Rates of interest are competitive and fixed at the outset. Government policies now restrict local authority fund-raising and currently there are few stocks available.

Longer period stocks are issued from time to time for one to four years maturity and must be held to maturity. These are known as 'tap bonds' or 'over-the-counter'. As the bonds are issued at par there is no capital gain.

Eurobonds

These are foreign currency bonds and are very flexible, with minimal regulations. The main features are:

- they are in bearer form with detachable coupons for interest;
- interest can be fixed or variable;
- 'straights' are conventional bonds with coupons and fixed redemption dates;
- other bonds have developed features to meet demand such as capped interest, interest in several currencies etc;

- the investor must be aware of the currency risk as well as the yield;
- it is usually cheaper to purchase Eurobonds through the subsidiary of a UK bank rather than a stockbroker.

Preference Shares

In that these shares have a fixed return, they have characteristics of corporate bonds – see Section 3.6, *Shares.*

Permanent Interest Bearing Shares

See Section 3.5.

Taxation Aspects

Interest is subject to income tax and is paid net of lower rate tax. Non-taxpayers can reclaim tax deducted at source. For basic rate taxpayers, where their total income, including savings income, does not exceed the upper limit of the basic rate band, they will only pay tax at 20% on those savings.

Where total income exceeds the upper limit of the basic rate band, then for this purpose the gross savings will be treated as the top slice of income (with dividend income being treated as the highest part of that savings income) and the excess over the threshold will be subject to higher rate tax.

There is no CGT on gains on sale and losses are not allowable for CGT. Certain bonds are non-qualifying corporate bonds (eg non-sterling or convertible) and such bonds are subject to CGT and tend to be used in corporate takeovers to facilitate tax planning on the disposal. However, losses on such bonds are allowable if the bond has become of negligible value or the redemption date has passed and the loan is irrecoverable. This includes unquoted bonds and non-convertible sterling bonds and options to acquire them. Anti-avoidance provisions will tax as income accrued interest accruing to date of sale on stock held by those resident in the UK.

Where a 'deep discount' security, which has been issued at a discount of more than half a point a year or 15 points overall, any profit on disposal or redemption is taxed as income in the tax year of disposal. There is no CGT charged on disposal or redemption of discounted securities. For securities acquired before 27 March 2003, investors are charged to income tax on profit made after deducting the expenses of acquisition and disposal. Losses made on the disposal of securities acquired before that date, may be set against other income of that tax year. For securities acquired on or after 27 March 2003, no deduction is allowed for the incidental costs of acquisition or disposal, no relief is available for losses made on disposal or redemption. Current securities which are convertible into ordinary shares of the issuing company and give the investor the option to put the bond back to the issuer (usually at a premium) and which meet certain other conditions will be 'qualifying' convertible securities and so outside the 'deep gains' legislation.

CROSS REFERENCES

Government Fixed Interest Stock – 'Gilts' **3.3**
Permanent Interest Bearing Shares **3.5**

3.5 Permanent Interest Bearing Shares (PIBS)

Description	PIBS are building society shares which are listed and traded on the London Stock Exchange. They serve to increase the societies' Tier I capital, the level of which constrains the extent to which a society can take deposits and make loans. PIBS are irredeemable, which means that the principal will only be repaid upon a winding-up of the society, subject to the prior rights of other creditors including deposit holders. Perpetual subordinated bonds (PSBs) were originally issued as PIBS by building societies that have now converted to banks.
Suitable for	Those investors who require a relatively high income and are prepared to assume a degree of risk with the value of the underlying capital.
Ages	No minimum.
Advantages	1 Generally, a higher yield than that available from Government stocks. 2 The interest payments are fixed. 3 PIBS are traded on the London Stock Exchange, thus enabling capital gains to be realised. 4 PIBS are treated as qualifying corporate bonds and as such there is no CGT liability on disposal.
Disadvantages	1 Since the interest rate is fixed, the capital will fall in value if interest rates rise. 2 PIBS are irredeemable and the society is under no obligation to repay the principal; they can therefore be somewhat illiquid. 3 On a winding-up, PIBS rank behind other creditors of the society. 4 PIBS do not qualify for compensation under the Financial Services Compensation Scheme. 5 If interest payments are missed they are non-cumulative and will not be made up in later years. 6 Second-hand market not very liquid.
Investment limits	Minimum £1,000, but normally £20,000–£50,000.
Charges	Usually gilt dealing commissions of 1%–1.5%.

FURTHER DETAILS

Although PIBS are termed as shares, they have certain distinct characteristics. They have no fixed redemption date and pay interest twice yearly at a predetermined rate set at the issue launch. If in any half year, the society considers it financially imprudent to pay the interest then it need not do so; such unpaid interest would be non-cumulative. PIBS are registered and transferred in the same way as shares except that settlement is effected seven days after dealing and shares are transferred in specific minimum amounts. It is possible to access PIBS through a collective fund, thus enabling a broader spread of investment and minimising risk.

Taxation Aspects

Interest is paid gross. For basic rate taxpayers, where their total income, including savings income, does not exceed the upper limit of the basic rate band, they will only pay tax at 20% on those savings.

Where total income exceeds the upper limit of the basic rate band, then for this purpose the gross savings will be treated as the top slice of income (with dividend income being treated as the top part of that savings income) and the excess over the threshold will be subject to higher rate tax.

Any gains are exempt from CGT.

CROSS REFERENCES

Corporate Bonds   **3.4**
Shares   **3.6**

3.6 Shares

Description	Investing in the issued ordinary share capital of companies, listed on the UK or other world Stock Exchanges. Most of the world's stock exchanges have both main and secondary markets according to size or other criteria for stock and it is important to ascertain before purchasing stock what are the marketability, costs and reputation of the market on which a particular stock is listed.
Ages	No one under 18 can hold shares in their own name. There is no maximum age limit.
Suitable for	Those with available funds able and prepared to accept varying degrees of financial risk in return for income and capital gain opportunities.
Advantages	1 Potential for growth in investment income and capital values.
	2 Large selection of available investments.
	3 Information on value of very many shares and underlying companies usually available on daily basis.
	4 Ready market normally available for shares.
	5 Worldwide investment opportunities.
	6 Discounts and other benefits available to shareholders in certain companies.
	7 Husband and wife each have annual CGT exemption (£10,100 for 2010/11).
Disadvantages	1 Risk of loss of income and capital values.
	2 Fairly high transaction costs on small (under £7,000) purchases and on overseas shares.
	3 Value of investment influenced by general market factors possibly not related to performance of company in question.
	4 Smaller or newly formed listed ('quoted') companies may be traded in narrow markets with wide dealing spreads as may be some stocks on main market and overseas markets.
	5 CGT (subject to annual exemption) on the profit on disposal of shares.
Investment limits	Minimum investment is about £600–£1,000 on any one purchase to avoid the impact of minimum commission. There is no maximum.
Charges and commission	0.5% stamp duty on purchases (not sales) in the UK plus stockbrokers' commission. The CREST settlement system involves the de-materialisation of paperwork and all shareholders should become non-certificated in due course. The settlement period has reduced to three days with the introduction of CREST.

FURTHER DETAILS

Commercial Aspects

Ordinary Shares

An ordinary share portfolio offers an individual who has a reserve of liquid funds a means of purchasing assets aimed at producing a real (net of inflation) return from a combination of capital and income growth. Professional advice is essential in establishing a portfolio and above all in the timing of purchases and sales, both insofar as the portfolio as a whole is concerned and in respect of individual stock holdings.

Ordinary shares represent a direct investment in the equity of a company. The investment is necessarily speculative – to a greater or lesser degree – since its value is dependent upon many factors and can rise or fall sometimes by significant relative amounts.

The price of shares can be influenced by past and projected profits of the company or market sector, the perceived quality and record of management, external economic and political factors, takeover rumours, press tips and other speculation.

The investor can follow the market and make necessary investment decisions. He can consult a stockbroker or investment manager before taking action or he can delegate full discretion to one of a number of stockbrokers, merchant banks or other investment advisers who will manage his portfolio either on an individual basis if it is over a minimum size or on a pooled basis if it is below that stockbroker's minimum size.

A varied choice is available to the investor, since investment can be made in any stock market in the world, almost any industry or economic sector and in shares which may be expected to provide a steady income or capital growth or a combination of both. Hence the investor is able to purchase shares satisfying his risk profile and aimed at providing him with the combination of yield to capital growth he requires.

An alternative to investing directly in overseas shares is to hold units in a unit trust specialising in the overseas market or shares in an investment trust or open-ended investment company (OEIC).

Preference Shares

Preference shares pay a fixed rate of dividend and are attractive for those dependent on having certain income, as they are paid in priority to dividends on ordinary shares. They can carry restricted rights to dividends, but are normally repaid in preference to other shareholders in a liquidation. They normally have no voting rights until the dividend is in arrears and may have rights to convert to ordinary shares at certain times.

Convertibles

Convertible loan stock is a form of corporate bond issued by a company which at a future date is redeemed for an issue of ordinary or preference shares. It may be attractive to those wanting income in times of low interest rates and offers the long-term prospect of capital gain after conversion has taken place.

Shareholder Perks

A minimum holding of shares may entitle a shareholder to substantial discounts on some companies' products, for example holidays, motor cars, clothing, hotel accommodation.

The Alternative Investment Market (AIM)

AIM is designed primarily for small companies. Although AIM is regulated by the London Stock Exchange it has less demanding rules than the Stock Exchange Official List.

During the first period of AIM there have been some fairly spectacular successes and failures, but AIM has now grown to well over 2,000 companies. The AIM is a less liquid market than that of the Stock Exchange.

Assessing the Performance of Ordinary Shares

Frequently, the performance of ordinary shares is judged by the use of a number of ratios:

– Price earning ratio (P/E ratio) = $\dfrac{\text{Current share price}}{\text{Earnings per share}}$

The main use of a P/E ratio is to compare one share with another, ie a high P/E ratio often denoting a sector of company with good growth prospects.

– Dividend yield = $\dfrac{\text{Gross dividend per share}}{\text{Share price}} = 100$

Useful for identifying companies with above average yield and therefore offering value.

– Net asset value = $\dfrac{\text{Net asset value}}{\text{Issued ordinary shares}}$

Used widely when judging investment trusts, many of which trade at a discount to NAV but can also trade at a premium to NAV.

Taxation Aspects

Capital Gains Tax

Each investor is liable to CGT on gains arising on the sales of shares. Each individual of whatever age is entitled to one annual CGT exemption and this is £10,100 for 2010/11. It is applied on the net chargeable gain.

Reinvestment Relief

Gains in quoted shares can be deferred by reinvestment into EIS. Since 6 April 2004, it has no longer been possible to defer gains by reinvestment into VCT shares issued after that date. New issues of certain AIM shares qualify. Reference should be made to Section 4.10, *EIS Deferral Relief*, Section 3.12 *Enterprise Investment Scheme*, and Section 3.13, *Venture Capital Trusts*.

Inheritance Tax

Holdings of shares in quoted companies which, by themselves or in conjunction with other holdings owned by the holder or his spouse, give voting control of the company, qualify for 50% business property relief.

AIM stocks are treated as unquoted and subject to certain rules can qualify for 100% business property relief once held for the minimum two-year qualifying period.

Income Tax

Dividends are grossed up by a tax credit equal to one-ninth of the cash amount, ie dividend received of £90 is grossed up by £10 to reach taxable dividend of £100. The grossed up dividend is deemed to be the highest part of the income, followed by other savings income, then all non-savings income such as earnings.

The tax credit is offset against the tax liability on the dividend to reduce the effective liability to nil for basic rate taxpayers or to a rate of 25.5% for higher rate taxpayers.

The tax credit is not recoverable even if the taxpayers' rate falls below 10%.

Non-UK dividends must be grossed up by the overseas tax credit. The tax credit can be offset against the UK tax liability to the extent that it is allowed under the double tax agreement.

CROSS REFERENCES

3.7   Investment Trusts

Description	A means of investing in a 'portfolio' of shares managed by professional investment managers via a purchase of the shares of a public company (known as an investment trust) whose assets consist wholly of shares in other companies.
Suitable for	Small or large investors seeking a spread of investments professionally managed or seeking to invest in an area or sector or to obtain geographic spread.
Ages	No limits, unless restricted by the Articles of Association, although under 18s cannot hold shares in their own name.
Advantages	1 Risk reduced by investment spread.
	2 Useful means of investing in individual market sectors/overseas securities where specialist knowledge provided by managers.
	3 Investment management is handled by professional managers.
	4 Gearing in a successful trust can boost the value of the holding.
	5 Monthly regular savings plans available – many linked to ISAs.
Disadvantages	1 CGT arises on the sale of shares by the investor.
	2 Dividends are subject to deduction of lower rate tax at source.
	3 Gearing in an unsuccessful trust can result in a substantial loss in value.
	4 Conventionally regarded as a long-term investment.
Investment limits	No minimum, although dealing costs can be high on investments below £1,000, particularly via stockbrokers.
Charges	Annual management charge on trust assets may be 0.5%–1%.
	Other normal costs of dealing on the Stock Market.

FURTHER DETAILS

Commercial Aspects

Investment trusts enable those often with modest resources or seeking geographic or sector spread to benefit from investing in a wide range of stocks and shares. The investor purchases shares in the trust company, which in turn invests the majority of its assets (in most cases) in stocks and shares of other companies. The individual therefore has a share of the investment trust's portfolio and a share in the income produced therefrom.

In many cases the shares of the investment trust stand at a 'discount' below the net asset value per share, thus providing the investor with a potentially higher level of income and capital growth than could be expected when investing the same amount of money in the same shares directly or through unit trusts. Part of the discount may also reflect the management expenses of the trust. Warrants are usually provided when new issues are made to offset the impact of an immediate discount.

Investment trusts offer expert investment management at low cost, comparing favourably with the charges levied on investment in unit trusts. The costs of management are borne by the trust company. The only costs borne by the investor are those associated with the sale and acquisition of the shares themselves. Shares are normally acquired on the Stock Exchange although direct dealing is becoming more available.

Investment trusts can benefit from 'gearing'. This means that they can borrow to purchase shares, thereby giving the opportunity for greater growth potential, although it should be noted that in a falling market high gearing depresses investment performance.

Some trusts are income-producing, specialising in high yielding shares. Others produce little income, the emphasis being on capital appreciation.

There are also some 'split-level' trusts, where the whole of the income is attributed to one class of shares (the 'income' shares) and the whole of the capital gain is attributed to a second class of shares (the 'capital' shares). This structure has evolved now with the introduction of intermediate classes of shares, giving different balances of income and capital, eg zeros paying no income but a pre-calculated rate of return on the wind up of the trust, or stepped preference shares which provide a growing income entitlement. In general these trusts are more suitable for experienced and sophisticated investors who need to be certain they have an exact understanding of the time frame, gearing and risk parameters relating to the anticipated returns sought.

It is also possible to invest in 'Fund of Fund' arrangements, either via investment trusts or unit trusts.

An increasing number of investment trust groups have made their trusts available within an ISA.

Differences between Investment Trusts and Unit Trusts

A quoted investment trust is a Stock Market company, and as the number of shares available is always the same it is said to be 'closed ended', unlike unit trusts where the unit trust managers can issue more units or repurchase (ie effectively cancel) units according to demand and thus run an 'open ended' fund.

In turn this means that the investment trust manager, unlike the unit trust manager, does not have to make his investment decisions in the light of sudden inflows/outflows of money and so can plan ahead more easily.

Investment trusts can borrow, whilst unit trusts cannot, and hence the former have the ability to generate gearing, which could improve asset and income growth if the underlying investments bought via the borrowing do well.

The greater freedom of investment policy allowed to investment trusts does not restrict back-to-back borrowing when hedging currency fluctuations. Unit trusts are restricted from such borrowing.

Investment trusts can generally invest in a wider range of companies than unit trusts.

Taxation Aspects

The Trust

Approved investment trusts are exempt from CGT on gains realised within the trust. Capital gains cannot be distributed to shareholders in the form of dividends, and are therefore reinvested in full. Investment trusts which are unapproved do not have this CGT exemption, and on liquidation a double charge to CGT will arise, first on the company and secondly on the shareholder. Care should be taken to ensure that this difference between approved and unapproved trusts is clear before any investment is made.

Corporation tax is paid on unfranked income received by the trust, generally at 30%. However, this liability may be offset by payments by the trust such as debenture interest, overseas loan interest and management charges.

Dividend income from UK companies, ie franked investment income, is not subject to corporation tax.

Individual investors in certain unauthorised investment trusts (eg venture capital trusts) should take specialist tax advice on the relevant tax position applying.

The Investor

Dividends are grossed up by a tax credit equal to one-ninth of the cash amount, ie dividend received of £90 is grossed up by £10 to reach taxable dividend of £100. The grossed up dividend is deemed to be the highest part of the income, followed by other savings income then all non-savings income such as earnings.

The tax credit is offset against the tax liability on the dividend to reduce the liability to nil for basic rate taxpayers or to a rate of 22.5% for higher rate taxpayers.

The tax credit is not recoverable even if the taxpayers' rate falls below 10%.

On the sale of shares, a liability to CGT arises subject to the annual exemption, although the gains within the trust are exempt.

CROSS REFERENCES

Shares **3.6**
Unit Trusts and OEICs **3.8**
Venture Capital Trusts **3.13**
Stock Market Warrants **3.21**
CGT – Taper Relief **4.12**
The Young **5.2**

3.8   Unit Trusts and OEICs

Description	A means of investing in a 'portfolio' of shares managed by professional investment managers.
Suitable for	Small or large investors seeking a spread of investments professionally managed, or seeking a spread of investments in a volatile area or one which is difficult to research or seeking geographic spread.
Ages	No minimum.
Advantages	1 Investment is managed by professional investment managers at a reasonable cost.
	2 Investment in UK and overseas markets is available.
	3 Risk reduced by investment spread.
	4 Availability of different trusts to suit different investment objectives including some guaranteed and protected trusts.
	5 Performance has been better overall historically than unit-linked insurance products.
	6 The currency risk inherent in overseas investments is dealt with by the investment managers.
	7 Regular monthly savings plans available – many linked to ISAs.
Disadvantages	1 Not suitable for short-term investment because of initial cost structure.
	2 Speculative gains are unlikely.
	3 Income tax is deducted at source on dividends.
	4 CGT arises when the investor sells units.
	5 If quoted on a bid basis the bid–offer spread may be high.
Investment limits	Minimum investment is £500–£2,500 for most unit trust managers. There is no maximum.
Charges	Approximately 1%–1.5% pa management charge and the bid–offer spread averaging 5%. Discounts may be available for large investments and discount brokers.

FURTHER DETAILS

Commercial Aspects

Unit trusts are a good way of investing on the Stock Market, in the UK or overseas, for anyone who lacks the time or expertise to manage his own investment portfolio. Section 3.7, *Investment Trusts* sets out a comparison of investment and unit trusts. As is the case with investment trusts, they can be linked to ISAs.

The investment decisions are entrusted to professional investment managers who manage the funds on a daily basis and pool together the capital subscribed by investors.

There are nearly 3,000 different unit trusts available, covering all the major world stock markets and several of the emerging countries too, and the various industry sectors or specialisms such as gold or ethical investments. Funds can be invested in trusts specialising in providing income or capital growth or a combination of both, depending on the individual's requirements.

The investor buys units (in a trust) the price of which is determined by the value of the underlying securities in which the trust invests. The money invested by a new investor is used to buy further securities, and so more units are created for sale by the managers. The reverse occurs when units are sold back to the managers.

On disposal the investor's holding is bought back by the managers at the price ruling at that date. Units can be bought and sold over the telephone with the managers issuing contract notes and certificates in the normal way.

The price of the units is reported in many newspapers. Two prices are shown, the bid price which indicates the price the investor will receive on sale of the units to the managers and the offer price which is the price at which the units can be bought. The spread between the two prices which usually varies between 4% and 6% reflects the initial charge from the managers – commonly known as the bid–offer spread. These changes can often be reduced by purchasing unit trusts through a 'funds supermarket'.

The unit holder will normally receive half-yearly reports (an interim and a final) from the managers, which review the performance of the trust and provide statutory information about it.

Regular savings plans are available with a number of unit trust groups, and these schemes compare favourably with the more traditional unit-linked endowment policy.

As well as satisfying the necessary tax legislation to qualify as a unit trust (see below) if a unit trust is to be eligible for cross-border marketing within the EC it must be open ended and have at least 90% of its assets in quoted securities (shares, Government stock, or bonds) and, to be listed in the UK, EC funds must apply for recognition under the FSA although non-UK funds will not be covered by UK compensation schemes. Unit trusts are known as Undertakings for Collective Investments in Transferable Securities (UCITS) if these requirements are met. Many unit trusts are now converting to Open Ended Investment Companies (OEICS) because of these requirements but to do so, consent is required from a majority of the holders. Please see section later in this chapter.

Types of Trust

For the first-time investor, a fund with a balanced investment policy of some income and some capital growth may be the best choice. However, there are a number of other types of trust as follows:

Income Funds   These funds invest primarily in higher yielding investments and are suitable mainly for those who depend on maximising their income and are not higher rate taxpayers. Fixed interest and convertibles funds achieve the same objective but may not match the overall performance of the pure income funds.

Capital Funds   These funds produce low income as they are geared to capital growth.

Overseas Funds   These invest primarily overseas either in world markets or in one specific area, for example Japan, and are an ideal way for an individual to enter these markets, as the investment managers will have resources and research capability which cannot normally be matched by the private investor. There is an increasing trend for such funds also to be structured to either produce income, or to concentrate on capital growth opportunities.

Offshore Funds   See Section 3.10.

Accumulation Funds   The investment aim of these trusts, whether investing principally in the UK or overseas, is usually capital growth; they are therefore aimed at higher rate taxpayers who seek capital gains rather than income. The income, which is normally insignificant, is reinvested on behalf of the unit holders. The amount reinvested is the amount net of basic rate tax, since although not distributed, the income is still treated as a distribution which suffers tax.

Property Funds   Property funds are available, providing investors with a wide spread across the commercial, industrial and, increasingly, the residential sectors.

Future and Options Funds   These funds are also available, and should enable individuals and fund managers to ride out market downturns by providing a hedging mechanism. These are sometimes referred to as guaranteed or protected funds.

Other Funds   Some funds are specifically established to invest in specialist markets such as 'green' or ethical investments, gold or commodity shares. They may be suited to the investor with risk capital.

Cash funds are now available to warehouse cash deposits awaiting investment. By using them for cash generated from sales of the same management group's unit trusts, the investor not only gets a highly competitive interest rate but qualifies for a substantial reduction to the bid–offer spread (see above – *Charges*) if he reinvests into other units of that group's range of trusts.

Index tracking funds aim to allow investors to replicate the performance of a particular world stock market index (for example, the US's Standard and Poors Composite Index) and so offer investors a guarantee in effect that their core portfolio, or a part of it, will perform in line with the particular chosen index and hence permit them to take a slightly more speculative approach with some of their other investment monies. The attraction of such funds follows from the fact that overall only about 20% of unit trusts beat the index each year. From 1 April 2004 a unit trust can offer different classes of units in the same way as OEICs – see below.

Open Ended Investment Companies

The 'OEIC' is a cross between a unit trust and an investment trust.

An OEIC can issue shares similar to an investment trust, but is open ended, similar to a unit trust. Furthermore, it has the advantage of single pricing of shares rather than the bid-offer spread of a unit trust and it offers the opportunity for the OEIC manager to issue different classes of shares (with different charging structures attached).

The OEIC is very similar to the SICAV (société d'investissement à capital variable) which are preferred by foreign investors who do not necessarily favour the unfamiliar bid–offer spreads and complex trust deeds of the UK unit trust. OEICs, like SICAVs, may be set up as umbrella funds, enabling investors to choose one fund whilst retaining the ability to make several switches each year between different asset classes and geographical regions.

Unit trusts can apply for UCITS status, ie as being an Undertaking for Collective Investments in Transferable Securities. This enables marketing throughout the European Union. Many unit trusts are converting to OEICs.

Taxation Aspects

Authorised Unit Trusts

Authorised unit trusts are those authorised as such under the Financial Services and Markets Act 2000 and now all authorised unit trusts pay corporation tax at a rate equal to savings rate (ie 20%) income tax and get relief for their management expenses and interest paid. This treatment is advantageous where most of the income is by way of dividends from UK companies, ie franked investment income, as the dividends flow through the company with no further tax deducted. Interest and unfranked income charged to corporation tax, generally at 30%, after deducting management and other administrative expenses and interest cost of borrowing such as non-UK dividends are taxed at 20%.

Dividends are grossed up by a tax credit equal to one-ninth of the cash amount, ie dividend received of £90 is grossed up by £10 to reach taxable dividend of £100. The grossed up dividend is deemed to be the highest part of the income, followed by other savings income then all non-savings income such as earnings.

The tax credit is offset against the tax liability on the dividend to reduce the liability to nil for basic rate taxpayers or to a rate of 22.5% for higher rate taxpayers.

The tax credit is not recoverable even if the taxpayers' rate falls below 10%.

Capital gains accruing to authorised unit trusts are exempt from CGT. On the disposal of units by the investor any gain will be liable to CGT.

Unauthorised Unit Trusts

The income of the trust is subject to basic rate tax on the trustees, and the unit holder is liable to higher rate tax on amounts paid out to them or reinvested. The trustees are liable to CGT on disposals, and the unit holder is liable to CGT on disposals of units.

OEICs

OEICs are taxed in the same way as authorised unit trusts. There is no CGT within the fund, but switching between the different classes of shares may trigger a CGT liability.

CROSS REFERENCES

3.9 Guaranteed Investment Products

Description	Guaranteed performance bonds/trusts or equity protected investments that guarantee investment performance over a set time span. They do this by investing part of each deposit in fixed rate bonds giving a defined return and making a small deposit in an options contract to provide linkage to a stock market index in order to offer some upside potential (to the guarantee to return all or the vast majority, say 90%, of the initial deposit).
Suitable for	Provided the company offering the product is a reputable one with experience in these products, they should be suitable to a wide range of investors seeking a guaranteed minimum amount of their capital returned (say 90% to 100%) but wanting the chance for some benefit in a rising stock market, even if this is limited by the product's terms. In fact for some years the appeal is likely to be more for the sophisticated investor than the nervous investor for whom the products are largely targeted.
Advantages	1 Returns of all or a fixed percentage of capital guaranteed at outset. 2 Possible investment gains to be made over guaranteed return. 3 Professional management allows individuals access to investment techniques and products otherwise restricted to institutions. 4 Time span fixed. 5 Permits linkage to index tracking funds and to overseas investment markets.
Disadvantages	1 New product of complex technical construction, inhibiting the cautious investor for whom it is specifically targeted. 2 Relatively high charges, particularly for those having to withdraw from the product, or dying during its term. 3 Sophisticated investment techniques required, particularly to generate the upside, means range of providers may be limited and credentials of those offering these products need thorough examination. 4 Complex new products tend to result in unforeseen difficulties, and investors will require a higher level of specialist advice before embracing them so that the security angle in particular can be fully explored by them.

Investment limits	Length of term of product is usually one to five years fixed term. Minimum investment sum is usually £5,000 and sometimes more.
Charges	Usually at least 5% up front and probably a performance fee too, ranging from 2%–5% of gains made. Charge structures can be complex and hard to identify.

FURTHER DETAILS

Commercial Aspects

These products aim to eliminate risk totally, or to guarantee a given percentage from equity investment. The risks are eliminated by the bulk of the investment monies being used to purchase fixed interest securities (often certificates of deposit (CDs)) which in turn generate interest which is used to purchase call options via a stockbroker on, eg the Nikkei Stock Average, Standard and Poors 500 or the FTSE 100 index. This provides the performance element and is exercised if the index rises. If it falls the option is left unexercised, the cost is lost but the underlying return guaranteed is nevertheless available on maturity of the CDs.

This structure varies in the products available – usually they are offered for a few weeks prior to the critical closing date on which CDs and options are purchased – but most offer lower returns for a higher level of guarantee as less of the investment monies are available to purchase the options providing the upside.

Sometimes the structure is such that a fixed percentage return is offered, or if larger the increase on a stock market index over a given period is offered.

Encashment during the life of the bond is likely to lead to severe penalties, and sometimes this can also apply to death during the investment period.

These products are likely to be developed further over the next few years, and should offer a very attractive range of investment media in due course.

These funds have begun to feature in pension planning, offering a guarantee and slightly more potential upside than the traditional pre-retirement fixed interest or cash funds.

Taxation Aspects

Normally the investments grow free of tax within the bonds which are offered by offshore entities, albeit in designated countries with investor protection legislation acceptable to the FSA. Proceeds are paid gross to investors, and UK residents will be subject to income tax on them on maturity. Some are now subject to CGT as capital gains on the profit; however, HMRC approval is generally required at the outset and rarely provided.

CROSS REFERENCES

Pension Planning and Practicalities   **2.12**
Offshore Funds   **3.10**

3.10   Offshore Funds

Description	Open-ended investment funds investing in equities or foreign currency or foreign Government stocks. They are resident outside the UK, usually in a recognised tax haven, and are structured either as investment companies or as unit trusts. Depending on their tax status under UK law, funds are described as having 'distributor' status or not.
Suitable for	Investors permanently or temporarily non-UK resident; residents of the UK wishing to invest via a vehicle providing exposure to foreign currency or to obtain a gross return (eg for independent taxation planning); or those wishing to shelter income in a 'roll-up' fund until their tax rate drops, eg on retirement or on becoming non-resident.
Advantages	1 Profits and gains of the fund itself are not subject to UK tax and the fund is outside UK controls. 2 The dividends paid by distributor funds are paid gross. 3 Roll-up funds can be used to shelter income in appropriate circumstances.
Disadvantages	1 Income from distributor funds is subject to income tax on the UK resident and domiciled investor when paid out. 2 Gains of the UK resident and domiciled investor are subject to CGT (and losses will be allowable) if a fund has distributor status. Non-distribution (roll-up) funds attract income tax with no CGT exemption in the year that the investor realises the investment. 3 Exchange gains or losses may also occur on the conversion of funds into sterling. 4 Investor protection comparable to UK standards may not be available. 5 Careful planning is required before higher rate UK resident taxpayers invest in roll-up funds. 6 Performance, in sterling terms, has not necessarily been better than onshore funds, mainly because the charges tend to be higher offshore. 7 Some offshore funds actually invest in UK shares.
Investment limits	Minimum investment variable from £100– £25,000 and investment may be made direct via the fund managers, via a stockbroker or other intermediary. Prices are quoted in the financial press.

| **Charges** | Initial and annual management charges. Some charges are less transparent than with onshore funds. |

FURTHER DETAILS

Commercial Aspects

Location

The funds are located outside the UK, usually in a recognised tax haven such as the Channel Islands, the Isle of Man, Bermuda, Hong Kong, Luxembourg and the Bahamas.

The Channel Islands or Luxembourg are often the investor's first choice because of the available investment expertise and ease of communication.

Regulatory Consents

Before they can be marketed in Britain they have to be authorised under the FSA legislation via one of the following routes:
1   the fund is registered in an area with 'designated territory status', ie investor protection here equates broadly to that in the UK, eg Jersey, Bermuda;
2   the fund management company applies directly for authorisation under Financial Services and Markets Act 2000 in the UK;
3   the fund becomes a UCITS (Undertaking for Collective Investments in Transferable Securities) fund which implies being a European-based fund which has satisfied requirements at least as onerous as in 1 above.

Structure

The fund will usually be established as an open-ended investment company with share capital. A small number of ordinary shares will be issued to a management company which thereby has control, and the remainder of the capital will be available to investors as participating preference shares on which a dividend is payable.

The day-to-day management of the fund is undertaken by the management company, which will also be situated outside the UK. These professional managers are responsible for matters such as payment of dividends and implementation of investment decisions. Investments are made in a combination of equities, currencies and bonds in various world markets. As they are not UK regulated they can invest in a wider range of assets than onshore unit trusts.

Umbrella funds allow an investor who has purchased units in one of the sub-funds under the umbrella, eg European, later to switch cheaply and efficiently into another sub-fund, eg North American, or to a currency sub-fund or a bond fund.

Hedge Funds

Whereas fund managers tend to focus on the long-term potential of investment, hedge fund managers seek to balance the good long stock selection with a stock selection on which the risk is managed. By appropriate leverage or gearing, the profits can be maximised. In a rising market, the hedge fund manager will seek to select those good stocks rising more than the market together with a short position on stocks which are rising less than the market. In a falling market, the good long stocks fall less than the market and the shorts fall more than the market.

There is a wide range of hedge funds including:

macro	–	which take positions on world macro economic conditions;
global	–	which take world politics including emerging market;
long only	–	which buy undervalued securities, but do not hedge;
short only	–	which sell overvalue securities, but do not hedge;
market neutral	–	which take offsetting position in closely related financial instructions, arbitrating price differences;
sectoral	–	particular industries;
event driven	–	mergers or liquidations;
fund of funds	–	invest in other hedge funds.

The number of hedge funds has grown significantly over the last few years.

Most of the funds are based offshore. The managers may use a variety of investment techniques to seek to achieve their objectives, and it may be difficult for the investor to know the risks which are likely to be involved. By gearing up with borrowing, the risks can be magnified if things go wrong. These funds are primarily for high net worth individuals with high-risk profile in which the hedge funds would form a part of the investment portfolio. Recently, a range of hedge 'Fund of Funds' has entered the market. However, these types of investments are still only suitable for experienced investors.

Taxation Aspects

Generally

Gains made by most UK resident investors in 'roll-up' funds will be subject to income tax together with the income which has been rolled up. This charge to income tax is reduced to a CGT charge if the fund has 'distributor status'. The main test for this is that it distributes 85% of its net income after charges and other expenses which would have been charged to corporation tax if it had been resident in the UK. Commodity funds are treated more favourably.

Distributor status is achieved on a year-by-year basis by agreement with the UK HMRC.

The fund itself will normally suffer only a nominal charge to corporation tax in the tax haven and possibly also some irrecoverable withholding tax, particularly if, for instance, UK shares are held. Fixed interest funds investing in gilts and Eurobonds avoid this problem for the time being.

UK Resident Investors

Funds with Distributor Status Dividends from the fund are paid gross to investors and are taxable under Sch D Case V. The individual will be liable to income tax at both basic and higher rate on the dividend received. Dividends are subject to the 10% rate for lower or basic rate taxpayers and 32.5% for higher rate taxpayers.

CGT will be payable in the normal manner on profits arising on the disposal of shares by the investor.

These funds are often not available to minors.

Funds without Distributor Status, for example Roll-up and Other Funds

Where no dividend is paid (as with accumulation shares) the gross income is accumulated within the fund until the investor sells his shares.

There is an income tax charge on the income rolled-up (accumulated) but this is not assessed until the fund units are sold. This charge effectively replaces any CGT charge, and the loss of taper relief compared to other investments needs to be taken into account.

As the income assessable on holders of roll-up and non-distributor status fund units is taxed under Sch D Case VI; if the disposal of a material interest in an offshore fund results in a loss then the unindexed gain is treated as nil. Where the disposal results in both an income gain and capital gain, the income gain is set off against the capital gain; however CGT annual exemption cannot be used to mitigate the tax liability.

Investors resident but not domiciled in the UK for tax purposes will be subject to UK tax only on income and gains to the extent of remittances.

Overseas Investors

There is no liability to UK tax, and overseas investors in funds with or without distributor status will be taxed according to the laws of the country in which they are resident.

Offshore Portfolio Bonds

The tax treatment should be contrasted with that pertaining to offshore portfolio bonds (see Section 3.16).

CROSS REFERENCES

3.11   Employee Share Schemes

Description	Schemes which enable directors and employees to acquire shares in their employer companies in a tax-efficient manner.
Suitable for	Companies who wish all employees or selected employees to participate in and help to ensure the future growth of their company.
Advantages	1 Gives employees a sense of identity with their company and an incentive to increase their personal value to the company.
	2 HMRC approved schemes confer tax advantages for employees.
	3 Under some schemes shares can be acquired at less than their market value.
	4 Some schemes allow shares and options to be given to selected employees only.
	5 Some schemes give entitlement to dividends and voting on allotment of shares.
	6 Some schemes will give a corporation tax deduction for the 'profit' the employee receives for receiving the shares at less than their market value.
	7 EBTs can create a market for unlisted shares.
Disadvantages	1 Some schemes must satisfy detailed conditions.
	2 Some schemes must allow all employees in certain classes to participate.
	3 The employee may be required to provide funds for the purchase.
Investment limits	Vary considerably depending on the type of scheme.
Charges	One-off professional costs in setting up the scheme, although these will usually be tax deductible.

FURTHER DETAILS

Company Share Option Plans (CSOPs)

These schemes are attractive to any company wishing to reward and motivate its personnel by providing them with the opportunity to participate as shareholders in the success of their company. Generally, there is neither an income tax charge nor a Class 1 National Insurance liability on the grant or exercise of an option under these schemes, and so most companies will find their introduction attractive. Such schemes are also beneficial, as companies can select and award individuals entirely at the discretion of the Board. Specific conditions can be set which must be met before an individual is entitled to exercise his or her option.

HMRC approval is required before any options are granted. All employees and full-time directors of the company (or group company) may participate. Full-time for directors means 25 hours per week excluding meal breaks. No person who personally, or with associates, owns more than 25% of the shares may participate if the company is a close company for tax purposes. Quoted and unquoted companies may establish schemes.

The shares available under the scheme must be fully paid, non-redeemable ordinary shares in the ultimate parent company and not subject to restrictions which do not attach to all shares of that class. The one exception is that an employee leaving the company can be required under the company's articles to dispose of the shares on leaving.

Options may not be transferred and must generally be exercised between three and ten years after they are obtained, if a tax charge on the exercise of option is to be avoided. The total value of shares subject to an employee's option held under the CSOP or other approved discretionary scheme must not exceed £30,000 (at option price). The option price must be stated at the time the option is granted and must not be less than the market value of the shares of the company at that time. If the company is unquoted, the share value will need to be agreed with HMRC before options can be granted.

Options granted in excess of £30,000 can be held as Unapproved options. Unapproved options are not subject to income tax relief.

A participant will be required to fund the purchase of the shares on the exercise of the option. Normal methods would include an immediate sale of some of the shares or funding from the employing company by way of a cash bonus or loan. It should be noted that company law now allows loans to directors, but only if certain conditions are met.

Enterprise Management Incentives (EMI)

The EMI scheme is aimed to help small companies attract and retain the key people they need and to reward these employees for taking a risk and investing their energy and skills in helping the company achieve its potential.

The EMI scheme is a tax-advantaged share option scheme under which an employee can be granted options over shares worth up to £120,000 (with effect from 6 April 2008) at the time of grant. Generally, the grant and exercise of the option is tax-free with CGT being chargeable on the ultimate disposal of the shares, (assuming the shares themselves are free from restrictions or other artificial influences).

To be a qualifying option, it must be granted for commercial reasons to retain or recruit an employee; the employee must not hold more than £120,000 of unexercised EMI options (unexercised CSOP options count towards this limit) this is the maximum limit in a three-year period starting with the date of grant of the options. Employees with £120,000 of EMI options who exercise those options within three years of that date are not able to 'top up' their EMI options until the three-year period has expired. The total value of unexercised options granted by the company (or group company) must not exceed £3m.

Employees must:
- be an employee of the company or of a qualifying subsidiary;
- work 25 hours per week for the company or, if less, 75% to the company or the group of his total working time;
- not have a material interest in the company or the group which with associates must not exceed 30%.

Options must be over shares which are fully paid up, non-redeemable ordinary shares, and the option must be in writing and capable of being exercised within ten years of the date of grant and non-assignable (except on death).

A company can grant EMI options only if it meets all the qualifying conditions at the time the options are granted:
- The company must be independent and not under the control of any other company. A wide definition of control is used, and groups of family shareholders with associated companies should check this carefully.
- The company must ensure that any company it controls is a 51% subsidiary (or a 90% subsidiary if it is a property managing subsidiary). Again a wide definition of control and connected persons is used.
- The value of the company's gross assets must not exceed £30m and where the company is a parent company the aggregated value of the group's assets must not exceed £30m and, from 21 July 2008, they must have fewer than 250 employees.
- The trading activities of the company (or group) must be the carrying on of one or more qualifying trades. No substantial part of the business may consist of non-qualifying activities, ignoring incidental activities which have no significant effect.
- It must exist for the purposes of carrying on a qualifying trade. Most trades will qualify, but there are some, for example leasing, financial activities, farming and property development, which are excluded and, from 2008, shipbuilding, coal and steel production. There is no requirement for the company to be resident in or incorporated in the UK, but to qualify for EMI, the company's trading activities must be carried out wholly or mainly in the UK. With a group it is sufficient if one group company trades mainly in the UK.

Unlike other tax advantaged share schemes, there is no requirement for advance approval to be sought from HMRC. Instead, each time an option is granted a notice must be given by the company to HMRC within 92 days of the grant, confirming that the requirements of the EMI legislation have been met. There is no need to notify HMRC of alterations to share capital. Alterations which do not increase the value of the shares or where the increase is merely a side effect from some other purpose will not negate an EMI option.

Share Incentive Plan (SIP)

The SIP legislation provides for three main types of plan. They are:
- *free shares* – employers can give each employee free shares worth up to £3,000 each
- *partnership shares* – employees can use up to £1,500 per year out of pre-tax and pre-National Insurance contributions (NICs) pay to buy partnership shares

- *matching shares* – employers can give matching shares at a ratio of up to two matching shares for each partnership share bought by the employee. Various combinations of types of plan share can be used, for example, free shares only, or partnership with or without matching shares, or another combination to suit the business needs of the company.

The purpose of the plan must be to provide benefits to all eligible employees of the company (or participating group). Broadly, eligible employees are employees of the company or participating group company. The company can impose a minimum service requirement of not more than 18 months. 'Group' extends to any company a company controls. All eligible employees who are resident and ordinarily resident in the UK must be included, and others may be included. Employees must not have a material interest in the company awarding the shares, a company controlling that company or a consortium which owns the company. Material interest is control directly or indirectly of 25% of the ordinary share capital.

Participation must:

- be on the same terms (although free shares can be geared to remuneration, length of service etc);
- not allow directors or higher-paid employees to have preferential treatment;
- not impose further conditions; and
- not be associated with loan arrangements for the employees.

An employee cannot participate in more than one SIP at the same time.

Free shares up to a value of £3,000 may be awarded in any tax year and must be held by trustees for a period of three to five years. Objective performance measures may be used and, if used, must apply for all qualifying employees, and employees must be notified of the measures.

Partnership shares may be purchased by the employee under the plan by means of salary deductions. Annual contributions must not exceed the lower of 10% of salary and £1,500. The company may set a minimum contribution of not more than £10. The deductions are made before tax out of gross income.

Matching shares may be awarded alongside partnership shares up to a maximum of 2:1, ie shares worth a maximum of £3,000. The provision of these shares is free of income tax and NIC.

Dividends received on shares may be reinvested in shares up to a total of £1,500 pa.

Shares must be ordinary shares, fully paid up and not redeemable and only certain restrictions on the shares are permitted, including pre-emption rights contained in the company's articles. Shares must be listed or in a company not under the control of another, or in a non-close company under the control of a listed company.

The SIP must be sent to HMRC for approval. A UK trust must be established to administer the various shares and monies held under the plan.

Savings Related Share Option Schemes

These schemes enable participants to subscribe for shares in their employing company or group under an approved share option scheme out of a linked accumulated savings arrangement which the participant has made under a bank or building society save-as-you-earn (SAYE) contract.

HMRC approval is also required for this type of scheme. SAYE share option schemes allow employees to save between £5 and £250 per month and use the proceeds to buy the shares after three, five or seven years. A tax-free bonus is paid at the maturity of the SAYE contract. This can also be used to exercise the option.

The bonus rates are set by HM Treasury in accordance with a formula linked to market rates.

The scheme has to be open to all eligible employees of the company. A qualifying period of employment can be set but this must be no greater than five years. The majority of companies operating a SAYE scheme include all those employed as at the date of invitation.

The option price for shares under an SAYE scheme can be at a discount of up to 20% of the market value of the shares at the date the option is granted. Historically, employers have granted options at the full 20% discount.

Individual Savings Accounts

Shares received on the exercise of SAYE share options, and shares still held at the end of the five-year SIP 'retention period', may be transferred, within 90 days into an ISA without any liability to CGT, provided that the market value of the shares may not exceed the available ISA subscription limit (£10,200 from April 2010).

Unapproved Share Schemes

Given the statutory limits and other conditions that apply to approved share schemes, many companies will consider operating an unapproved share scheme whether to top-up options under a CSOP or EMI scheme or to replace them where those schemes are not available or appropriate. As they are tax unapproved, there is considerable flexibility in how these schemes are designed. Nil cost options, joint-share and growth-share ownership plans are popular variants.

EBTs

Employee benefit trusts (EBTs) are discretionary trusts set up for the benefit of employees, former employees and their dependants. Generally, the trustees of an EBT have wide powers to provide benefits in such manner and to such beneficiaries as they see fit. Some EBTs are limited to providing share related benefits (sometimes called employee share ownership plans or ESOPs). While these trusts can operate alone, they are often linked to one of the forms of share scheme discussed above. An EBT has a variety of uses. For example, it may enable an unlisted company to provide a market in its shares thereby bringing to life employee share incentive schemes in such companies. EBTs are also becoming an important element in management buy-ins. There are significant advantages for listed companies which establish an EBT, eg the facility to 'warehouse' shares at an advantageous price for distribution to employees at some stage in the future.

General

The tax treatment of the various share schemes is summarised below. However, there are a number of other considerations when establishing a share scheme and these are briefly listed below:

1 company law aspects must be considered, for example the need to obtain shareholder approval, shareholder pre-emption rights and financial assistance;
2 the impact of the Financial Services and Markets Act 2000;
3 for listed companies, the Listing Rules must be considered. Broadly these require most forms of share schemes to be approved by shareholders in general meeting;
4 for listed companies, the attitude of institutional shareholders and their representative bodies. In particular, the Association of British Insurers and the National Association of Pension Funds produce guidelines of the operation of share incentive schemes;
5 the accounting implications of any scheme. Financial Reporting Standard 20 'Share-based Payment', which applies to all UK companies other than 'small' companies exempted by FRSSE, requires a company to charge to profit and loss the cost of making share awards.

Each of the above is outside the scope of this publication, but nonetheless they should not be overlooked.

Taxation and National Insurance Aspects

CSOPs

No income tax or National Insurance is charged on the grant of the option. Income tax is not charged on exercise provided the option is exercised more than three years after grant or if the option holder is a 'good leaver'. A good leaver is one who leaves employment due to injury, disability, redundancy or retirement. In all other cases an income tax charge will arise on exercise. The charge will be on the difference between the market value of the shares at the time of exercise and the exercise price. If the shares are 'readily convertible' on exercise the amount of income tax must be accounted for under PAYE. In addition, a liability to National Insurance contributions will also arise. When the shares are sold, CGT will arise on the excess of the disposal proceeds over the exercise price (or if income tax was charged on exercise, on the excess of the disposal proceeds over the market value at exercise).

Enterprise Management Incentives (EMI)

No income tax or National Insurance is charged on the grant of the option. There are a number of conditions that must be satisfied both at the date of grant and through the life of the option. Provided these are satisfied, the option is exercised within ten years of grant (no minimum holding period required) and the exercise price is at least equal to the market value of the shares at the date of grant, no income tax arises on the exercise of the option. An option exercised more than ten years after grant is taxable under the normal rules relating to unapproved share options.

The EMI rules allow for the use of nil cost and discounted options. However, in these circumstances there is both an income tax charge at exercise on the difference between the exercise price and the lower of the market value at the date of grant and the date of exercise. If there is a market for the shares on exercise the income tax must be accounted for under PAYE. A liability to National Insurance contributions will also arise.

CGT will be charged on the gain when the shares are sold. For disposals after 23 June 2010, CGT will be charged effectively as a top slice of income, with a rate of 18% on gains within the available basic rate band and 28% on the excess.

However, in a relatively small number of situations a participant may be able to qualify for 'Entrepreneurs' Relief' and be able to benefit from a 10% rate of CGT. The 10% rate will apply to an individual's first £5 million of chargeable gains (post 23 June 2010) where certain conditions are met, namely:

(i)   the business is an unquoted trading company;
(ii)   the Participant is an officer or employee of the company;
(iii) the Participant holds at least 5% of the ordinary shares in the capital of the company as well as 5% of the voting rights; and
(iv)   the Participant has held the qualifying interest, obtained on the exercise of the option and acquisition of the underlying shares, for a period of 12 months before the date of disposal of those shares.

The EMI rules allow an employee to receive no more than £120,000 of EMI options in a three-year period starting with the date of the grant of the options which took the employee to the limit. Employees with £120,000 of EMI options who exercise those options within three years of that date are not able to 'top up' their EMI options until the three-year period has expired. As well as EMI options, employees will also be able to hold options under the SAYE savings related share option scheme. Where an employee holds approved share options under ITEPA 2003 Sch 4 (CSOPs), other than SAYE options, any unexercised options under that scheme are treated as unexercised qualifying options under the EMI. This means that it will not be possible to hold options of £120,000 under the EMI and £30,000 under an approved share option scheme.

Share Incentive Plan

No income tax or National Insurance is charged when shares are awarded or acquired as partnership shares.

Employees who keep their shares in the plan for five years will pay no income tax or National Insurance on the value of the shares. If they keep the shares in the plan for more than three years but less than five years, they will pay income tax on the lower of the market value of those shares at the time and the initial market value of those shares. If there is a market for the shares, the income tax must be collected under PAYE and a liability to National Insurance contributions will also arise. However, any increase in the value of the shares while in the plan will be free of income tax and National Insurance. In limited circumstances shares may leave the plan within three years. In this case income tax is due on the market value of the shares at that time (and if relevant, PAYE and National Insurance contributions will also be due). Employees who sell their shares will be liable to CGT only on any increase in the value of their shares after they have come out of the plan.

Employers will get corporation tax relief on the costs of setting up and running the plan, including the cost of any free or matching shares, and the cost of providing partnership shares to the extent that this exceeds contributions received from employees.

Savings Related Schemes

Generally, no income tax or National Insurance arises on the grant or exercise of the option. However, in the event of an early exercise of options within three years from the date of grant, the employee may have to pay income tax on any gain. CGT only will be charged on the excess of disposal proceeds over the amount paid for the option shares. There is no tax on SAYE proceeds.

Unapproved Share Option Schemes

No income tax is charged on the grant of the option.

On exercise of the option, income tax will be charged on the difference between the exercise price and the market value of the shares. If there is a market for the shares, the income tax must be collected under PAYE and a liability to National Insurance contributions will also arise. On the subsequent sale of the shares CGT is chargeable on the sale price less the market value on the date of exercise. See however below where the tax treatment is varied if the underlying shares themselves are 'restricted' shares.

For some companies with highly volatile share prices, the unpredictability of the employer's National Insurance liability which would arise on unapproved option share option gains was of real concern. In particular, companies were concerned that there would be an adverse effect on their reported results and cash flow. In response, law has been introduced allowing the employer to agree with the employee that the employers charge should be picked up by the employee. If the employee agrees, he is able to claim tax relief for the additional expense incurred.

Unapproved Share Arrangements

With unapproved share arrangements which are not in the form of options, the basic rule is that if the shares are obtained by reason of employment, the recipient is liable to income tax on the difference between the price paid for the shares and the market value of the shares when acquired. If the shares are 'readily convertible' when acquired, the income tax will have to be collected through PAYE and a liability to National Insurance contributions will also arise.

Special rules apply if the shares are acquired subject to restrictions, for example on the ability to vote the shares or receive dividends, or if the recipient is at risk of losing the shares, for example on leaving employment. Depending on the circumstances, all or part of the income tax charge may be deferred until the relevant restriction is lifted (and be based on the value at that time). Alternatively, it is sometimes possible to elect to be taxed in full at the outset (with any subsequent growth in value being subject to CGT). Any such election must be made jointly by the employee and employer and within 14 days of acquisition.

Special rules also apply if the shares are convertible. In this case part of the tax charge is deferred until the shares convert, but is then calculated based on the value of the shares at that time.

Employee Benefit Trusts

A tax deduction for contributions made to an EBT is generally only available where the EBT makes corresponding payments to beneficiaries which are both subject to PAYE and liable to National Insurance contributions (or where they are used to meet certain qualifying expenses).

Corporation Tax Relief

Broadly, corporation tax relief is available for an amount equal to the market value of shares awarded to employees (or shares acquired on the exercise of options), less any amount paid for the shares. The deduction is available to the employer and is intended to mirror the amount on which the employee is liable to income tax (or would be but for the fact that the scheme is tax approved). The deduction is available even though there may be no actual expense incurred by the employer (for example if the shares are issued direct to the employee).

There are a number of conditions that must be met which primarily relate to the shares. Broadly if the shares are ordinary shares, fully paid-up and non-redeemable and the company is not under the control of another company (or is under the control of a listed company), tax relief should be available.

PAYE and National Insurance

Employers are obliged to apply PAYE tax and National Insurance contributions where a liability to income tax arises in connection with share options and share awards to employees except where the shares/options are obtained under HMRC approved schemes (there are limited exceptions).

In practice, the requirements will only catch shares/options where the shares are quoted on a recognised stock exchange or where the shares are 'readily convertible assets'. Quoted company schemes will therefore almost always be caught, as will shares where trading arrangements are in place, or are likely to come into existence. This is likely to include schemes with an EBT, or where a company sale or flotation is anticipated. Unquoted shares may therefore also fall within the provisions. Shares where the employing company is not eligible for corporate tax relief in respect of the shares, are also automatically treated as readily convertible assets. This would capture shares in overseas companies and shares in the subsidiary of an unquoted company. Consequently, only shares in an unquoted parent company are capable of not being readily convertible and therefore being outside the scope of PAYE and National Insurance contributions.

CROSS REFERENCE

Shares   **3.6**

3.12 Enterprise Investment Scheme

Description	The EIS provides income tax and CGT relief to encourage outside equity investment in unquoted trading companies. The scheme is also suitable for 'business angels' who want to provide expertise as well as finance by becoming paid directors.
Suitable for	Basic or higher rate taxpayers interested in speculative equity investment over the medium to long term. Those who wish to defer CGT.
Ages	No practical limit.
Advantages	1 Income tax relief at 20% on qualifying investments up to £500,000 in any tax year, must be held for three years. Income tax relief can be carried back to the previous tax year.
	2 Any increases in value of the EIS shares will be capital gains tax free, generally, if sold after being held for three or more years.
	3 If **any** (business or investment) capital gains are made on other assets within one year before and/or within three years after the EIS share subscription, any part of that gain can be elected to be deferred into the new shares.
	4 Any amount of CGT deferral relief can be claimed which is only limited to the amount of EIS shares subscribed for.
	5 Income tax or CGT relief can be claimed for losses made on disposal of qualifying shares.
	6 Allows unconnected investors to become paid directors while still qualifying for relief.
	7 The EIS shares should qualify for 100% IHT relief after being held for two years or more, exempting them from IHT.
Disadvantages	1 Income tax relief is limited to 20% on investments of up to £500,000 per tax year.
	2 High risk strategy involving investment in companies with limited asset backing.
	3 Certain trades do not qualify.
	4 Minimum three-year lock-in period if income tax relief or CGT exemption not to be lost.
	5 No clearly defined exit route.
	6 Maximum permitted shareholding of 30% in any single company, directly or indirectly.
Investment limits	Maximum £500,000 per tax year for income tax relief, no upper limit for CGT deferral.
Charges	None if private issue.

FURTHER DETAILS

Commercial Aspects

As with any investment which has tax advantages, the investor must consider the merits of the investment without those reliefs. The following matters should be considered:

- investment in smaller unquoted trading companies should be regarded as high risk with the possibility of capital being lost – asset rich companies are excluded;
- sponsored schemes may have costs which are disguised by the tax relief;
- the investment must be held for at least three years;
- it may be difficult to realise the investment as the market may be illiquid or non-existent;
- there are detailed rules to be observed (see below);
- can now invest in AIM listed company.

Taxation Aspects

Capital Gains Tax

This is set out in detail in Section 4.10, EIS Deferral Relief, together with the rules for qualifying investments and companies, which also apply for income tax.

Income Tax

A maximum of £500,000 subscribed for newly issued fully paid up ordinary shares for cash in an EIS will qualify for tax relief for each individual in any tax year. Husband and wife are each entitled to £500,000. Tax relief is given at the lower tax rate (20%) and is given before certain other reliefs and allowances. This may result in the loss of those reliefs and allowances if there is insufficient income in that year. The Income tax relief can be carried back to the previous taxyear if the maximum relief has not been attained.

Claims can be made once the qualifying trade has been carried on for four months, and must be made within five years of 31 January after the tax year in which the shares were issued.

The individual does not have to be resident in the UK but merely have a UK income tax liability against which to claim the relief. Trustees are not eligible to claim income tax relief on EIS shares, and will only be able to claim the CGT deferral.

There are complex rules preventing relief for investors (generally employees) connected with a company covering relationships with individuals and exclusion if more than 30% of the company or subsidiary can be acquired. Where the connection is by virtue of being a paid director, the relief is generally available provided the investor was not connected to the issuing company or involved in carrying on the trade in any capacity during the two years before and three years (five years for shares acquired pre-6 April 2000) after the issue or commencement of the trade if later.

Anti-avoidance legislation is in place to prevent relief for loan interest where monies are borrowed to make the investment.

Relief is withdrawn at the time of disposal if the disposal is made within three years of the share issue – or date it starts to trade if later –

(five years for shares acquired before 6 April 2000), and there are special identification rules. Any income tax relief initially given will not be clawed back for disposals after that period. Withdrawal of relief will take place if the investor receives value from the company. Transfers of EIS shares can be made between husband and wife and the recipient stands in the shoes of the transferor.

There is a gross assets test such that the value of the gross assets of a company and its subsidiaries must be less than £7m before, and no more than £8m after, the investment. For EIS shares issued on or after the date of royal assent of the Finance Act 2007 (estimated to be mid-July 2007) – the company must have less than 50 full-time equivalent employees at the date the EIS shares are issued. A full-time equivalent employee is calculated by adding all the full-time employees plus a just and reasonable addition of the part-time staff. Again from royal assent, the company must have raised £2m or less by issuing shares in the 12 months immediately prior to the new EIS share issue.

CROSS REFERENCES

Venture Capital Trusts   **3.13**
Income Tax – Exemptions and Reliefs   **4.3**
CGT – EIS Deferral Relief   **4.10**

3.13   Venture Capital Trusts

Description	A quoted company which invests at least 70% in qualifying unquoted companies which can include those listed on the Alternative Investment Market. Subscribers for VCT shares receive generous tax reliefs.
Ages	Taxpayers over 18.
Suitable for	Basic or higher rate taxpayers who seek tax efficient exposure in the small companies sector.
Advantages	1 A 30% income tax refund on up to £200,000 invested, as long as shares retained for five years.
	2 CGT deferral for shares issued before 6 April 2004.
	3 Tax-free income distributions.
	4 No CGT on any gain in VCT shares.
	5 Exposure to the high risk/reward small companies market through a collective vehicle with the buffer of tax reliefs.
	6 Up to 30% may be non-qualifying stocks including blue chip equities, fixed interest and even gilts.
Disadvantages	1 Income tax relief and CGT deferral relief (for shares issued before 6 April 2004) are only available for subscriptions for new shares.
	2 CGT on gains reinvested on shares issued before 6 April 2004 is only deferred, and remains payable on the ultimate disposal.
	3 No business property relief from IHT.
	4 No defined/guaranteed exits available.
	5 Possible shortage of genuinely good investment opportunities.
	6 High risk.
	7 £200,000 limit per individual per tax year.
	8 To gain income tax relief shares must be held for five years; if less, tax relief can be reclaimed.
Charges	Typically, charges are 5% initial and can be up to 3% annual.

FURTHER DETAILS

Commercial Aspects

To qualify for a VCT:

- the VCT's income must derive mainly from shares or securities and it must not retain more than 15% of the income;

- at least 70% of the value of the VCT's investments is represented by shares or securities in qualifying unlisted trading companies including AIM companies;
- no individual holding represents more than 15% of the VCT's investments;
- the VCT is listed on the London Stock Exchange or on any EU regulated market;
- investments of the VCT are made within three years of approval as a VCT;
- the investments must be used wholly for the purpose of a qualifying trade to be carried on by the target company or its 90% subsidiaries and used by the trading company within certain time limits;
- loans guaranteeing the VCT to receive monies are prohibited;
- 10% of each holding must be in qualifying shares and to achieve good performance a VCT manager will have to find a regular qualifying deal flow – there is a real danger that in seeking to be 70% invested in qualifying unquoted companies within three years (to ensure no loss of tax benefits to investors), a manager might be forced to consider investments which he would not normally consider;
- the target company and its 75% subsidiaries must not have gross assets exceeding £7m immediately before the time of the investment;
- bona fide paper for paper exchanges which result in the company shares becoming a subsidiary and conversion of convertible shares and securities which qualified will both continue as qualifying investments.

All the above will be dealt with by the VCT manager.

Although the minimum VCT holding period is five years (five years for shares acquired before 6 April 2000, and three years thereafter up to 6 April 2006), it is often difficult to see a clear exit at the three-year point. Tax reliefs are only available to subscribers for shares and not to those who buy in the market, and this may greatly reduce the demand for existing shares. Some VCT managers may liquidate portfolios to provide an exit, but this could possibly be against the interest of those wishing to stay in, especially if top-performing shares had to be sold to provide the required funds.

Taxation Aspects

Income Tax

Subscription in the shares of a VCT entitles an individual aged 18 or over to an income tax refund of 30% of the amount subscribed, subject to the amount of tax paid during the year. The maximum relief is £200,000 × 30% = £60,000 for the 2007/08 tax year. For shares issued between 6 April 2004 and 5 April 2006 the maximum relief was £100,000 × 40% = £40,000. These increased reliefs applied for the tax years 2004/05 and 2005/06 to compensate transitionally for the loss of the CGT deferral relief. For shares issued prior to 6 April 2004 the maximum relief was £100,000 × 20% = £20,000.

Distributions made by a VCT remain free of income tax. The dividend exemption will only apply if the VCT shares were not acquired for avoidance of tax. Disposals of the shares in the VCT within five years of issue will cause withdrawal of relief (three years for shares issued after 5 April 2000 and before 6 April 2006).

A major disadvantage of VCTs is the absence of business property relief (BPR) from IHT. As the VCT is itself quoted, then BPR is denied, whereas had the individual invested directly in many of the underlying companies, relief at 100% would have been available after two years.

Capital Gains Tax

See details under EIS Deferral Relief, Section 4.10, but note that VCT CGT deferral relief was withdrawn for shares issued on or after 6 April 2004. Deferral relief could be claimed in 2004/05 for shares issued up to 12 months prior to the disposal giving rise to the gain. This was the last date for deferral relief.

CROSS REFERENCES

Enterprise Investment Scheme   **3.12**
Income Tax – Exemptions and Reliefs   **4.3**
CGT – EIS Deferral Relief   **4.10**

3.14   Unit-linked Single Premium (Investment) Bonds

Description	A non-qualifying life assurance policy in which lump sums are invested. There is minimal life cover.
Ages	No minimum or maximum, although some product providers have an upper age limit.
Suitable for	Higher rate taxpayers who will become basic rate taxpayers, discretionary trusts and Accumulation & Maintenance Trusts. Those who are likely to gift (assign) the investment to others.
Advantages	1 There is no tax charge on withdrawals from the bond for basic rate taxpayers; higher rate taxpayers can defer or avoid the charge in certain circumstances. This is a maximum 5% cumulative tax deferred withdrawal from the initial investment.
	2 There is normally no CGT liability on the policy proceeds in the hands of the investor.
	3 An offshore version is available, where CGT and income tax can be deferred indefinitely providing collective investment funds are used within the bond structure.
Disadvantages	1 A potential charge to higher rate tax can arise. Note that this can occur when no profit (or even a loss) has been made.
	2 Income tax and CGT will be deducted from the bond's underlying income and gains within the life company's funds.
	3 Capital losses cannot be offset against an investor's capital gains elsewhere for CGT purposes.
	4 Currently a basic rate tax credit is given for higher rate taxpayers at 20%, meaning that 20% (40–20) extra tax is payable. With similar investments such as Fixed Rate Bonds an additional 20% (40–20) is also due. Unit trust and investment trust dividends are subject to an additional 22.5% charge on the gross dividend, which is the dividend received plus the tax credit (10%).
Investment limits	Minimum investment typically £5,000. No maximum.
Charges	Approximate charges – initial 5% of investment plus 1% annual management charge thereafter.
	Usually, the first switch each year is free. Thereafter, there is a 'switching' charge of £15 to £25 or 1.25% to 1.5% of the bid value of units switched for second and subsequent switching of funds.

FURTHER DETAILS

Commercial Aspects

Single premium bonds are investment contracts with a minimal life assurance element and can be used either to accumulate a growing capital fund for use in the future or to provide a more tax-efficient 'income' (return of capital) for the investor on a regular basis. Withdrawals from single premium bonds can be taken yearly, quarterly, and in some instances monthly, by periodic part surrenders of the bond.

Single premium bonds can have their underlying investments in either conventional life assurance or unit-linked funds, the latter being more popular due to their greater profit potential.

The investor in a unit-linked bond can choose a number of funds in which to place his investment. These are commonly equity, international, gilt, property, money and managed funds. A number of life companies also offer a with-profits fund link.

Each investment in a fund is normally subject to a minimum value of units, approximately £150–£250. The values of each fund are regularly published in the press, enabling the investor to monitor the progress of the investment.

Within trusts insurance, company bonds reduce the requirement for complex annual accounting, and the ability to assign segments of the bond to beneficiaries so that the proceeds are taxable in the beneficiaries hands can be useful.

Some single premium bonds allow the fund to be 'self-administered', through the investor's adviser. However, see below for the taxation penalties now being introduced. In addition the investor's own assets could be transferred into the bond, although a CGT liability could arise. Single premium bonds should be viewed as a medium- to long-term investment.

The life funds are subject to tax on both income and capital gains. Some life companies can write the policy on the life of a child, and there are attractions for school fees plans. Further, some bonds have been designed with no CGT arising on the fund. Distribution bonds pay out only the income arising on the bond, leaving the capital intact – subject to the value of the capital fluctuating. From a pure investment viewpoint, higher rate taxpayers should consider whether direct investment into unit or investment trusts would produce a greater after tax return.

A further point for any investor contemplating a with-profits investment bond is the application of the Market Valuation Adjustment (MVA). This enables the life company to revalue the investment if a large number of policyholders decide to withdraw their funds. Therefore, if the policy is surrendered the investor may receive less than the current value.

Comparison to unit trust investments may improve next year: this is because the internal rate of tax within an insurance company bond may become more effective than the tax on next year if/when the 50% rate is brought in.

Uses of Single Premium Bonds

1   Provision of tax-efficient 'income'.
2   Together with a ten-year maximum investment plan, the conversion of capital into either a tax-free income or the tax-free appreciation of the original capital invested.

3   The provision of school fees (see *The Young – School Fees* in Section 5.2).
4   Investment.
5   IHT mitigation.

Taxation Aspects

There is no tax charge on withdrawals from the bond for a basic rate taxpayer. However, care must be taken that withdrawals or encashment of the bond will not affect an individual's claim to full age allowance, if appropriate. The savings income arising on the underlying investment of the bond within the life company's fund is taxed at 20%. Capital gains arising are taxed at 20%, unless the bond is linked solely to government securities, in which case no charges to CGT arise. There is no annual CGT exemption in the bond.

Higher rate taxpayers can defer the charge to higher rate income tax for 20 years if they withdraw no more than 5% each premium year of their original investment. The unused annual 5% cumulative allowances can be carried forward and used in later years. For example, if no withdrawals are made in years one to four, in year five up to 25% of the original lump sum could be withdrawn without a charge to income tax arising at that stage.

Withdrawals in excess of 5% per annum are subjected to the difference between the higher rate tax and the basic rate tax credit, even when there has been no capital gain or, indeed, when there has actually been a loss. The procedure is followed on the eventual withdrawal of 100% of the original premium, total encashment of the bond, the death of the life assured or the assignment of the policy for money's worth. It must be noted that withdrawals in excess of the 5% could have an effect on the age allowance (for those over 65). The age allowance for 2007/08 is £20,900.

A measure of relief from the charge to higher rate tax is available if top slicing relief is claimed. It is possible to maximise this relief if the bond purchased is segmented into a number of individual policies. Withdrawals can therefore be made by the complete surrender of individual policies as opposed to a partial surrender of one single policy. For further details see Section 1.13, *Life Assurance Taxation*.

For the taxation aspect of offshore bonds see Section 3.16, *Offshore Bonds*.

As a general rule, losses cannot be offset against income. However, there is one exception. On final encashment of the policy, where the result of the chargeable gain calculation is a loss (deficiency), then the amount allowable as a deduction from income is the lower of the 'deficiency' and the total of chargeable gains previously attributed to the policy.

CROSS REFERENCES

3.15 Guaranteed Income/Growth Bonds and High Income Bonds

Description	A lump sum investment usually into a non-qualifying life assurance policy or combination of policies which guarantee a fixed rate of return throughout the policy term, usually one to five years. Returns are net of basic rate tax.
	Policies can either provide an income for the investor or provide capital growth over the policy term.
Ages	Minimum 16, no maximum.
Suitable for	Basic rate taxpayers who can tie up a lump sum for the policy term and who have a low attitude to risk.
Advantages	1 There is no liability to CGT or basic rate income tax on the bond proceeds.
	2 Competitive rates of interest can be offered. However, those with higher rates are closed to new business at certain levels.
	3 There is a fixed level of interest throughout the term of the bond.
	4 Medical evidence is not required.
	5 A high income version is available.
Disadvantages	1 A liability to higher rate tax may arise on the annual payments from the bond, on surrender or maturity of the bond or on the death of the investor during the term of the bond.
	2 The fixed return offered may become less attractive if interest rates rise or in times of high inflation.
	3 Surrender values before maturity date are not guaranteed.
	4 High Income versions contain capital risk. Capital sum will only be repaid at the end of the term if the underlying investment/ indices has performed within restricted range. Underperformance can lead to significant geared losses.
	5 When High Income Bonds contain a derivative, there will always be a risk that the counterparty may default.
Investment limits	Minimum investment typically £5,000. Usually no maximum.
Charges	None explicit.

FURTHER DETAILS

Commercial Aspects

These bonds are often issued to satisfy the insurance company's need for an immediate cash injection. Thus the offer period may be very short, the bond being withdrawn when the cash need is satisfied.

There are two types of guaranteed bond which both have policy terms ranging from one to ten years.

Growth Bonds

These are usually non-qualifying single premium endowment policies providing a guaranteed compound return per annum. On death or maturity of the policy, the original sum invested plus the compound guaranteed interest rate will be paid for each year during which the bond has been in force. Guaranteed Growth Bonds benefit from the underlying guarantees provided by the Financial Services Compensation Scheme.

Income Bonds

These are normally non-qualifying single premium endowment policies, the income being produced by part surrender of the policies, or a series of non-qualifying single premium endowment policies, each of which is consecutively surrendered to provide the guaranteed annual income over the term of the policy.

High Income Bonds

A number of insurance companies have offered high income bonds, typically providing income well in excess of that available from other investment products.

However, there is always a risk to the underlying capital which will only be returned in full if (usually) two world share indices, typically the FTSE 100 and S&P 500, do not fall over a pre-determined fixed term.

Due to the use of derivatives, there is normally a very high gearing on the downside with high income bonds. For example, a 5% fall in either index over five years can lead to a 40% to 50% fall in original capital returned to the investor.

Taxation Aspects

In all cases, non-taxpayers are unable to reclaim any element of tax paid within the fund.

Growth Bonds

On maturity or early encashment, or death of the policyholder during the term of the bond, a charge to income tax will apply on the policy 'gain' or 'profit' at a rate between the higher and basic rates of tax.

Income Bonds

Liability to tax will arise when more than 5% of the original lump sum is withdrawn annually as described above. At the end of the term or earlier death, the portion not previously taxed will also be subject to tax.

No liability to tax will arise on a basic rate taxpayer unless the return on the policy places him within the higher rate band. Some income bonds will contain an option for the investor to extend the bond on maturity on the terms the life office has available. However, this no longer defers any tax liability on maturity as a result of changes introduced by FA 2003.

The income payments are deemed to be net of basic rate tax and therefore an additional liability arises to higher rate taxpayers.

High Income Bonds

Tax treatment depends upon the underlying structure of the bond. So please check. If the structure is an insurance company bond, the liability to tax will arise when more than 5% of the original lump sum is withdrawn annually as described above. At the end of the term or earlier death, the portion not previously taxed will also be subject to tax.

No liability to tax will arise on a basic rate taxpayer unless the return on the policy places him within the higher rate band. Some income bonds will contain an option for the investor to extend the bond on maturity on the terms the life office has available. However, this no longer defers any tax liability on maturity as a result of changes introduced by FA 2003.

The income payments are deemed to be net of basic rate tax and therefore an additional liability arises to higher rate taxpayers.

CROSS REFERENCES

Life Assurance Taxation   **1.13**
Unit-linked Single Premium (Investment) Bonds   **3.14**

3.16 Offshore Bonds

Description	An investment in insured funds or other collectives, or indirect stocks held within an insurance company contract. The assets within the band are held by an insurance company based offshore, often being the offshore arm of a UK-based insurer.
Ages	Minimum 18.
	Suitable for higher rate taxpayers, especially those using their CGT exemption.
Advantages	1 No income tax liability until bond is surrendered or matures – this gives gross roll-up other than a small amount of withholding tax etc suffered on dividends and fixed interest stock held within the bond.
	2 No CGT.
	3 In many cases it is possible to switch between different collective investments at an extremely low or non-existent bid–offer spread.
	4 Proceeds from a maturing or surrendered offshore bond can be taken completely free of tax when combined with the period of non-residence.
Disadvantages	1 Costs are generally higher than for the onshore variety.
	2 Personalised bonds have come increasingly under attack from HMRC and some are now subject to a tax on deemed gains.
	3 Tax is not avoided for UK residents, it is merely deferred.
Investment limits	Minimum typically £25,000 – offshore bonds often carry investments well in excess of £10m.
Charges	Varied and depending on the amount of commission taken by the intermediary. If advisory remuneration limited to 1% then often 100% allocation rates are available with annual management charges of less than 1% in the first five years and less than 0.5% thereafter. There are also the underlying charges of any investment manager if collectives are used and these can be as high as 2%–3% per annum in the case of genuine offshore funds. If advisory remuneration is set as high as, say, 6% and the initial allocation rate can be reduced to as little as 94% or insurance company annual management charge may increase to approximately 2%.
	Overall, charges on large offshore investment bonds tend to be negotiable.

FURTHER DETAILS

When used intelligently, offshore bonds can offer a useful tax shelter. The assets within the bond are held by an insurance company based offshore, often being the offshore arm of the UK-based insurer. The UK resident investor merely holds a life insurance policy – the actual assets belong to the insurance company and hence no income tax is payable until the policy is surrendered or matures. The offshore insurance company has no liability to UK tax and therefore it does not have to account for corporation tax on income on an annual basis. In practice, this advantage may be fairly limited, as many dividends are received net of withholding tax or imputed taxes which are not reclaimable due to limitations on double tax treaties in the tax havens in which the offshore insurance companies are based – often the Isle of Man or Luxembourg.

Often the funds used are UK based, circumventing the problem of higher annual management charges. As many will be high growth/low yield funds, the disadvantages of withholding tax as mentioned above are fairly limited and easily compensated for by the ability of the fund manager running the portfolio to trade free of CGT.

Taxation

It has been widely accepted that HMRC have not liked offshore bonds for a number of years. They sought to use existing anti-avoidance legislation in the *Willoughby* case (*IRC v Willoughby* [1997] STC 995). HMRC lost the case and one of the key issues was that the owner of the bond merely has rights under the bond. It is the insurance company which owns the underlying assets.

HMRC has specific anti-avoidance measures targeted against personal portfolio bonds.

A personal portfolio bond (PPB) is a life policy where some or all of the property (ie assets) or index may be selected by the policyholder or a person connected with him. Direct investment in quoted and unquoted shares and securities are deemed to be selected and caught by its legislation.

Most offshore bonds invest in funds open to different classes of investment, and will therefore not be caught by the legislation. PPBs that are caught by the legislation will be subject to a 15% yearly charge geared to the policy year. The charge is compounded and is broadly 15% of the original investment plus 15% of notional or actual 15% charges since the bond was taken out. It may bear no relation to the investment performance of the bond.

The first actual charge is at the end of the policy year after 5 April 2000. For bonds taken out after 16 March 1998, most pooled investments are allowed. For bonds taken out before 17 March 1998 direct investment in quoted shares and less than 10% holdings in AIM or USM shares are also allowed; investments outside these categories will be allowed so long as no benefits have been determined by the disallowed investment since 5 April 1994.

Existing bonds should be reviewed prior to return to the UK after non-residence, and for UK residents to consider non-residence as a means of exiting from them. The surrender of a bond will be a chargeable event for income tax purposes, and not be subject to the five-year non-residence rule required for CGT.

On death, the income gain is calculated on the difference between the base cost and the surrender value immediately before death. If the offshore bond is held in a trust, the gain is treated as relevant income for tax purposes and a resident recipient or beneficiary would be subject to tax. A non-domiciled beneficiary is not able to claim the remittance basis.

CROSS REFERENCES

Offshore Funds   **3.10**
Income Tax – Overseas Aspects   **4.5**
CGT – Overseas Aspects   **4.13**

3.17 Traded Endowment Policies

Description	A with-profits insurance policy that has been sold to a market maker in such policies rather than surrendered back to the originating insurance company.
	Suitable for individuals wishing to gain access to the with-profits market without the high initial set-up charges associated with new policies.
Advantages	1 Smooth performance of the with-profits fund.
	2 Any initial charges on new policies are avoided.
	3 The vast range of policies available makes TEPs suitable for a number of purposes.
	4 Can be attractive for tax planning purposes.
	5 Managed portfolios of TEPs are now available.
Disadvantages	1 It is difficult to know whether the estimated maturity proceeds are realistic.
	2 Price of the policies is normally based on estimated maturity proceeds discounted backwards. This makes it difficult to assess whether a fair price is being charged for the policy.
Investment limits	Normally £5,000 capital sum upwards together with regular premiums of £20 per month upwards.
Charges	Often 2%–3% initial with underlying charges of insurance companies' with-profit funds and administration.

FURTHER DETAILS

The second-hand market in traditional with-profits endowment policies is more than 150 years old. From 1843 to the late 1980s it was conducted by a single auction house in London and total market turnover had reached only £5m by 1989.

The traded endowment policy (TEP) market makes it possible for policyholders to obtain more money by selling their policy than they would get from the life company if they surrendered it, and for investors to acquire a mid-term policy with attaching bonuses at a price which may give them a very attractive return with limited risk.

The main reason the TEP market exists is because many life companies' surrender values do not reflect the full inherent worth of their policies as continuing contracts. There is inevitably some penalty for the unilateral cancellation of a long-term contract by the policyholder. The fact that there is a shortfall, ie a difference between the life company surrender value and the policy's real worth, is what has created the TEP market.

TEPs are traditional with-profits policies with a guaranteed sum assured and attaching annual and terminal bonuses. When purchased, the guaranteed sum assured together with the annual bonuses paid thus far is guaranteed. Future annual bonuses and terminal bonuses are not guaranteed. Estimates are provided by market makers based on previous history, prevailing market conditions and expectations of future market conditions.

An investor in a TEP pays a capital sum together with the agreement to pay all future premiums until the policy matures. They will then be entitled to the maturity proceeds on maturity of the policy.

Taxation aspects

Qualifying Policies

These are subject to CGT, with the gain calculated as maturity proceeds less purchase price together with premiums paid. The CGT is assessed in the same way as it is for other assets. The receipt of benefit by the TEP holder in the event of death (of life assured), maturity, surrender or subsequent sale will give rise to a disposal for CGT purposes.

Qualifying policies can be transferred between spouses without charge to CGT, with the donee then receiving the proceeds free from CGT. Furthermore, it is possible to sell policies back to the main market makers and then purchase a very similar policy shortly afterwards so as to increase the base cost for CGT purposes, although taper relief should be considered.

Non-Qualifying Policies

These are subject to income tax with top slicing rules applying. Calculation is maturity proceeds less premiums actually paid on the policy from inception to maturity. Higher rate taxpayers will pay the difference between higher rate tax and basic rate tax. For basic rate taxpayers no further liability is due. Furthermore, CGT will also apply and the gain will be assessed as maturity proceeds less purchase price together with premiums paid by the investor, and also less the profit already charged to income tax. It should be borne in mind that age allowance may be affected for a basic rate taxpayer who is over or due to become 65 in the tax year of maturity.

Finance Act 2003

It is now not possible for an allowable capital loss to be generated which exceeds the amount of any economic loss. Furthermore, gains will not escape CGT because the disponer received the policy as a gift.

It was also previously possible for a basic rate taxpayer to vary the policy after purchase such that they may avoid a future CGT charge by making the policy non-qualifying. Although a chargeable gain would arise on subsequent disposal, there would be no tax charge for a basic rate taxpayer. For disposals of non-qualifying policies after 9 April 2003, the gain would be allowable against the taxable (income tax) capital gain, but that relief is limited to the economic loss (if any).

CROSS REFERENCES

3.18   Investment Property

Description	The acquisition of property to hold as an investment which will show real appreciation against inflation or provide an income, or both, and utilisation of the tax allowances and relief which are available.
Suitable for	Those who see property as providing balance to their investments and can take a long-term view and cope with the illiquidity if property is held directly.
Advantages	1 Property values have given good returns provided a long-term view is taken.
	2 A portfolio of let property creates annual income flow.
	3 No CGT on main residence.
	4 Interest relief on loans to acquire let properties.
	5 Substantial tax allowances for enterprise zone properties.
	6 Tax relief for furnished holiday lettings.
Disadvantages	1 Direct holdings of properties are relatively illiquid.
	2 Costs associated with management of the properties.
	3 Properties may fall vacant in times of recession.
	4 Enterprise zone properties can be high risk.
Charges	Stamp duty on purchase price of property, legal, management, sale and purchase cost.

up to £125,000 (or up to £250,000 for first time buyers)	Nil
£125,001–£250,000	1%
£250,001–£500,000	3%
£500,001–£1,000,000	4%
more than £1,000,001	5%

	The stamp duty threshold for non-residential purchases of land increased to £150,000 in December 2003. Properties bought in areas designated by the government as 'disadvantaged' have historically qualified for Disadvantaged Areas Relief (whereby the SDLT threshold was higher than for other residential properties). This relief will not apply for property purchases between 3 September 2008 and 31 December 2009 inclusive. Instead, the SDLT threshold will be the same as for all other property as shown above. The new threshold is higher than the previous disadvantaged Areas Relief threshold of £150,000.
Investment limits	For indirect holdings, say £1,000, and direct holdings of property, say £50,000, depending on location.

FURTHER DETAILS

This section gives details of the ways in which property can be held. Both the commercial and taxation aspects are described under each property heading.

Let Property

In its simplest form, an investor will acquire a property and let it out to tenants on a commercial basis. The acquisition would incur a number of costs including stamp duty, surveying fees, legal costs and possibly financial costs.

It is normally prudent to ensure that the properties are let under assured short-hold leases which are structured to run for specified periods only. If they are not short-hold leases, the tenant can have the right to occupy the property so long as they continue to pay the rent. This latter situation creates great difficulties when seeking to improve or dispose of the property.

All the initial costs are deemed to be capital, and will not be allowed as deductions for income tax. They will, however, be added to the cost of the property in calculating the capital gain on the property on its eventual disposal.

The normal method of acquisition of a property is by way of loan, and lenders will normally lend up to 75% of the value of reasonable properties. The interest payable can be claimed as a deduction against the rental income received on the property, substantially reducing the real cost of the borrowing. For higher rate taxpayers, the rate of relief can now be as high as 50% on the interest on the whole borrowing.

The rental income received is treated as taxable income, from which can be deducted all the normal expenses incurred in running the property, including insurance, maintenance, property taxes, interest costs, agents and accountants' fees, etc. The income is taxed under the property income rules in accordance with the rules applying to normal trading businesses.

All the UK properties are treated as one business except for properties which are not let at a commercial rent which are treated separately. For properties let at a normal rent, if the computation shows a profit, tax will be paid as part of the self-assessment procedure. If the computation shows a loss including the interest on the borrowing, this loss will be available to set against future income from that rental income business. Losses incurred on properties not let at a commercial rent can only be carried forward to be set off against future income from that property. It is not normally possible to charge a substantial salary or remuneration against the property, as HMRC do not consider that high remuneration is called for in managing such properties. The individual would need to be very involved with the running of the properties to be able to charge remuneration and even then the remuneration would have to be paid to someone else, possibly a spouse.

On eventual disposal, the gain will be subject to CGT. The base cost will be the initial acquisition costs including professional fees, plus any subsequent enhancement expenditure which was not allowed for income tax. The properties will not normally have been treated as business assets and therefore reliefs such as entrepreneurs' relief will not be available except in the case of furnished holiday lettings.

Gains on properties cannot be rolled over into the acquisition of new properties, as such new properties are not deemed to be trading assets. The chargeable gain can, however, be deferred by reinvestment into the shares of an EIS. If the property is acquired with the intention of making a gain on the property rather than letting it out, then HMRC could argue that any gain should be taxed as income as it will be treated as an adventure in the nature of the trade.

The task of managing and letting the properties is considerable if a number of properties are involved. It will be prudent to find a good agent to carry out this task on agreed terms. The matters to consider would be a balance between the quality of service which could be provided by the agent and the level of fees charged for this.

Again it would be best to have a portfolio of properties so as to balance the risk in, say, having one property unlet for a period. Before acquiring any property, it is prudent to prepare a profit forecast or cash flow on the property, taking into account estimated maintenance which may depend on the age of the property and the amount of rental income that can be obtained. In turn, this would depend on the quality of the property. Also the potential for capital growth needs to be considered carefully.

Furnished Holiday Lettings

This is a special type of letting to encourage the holding of property in leisure areas. The main advantage is provided by specific tax reliefs, and the net rental income from a UK holiday furnished letting is taxed as earned income. This enables a claim for entrepreneurs' relief (in certain circumstances) and roll-over relief to be claimed for CGT purposes on the sale of the property, and hold-over relief to be claimed for CGT purposes on the gift of the property. As the income is treated as earned, it qualifies as net relevant earnings, and therefore pension payments can be made against the income. If plant and equipment are purchased in connection with the holiday letting, capital allowances are available to provide a measure of tax depreciation. In addition, losses arising on the holiday letting are available to set against other income.

In order to qualify, accommodation must be available to let commercially to the public for 140 days per tax year and be let for 70 days. The property must not be occupied by the same person for more than 31 days during seven months within the year.

The new coalition Government has proposed changes to the special tax rules for furnished holiday lettings and issued a consultative paper in July 2010 on which responses were needed by 22 October 2010 so some fundamental changes will be taking place but these will not be effective until 6 April 2011.

Enterprise Zone Properties

Substantial tax allowances are available for long-term investment in properties located in designated enterprise zones. The tax relief is up to 100% capital allowance on the costs of acquiring the building. This can be set against the investor's taxable income with no upper limit.

The element of the purchase price that relates to land does not qualify for the capital allowance. Interest on loans taken out to acquire the property is treated as a deduction from the rental income. The rental income is taxed under the property income rules, which follow the lines, set out above.

The intention in the legislation was that property should be held for a period of at least 25 years, and this is therefore a very long-term investment. It is possible to create an effective sale after seven years by disposing of a very long leasehold interest in the property which is equivalent to the freehold, eg a period of, say, 999 years. If there is a complete disposal of the property within 25 years, then the capital allowance is withdrawn with a balancing charge.

On the commercial side, these acquisitions are generally high risk and only for the sophisticated investor with substantial taxable income against which to set the allowances. The quality of the rental income is often variable and occasionally non-existent. For this reason, a number of enterprise zone schemes provided a guarantee for the rental income for a number of years. However, after that period, the rental stream will depend on the appeal of the property to potential tenants. Often the enterprise zones are structured or located because of the unattractiveness of the area, and therefore a continuing rental income may be difficult. This causes problems if a loan has been taken out to acquire the property, as the interest on the loan will only be allowable against the rental income.

When the property is disposed of, the main attraction of the enterprise zone property disappears. The purchaser of a second-hand enterprise zone property is not entitled to 100% allowance on his acquisition costs, but only a 4% annual writing down allowance. This relief is being phased out and for 2009/10 will be at 1% and will be withdrawn completely from 6 April 2011. The prospective purchaser would therefore take this into account when structuring his price for the acquisition of the property.

Larger investors may be able to acquire the entire interest in an enterprise zone property, but enterprise zone trusts are available for smaller investors to take a portion of a property. The potential investor should look carefully at the terms of the trust to make sure of his rights when circumstances change.

Urban Regeneration

From 11 May 2001, renovation and conversion expenditure to convert vacant or under-used space over shops into flats for rent will qualify for 100% capital allowances on that expenditure. The focus is on urban regeneration in traditional shopping areas and availability to all property owners and occupiers, as long as they have an interest in the property.

The property must have been built before 1980; be not more than five floors including roof but excluding basement; the upper floors originally must have been constructed as residential; the ground floor at the start of conversion work must be rated for most business purposes; and, the upper floors must have been empty or used for storage for at least one year before conversion.

Conversion must take place within existing borders, and only access extension will qualify. Each new flat must be self-contained, with external access separate from the ground floor. Each flat must have no more than four rooms excluding kitchen, bathroom, cloakrooms and some hallways. High-value flats are excluded and are based on a notional rent table.

100% capital allowances will be allowed on the expenditure, and there will be no clawback of the allowances if the flat is sold, ceased to be used for letting, etc more than seven years after the flat is complete and ready for letting.

There will be a stamp duty exemption for land situated in disadvantaged areas as specified by the Treasury. It is not clear that this relief will have the same geographic boundaries as the capital allowances.

The rate of VAT is reduced to 5% on the costs of:

- renovating dwellings which have been empty for two years or more;
- converting a home into flats;
- converting non-residential property into a dwelling or number of dwellings; and
- converting a dwelling into a care home or house into multiple occupation.

The zero rate of VAT will be adjusted by Statutory Instrument to provide relief for the sale of renovated houses that have been empty for ten years or more.

Properties in Pension Funds

Commercial properties and certain tied residential properties may be held within a small self-administered scheme or self-invested pension plan. This is often a very effective way for the owner-managed business to acquire its trading premises. Details are covered in the relevant pensions sections of Part 2 of this Manual.

Main Residence

An individual's main residence is not subject to CGT on disposal. Where such a property is held over a long period, there would normally be real growth over inflation. By careful selection, it may be possible to obtain such tax-free growth over a short period either by speculating on properties which are expected to rise substantially in value because of local factors, or by taking a property and considerably improving it for 'on-sale'.

If part of the property is used exclusively for business purposes, then the capital gains exemption will be scaled down accordingly on disposal. It is therefore sensible to ensure that no part of the property is used exclusively for business purposes. In addition, it is possible to let part or all of the property without necessarily damaging the overall CGT exemption. The let should be on a residential basis.

Very substantial properties may have a restriction on the capital gains exemption, eg where the garden exceeds 0.5 hectare, but in these circumstances any amount of excess land should be taken at agricultural value rather than residential property value.

Where more than one property is held, it is possible to make an election within two years of the acquisition of the second property so that one of these properties shall be deemed to be the individual's main residence. This is an extremely valuable election, as the property does not then have to be used as the individual's main residence, although it may be necessary to justify to HMRC that the property is used as a residence. In most circumstances the property selected under the election to be the main residence will be the one to be sold in due course at the greatest gain. The property that is not subject to the principal private residence election, is very often held until death, when there will be no CGT in any case. Provided that an election is made, it can be varied in the future. This can, with careful planning, enable the last three years of ownership of a property to qualify for exemption with a more limited loss of exemption on the other property.

There are special rules where couples get married each owning a property, and these are set out in Section 5.4, *Married with No Children*. Also when married couples divorce or separate, there are specific rules again, and these are set out in Section 5.6, *Married with Older Children*.

Freehold Reversions

This concerns the purchase of a freehold over which a lease has been granted and which will expire in due course. The value of the freehold will be discounted, depending on the length of the lease that is remaining. Thus, the longer the lease, the lower will be the cost of the freehold. On eventual expiry of the lease, the leasehold interest and freehold interest merge together and become a much more valuable asset.

These investments are passive long-term non-income producing investments and any eventual profit will be subject to CGT in the normal way.

It is prudent to obtain legal advice when acquiring such reversions, to ensure that the implications of tenants' security or right to buy do not negate the acquisition.

Collective Investments

Given the cost of property, it is often not possible for an individual investor to be able to acquire very attractive properties or sufficient properties to create a balanced portfolio. The alternative is to consider acquiring shares or units in property companies or unit trusts. It is now possible to hold property shares directly or indirectly with the tax advantages of an ISA.

Shares

For the investor with a balanced share portfolio, investment could be made into shares in companies specialising in properties. It should normally be possible to select property companies providing the desired investment objective in line with that of the individual investor.

Unit Trusts

For those seeking a spread of investments, there are a few property unit trusts which hold investments directly in property. As with all authorised unit trusts, there is no CGT on investments within the fund and the investor is only subject to CGT on the disposal of the units themselves.

Real Estate Investment Trusts (REITS)

A company which is publically listed on a recognised stock exchange and will invest in commercial property. As long as at least 75% of the company's activity relates to the ring fenced property letting business both in terms of income and assets, it will benefit from favourable tax treatment.

Insurance Company Funds

The funds are structured on a unitised basis with the values fluctuating as the property values change and any gains are subject to tax at the life fund rates, which may make them less attractive than unit trusts.

Pension Funds

Property may be held in the tax-free environment of Self-Invested Personal Pensions or Small Self-Administered Pension Schemes (see Sections 2.5 and 2.10).

Personal Company

If properties are held in a personal company, it may be attractive on ultimate disposal to sell the whole company and thus save the purchaser stamp duty of up to 3.5% on the price at the rate of duty on stocks and shares of only 0.5%. Stamp duty on the shares of property owning companies is under consideration, and future changes to prevent the use of special purpose vehicles to minimise stamp duty on property transactions cannot be ruled out.

CROSS REFERENCES

3.19 Traded Options

Description	An option gives the right (but not the obligation) to buy or sell existing shares in a specific company at a fixed price up to and including a specific expiry date. With a traded option this right can itself be bought or sold, and its value will rise or fall according to the movement in the price of the underlying share and the length of time the option has to run.
Suitable for	Investors seeking to adjust the risk exposure of their Stock Market portfolios to take account of short- and medium-term expectations of market movements without having to borrow to purchase stock or to sell stock to generate cash. Most investors will seek professional advice before dealing.
Ages	Over 18. No maximum.
Advantages	1 Relatively low capital outlay required.
	2 The option to forward buy the underlying security can be profitable in a rising market and increases gearing.
	3 The ability to write call options enables a portfolio holder to provide limited insurance against an overall market decline.
	4 The FTSE 100 Index option and the gilt contract allow investors to hedge the main UK market, the main currency market and the gilt market.
	5 Traded options overcome the disadvantage of traditional options, viz limited time scale and limited gearing. Traded options also have the ability to be traded, an option not available on traditional options.
	6 No CGT on gilt options or on those on qualifying corporate bonds.
	7 Can be used defensively.
Disadvantages	1 Range of shares in which traded options available is limited.
	2 Good quality professional advice may be hard to find.
	3 Non-professionals find options hard to understand.
Investment limits	No maximum, subject to availability of cash or stocks to satisfy margin requirements for uncovered writers. Minimum dealing size is one contract (usually for 1,000 shares) where the option premium cost can be under £1,000.
Charges	Charges are generally negotiable and are exempt from VAT.

FURTHER DETAILS

Commercial Aspects

A traded option is a negotiable contract between the buyer and the seller. The buyer is willing to purchase or sell a specific number of shares of a Stock Market listed company at a fixed price over an agreed period for a price (ie the option premium). The seller is under an obligation to meet the requirements of the contract at any time.

A call option grants the purchaser the right to buy shares from the seller (ie writer) whilst a put option grants the purchaser the right to sell shares to the option seller.

In addition to over 70 contracts based on shares, there are contracts based on the FTSE 100 Share Index and contracts on LIFFE for gilt futures, Eurodollar futures, short sterling futures and Bond futures options.

When discussing options, the term 'risk management' is often used. It is important to note that options can be used to protect a position, ie to insure against a fall in price of the underlying security index. In fact this is arguably one of their best uses, but they have received far less publicity than one or two spectacular calamities.

Basic Option Strategies

1   Purchase call options by investor seeking right to purchase stock at a predetermined price in view of anticipated market rise.
2   Sell call options by investor seeking to insure himself against overall market fall.
3   Purchase put options by investor seeking right to sell shares at specific price for given period in anticipation of market fall.
4   Sell put options by investor seeking to acquire additional shares at a predetermined price below current price.

Taxation Aspects

Overall the CGT position is the same as for any security/investment. Options are assets for CGT, and when shares are acquired by exercising call options the option cost is treated as part of the cost of the shares[1]. Similarly, when shares are disposed of by exercising put options the option cost is deducted from the sale proceeds.

When shares are disposed of under a writer's call option the premium is treated as part of the sale proceeds, and when shares are purchased under a writer's put option, premiums are deducted from the share price.

Generally, the option and equity trades are now treated separately. For example, if a client purchases a £500 call for £1,000, the £1,000 is treated as a loss, if the option is exercised. The purchase of shares takes the £500 exercise price as the basis for CGT calculations.

The wasting assets rules do not apply to the option.

Where an option is not exercised, the chargeable gain or allowable loss (ie the difference between cost and proceeds) is treated as a disposal of an asset with a nil cost. Where a contract lapses at expiry the whole proceeds are CGT chargeable on the option grantor.

However, there is no CGT (and no CGT allowable loss) for gains/losses on options over UK Government stock (gilts) or qualifying corporate bonds.

Transactions in options which are structured to produce guaranteed returns are taxed under Sch D Case VI.

CROSS REFERENCES

Shares   **3.6**
Financial Futures   **3.20**
Stock Market Warrants   **3.21**
Commodities   **3.22**

3.20 Financial Futures

Description	A future is a legally binding contract between two parties to receive/supply a financial instrument at the agreed price dealt in the market. Financial futures have two major uses. The first is to allow investors to hedge their asset or liability positions against adverse interest rates, currency fluctuations and share index movements. The second is to trade in the contracts offered, in order to produce a profit based on market performance.
Suitable for	The very sophisticated personal investor usually with substantial assets. Sometimes also used by active smaller investors with a speculative interest.
Ages	Minimum age 18. No maximum.
Advantages	1 Allows investors to lock into a future lending or borrowing rate and hence reduce the risk of loss through adverse price movements in interest rates, currency rates or share prices by taking a position in future contracts which is equal and opposite to an existing or anticipated position in the cash market.
	2 Contracts are standardised, with buyer and seller knowing exactly what they are trading, and can be freely bought and sold at any time on LIFFE.
	3 The market is highly liquid but there was no indication of where it goes.
	4 Prices are highly competitive.
	5 Although margins have to be deposited, the minimum level may range from 0.1% to 6% of the face value of the contract.
	6 No CGT on gains in gilt or qualifying corporate bond contracts.
Disadvantages	1 A market mainly appealing to professionals and sophisticated individual investors.
	2 Standardisation of contracts can lead to lack of flexibility to completely hedge an individual's asset liability position.
	3 Price fluctuations can be volatile and large margin calls may ensue.
	4 No income.
	5 Unlimited liability on straight (eg not hedged) futures positions.
Investment limits	Minimum size is one contract and there is no maximum, provided margin requirements met.
Charges	Commissions are negotiated.

FURTHER DETAILS

Commercial Aspects

Commodity Futures Exchanges grew out of the need for a mechanism to protect producers and users of commodities from the effects of fluctuations in prices. Hedging is a defensive tactic used by investors to protect themselves against adverse interest rates, currency fluctuations and share movements in order to reduce the risk of a loss. This is done by taking a position in futures contracts equal and opposite to one's position in the cash market, for example where one will be receiving cash from a long-term investment in three months' time one can, rather than waiting to see what the prevailing interest rate will then be, lock into existing quoted rates by buying a financial futures contract at today's price which will mature in three months' time. Purchasing such a contract at currently prevailing rates locks one into these rates, and if they then move in the opposite direction to that expected, there will be a loss offsetting the corresponding gain in the cash market. Either way the investor will have locked himself into the rate prevailing when he purchased the futures contract.

Futures markets can also be used to trade and produce a profit based on one's view of where the market will go.

There are currently contracts on the London International Financial Futures Exchange (LIFFE) for interest rate futures, a three months' Sterling contract, a 20-year gilt interest rate contract and a US Treasury Bond interest rate contract.

An investor's order to a LIFFE member firm is executed electronically, and both buyer and seller have to put up a margin to the Clearing House in the form of cash or collateral to provide a cushion against adverse price movements for the futures contract. This margin varies every day, dependent on the movement of the futures contract. If a contract is held until delivery, then the buyer has to pay the seller the full value of the contract.

Futures contracts are geared instruments, since positions can be taken in the underlying asset by means of small cash outlay (the initial margin).

Taxation Aspects

Profits from transactions in futures (provided they are not regarded as being part of a trade) will be charged to CGT. The charge to CGT will apply to gains outside of the course of trade.

Transactions in financial futures which are part of an existing financial trade will continue to be taxed under Sch D Case I as trading income, although it will be somewhat unusual for private investors to be so assessed. Transactions in financial futures which are structured to produce guaranteed returns are taxed under Sch D Case VI.

There will be no CGT (and no CGT allowable loss) for gains/losses on futures contracted in UK Government stock (gilts) or qualifying corporate bonds.

CROSS REFERENCES

Traded Options   **3.19**
Stock Market Warrants   **3.21**
Commodities   **3.22**

3.21 Stock Market Warrants

Description	Warrants give the right (but not the obligation) to buy an ordinary share in certain listed Stock Market quoted companies at a fixed price on a fixed future date. Also 'put' warrants give the right to sell. The underlying warrants can, however, be traded and sold separately from the shares.
Suitable for	Individual investors wishing to obtain geared returns for relatively modest outlay. Even experienced investors would normally seek professional advice before dealing.
Ages	Over 18. No maximum.
Advantages	1 Market not dominated by institutions. 2 Returns are geared. 3 Limited amounts of capital required. 4 Many warrants attached to investment trust shares, thus giving an interest in companies with the underlying risk widely spread.
Disadvantages	1 Limited information available, so hard to follow. 2 Market can be very narrow and difficult to deal in. 3 Warrant holders get no rights to dividends or to vote and may lose all value if the underlying company is taken over. 4 Losses are geared if price moves wrong way. 5 No income.
Investment limits	Minimum size can be a few hundred pounds and whilst maximum may be many thousands, often stock availability curtails it.
Charges	Brokers' commission.

FURTHER DETAILS

Commercial Aspects

Warrants give the right to buy shares at a certain price (the exercise price) at specified future dates. Usually there is a final date by which they have to be exercised prior to lapsing and becoming worthless.

Warrants are a geared investment, ie movement in the price of a warrant is proportionately greater than the increase in the underlying share price. However, the gearing effect works both ways, not just on the upside.

The warrant price can reflect a mixture of two values, ie an intrinsic value in relation to the share price and a time value representing the opportunity to exercise it. By calculating how quickly the share price needs to rise between the date of purchase and final exercise date in order to make exercising the warrant worthwhile, an investor can judge whether the warrant is good value.

When share prices are falling the effect can work in reverse and investors need to be extremely cautious in such markets, and a lack of dividend is a further deterrent to investors requiring income.

The value of a warrant can be assessed by adding its current price to its exercise price and comparing the result with the current ordinary share price. This will almost always be greater than the existing share price, and the most attractive warrants are those which have the smallest premium and the longest time prior to the warrant expiring.

The warrant price takes into account expectations that the underlying share price will rise over the years prior to the final warrant exercise date.

Taxation Aspects

The investor will be liable to CGT on gains arising on the sale of his warrants, subject to the annual CGT exemption.

Warrants can be cash-settled and physically settled. Cash-settled warrants are simpler and more cost effective to exercise than physically-settled warrants because the investor simply receives cash from the issuer, but without the need to buy the stock and to pay stamp duty. Exercising a call warrant physically means that the investor acquires the stock and will have to pay dealing commissions and stamp duty.

Capital losses can be offset against other gains realised in the year; any excess over gains can be carried forward against future capital gains.

CROSS REFERENCES

Investment Trusts   **3.7**
Unit Trusts and OEICs   **3.8**
Traded Options   **3.19**
Financial Futures   **3.20**

3.22   Commodities

Description	A means of generating profits by investment in commodities, the prices of which fluctuate with world supply and demand.
Suitable for	Wealthy individuals with a very high-risk profile.
Ages	Minimum 18; no maximum.
Advantages	1 Potential for high investment return.
	2 Only 10% of the total investment needs to be 'put up' initially.
	3 There is the availability of managed portfolios and specialist unit trusts.
	4 Dealing costs are low.
Disadvantages	1 A very risky investment.
	2 Returns on physicals trading are treated as income rather than capital gains for tax purposes.
	3 Investment through a broker or futures market results in income being treated as investment income.
Investment limits	Minimum investment above £5,000, but since minimum is usually expressed in terms of quantity of a particular commodity, the minimum investment depends on the price ruling at the time. There is no maximum.
Charges	Buying and selling commission is commonly around 0.5% of the value of the commodity.

FURTHER DETAILS

Commercial Aspects

Commodities broadly fall into two categories: 'soft' (eg coffee and sugar) and 'metals' (eg copper, tin). Both categories are further subdivided, into 'physicals', where a delivery of a commodity would be expected and 'futures', where the contract would normally be terminated before delivery.

Speculators invest mainly in the futures market, ie they agree to purchase a commodity in, say, six months' time at a predetermined price. The speculator is counting on the price within six months' time being higher than the agreed price at which point the commodity is sold prior to its delivery. The majority of investment purchases are of futures.

For those who do not wish to make their own investment decisions, commodity brokers operate discretionary accounts. Here the investor deposits a lump sum and the broker deals with that money on the client's behalf.

As an alternative to discretionary accounts, the smaller investor can become a member of a commodity syndicate which then delegates its management to a commodity broker.

There are a number of UK authorised unit trusts which invest in commodity company shares, enabling the investor to spread his risk. Investment may also be made in unauthorised unit trusts and similar vehicles located outside the UK, but the additional risks should be carefully examined.

A number of commodity brokerages have introduced funds aimed at the public with a minimum of around £10,000 investment. These are structured so that there is a guarantee that the entire initial investment will be returned after an initial four- or five-year period. Part of the initial sum will be invested in a zero coupon security issued at a discount but maturing at the full value. Meanwhile the balance of the initial investment will be used to trade the futures markets (Financial and Commodity). Note the four/five-year lock-in period.

Taxation Aspects

Physicals

When the investor has made his own trading decisions, the profit may be treated as trading income under Sch D Case I. It is a question of fact as to whether a trade is being carried on.

When the trading decisions are delegated to a broker, the profit has normally been treated as income assessable under Sch D Case VI.

Futures

Profits from futures dealing, which is not part of a trade, will be taxed as capital gains with losses allowed as capital losses.

Generally

Commodities which are structured to produce guaranteed returns are assessed under Sch D Case VI The disadvantage of assessment under Sch D Case VI is that losses can be relieved only against other profits assessable under Sch D Case VI in current or future years.

Gains on the disposal of units in unit trusts by the investor will normally be taxed as capital gains. Where the unit trust is located overseas, any gain on the disposal of units will be assessed to income tax, unless the fund has distributor status. For commodity funds, the distributor status rules are modified.

CROSS REFERENCES

3.23 Endowment Assurance

Description	A life assurance contract which pays a sum assured on a predetermined maturity date or prior death.
Ages	12–75.
Suitable for	All taxpayers who wish to build up a tax-free lump sum over a long term.
Advantages	1 Proceeds of ten-year qualifying policies can be withdrawn free of all taxes after seven and a half years; longer term policies are free of tax after three-quarters of the term or ten years, whichever is earlier. 2 Relatively low risk investment medium for those wishing to build up capital over periods of ten years or more.
Disadvantages	1 Potential charge to the higher rates of tax may arise on surrender. 2 Surrender values are low during the first few years of the policy, especially with low cost endowments. 3 Corporation tax and CGT will be charged on the income or capital gains arising on the life company's funds. 4 Sum assured may prove inadequate in times of inflation. 5 Evidence of health is required, and cover may be expensive or unavailable for those in poor health and/or the elderly.
Investment limits	Minimum investment approximately £20 per month. No maximum.
Charges	For unit-linked policies, approximately 5% initial charge plus approximately 1% annual management charge and a monthly policy fee of approximately £1.50–£2.00 – fixed policy fee of approximately £2 per month for a with-profits policy.

FURTHER DETAILS

Commercial Aspects

The following endowment policies are currently available.

(a) With-profits

These policies are often the most expensive form of life assurance in relation to the initial sum assured, since the latter is increased by the regular addition of 'profits' or 'bonuses' periodically declared by the life company. The level of bonus is not guaranteed and, therefore, the future anticipated return from the policy can be assessed only on the past bonus declarations made by any one company. However, care needs to be taken when assessing a company's past performance, as there is no guarantee of future investment returns. With-profits policies can reduce the effects of inflation. The majority of life insurance companies pay two types of bonus (profits). Reversionary bonuses are usually declared annually and once added, they form part of the emerging policy proceeds and are guaranteed. In addition, many companies pay a terminal bonus at the maturity of the policy (and in some cases on earlier surrender). Some companies also pay special bonuses. Results may be smoothed over a number of years to ensure a good performance in bad years. Considerable disquiet is currently being expressed about the performance and lack of transparency of with-profits funds.

Unitised with-profits policies are structured so that bonuses are allocated proportional to each unit depending on its current value. It is more transparent to policyholders and they also have the facility to switch between unit-linked funds.

(b) Without-profits

With these policies the sum assured remains the same throughout the term of the policy and, therefore, the return will decline in real terms in times of inflation. The premiums are, however, much lower than those for the same initial sum assured under with-profits policies. Relatively few policies of this type are now issued.

(c) Low Cost

Such policies are a combination of a with-profits endowment and a decreasing term assurance, and were developed in connection with mortgage loans as an alternative to with-profits endowment mortgages. The endowment policy has a sum assured less than the outstanding capital under the mortgage, but by the maturity date the additional profits on the policy should have increased the sum assured sufficiently to repay the loan, but this is not guaranteed. The decreasing term assurance provides repayment of any shortfall under the endowment policy should death occur before the maturity date.

A variant known as 'low start' low cost endowment reduces the initial outlay even further, though the premium then increases each year, usually levelling off after the fifth year. There have been problems with these policies where, due to high initial commission and poor investment performance, it has become clear that the required maturity sum will not be achieved. In many cases premiums have been reviewed and increased quite sharply.

(d) Pure Endowment

These policies pay a sum assured on survival to a specified date. No return is, however, made should death occur during the term. These policies are now rarely used except in connection with some capital tax mitigation arrangements.

(e) Unit-linked

The premiums for a unit-linked contract may be invested in a variety of insurance company funds and sometimes unit trust funds, usually consisting of equity, international, property, money, gilt, managed and other specialist funds and also with-profits funds. The sum payable on maturity or earlier surrender reflects the underlying value of the particular units held.

There is a facility for switching the invested premiums between the various funds in order to take advantage of prevailing investment conditions. Most companies permit one free switch between funds each year, and thereafter charge either a fixed fee of approximately £15 to £25 or half a per cent of the bid value of the units switched for subsequent switches. If the investor does not wish to take an active role in managing his investment the premiums can be invested in the managed fund, the insurance company fund managers deciding for him the proportion of his premium to be invested in the various market sectors.

Unitised funds give the small investor the opportunity of investing in a mixed portfolio with the facility of professional management.

It should be noted that the maturity and surrender values are unknown and are dependent upon the performance of the units, which can go down as well as up.

A number of life companies offering ten-year unit-linked contracts include the option to take a tax-free income once ten years have elapsed. If such an option is effected, the capital sum on maturity is retained within the unitised funds, part surrenders being made by the policyholder as and when an income is required and to fund the continuing premiums required to maintain the qualifying status of the policy. The balance of the capital sum therefore grows within the unitised funds. No personal liability should fall upon the policyholder, as he will be receiving the proceeds of a qualifying life policy which are tax-free.

(f) Flexidowments

Such policies are written on flexible terms, say to age 65, but with the ability to cash them in after ten years with no surrender penalty and no loss of terminal bonus.

(g) Short-Term Savings Plans

These are applicable to non-higher rate taxpayers or those who will not be higher rate taxpayers on maturity. They typically run for five years, and because they are not qualifying policies they can have very flexible terms with variable premiums, minimal life cover and high investment content. On encashment or maturity, any gain will be subject to tax if higher rate or transferred into a single premium policy which defers any tax charge.

General

Endowment policies can be written on a joint-life, first-death or last survivor basis. Joint-life policies are generally cheaper than two single life policies. If the sum assured is due on the first death of one of the joint lives, it will be termed joint-life first-death, and if payment is due on the second death of the joint lives it will be termed last survivor.

It is possible to insure another's life but only if there is sufficient 'insurable interest'. The sum assured is paid to the owner of the policy on the death of the life assured. In the case of husband and wife, each spouse is deemed to have an unlimited insurable interest in the other's life.

The premiums for endowment policies will be lower, the younger and healthier the life assured. Female lives are generally underwritten at lower rates than male lives to reflect that on average, they tend to outlive males by approximately four to five years.

Uses of Endowment Policies

The main uses are for mortgages, school fees and pure savings and investment – but see also the cross references listed below.

Taxation Aspects

There is a potential charge to income tax on surrender of the policy (in part or in whole) within the shorter of ten years or three-quarters of the policy-paying term where the holder is a high rate taxpayer.

The encashing of accrued bonuses on with-profits policies is treated as a part surrender. If surrender of the policy occurs outside the limits mentioned above, the policy proceeds will be free of all taxes.

There may, however, be a policy charge imposed by the life company upon early encashment. When taking out policies it is prudent to segment the policies into a number of smaller policies to enable some policies to continue when others are cashed in.

No charge to CGT should arise on the payment of the policy proceeds.

CROSS REFERENCES

3.24 Maximum Investment Plans

Description	Ten-year qualifying unit-linked life assurance policies – the life cover being reduced to a minimum (although sufficient for the policy to obtain qualifying status), a high percentage of the premiums being invested in unit-linked funds.
Ages	Minimum 12, maximum 80.
Suitable for	Higher rate taxpayers who wish to build up a tax-free capital sum.
Advantages	1 The proceeds of the policy can be withdrawn free of all taxes after seven and a half years. 2 A tax-free 'income' can be taken after ten years provided the policy is maintained by continuing premium payments at a level no lower than 50% of the original premium. 3 An offshore version is available for non-UK residents, and if this is converted into a UK qualifying policy within 12 months of return to the UK, benefits can be taken free of tax.
Disadvantages	1 Potential charge to higher rate tax on early surrender. 2 Income tax and CGT will be deducted from the income within the life company's funds. 3 Medical evidence is required, and cover may be expensive or in some cases unavailable where the individual is in poor health.
Investment limits	Minimum investment £20–£50 per month. No maximum.
Charges	Approximate policy charges – initial 5% deduction plus annual management charge of 1% of the fund value and a monthly plan fee of approximately £1.50–£2.00. Switching charges between investment funds – £15–£25 or 1.25%–1.5% of the bid value of units switched for second and subsequent switches in any one year; usually one free switch permitted each year.

FURTHER DETAILS

Commercial Aspects

Maximum investment plans are designed mainly with investment, rather than life assurance, in mind. The life cover is, however, sufficient for the policy to be qualifying and therefore the policy guarantees a minimum death benefit for this purpose. Should death occur within the ten-year policy term, the greater of the guaranteed death benefit or value of the unitised investment fund will be paid.

The investor has a choice of funds in which to invest premiums and at least equity, international, money, gilts, property and managed funds are normally available. It is possible for the investor to switch between the various funds without a tax charge arising. Alternatively, he can invest in the managed fund, where investment fund managers will decide what proportion of the premium should be invested in the various funds. Unitised funds give the small investor professional management of a mixed portfolio.

At the end of the ten-year period the investor usually has one of the following options, or a combination thereof:
(a) to take the policy proceeds free of all taxes;
(b) to take a tax-free 'income' from the plan provided the policy is maintained by continuing premium payments at a level no lower than 50% of the original premium;
(c) to leave the capital to grow for future use;
(d) to continue paying premiums for a further ten years.

These policies can be written on a joint-lives basis, with the sum assured being paid out either on the first death or the death of the survivor.

It is possible to insure another's life if there is sufficient insurable interest. The life assured in that event would have no benefit from the contract, the sum assured being paid to the owner of the policy on the death of the life assured.

Use of Maximum Investment Policies

1   Provision of a tax-free capital sum.
2   Provision of a tax-free income.
3   Future provision of school fees (see *The Young – School Fees* in Section 5.2).
4   Funding any IHT liability which may arise on the death of the life assured. The policy in this case will need to be written in trust. (See Section 4.30, *Insurance for IHT.*)
5   These types of policy are also suitable for gifting amounts to minor children in order to mitigate IHT by writing the policy under trust and utilising the IHT exemptions. No liability to income tax for the parent would arise on the payments as life assurance policies are regarded by HMRC as non-income producing assets.

Taxation Aspects

If surrender of the policy occurs before seven and a half years have elapsed, a higher rate taxpayer will be liable to tax on the gain from the policy. If surrender occurs after this time the policy proceeds will be free of all taxes.

CROSS REFERENCES

Life Assurance Taxation   **1.13**
Unit Trusts and OEICs   **3.8**

3.25 Friendly Society Policies

Description	Qualifying life policies offered by registered friendly societies which provide a tax-free lump sum on maturity or prior death – ISA friendly.
Ages	No minimum, maximum 80.
Suitable for	All taxpayers requiring regular savings.
Advantages	1 The investment fund is exempt from income and corporation tax and CGT.
	2 The policy proceeds are free from all tax after ten years.
	3 Investment limits are available to both husband and wife and to each child.
	4 With-profits and unit-linked policies are available.
Disadvantages	1 Limits: £270 per annum/£25 per month premium in respect of life policies.
	2 Often there are high administration and management charges which detract from the fund performance.

FURTHER DETAILS

Commercial Aspects

Despite the relatively low maximum investment limits, friendly society policies have become increasingly popular as a savings vehicle. They are permitted investments for ISAs, although it would have been sensible to increase the limit from £270 to £1,000. Friendly society policies can no longer recover the 10% tax credit on UK dividends received after 6 April 2004.

CROSS REFERENCES

Whole Life Assurance **1.3**
Endowment Assurance   **3.23**
Individual Savings Accounts (ISAs)   **3.27**
The Young   **5.2**

3.26 Savings Accounts

INTEREST EARNING ACCOUNTS

Deposit account An account into which funds are placed sometimes subject to a period notice for withdrawal. Interest is variable and is usually added to the account on a half-yearly basis. The minimum deposit is generally £1; where there is a notice period funds can be withdrawn on demand, but interest equivalent to that which would be earned during the notice period is lost.

Qualifying Term Deposit account A lump sum investment for a fixed term at a fixed rate of interest. Minimum investment is approximately £2,000–£29,000. Interest is normally paid at the end of the term and therefore compares unfavourably with, for example, Money Market deposit. Interest may be paid without tax being deducted by UK resident banks to UK ordinarily resident individuals who deposit sums of £50,000 or more on fixed terms of seven days or more.

Seven-day and 28-day and 90-day access account Suitable for lump sums and often termed 'gold' or 'premium' accounts. Minimum notice for withdrawal is seven, 28 or 90 days, during which period interest is lost if withdrawals are made. Interest rate is higher than the share account. Minimum investment is usually £1,000/£500 and many now offer immediate access to money, although interest on the amount withdrawn will be lost.

Quick access term shares Suitable for lump sums which are invested for terms of one to six years. Up to three months' notice required for withdrawal, during which period interest may be lost. Interest usually 1%+ above the share account rate, and is guaranteed throughout the length of the term. The minimum investment is £1,000. Extra premium accounts are a derivative offering higher interest on deposits in excess of £5,000 or £10,000 over a fixed period with no additions being permitted.

High interest cheque account A savings account paying nearer money market rates than a conventional deposit account and having a chequing facility. The minimum investment is typically £1,000 or £2,500. Some accounts require minimum cheque withdrawals to be £200 to £500. A cheque guarantee card is often available.

Money Market account Funds deposited for a fixed term normally. Money cannot be withdrawn before notice given or term expired. Rate of interest is higher than deposit account and varies with amount invested. Minimum approximately £10,000 – no maximum.

Money Market and deposit accounts in the Channel Islands Interest rates obtainable are sometimes slightly lower but the interest accruing is credited without deduction for tax (see below).

Currency account   Deposit made in sterling and converted to the currency of choice. Account withdrawals can be made with notice, ranging from call to 12 months. The longer the term the higher the interest. At the end of the term, there may be a charge on converting the currency to sterling. Minimum investment £500.

Save As You Earn account   Regular monthly payment made into a Save As You Earn (SAYE) account earning 0.75%+ above the share account interest rate, often with a terminal bonus added after five years.

Save As You Earn transfer account   Enables a lump sum to be paid into an account from which monthly payments are made by the building society into an SAYE account.

Linked account   A conventional current account offering an automatic transfer or 'sweep' of surplus cash over a fixed figure to be credited to a bank deposit or building society share account earning interest.

Children's account   A deposit account for those under 18 (see Tax below).

OTHER FACILITIES

Gold Card account   Links overdraft facility (typically to £10,000) to charge card plus a range of 'executive' extras.

Budget account   Helps spread effect of household bills over 12 months. The customer estimates the expected outlay for the next 12 months, and a monthly standing order is established from his current account for one-twelfth of the estimated figure. Bills can be paid on receipt using overdraft facilities. At the end of the year the balance should be nil. Charges are the same as those on a current account plus a small annual service charge. No credit interest is paid and if the account is in credit, charges will be reduced.

Revolving credit facility   For regular monthly savings and providing an overdraft up to about £3,000 or 30 times the monthly amount saved.

Card cash account   Operated through a hole in the wall ATM cash dispenser by using a personalised plastic card with a PIN number, these accounts allow withdrawal or credit of cash and will provide balance and mini statement services as well as standing order, bill paying and fund transfer services.

Internet Banking   Banking via the Internet, often with better rates to reflect the lower administration costs. There are concerns over security and confidentiality.

INCENTIVISED ACCOUNTS

Individual Savings Accounts (ISAs)   See **3.27**

National Savings   See **3.28**

TAX ON SAVINGS ACCOUNTS

Income Tax

Interest is subject to income tax. Non-taxpayers can reclaim tax deducted at source, they can elect to have the interest paid gross by completing form R85. For basic rate taxpayers, where their total income, including savings income, does not exceed the upper limit of the basic rate band, they will only pay tax at 20% on those savings.

Where total income exceeds the upper limit of the basic rate band, then for this purpose the gross savings will be treated as the top slice of income and the excess over the threshold will be subject to higher rate tax. Dividends will be treated as the highest part of that savings income. There is a facility for account holders to certify then that they are not liable to income tax so that a bank, building society or other deposit-taking institution can pay interest to them gross. Taxpayers who are not UK ordinarily resident may apply to receive interest on a gross basis.

Gross Interest

Deposits in the UK of sums of £50,000 or more for seven days are paid gross. Such accounts are normally treasurers' deposit accounts and as they are renewed monthly, they are taxed on an arising basis.

Interest on deposit with overseas banks and institutions is paid gross and taxed on a current-year basis.

Capital Gains Tax

Where currency accounts are operated other than for personal expenditure, a CGT charge can arise as a disposal, for CGT takes place on every withdrawal.

CROSS REFERENCES

Offshore Funds   **3.10**
Individual Savings Accounts (ISAs)   **3.27**
National Savings   **3.28**
The Young   **5.2**

3.27 Individual Savings Accounts (ISAs)

Description	An easy access, tax-favoured account which can contain cash, stocks and shares, life assurance and National Savings to replace TESSAs and PEPs, designed to encourage those on more modest incomes to save.
Ages	Any UK resident individual over 18 years of age, and certain ISAs for 16 and 17-year-olds.
Suitable for	All individual investors, but particularly those paying 40% tax on income and gains.
Advantages	1 No minimum level of savings and ability to withdraw funds without disadvantages. 2 Include cash, equities and assurance. 3 Pre-April 1999 TESSAs and PEPs can continue alongside. 4 No income tax or CGT. 5 Guaranteed to run until 2010. 6 Some ISAs offer to benchmark Charges, Access and Terms (CAT mark). 7 No lifetime, maximum limit. 8 £10,200 limit (up to £5,100 of the limit can be invested into cash ISA element). 9 Post April 2008 ISA investors can move funds from Cash ISAs into Stocks and Shares ISAs.
Disadvantages	1 Maximum limit per individual per year. 2 Limited to contribution of £10,200 per year. 3 Question wisdom of those with lower savings to invest in equities.
Charges	Depends whether or not CAT marked, as regards Charges, Access and Terms, otherwise similar to PEPs.

FURTHER DETAILS

Commercial Aspects

ISAs became available with effect from 6 April 1999 to encourage long-term savings, particularly for those of modest means. New PEPs and TESSAs are no longer available, although existing PEPs can continue alongside ISAs.

There are four types of ISA with differing investment components:

- CAT standard cash ISA;
- non-CAT standard cash ISA;
- CAT standard stocks and shares ISA;
- non-CAT standard stocks and shares ISA.

The CAT standard is a Government initiative and represents reasonable Charges, easy Access and fair Terms. The limit on charging does mean that the majority of the CAT-marked ISAs tend to be cash based and not invested directly or indirectly into equities.

Mini and Maxi ISAs no longer exist. The following is applicable from 6 April 2008.

The ISA investment allowance is currently £10,200.

Up to £5,100 can be saved in cash with one provider.

The remainder of the £10,200 can be invested in stocks and shares with either the same or different provider.

From 6 April 2006 the scope of qualifying investments will be widened to allow all retail collective investment schemes authorised by the FSA, as long as the saver's ability to access the funds is not restricted. Investments in FSA authorised overseas retail schemes will also be permitted.

Stocks and Shares – ISAs are more identifiable with PEPs in that the whole allowance £10,200 may be invested in the stocks and shares element.

Caution must be exercised with ISAs as it is not possible to cancel one ISA in favour of the other.

The insurance element has been abolished since 6 April 2005, and life insurance components will generally now qualify for inclusion in a stocks and shares component. It will therefore be possible to invest up to £10,200 in life insurance policies in a stocks and shares ISA, less any investment in a cash ISA.

Those aged 16 and 17 can hold cash ISAs and the cash component of a stocks and shares ISA.

Taxation Aspects

There is no income tax or CGT to pay on ISAs. Dividends on the stocks and shares element of ISAs did receive tax credits at a rate of 10% gross dividend until 5 April 2004. This is now ceased.

Non-residents cannot hold ISAs, although they may continue to hold them if they become non-resident. They will be entitled to a 10% tax credit on dividends for UK shares for the first five years. Income and gains on the insurance element of ISAs will be tax free.

CROSS REFERENCE

Friendly Society Policies **3.25**

3.28 National Savings

Quick Guide for Financial Advisers

19 July 2010

All interest rates are pa. ● Gross is the taxable rate of interest without deduction of Income Tax. ● AER (Annual Equivalent Rate) is a notional rate which illustrates what the gross rate would be if interest were paid and compounded each year. Where the AER is not specified, it is the same as the quoted rate. ● Tax-free means free of UK Income Tax and Capital Gains Tax at all rates of tax. ● Coloured type indicates changes since last edition.

		Rate	Tax	Key benefits	Min	Max	Who for	Access
Tax-free	**Direct ISA** *from 19 August 2009*	**2.50%** AER (+**5.00%** gross for additional rate taxpayers, **4.16%** for higher rate taxpayers, **3.12%** for basic rate taxpayers). Rates variable.	TAX FREE!	• Tax-free • Managed by phone and online	£100	**£5,100** per tax year.	Individuals 16+ resident in UK for tax purposes.	Repayment by BACS. Min withdrawal £50.
	Premium Bonds *from 1 October 2009*	Rate for prize fund **1.50%** (variable). The odds of each £1 unit winning a prize are 24,000 to 1 each month.	TAX FREE!	• One £1 million jackpot • Over 1 million prizes each month • Chances to win every month (Bonds eligible for prize draws one clear month after purchase) • All prizes tax-free	£100	**£30,000**	Individuals 16+. Under 16, by parents, guardians, (great) grandparents.	Funds normally received within 8 working days by BACS or crossed warrant.
	Fixed Interest Savings Certs. No Issues currently on sale.		TAX FREE!	• Tax-free • Guaranteed returns • Choice of terms • Investment options at maturity*	£100	**£15,000** per Issue. No limit on reinvesting matured Certificates.	Individuals (also jointly), trustees, charities, some clubs and voluntary bodies.	Funds normally received within 8 working days by BACS or crossed warrant. No interest if repaid in first year (except Reinvestment Certificates). If held less than full term, see terms and conditions.
	Index-linked Savings Certs. No Issues currently on sale.		TAX FREE!	• Tax-free • Inflation beating • Choice of terms • Investment options at maturity**	£100	**£15,000** per Issue. No limit on reinvesting matured Certificates.	Individuals (also jointly), trustees, charities, some clubs and voluntary bodies.	Funds normally received within 8 working days by BACS or crossed warrant. No interest or index-linking if repaid in first year (except Reinvestment Certificates). If held less than full term, see terms and conditions.
	Children's Bonus Bonds Issue 34 *from 19 August 2009* *Fixed Interest*	**2.50%** AER compound guaranteed over first 5 years, including bonus. New fixed rates notified each 5th anniversary to age 21. Guaranteed bonus every 5 years, and final bonus on 21st birthday.	TAX FREE!	• Tax-free – even if children become taxpayers • Guaranteed rate • Bonus every five years and final bonus on 21st birthday • No tax for parents to pay	£25 Then in units of £25.	**£3,000** per Issue, per child.	Anyone 16+ for individuals under 16.	Funds normally received within 8 working days by crossed warrant. No interest if repaid in first year. Otherwise 1.85% if repaid before 5th anniversary.
Growth	**Guaranteed Growth Bonds** No Issues currently on sale.		Tax (at 20%) deducted at source. No further liability for basic or lower rate taxpayers.	• Guaranteed rates • Choice of terms • Interest taxable, paid net	£500	**£1 million** – all Bonds held (sole or joint), including any amount held in Guaranteed Income Bonds and previous issues of Fixed Rate Savings Bonds.	Individuals 16+, or 2 jointly; trustees for not more than 2 individuals.	Funds normally received within 8 working days by BACS. No penalty for repayment at full term. Otherwise penalty equivalent to 90 days' interest.
Monthly income	**Guaranteed Income Bonds** No Issues currently on sale.		Tax (at 20%) deducted at source. No further liability for basic or lower rate taxpayers.	• Guaranteed monthly income • Choice of terms • Interest taxable, paid net	£500	**£1 million** – all Bonds held (sole or joint), including any amount held in Guaranteed Growth Bonds and previous issues of Fixed Rate Savings Bonds.	Individuals 16+ or 2 jointly; trustees for not more than 2 individuals.	Funds normally received within 8 working days by BACS. No penalty for repayment at full term. Otherwise penalty equivalent to 90 days' interest.
	Income Bonds *from 19 July 2010*	£500-£25,000 **1.45%** gross/**1.46%** AER £25,000+ **1.75%** gross/**1.76%** AER Paid monthly. Rates variable.	Taxable but paid in full without deduction of tax at source.	• Regular monthly income • Competitive interest rate • Higher rates of interest on investments of £25,000+	£500	**£1 million** (sole or joint).	Individuals, or 2 jointly; trustees for not more than 2 individuals.	Easy access (no notice, no penalty). Repayment by BACS or crossed warrant.
Savings accounts	**Investment Account** *from 18 March 2009*	0.20% to 0.30% Rates gross/AER and variable.	Taxable but credited in full without deduction of tax at source.	• Passbook • Tiered interest rates	£20	**£1 million** (sole or joint).	Individuals, or 2 jointly; trustees.	Easy access (no notice, no penalty). Repayment by crossed warrant up to £2,000.
	Easy Access Savings Account *from 19 February 2009*	0.30% to 0.70% Rates gross/AER and variable.		• Telephone service • Cash card • Tiered interest rates	£100	**£2 million** per person.	Individuals, or 2 jointly.	Instant access up to £300 per day at POs and ATMs.
	Direct Saver *from 19 July 2010*	1.75% Rates gross/AER and variable.	Taxable but paid in full without deduction of tax at source.	• Managed by phone and online • Attractive interest rates	£1	**£2 million** per person.	Individuals, or 2 jointly, 16+.	Repayment by BACS. Min withdrawal £1.

*Fixed Interest Savings Certificates which matured before 8 October 2001, and have not been cashed-in or reinvested, earn the variable General Extension Rate at 0.09% pa from 1 April 2009 for each complete period of 3 months held.
**Index-linked Savings Certificates which matured before 8 October 2001, and have not been cashed-in or reinvested, earn index-linking (plus 0.5% pa interest for 3rd + 4th Issues) for each complete month. 2-year Index-linked Savings Certificates maturing on or after 29 April 2009 (until further notice) will earn index-linking plus 1.0% pa compound if held for a further two years.

Call us for brochures/application forms - or use the fax sheet overleaf.
Financial Advisers' Faxline 01253 832025
Internet: nsandi.com/ifa
e-mail: ifa@nsandi.com

†Calls from mobiles may not be free. Calls may be recorded.

For all information, please call us free on

0800 092 1228†

IFA111

Available 7am until midnight, 7 days a week

3.29 Farming

Suitable for	Wealthy individuals, partnerships.
Advantages	1 Favourable income tax, CGT and IHT treatment.
	2 A particular way of life, which despite generally poor financial returns, can be attractive.
Disadvantages	1 Returns are variable depending upon the quality of the land, the farmer's ability and the weather.
	2 Subject to political intervention which can affect profitability.
	3 Low return on capital employed.

FURTHER DETAILS

Commercial Aspects

Many farmers conduct their business as sole traders or partnerships, but a significant number, particularly the larger enterprises, operate through a limited company. An increasing number of farmers are involved in shared farming arrangements. Under these agreements, which are not partnerships, two or more individuals undertake to provide the capital, equipment, expertise and labour for the enterprise. Share farming is treated as a business, provided a certain level of activity is reached and there is business risk for both parties.

GRANTS AND COMPENSATION

A number of grants and compensation arrangements are available to assist farmers, including:

- *BSE Compensation* – This comprises five different schemes and the compensation is taxable, although where the compulsory slaughter concession applies, it may be spread over three years.
- *European Agricultural Support Regime* – There are numerous schemes under this heading, most of which are a sales subsidiary and are therefore taxed as income. The principal subsidy is The Single Payment Scheme. This allows farmers more freedom to farm the demands of the market, as the subsidy is no longer linked to production, but rather farming practices (known as cross compliance). Environment Scheme grants are also taxed as income, as they compensate for the reduction in productivity.
- *Agricultural Tenancies* – Monies received for the surrender of an agricultural tenancy are subject to CGT, but a compulsory surrender under an Agricultural Holdings Act 1986 tenancy will be exempt compensation.

- *Milk* – Compensation for temporary cuts in quotas are taxed as income, and for permanent cuts are taxed as capital. The latter gain may be deferred by reinvestment.

Taxation Aspects

The following taxation notes focus on the rules for individuals and partnerships. Many of the provisions are mirrored in the tax rules for farming companies, but there are important differences.

Income Tax

Losses can be offset against other income or carried forward against future profits. In some instances the losses can be carried back against other income. Subject to certain important restrictions, losses can also be set against capital gains.

In most situations, if there have been losses, before capital allowances, in the previous five fiscal years, a loss in the sixth and subsequent years can be carried forward only against future profits of that farming activity. Once a profit has occurred in a subsequent fiscal year, the six-year cycle for disallowance of losses recommences.

Following a 'herd basis' election, the values of production animals are not included in computing trading profits. The cost of the original herd and of additions to that herd is not deductible – equally the sale of the herd or a substantial (in excess of 20%) part of that herd is not taxable, providing there is no replacement within five years. In contrast the profit or loss on the sale of individual animals or other insubstantial parts of the herd is subject to income tax.

HMRC has stated that where there is a minor disposal without replacement, ie less that 20% of herd, the profit, if any, will be calculated by reference to the cost of the animal, rather than the old historic cost basis.

All farming carried on by the same individual or partnership is treated as the carrying on of one trade. In certain circumstances, profits can be averaged over two years.

Capital Allowances are granted on the cost of agricultural buildings. However, from the 5 April 2008 this relief (ABAs), along with all forms of Industrial Buildings Allowances (IBAs) were being phased out over a four-year period.

Historically, one-third of farmhouse expenses (eg business rates, light and heat, repairs) could be deducted from farming profits, but depending upon the size of the farmhouse, HMRC now seek to agree a basis on the actual usage.

Capital Gains Tax

If land, buildings and certain other assets such as milk quota are used exclusively for the purpose of carrying on a farming trade are sold and the proceeds of sale are reinvested in other assets used only for the purpose of the trade, then a roll-over relief election may be made to defer the CGT, by offsetting the gain otherwise chargeable on the old asset against the acquisition cost of the new asset.

Expenditure on the new asset must normally be incurred within one year before, or three years after, the disposal of the old asset. Special rules apply where there is only a partial reinvestment of the proceeds, where the asset has been used partly for non-business use or where the new asset has an expected life of less than 50 years, or will have such an expected life within the next ten years.

If the farmhouse is the farmer's main residence, the whole or part of the gain on the disposal of the farmhouse may be covered by the principal private residence exemption.

Inheritance Tax

Relief from IHT is available on chargeable transfers of qualifying agricultural property. Where agricultural relief is not given, business relief may be available (see Section 4.20, *IHT – Agricultural Property Relief* and Section 4.19, *IHT – Business Property Relief*).

IHT arising on transfers of agricultural property on death can be paid in annual instalments over a period of ten years. Further, if the payments are made by the due date, they will be interest-free.

Subject to certain requirements, tenanted land qualifies for IHT agricultural relief.

CROSS REFERENCES

Investment Property   **3.18**
Woodlands   **3.31**
IHT – Agricultural Property Relief   **4.20**

3.30 Lloyd's

Description	Participation in a number of insurance syndicates directly, through a limited liability vehicle, or through a 'unit trust' vehicle at Lloyd's of London, with a view to producing an additional income.
Suitable for	High risk-taking wealthy individuals with substantial capital, of which a sufficient part is in readily realisable assets or cash.
Advantages	1 The opportunity to obtain a second return of income on existing assets, or an income on non-income producing assets.
	2 To participate as a Name, the individual does not have to dispose of existing assets and retains control over those assets.
	3 Treated as a business for IHT purposes.
	4 The ability to shelter the tax liability on Lloyd's income in profitable years.
	5 Availability of limited liability vehicles make the risks more manageable.
	6 Opportunities for existing Names to convert to one of the new vehicles.
	7 Names can make contributions to pension scheme.
Disadvantages	1 More emphasis on limited liability vehicles reduces opportunities for individual Names.
	2 Unlimited liability can result in huge personal losses as experienced in last decade by Names.
	3 Significant cash outlay to defray any expenses before first profit cheque and on an annual basis.
	4 Delay in withdrawing from investment.
Charges	Could be as high as £20,000 before any return on investment is received.

FURTHER DETAILS

Commercial Aspects

Reconstruction and Renewal

The Corporation of Lloyd's conducts its business through a Council elected by the Members, and this Council has the responsibility for regulating, controlling and managing the insurance market of Lloyd's. Lloyd's is regulated by the Lloyd's Act 1982 and by the Financial Services and Markets Act 2000.

Profitability

Lloyd's is a cyclical business driven by demand and supply. Demand is relatively constant, but does increase after catastrophes, which heighten awareness for the need to increase cover. Supply is provided worldwide by insurance organisations. After catastrophes, rates increase and business becomes profitable. That profitability encourages others (ie non-traditional insurers) to enter the market, which increases the capacity and forces the rates down. If this increased capacity coincides with low claims in the absence of catastrophes, then rates reduce to levels below which a profit can be made.

Structure

Syndicates are groupings of Members formed so that the resources of those Members can be combined into a single unit to enable much larger sums to be underwritten. Each Syndicate has one or more expert underwriter who negotiates and accepts risks on behalf of the Syndicate. Each Syndicate usually accepts risks for a particular sector of the market – mainly marine, non-marine, aviation and motor – but, subject to certain restrictions, can accept other sector risks. Syndicates are run by managing agents. Names are advised by Members' agents on their Syndicate participation. Brokers place business with the Syndicates.

Managers and Members' agents can be under common control; Members' agents and brokers can be under common control; brokers and managing agents cannot.

Participating in Lloyd's

Traditionally, Members participated as individuals with unlimited liability. There are now a number of ways in which to participate, which are outlined below.
- *Individually* – Traditional; unlimited liability; advised by Members' agents; able to underwrite four times the Funds at Lloyd's requirement and able to set losses against other taxable income. An individual can transfer up to 50% of commercial profits into a special reserve fund to reduce taxable profits. There is an automatic withdrawal in a year of loss, or on cessation, which is taxed as income.
- *Individually via MAPA* – As above, but the Name participates through the Members' Agents' Pooling Arrangements, which enable Names to have a wider spread of Syndicates in their portfolio.
- *Scottish Limited Partnership* – Scottish partnerships have a corporate persona and thus qualify as corporate vehicles able to participate in Lloyd's Scottish. Limited partnerships have up to 19 partners who contribute capital as partners but are not allowed to participate in the management of the partnership. There is a general partner who runs the partnership – normally the managing agent. The partnership participates in the Syndicate and profits and losses are shared amongst the partners, but a limited partner cannot lose more than his contribution to the partnership. Losses can be set against other income of Names up to the amount of the contributions of the Name. The partnership is able to underwrite two times the contributions made. From 6 April 2004 Names can carry forward old losses on transferring

their Lloyd's business into the partnership. Relief is then given against the partner's income from the partnership.

- *Limited Liability Partnerships* – Limited liability partnerships were admitted to Lloyd's from December 2005 with first participation in the 2007 underwriting year. Unlike Scottish limited partnerships(SLP) the member has control over underwriting decisions. Liability is limited to the contributions which may be required under the Limited Liability Partnership Act 2000. There must be at least three members who can be individuals or companies.
- *Corporate vehicle* – Individuals invest in the corporate, which invests in Syndicates at a ratio of two times the contributions made. Companies may be dedicated to one Syndicate or spread amongst a number of Syndicates. Liability is limited, but the participation in Lloyd's is remote. Existing Names may transfer their Lloyd's business to the company under a route called transition, in which the Name reinsures his underwriting liability into the company. A second method of transfer called interavailability is used, whereby the funds at Lloyd's support the corporate vehicle and the Names continuing or with past obligations to Lloyd's.
- *Listed vehicles* – A more passive and remote investment trust type vehicle.

The trend is for the traditional Names to reduce in numbers, although Lloyd's has confirmed that it wishes individuals to continue. A more reflective view may be taken in due course once the reaction of corporate Members to poor years is known.

Taxation Aspects

Finance Acts 1993 and 1994 set out the main legislation for the taxation of participation at Lloyd's. An underwriting year runs for a calendar year, not a fiscal year, and is normally closed by reinsurance forward for a further two years so that claims can be accepted against the risks written on that account. The 2005 account closed on 31 December 2007, with commercial results published and distributions made in the summer of 2008. The result will be declared on the 2008/09 tax return.

Income Tax

Lloyd's syndicates must either discount their premiums paid to close syndicate years, or face an interest charge if the settlement figures are lower than the premiums paid. Minor excess premiums by syndicates or minor amounts borne by individual members will be exempted.

Individuals can pay into a special reserve fund which will be paid out in years of losses. 50% of Lloyd's profits can be paid in, which can accumulate up to an aggregate of 50% of that Name's overall premium limit.

All Lloyd's income is treated as earned income. This enables personal pensions to be taken out against the earnings, and this includes all the non-Syndicate investment income.

In addition, Class 2 and Class 4 National Insurance contributions will be due on any income unless an exemption or deferment applies through age or other earnings.

For Scottish limited partnerships the regulations relating to earned income were disapplied and therefore earnings are not relevant (UK) earnings and therefore not subject to NIC or eligible for relief for pension contributions.

This is because the limited partners in SLPs are not permitted to have a role in the management of the SLP.

The regulations were not disapplied for LLPs which are treated as earned income.

Losses can be set against other income of the tax year or the previous year, or carried forward against future underwriting profits. Limited partners cannot offset losses in excess of their contribution to the partnership, but can take the first four years of partnership losses back against other income in the previous three years. Capital losses on shares subscribed to corporate vehicles may be set against other income.

When a Lloyd's Name converts from unlimited personal liability to limited liability status from 6 April 2004, trading losses can be carried forward and relieved against remuneration and dividends received by the Name from the company. The company must be under the control of the Name.

Capital Gains Tax

Capital appreciation or losses on the investment of the invested premiums are part of the Lloyd's results and taxed as income.

As underwriting income is now deemed trading income for all Names, retirement will involve the sale of Syndicate capacity at auction. Such a disposal will give rise to a capital gain or a capital loss. Roll-over relief is available on a qualifying reinvestment.

Inheritance Tax

In normal circumstances, when a Name ceases underwriting, the final year of assessment is usually that in which the Lloyd's deposit is repaid. If there is no Lloyd's deposit to be refunded, the final year of assessment is the later of either the calendar year during which the results of the final account of the last open Syndicates are declared, or the end of the year of account during which membership ceased by the usual rules and practice of Lloyd's.

In the same way that a Name's underwriting interest is treated as a business for pension and CGT purposes on death, provided that certain requirements are met, relief from IHT is available through business property relief. In addition, the personal representatives will have the option of paying the IHT in respect of the Lloyd's interest either immediately (before probate), 12 months after the death, or, subject to certain requirements, by instalments.

The tax treatment of a deceased Name will depend on the date of death. If this occurred on or after 6 April 1994, the Name's underwriting business is continued by the personal representatives until the rules detailed above relating to cessation can apply. Previously, any Lloyd's income or expenditure was related back to the final year and included in the Member's Lloyd's profit or loss for that final year.

There are special reliefs given to those Names who commenced underwriting before 1 January 1972.

CROSS REFERENCES

Investment Property **3.18**
CGT – Taper Relief **4.12**
IHT – Business Property Relief **4.19**

3.31 Woodlands

Description	The ownership of woodlands with a view to capital appreciation over the long term.
Suitable for	Wealthy individuals.
Advantages	1 A safe long-term investment.
	2 Any income derived from sales of timber can be non-taxable both to income tax and CGT.
	3 The ownership of woodlands is treated as a business for IHT purposes and can therefore attract 100% BPR.
	4 Valuable government grants are available to reduce planting costs on marginal arable land.
Disadvantages	No income tax relief on expenditure incurred on newly purchased woodlands.
Investment limits	Minimum investment £5,000 via a syndicate or £50,000 for a direct holding.
Charges	SDLT on purchase of the land. Legal fees and managers' charges. Planting and upkeep costs.

FURTHER DETAILS

Commercial Aspects

Over the past 20 years, the proportion of Britain's forests and woodlands in private ownership has risen from less than 50% to over 60%. This striking increase reflects the success of the Government's policy to develop a strong private forestry sector. The UK is less than 25% self-supporting in timber products and world demand is estimated to exceed supply.

The investment should be considered long term, but on the basis of past performance gives the prospect of a real return in excess of the rate of inflation. Over recent years, there has been a discernible trend towards smaller investments in woodlands, although the market still ranges from major corporates to private individuals.

Grant Schemes

The English Woodland Grant Scheme (EWGS) is the Forestry Commission's suite of grants. EWGS is supported via the Rural Development Programme for England.

The key grants are: Woodland Planting Grant (WPG), Woodland Assessment Grant (WAG), Woodland Regeneration Grant (WRG), Woodland Improvement Grant (WIG) and the Woodland Management Grant (WMG). These grants apply to existing woodlands. New woodlands can receive a Woodlands Creation Grant (WCG).

The Scottish Forestry Grants Scheme closed on 31 August 2006 and was replaced by rural development contracts. In Wales there are grants available under the Better Woodlands for Wales (BWW) scheme.

Similar grants are available in Northern Ireland.

See the Royal Forestry Society Grants for Trees booklet at www.rfs.org.uk/grantsfortrees.asp.

The emphasis is on an incentive available to all woodlands investors, regardless of tax status.

Government Review

The UK Forestry Standard, published in January 1998, laid out the Government's approach to sustainable forest management.

The Forestry Commission had been sub-divided into three distinct agencies to enable the effective implementation of forestry policies.

- The Forestry Authority is responsible for protecting Britain's forests by setting standards, providing information and offering grants, eg the Woodland Grant Scheme, for expanding, regenerating and managing forests and woodlands.
- The Forest Enterprise agency is responsible for the efficient and sustainable management of the public forest estate.
- The Forest Research Agency provides high-quality scientific research to inform the development of forestry policies and practices to promote a high standard of sustainable forest management.

A revised edition of the UK Forestry Standard was published on 14 May 2004. Minor changes have been made to guidance on forestry practices, but a new approach is being taken in monitoring implementation. A further fundamental revision has been promised following consultation with stakeholders.

Taxation Aspects

Income is not taxed and losses not allowed for income tax.

Woodlands can qualify for agricultural property relief or business property relief for IHT purposes. The effect of this is that 100% of the value of the woodlands is excluded from the value of an estate on death. Advantage can be taken of a special IHT relief for woodlands, whereby for growing timber and underwood passing on death, IHT may be deferred until such time as it is actually sold, and is calculated by reference to the value of the timber at the date of sale.

Consideration for the disposal of trees or timber (but not for the land on which they stand) is exempt from CGT. Tax on land sales will be at the rate applicable to the vendor. CGT roll-over relief is available against land costs.

Stamp Duty Land Tax is payable on the purchase of woodland.

CROSS REFERENCES

3.32 Glossary of Investment Terminology

'A-Day'   The implementation date of the new simplified pension regime. This was 6 April 2006.

Advisory client   The extent of service varies. It is normally contrasted with either a discretionary service (where the broker takes investment decisions on the client's behalf without consultation), or a dealing only service (where the broker does what the client tells him, without offering advice).

Allotment letter   An allotment letter is sent to successful applicants when a company offers shares to the public. (See *Renounceable documents* below.)

Alternative Investment Market (AIM)   A market for trading smaller company shares with less onerous reporting requirements than required by a full listing.

Application form   When companies offer shares to the public, any person who wants to apply must use the official application form. The application form is part of the prospectus.

Arbitrage   The purchase of securities, commodities, etc in one market for immediate resale in another to profit from a price discrepancy. *Convertible arbitrage* generates profits from the fixed income security and the short sale of stock, whilst the principal is protected from market movement. *Fixed income arbitrage* seeks to profit from price anomalies between related interest rate securities, often globally. *Risk arbitrage* involves, say, taking a long position of the stock of a merger target and a short position on the acquiring company.

Bear market   A market that is falling. (The opposite to a bull market.)

Bearer stock   Stocks or shares of which no register of ownership is kept by the company concerned. The certificate itself has the value.

Bid   On the stock market this is the price at which someone is willing to buy shares. (The offer price is the price at which he will sell them.)

Blue chip   Most secure investments by common regard.

Bond   Fixed interest security issued by governments and companies.

Bonus issue   A free issue of shares to shareholders.

Broker-dealer   A stockbroker who makes markets as well as buying and selling securities on a client's behalf.

Bull market   A market that is rising.

Call   Demand by company, or other issuer of shares or stock, for payment.

Capitalisation   The total value of a company's issued securities.

Cash dealings   Cash dealings must be settled the following day.

Central gilts office   An electronic system which records gilts transactions.

Chinese wall   Rules designed to prevent price-sensitive information seeping between dealing/fund management/corporate finance operations in an investment house.

Closing price   The price at the end of the day's trading.

Compliance   Self-policing by securities firms to make sure rules are being obeyed. Compliance officers within firms act as 'internal deputies' to the outside regulations authorities.

Consideration   The value of a transaction before adding commission, stamp duty and VAT.

Contract note   A stockbroker's notification of a deal to his client.

Coupon   The nominal rate of interest attached to a fixed interest security. This will differ from the yield, if the market price differs from the nominal price of the stock.

CREST   Computerised share dealing system making shareholdings non-certificated.

Dealing 'net'   When a client deals directly with a market maker the transaction is done for a net price. This means that the investor pays only the selling (bid) price or the buying (offer) price, ie there is no commission. This is the basis on which licensed dealers deal with clients. Most private clients will still probably deal on the old agency (commission) basis.

Discount broker   A securities merchant. Commission rates will be lower but this will probably mean no investment advice.

Dividend yield   Gross dividend divided by share price.

EASDAQ   The European Association of Securities Dealers modelled on NASDAQ.

EBITDA   'Earnings Before Interest, Taxes, Depreciation and Amortization'. This is a useful measure of a company's income for interest payments on loans. Also known as Operational Cash Flow.

Enhanced protection   Available to individuals who ceased active membership of all approved pension schemes before 'A-Day'. Provided they do not resume active membership, all benefits coming into payment will be exempt from the recovery tax charge.

Equity   The ordinary share capital of a company, as distinct from its preference or loan capital. Sometimes used as a synonym for ordinary shares.

FSA   The Financial Services Authority – responsible for the policing of investment business.

FT index   The Financial Times Ordinary Share Index. Based on 30 leading industrial and commercial shares.

FTSE 100 index   Index of 100 top UK shares – popularly known as FOOTSIE and updated throughout the day.

Gilts   Stock issued by the Government and both the capital and the interest are guaranteed. 'Long gilts' are those without a redemption date within 15 years. 'Medium gilts' are those with a redemption date between five and 15 years. 'Short gilts' have a redemption date within five years.

Guaranteed fund   An investment fund (often pension) with a guaranteed downside protection.

Hedge funds   A fund that invests in securities and liquid assets. The fund's activities are limited only by the terms of the contract governing the particular fund. Hedge funds are lightly regulated and can follow complex investment strategies. Invariably, the objective of a hedge fund is to generate absolute returns in all market conditions.

Index tracker   A fund that tries to replicate the performance of a particular index by mirroring its constituent parts.

Institution   Institutional investors are those who run investment funds, such as pension funds, life assurance companies, unit and investment trusts.

Inter-dealer broker   A go-between who provides a dealing service to market makers. IDBs will confidentially match up buyers and sellers, and so give market makers another trading outlet. A market maker could use an IDB to lay off risk or to sell short without the competition knowing. IDBs give the market added liquidity.

Lifetime allowance   £1.5m as at 'A-Day'.

LIFFE   London International Financial Futures Exchange which provides facilities for dealing in futures contracts.

Listing   Act of allowing particular securities to be traded on a stock market. In London companies which get a listing on the main London Stock Exchange sign a 'listing agreement', which sets certain standards of conduct, and can only get a listing provided they satisfy certain criteria – the listing requirements. Such companies are then described as listed companies. Companies joining the Alternative Investment Market have to satisfy less stringent criteria.

Market makers   Wholesalers of securities (stocks and shares). They fill securities orders from their 'book' – inventories of shares or gilts. As these dealers take positions in stocks, they also bear the risk. Market makers are committed to making a buying or selling price on demand. The aim is to provide liquidity.

Marketability   A share is freely marketable if one can buy or sell a large quantity (of the shares) without upsetting the market and shifting the price.

Middle price   The price half way between the two prices shown in the Stock Exchange Daily Official List. Newspapers also normally show the middle price.

NASDAQ   National Association of Securities Dealers Automated Quotation System. American screen-based system similar to SEAQ.

Net asset value   Net assets divided by issued ordinary shares.

New time Dealings in the last two days of an account can by special arrangement be settled as if they had been made during the following account.

Nil paid A new issue of shares normally through a rights issue on which to date no payment to the company has been made.

Nominee name Name in which a security is registered which does not indicate the beneficial owner.

OFEX An unregulated market run by a market maker for unlisted shares.

Official List The list of official Stock Exchange daily prices.

Open ended investment company (OEIC) A cross between a unit trust and an investment trust introduced as the preferred collective investment vehicle to trade in Europe.

Order driven market Brokers deal with other brokers to find a match for shares they want to buy or sell, eg NYSE and Tokyo SE.

Overhang If the stock market knows that a major investor (or group of investors, such as underwriters) wishes to sell a large line of shares in a particular company.

Oversubscription Excess demand for a new issue.

Partly paid shares Those where the original investors put up only part of the issued capital, thus remaining legally liable to further cash calls.

Preferential form On a new issue up to 10% of the shares on offer can be set aside for employees to apply for (or shareholders of the parent company). They are usually pink in colour and are also known as 'pink forms'.

Price/earnings ratio The share price divided by the earnings per share. Also known as the 'P/E ratio'.

Primary dealer Market maker in gilts.

Primary market The Stock Exchange's facilities to raise money through new issues.

Primary protection Protection will be available to the value of Pre-'A-Day' pension rights in excess of £1.5m. The Pre-'A-Day' value will be indexed in parallel with the indexation of the lifetime allowance.

Prospectus Document published by any company issuing shares to the public. Information in the prospectus is subject to legal and stock market regulations.

Proxy A person that a shareholder appoints to vote on their behalf at company meetings.

Quote driven market Market makers provide quotes for buying and selling shares and brokers transact with the market makers, eg LSE and NASDAQ.

Redemption date Date on which a redeemable bond or preference share will be repaid.

Renounceable documents　Used temporarily to prove ownership. An 'allotment letter' is sent to successful applicants when a company offers shares. A 'provisional allotment' is sent in the case of a rights issue and in the case of capitalisation. Each of these are 'bearer securities' and are valuable.

Rights issue　A rights issue is a means whereby a company can raise extra finance offered to existing shareholders.

Risk warning　A buyer-beware label to be imposed on risky investments by the Securities and Investments Board.

SEAQ　The Stock Exchange's electronic price display system. The initials stand for Stock Exchange Automated Quotations. Market makers are required to display buying/selling prices for equities or gilts dealt in. Brokers, as well as institutions, can follow these prices on computer terminals in the SEAQ network. Dealers will still receive orders and negotiate over the telephone.

SEATS plus　Similar to SEAQ for AIM stocks and stocks with only one market maker.

Secondary market　The Stock Exchange's market for investors to trade in issued securities.

Securities　The general name given to stocks and shares.

SETS　The Stock Exchange Electronic Trading Service, being an order-driven system for stock and shares.

Settlement　Settlement of the transaction shortly afterwards – in the UK three days after trade.

Société d'investissement à capital variable (SICAV)　A foreign-based investment company with single priced shares and commonly an umbrella structure – see OEIC.

Spread　Difference between a market maker's buying and selling prices.

Stamp Duty Reserve Tax　0.5% duty charged on the purchase price to the purchaser.

Stop-loss　Order to buy or sell shares or other securities at a particular price above or below the current price.

Striking price　Price at which shares are allotted in a tender offer for sale (a form of new issue). Everyone tendering at or above the striking price gets some shares at the striking price.

Takeover Panel　Self-regulatory City body which sets and polices the rules on takeovers embodied in the Takeover Code.

Technical analysis　Method of predicting future price movements by looking at patterns of past ones on charts.

Tender　Offer for sale in which investors are asked to bid for the stock in order to determine the striking price at which the shares will be sold.

Traded options　Options to buy or sell shares at a set price before the expiry date of the option.

Tradepoint   A computerised order driven alternative to the Stock Exchange.

UCITS   Undertakings for Collective Investments in Transferable Securities.

Underwriter   Investor agreeing for a fee to purchase any shares offered for sale if the public (or the relevant shareholders) do not.

Yield   The annual return on investment, based on the price of the security, and the amount paid via dividends.

Part 4   Tax Planning

4.1 Introduction

This chapter deals with taxation from a UK perspective. In the UK there are two main types of taxation – direct and indirect. Direct taxation is levied on an individual's income, profits, gains and assets. Indirect tax tends to be levied on expenditure or consumption. For example, value added tax, stamp duty, stamp duty land tax, airport passenger tax, insurance premium tax etc. The following focuses on direct taxation. The three direct taxes for individuals are income tax, capital gains tax (CGT) and inheritance tax (IHT).

Income tax is applied to an individual's income and profits which are assessed for a tax year which runs from 6 April to 5 April. The tax is progressive, starting at an effective nil rate granted by deductible personal allowances to a basic rate of 20% and a top rate of 40%. Tax due is payable either by withholding from earnings and certain investment income and the balance by direct payment to HM Revenue and Customs (HMRC).

Capital gains tax is applied to an individual's gains arising on the disposal of chargeable assets. Chargeable assets are those likely to produce a gain, eg an appreciating asset rather than an asset which depreciates in value such as a motor car. The Finance Bill 2008 significantly simplified the calculation of capital gains, abolishing concepts such as taper relief and indexation allowance. Gains are now calculated by taking the net proceeds and deducting the original acquisition cost.

A change in government in 2010 resulted in an emergency Budget on 22 June 2010 which resulted in changes to tax rates effective in the middle of a tax year.

Total chargeable gains less capital losses for a tax year to 5 April are taxed at an effective rate of nil for the first £10,100 (2010/11). The balance of gains arising in the period 6 April 2010 to 22 June 2010 are taxed at a flat rate of 18%. For gains arising in the period 23 June 2010 to 5 April 2011 the flat rate of 18% will continue to apply if an individual's total taxable gains and income are less than the upper limit of the income tax basic rate band. A rate of 28% applies to gains (or any parts of gains) above the limit.

Gains which are reinvested in certain businesses are deferred. Tax due is payable by direct payment to HMRC by 31 January following the end of the tax year in which the chargeable gain was made.

Inheritance tax is a tax on lifetime gifts and an individual's assets on death. Most lifetime gifts are exempt from IHT if the donor survives seven years from the making of the gift. On death, an individual is entitled to a nil-rate allowance of £325,000 (2010/11) and any excess of assets less liabilities is taxed at 40%.

Business assets are again favourably treated with 100%, or 50% of the value of qualifying assets being exempt from tax.

The planning involved to minimise the above taxes is dealt with in detail in the relevant sections. However, all planning to minimise direct tax follows the same broad strategy which is suggested as follows:

Residence and Domicile

An individual who is ordinarily resident and domiciled in the UK is assessed to tax on his worldwide income, gains and assets.

Non-resident individuals are broadly assessed to income tax on UK source income.

Non-resident and non-ordinarily resident individuals are exempt from CGT if they have been overseas for five years or more.

Resident but non-domiciled individuals are assessed to income tax on UK source income and are normally subject to IHT only on assets situated in the UK. From 6 April 2008 non-domiciled individuals will also be taxed on foreign income and gains whether remitted to the UK or not, unless a claim is made for the remittance basis to apply. The claim will attach a £30,000 charge payable to HMRC if the individual has been resident in the UK seven out of nine years preceding the year of assessment and is 18 or over and has foreign income of more than £2,000. Due to the £30,000 charge, the claim for remittance basis may or may not be beneficial. The claim can be made year on year, which in turn will require some planning, particularly where foreign income and gains might fluctuate year on year.

If an individual has non-resident status, or is not domiciled in the UK, the planner should try to retain that status and maximise its benefits subject to the overriding aims of the individual and individual's family. Again, the opportunity to attain that status should also be considered in view of the substantial taxation benefit which may be obtained. The benefits attaching to such special status are still extremely valuable to wealthy individuals, despite the £30,000 charge.

Alienation of Income and Assets

Once all the possibilities of non-residence and non-domicile have been explored, the next stage is to consider how to pass on the ownership of assets to avoid being taxed on income arising, or on the assets themselves.

Planning becomes easier if the individual has family members to whom assets can be passed. Every individual, even if they are a minor, is entitled to a personal allowance for income tax, and an annual allowance for CGT and IHT. If the assets can be passed to family members with lower rates of taxation or longer lives, then tax may be deferred or saved. However, anti-avoidance provisions operate to ensure that parents remain taxable on the income arising from assets given to their minor children.

It should also be noted that from 6 April 2008 strategies to alienate assets offshore, formerly standard pre-remittance planning, are now restricted by new legislation.

In considering this planning, the first consideration must be to safeguard the financial security of the donor and his dependants, both now and in the future. It will be imprudent to pass on assets on which the donor might need to rely or possess in the future. If retention of control is important, it is possible to use the medium of a trust to hold the asset outside an individual's estate and retain effective control as trustee. The use of trusts is explained in the Estate Planning section.

Tax Favoured Assets

Assets retained by an individual can then be reviewed to see if the holdings can be structured to maximise tax benefits. The two main classes of favoured assets are trading assets and tax favoured investments.

Trading assets are those employed in a qualifying trading business, or shares in a qualifying trading company which is deemed to be privately owned. Shares in unquoted companies and certain holdings in quoted shares where the individual is an employee and/or where the holding exceeds 5%, are also classed as business assets for CGT purposes.

For income tax, trading income becomes pensionable and monies can be paid into an approved pension fund, the payment is deductible by the business and the pension fund itself is tax exempt. Interest on borrowings to fund trading ventures is also allowable as a deduction against income when calculating income tax payable.

For CGT, gains on business assets may benefit from entrepreneurs' relief, which gives an effective rate of tax of 10% on a capped amount of gains, any gains above this cap are taxed at the flat rate in force at the time of disposal. Entrepreneurs' Relief applies to any disposals post 5 April 2008 and replaces reliefs such as taper relief. The capped amount is per individual and is a lifetime allowance and therefore not on every disposal. The capped amount for the period 6 April 2008 to 5 April 2010 was £1 million, then increased to £2 million for gains from 6 April 2010 to 22 June 2010 and to £5 million for gains after 22 June 2010.

For IHT, the value of trading assets may be exempt from tax or have only 50% of their value subject to tax.

Tax Favoured Assets

For income tax include the following:
- investments that qualify for a tax deduction on the making of the investment, eg Enterprise Investment Schemes or Venture Capital Trusts;
- those for which income arising is exempt from tax, eg personal equity plans, ISAs or certain National Savings;
- those where taxation is deferred, eg offshore funds;
- those subject to a lower rate of taxation, eg Life Assurance Investments.

For CGT the tax favoured assets are:
- certain assets attracting Entrepreneurs' Relief unquoted shares in trading companies;
- certain assets are exempt from capital gains, eg Gilts;
- others may be used as gain deferral vehicles, eg Enterprise Investment Schemes.

For IHT tax purposes the main tax favoured assets are:
- trading assets in woodlands and farming or trading businesses which may be taxed at a nil rate or 50% of the normal rate;
- assets in certain trusts which may not be subject to tax on death.

It may be possible to borrow against the security of a non-trading asset which does not qualify for business property relief at 50% or 100%, and use the borrowed funds to establish a trading asset which does qualify for such relief.

Deductions and Allowances

For income tax there are extensive rules allowing many deductions. For employment income, expenses are allowable if they are wholly, exclusively and necessarily incurred in the performance of the duties. For self-employed individuals, expenses merely have to be wholly and exclusively incurred by the individual. This subtle difference makes the scope of planning on self-employment income much more extensive. Where services are provided through an intermediary which would be an employment if provided directly, the service may be taxed as though an employment existed. For both types of earned income, the deduction for pension payments is the most extensively used and normally results in the greatest benefits.

For CGT, a popular option used to be to bed and breakfast shares to crystallise gains to use up the annual exemption or to generate losses to reduce taxable gains. With matching rules in place, the transactions now need to be 31 days or more apart and are therefore less effective.

For IHT, in a family situation assets can be transferred outside an individual's estate by using the annual exemption, small gifts exemption, transfers between spouses, gifts in consideration of marriage, normal expenditure out of income and dispositions for family maintenance. At present the most beneficial gifting route is by use of the potentially exempt transfer on which no IHT is chargeable if the donor survives seven years from the date of the gift.

Payment of Tax

The final stage is to be aware of the tax on the asset and income remaining in the hands of the individual.

It is prudent for any taxpayer to be aware of, and provide for, income tax and CGT liabilities. For IHT, the use of an appropriate life assurance policy in trust can place monies in the hands of beneficiaries to fund the tax on death and to leave the estate intact. The proceeds of the life policy may also escape taxation if properly structured.

Tax Planning

For those taxpayers with an appetite for mitigating their tax liabilities, there are always a range of tax planning ideas and structures available. These ideas can range in their complexity and the levels of tax mitigation they achieve. Appropriate tax planning can help to reduce or eliminate the income tax, National Insurance or CGT exposure for individuals, trustees and companies alike. As ever, the choice of tax mitigation strategy will depend on the particular risk profile of the taxpayer concerned. Inevitably, the greater the reduction in the tax liability the greater the risk of a HMRC challenge.

In recent years there have been a number of strategies to eliminate a liability to income tax. These have involved establishing a tax loss without a corresponding cash or economic loss. For example, past ideas have involved discounted loan notes and Government gilt strips. In a recent Special Commissioners case one of the earlier strategies was upheld, notwithstanding the intention to mitigate tax.

Similar structures have been devised to eliminate a liability to CGT (or corporation tax) by creating a corresponding capital loss, again without a cash or economic cost to the taxpayer. In many cases these have involved the use of insurance products.

Remuneration planning has been a very active market in recent years. In particular, there have been a number of structures intended to reduce and in some cases eliminate the income tax and National Insurance contributions associated with conventional bonus payments. In many cases these have involved converting cash bonus payments into dividends, the latter attracting a more favourable effective tax rate. Although once the preserve of companies in the financial services sector, these arrangements have now become more widespread.

New disclosure rules covering certain types of tax avoidance schemes were introduced in the Finance Act 2004. These rules require promoters of tax schemes to disclose their details to HMRC. Certainly their introduction will make it more challenging for tax practitioners to design and implement these types of structures. However, given that a general anti-avoidance rule has not been introduced, there should still be scope for the design and implementation of tax planning arrangements for taxpayers with an appetite for mitigation.

4.2 Income Tax – Self-Assessment

Description	Self-assessment requires the taxpayer to file any returns by a fixed date, calculate his own income tax and CGT liabilities and to pay the tax according to a strict timetable.
Advantages	1 The procedures for making returns and paying tax are simpler; no longer are assessments (estimated and amended) issued as a matter of course.
	2 The rules for working out an individual's tax liability are being simplified, where possible.
	3 Statements of Account are regularly issued by HMRC showing the taxpayer the tax which he owes, if any.
	4 Taxpayers have greater control of their own tax affairs.
	5 New simplified self-assessment form for individuals with simple tax affairs.
Disadvantages	1 The onus for getting things right is on the taxpayer and not HMRC.
	2 The format of the full tax return, requiring completion of the requisite supplementary pages, can be confusing.
	3 There can be strict penalties which can catch innocent errors.
	4 Random audits can result in taxpayers being involved in protracted correspondence for no apparent reason, with little form of redress.
	5 Strict rules for record keeping and source documentation.

Filing of Tax Return

If a return has been issued, the taxpayer is required to complete and file it by the filing date, normally 31 January following the end of the tax year if filing on line. Paper returns must be submitted by 31 October. If a return has not been received and the taxpayer has not paid the correct amount of income tax for the year, eg via PAYE, or if there is a CGT liability, then he must notify HMRC of his chargeability to tax by 5 October following the end of the tax year in which the tax liability arose.

Amendments to a return may be made within 12 months of the filing date, provided HMRC have not commenced enquiries into the return.

Provided the return is filed by 30 September, HMRC will normally calculate the tax payments due.

Documentary evidence and records supporting the return entries must be retained and be available for inspection by HMRC, if sought. The retention period is normally 12 months from the filing date but is extended to five years in the case of businesses and let property.

A fixed penalty of £100 will be charged if the completed return is not submitted by the statutory filing date. If the return is still outstanding six months after that date, then an additional £100 penalty will be imposed. The fixed penalty cannot exceed the tax liability for the year. In large cases where substantial amounts of tax are at stake, proceedings may be taken before the Tribunal to impose daily penalties for continuing failure.

Tax Payment Dates

Payments on account (POA) of an individual's income tax liability are required on 31 January in the tax year and 31 July after the tax year. A balancing payment of any residual income tax, CGT and Class 4 National Insurance (NI) is required on 31 January after the tax year-end.

Normally each POA is simply 50% of the previous year's income tax and NI liability after taking into account tax deducted at source and tax credits. There is no POA required for CGT.

Additionally, POAs for income tax are not required if one of two tests are satisfied:

1 that the income tax and NI liability for the preceding year, net of tax deducted at source or tax credits, was less than £1,000; or
2 that more than 80% of income tax and NI liability of the preceding year, was met by tax deducted at source or from tax credits.

Balancing payments are made on 31 January following the end of the tax year, although if the return has been issued late and there is no failure to notify, the due date is three months from the issue of the return. It may be possible to collect the balancing payment of £2,000 or less via a PAYE code number for the following year if the return is submitted prior to 30 September following the end of the tax year. Coding out an underpayment means that no POAs are required for the next year.

Interest is chargeable on any tax paid late on any POA, balancing payment or tax payable following an amendment to a self-assessment or a discovery by HMRC. Interest charges are automatically included on the Statement of Account, with no de minimis level.

A surcharge of 5% of the unpaid tax is applied to any balancing payments unpaid 28 days after the due date (normally tax unpaid by 28 February). Any amounts remaining unpaid after the six months (31 July) attract an additional 5% surcharge.

Capital Gains

The main changes under self-assessment relate to the way in which losses are claimed. A loss made after 6 April 1996 must be claimed, and losses are not allowable until notice has been given to HMRC. A loss can be claimed in the tax return or by writing to HMRC. The claim must be made within four years from the fixed filing date, whether the losses are used in that period or not.

Self-assessment losses must be identified separately from losses relating to 1995/96 and earlier, and must also be used in priority to earlier losses.

A potential problem exists where valuations may be required. Under self-assessment a valuation must be made; if not, HMRC could declare the return incomplete and charge penalties. As much information as possible regarding the valuation and its basis must be given, with the gain calculated as accurately as possible. If the return is not selected for random enquiry, the gain will be treated as final after the deadline, although the rules regarding later discovery are still valid. HMRC are prepared to check a proposed valuation once the disposal has taken place and before the return is filed if details are provided on form CG34.

Partnerships

Partnerships are required to submit a separate return giving details of the partnership's profits etc, and the individual partner's shares which he then enters on his self-assessment return. The individual partner is responsible for settling the liability on his share of profits under the normal self-assessment rules. The tax attributable to the partnership's profits is no longer a joint and several liability of all the partners' self-assessment.

Any claims in connection with the partnership business must be made on the composite partnership return; it is not possible to claim capital allowances or interest through the individual's return – relief will only be given through a valid partnership claim.

4.3 Income Tax – Exemptions and Reliefs

Description	Planning income and outgoings to minimise taxable income and maximise reliefs whilst retaining flexibility of action.
Suitable for	All but additional flexibility for families.
Advantages	1 Every individual entitled to their own allowances.
	2 Numerous basic reliefs endorsed by the legislation.
Disadvantages	1 Certain tax breaks may disguise the inherent risks of the investment.
	2 Relief may be withdrawn if investment is realised.
	3 May need to hold investment for a qualifying period.

FURTHER DETAILS

Tax Efficient Income

Dividends and Interest

Dividends are grossed up by a tax credit equal to one-ninth of the cash amount, ie dividend received of £90 is grossed up by £10 to reach a taxable dividend of £100. The grossed up dividend is deemed to be the highest part of the income, followed by other savings income, then all non-savings income such as earnings.

The tax credit is offset against the tax liability on the dividend to reduce the liability to nil for basic rate taxpayers or an effective rate of 25% for higher rate taxpayers.

The tax credit is not recoverable even if the taxpayers' rate falls below 10%.

Non-UK dividends must be grossed up by the tax credit and relief given in accordance with the appropriate tax treaty.

Most interest has 20% tax withheld at source. Non-taxpayers can reclaim this and lower rate taxpayers can claim the excess back. The 20% satisfies the basic rate tax liability and higher rate taxpayers have to pay a further 20% on the gross amount.

Where the higher rate threshold is being breached, consideration should be given to ensuring that the individual's spouse uses their capacity first.

Where substantial amounts of income are received and one spouse has not used up their personal tax allowances or lower and basic rate tax bands, then a joint investment will enable 50% of the income arising to be assessed on each spouse. It is possible to alter the percentages, but this requires the ownership of the asset itself to be similarly altered and this may not always be desirable or possible.

ISAs

ISAs have replaced PEPs and TESSAs from 6 April 1999. An individual who is aged less than 50 may invest in a Cash ISA, Stocks and Shares ISA, or both, provided the overall maximum limit of £7,200 is not breached (including a cash maximum of £3,600).

Finance Act 2009 introduced increased limits for individuals aged 50 or more, the overall maximum limit is £10,200 (including a cash maximum of £5,100).

National Savings

Certain accounts and certificates are tax-free.

SAYE

Bonuses from savings accounts which are linked to share option schemes are tax-free.

Pensions

On retirement from occupational pension schemes and after the age of 50 for personal pension schemes, a tax-free cash sum may be received with a reduced pension.

Approved Employee Share Option Schemes

The increase of the exercise price of the option over the value at grant of the option will be tax-free subject to the detailed rules.

Reliefs

Deduction from Income

Losses arising from a trade can be relieved as follows:
1   in the first four years of a trade by carrying them back over the previous three years to generate a repayment of tax;
2   against the taxpayer's other income of the year of the loss and/or the previous year;
3   a loss not fully relieved under item 2 can be extended to set-off against capital gains in the year of the claim;
4   and finally, carried forward against future trading profits.

Finance Act 2009 extended the period for which trading losses can be carried back. For unincorporated entities making losses in the tax years 2008/09 and 2009/10 losses can be carried back three years. An unlimited amount can be carried back to the preceding year, but a maximum of £50,000 per tax year can be carried back to the earlier two years.

Capital losses arising from sale, or negligible value claim on shares which had been subscribed for, can be relieved against total income for the year. To obtain relief, the shares must be in a qualifying company (similar to the qualifying company rules for EIS).

Gift Aid and Deeds of Covenant

Monies gifted to a charity may be deducted from total income upon completion of a Gifts Aid declaration which is given to the charity. There is no minimum donation level. Any amount gifted to charity under an existing Deed of Covenant will continue, but any changes will now fall into the Gift Aid Scheme.

From 2003/04 onwards, it is possible for an individual to give a tax repayment to a chosen charity using the self-assessment tax return. The gift will come within the Gift Aid provisions if the necessary declaration is made on the return.

EIS and VCT

Payments into an Enterprise Investment Scheme (EIS) and Venture Capital Trusts (VCTs) attract tax relief. For EIS this is at 20% on up to £500,000 for 2010/11. For VCTs the relief is at 30% for 2010/11 on investments up to £200,000.

Pension Payments

Pension payments into retirement annuities, personal plans or AVCs are deductible against income within the normal relief limits.

Interest on Loans

Interest payable on loans to purchase shares in family companies, interests in partnerships and property let out as rental property are allowable against income. The interest on property let out as rental property is only allowed as a deduction against the rent receivable.

Summary

The above is just a brief indication of the major exemptions or reliefs which are available.

CROSS REFERENCES

4.4 Income Tax – Borrowing

Description		Structuring of loans to maximise tax relief available for interest on borrowings to acquire certain assets or settle certain liabilities.
Advantages	1	Reduces cost of borrowing for the investor.
	2	Can assist in reducing IHT if security for borrowing is attached to certain assets.
Disadvantages	1	May deny other tax reliefs available, eg in respect of Enterprise Investment Schemes.
	2	May remove flexibility in structuring one's financial affairs.
	3	Relief not normally available for overdraft interest.

FURTHER DETAILS

Commercial Aspects

Interest charges at rate of minimum of 1% over LIBOR up to 3% or 4% above LIBOR depending on lender's view of the risk involved. May also be an arrangement fee charged.

Main Residence

The relief for interest on loans to acquire an individual's main residence was abolished with effect from April 2000.

Let Property

For income tax, any activity which exploits land in the UK to produce rents or other receipts is taxed as a business. Interest paid on loans or overdrafts to any rental business is treated as a deductible expense in the computation of the assessable profits of the rental business. This is a valuable and often under-rated relief. Losses including losses created by the interest deduction are carried forward against future rental profits.

Family (Close) Company

Tax relief is given on interest on loans to acquire ordinary shares in a close company or to make a loan (or replacement loan) to the close company which is used wholly and exclusively for business purposes. A close company is broadly a UK-resident company which is under the control of five or fewer participants with extended definitions of control and attributions of rights to those participants. Interest will continue to qualify for relief if the company ceases to be close.

There is no restriction of the available relief provided all the conditions are fulfilled. The conditions include the following.

- The individual on his own, or with associates, must own or control directly or indirectly more than 5% of the ordinary shares in the company or possess rights which would give him more than 5% of the assets of the company on winding up. Associates include relatives, partners and certain trustees where the individual or associate was the settlor.
- The company must carry on a trade on a commercial basis or invest in land which is let to persons, or relatives of persons, not connected with the company. Companies controlling such companies also qualify. The individual must either work for the greater part of his time in the actual management or conduct of the company or of an associated company.
- If the individual receives or recovers any capital from the company, that capital is deemed to reduce the principal borrowed, which will reduce the amount of interest eligible for relief pro rata.

For IHT planning, where a loan is secured on a business asset the loan is set off against that asset and only the net value attracts business property relief. Thus such loans should be secured against assets not qualifying for business property relief to maximise the IHT relief in the family company. If a company does not qualify for business property relief, it may be worth considering taking out a loan secured on that company to reduce the IHT value and invest in a company which does qualify for business property relief.

Co-operatives, Employee-Controlled Companies and Partnerships

Similar rules provide relief for interest on loans to acquire interests in co-operatives and employee-controlled companies and to lend money or acquire an interest in a partnership. A partner can only obtain relief while he is a member of the partnership. Salaried partners can obtain relief in the same way as general partners. Relief for limited partners will be restricted to the amount of the contribution made by the limited partner to the partnership.

Sole Traders

There are no specific provisions whereby sole traders can obtain relief for interest on loans to their business. Where the interest is on a loan which is wholly and exclusively used for the purposes of the business, then it is allowable as a business expense.

Loans to Acquire Plant and Machinery

Interest on loans taken out by partners or employees to acquire assets which qualify for capital allowances will qualify for tax relief. Employees can no longer claim capital allowances on cars used for business and so interest relief is not available either.

Interest relief will not be available more than three years after the end of the tax year in which the loan was taken out. Where the asset is only partly used for business purposes, an appropriate proportion of the loan interest will be available.

Other Loans

Relief is available on loans to pay IHT and certain life annuities (see Section 1.9, *Home Income Plans*).

Commercial Aspects

Loans may be with any lender whether in the UK or elsewhere. If loans are taken out in a foreign currency, eg to obtain a lower rate of interest, the potential higher repayment of capital must be carefully considered should the exchange rate move. For overseas lenders, the loan must be at no more than reasonable commercial rate.

Where security for the loan is provided on jointly-owned property, the joint owner should consider taking specific advice on the implications of using their partial ownership as security.

CROSS REFERENCES

4.5   Income Tax – Overseas Aspects

Description	Generally, UK taxation is charged on income from UK sources and worldwide income arising to individuals resident and domiciled in the UK, although there are numerous reliefs which enable certain taxpayers to reduce the burden of taxation.
Suitable for	All persons, particularly those who may have, or can establish, a non-UK domicile or non-UK residence status.
Advantages	1 Reduce income chargeable to UK taxation.
	2 May restrict chargeability to income remitted to the UK.
	3 May defer income arising and thus its immediate chargeability.
Disadvantages	1 Costs.
	2 Personal desires and commerciality.
	3 Sometimes complex structures.
	4 There is a cost to claiming remittance treatment, be it a minimum £30,000 tax charge and/or the surrender of UK tax allowances.

FURTHER DETAILS

The Basic Concepts

In the UK, the extent of an individual's liability to income tax depends on one's residence and domicile status.

If an individual is resident, ordinarily resident and domiciled in the UK, the UK charges income tax on income arising worldwide. A resident of the UK who is not domiciled or not ordinarily resident in the UK can make a claim to only be charged on foreign source income if it is brought into or enjoyed in the UK, referred to as the 'remittance basis'. Non-residents are only liable to UK taxes on UK source income.

It is important to understand the meaning of the concepts of residence and domicile before considering the planning opportunities available.

Residence and Ordinary Residence

Whilst the rules which determine residence and domicile are the same for everyone, it is usually helpful to look at these separately from the viewpoint of UK nationals who are overseas, or considering going overseas, and for non-UK domiciliaries coming to the UK.

An individual's residence is based on the amount of time the individual spends and intends to spend in the UK. Individuals become resident in the UK if they are physically present here for 183 days or more in the tax year or if they spend an average of 91 days or more in the UK over a four-year period. The Finance Act 2008 amended the day counting rules, so that if an individual is in the UK at midnight this counts as a day spent in the UK. This represents a significant shift from the old rules, where days of arrival and departure were ignored. Individuals should be very careful about monitoring their visits to the UK.

Ordinary residence depends on qualitative tests rather than quantitative tests. It refers to an individual's abode in a particular place or country which has been adopted for settled purposes for the regular order of life for a period, whether of short or long duration. This test is the prime one to satisfy for exemption from certain taxes, particularly where an individual seeks to absent him or herself for one tax year only. In most cases, ordinary residence will be determined by the days spent in the UK over a number of years and one's future intention.

Strictly, one is either resident or non-resident for the whole of a tax year; however by HMRC concession it is possible, under certain circumstances, to split the tax year into resident and non-resident periods if you leave or come to the UK part way through a tax year.

Leaving the UK

Anyone leaving the UK to take up full-time service abroad for a period which will encompass a complete UK tax year, will be regarded as not resident and not ordinarily resident from the day after departure to the day before they return, providing any visits back to the UK during their absence total less than 183 days in any one tax year and average less than 91 days per annum over the period of absence up to a maximum of four years.

Individuals who do not leave the UK for full-time service overseas but intend to stay away for at least three tax years, can obtain non-resident and not-ordinarily-resident status from the day after departure by agreement with HMRC if they present evidence of their intentions. To retain this status, the intentions must be fulfilled, and any visits to the UK must be within the 183-day and 91-day limits.

Coming to the UK for less than Two Years

Anyone coming to the UK for less than two years will be treated as not ordinarily resident for the duration of the stay. Their residence status will be determined year by year. If they spend 183 days or more in the UK in a tax year, they will be resident for the relevant tax year. If not, they will be not resident.

Coming to the UK for Two to Three Years

Individuals who come to the UK for at least two years, but less than three years, will be treated as resident but not ordinarily resident from the date of arrival for the duration of their stay, irrespective of the actual number of days spent in the UK in each tax year.

Coming to the UK for at least Three Years

Coming to the UK with an intention to stay for at least three years makes an individual resident and ordinarily resident for the duration of their stay, from the date of arrival.

Increased Length of Stay

Where the intended stay is extended, the individual's residence and ordinary residence status will be revised accordingly. The date from which this will apply depends on the particular circumstances.

Regular Visitors

Anyone visiting the UK for at least 91 days on average per year over a period of at least four years will be treated as resident and ordinarily resident from the start of the fifth tax year. However, if the visits are intended at the outset, the individual will be resident and ordinarily resident from the first year and each year thereafter.

Accommodation in the UK

Although owning accommodation in the UK will not automatically make one resident, anyone resident but not ordinarily resident will become ordinarily resident if they buy a property or acquire a leasehold that will exceed the third anniversary of their arrival. However, if they leave the UK before the third anniversary of their arrival, they can apply to have their not ordinarily resident status during their stay reinstated.

Domicile

Domicile is distinct from residence and ordinary residence. In simple terms, one is domiciled in the place considered to be one's home country. However, it is a complex area of general law rather than tax law, which means that the facts for each individual need to be studied in detail. There are three types of domicile as outlined below.

Domicile of Origin

A domicile of origin is acquired at birth, when it is determined by the father's domicile (or the mother's domicile if the father is dead or they are not married). It is possible to have a domicile of origin in a country one has never visited (eg if one is raised in a country where one's parents are not domiciled). In order to lose the domicile of origin one must obtain a domicile of choice or dependency, but it will automatically revert if the new domicile is lost.

Domicile of Choice

A domicile of choice is created when an individual settles in a country that is not their domicile of origin with the intention of making it their permanent home. However, it is not easy to evidence a domicile of choice, because one has to acquire such strong ties with the new country and lose so many ties with the old country that the change must be shown in many, if not all, aspects of one's life.

Domicile of Dependency

Whilst under the age of 16 and unmarried, a child's domicile will normally depend on the domicile of the relevant parent (as mentioned in the paragraph on domicile of origin). If the parent takes on a new domicile during this time, then the child will automatically take on a domicile of dependency in line with the parent's new domicile.

Women who married prior to 1 January 1974 also acquired their husband's domicile as a domicile of dependency upon marriage. This domicile of dependency can be shed by the woman leaving her husband and thus reverting to her domicile of origin or by taking on a new domicile of choice. This position no longer affects US national women who are married to UK domiciled men, as they retain their domicile of origin.

Women who were married after 1973 are able to retain or acquire a separate domicile from that of their husband.

Finance Act 2008

This Act introduced significant changes to the taxation of non domiciled or not ordinarily resident individuals.

For longer term UK residents (i.e. those UK resident for 7 out of the last 9 tax years prior to the year in question), all unremitted overseas income and gains will be charged to UK tax as they arise unless a claim for the remittance basis to apply is made and they pay a UK tax charge of £30,000 on nominated elements of the overseas income and gains. Note the claim can be varied year on year and should not affect domicile status.

Those making the claim for the remittance basis will also lose their entitlement to the UK personal allowance and capital gains annual exemption.

The £30,000 tax charge does not apply to under 18s, or if an individual has unremitted income of less than £2,000. The £30,000 tax charge should qualify for relief under Double Tax treaties where available, although there are anticipated problems with countries such as the US.

Payment of the £30,000 tax charge directly to HMRC from a foreign bank account will not count as a remittance.

For non domiciled individuals who do not exceed the '7 out of 9' threshold, then any claim for the remittance basis will mean the loss of their personal allowance and annual capital gains exemption.

The 2008 Finance Act also seeks to tackle techniques that existed to avoid falling into the definition of a remittance and will block many of these routes. The legislation aims to tax any monies that effectively are remitted by an individual, such that an individual or his close family has the use or enjoyment of those monies in the UK.

PLANNING

This section sets out some very broad thoughts on the key aspects in respect of overseas tax planning.

Status	Taxability of overseas investment income*
Resident Ordinarily Resident Domiciled in the UK	Taxable on arising basis
Resident Not UK Domiciled Ordinarily Resident	Taxed on remittance basis provided a claim has been made
Resident Not Ordinarily Resident Domiciled in the UK	Commonwealth and Irish citizens – remittance basis Non-Commonwealth citizens – taxable on arising basis
Resident Not Ordinarily Resident Not UK Domiciled	Taxed on remittance basis, provided a claim has been made
Not Resident Regardless of Domicile	Not taxable

* Irish source income is generally treated as arising in the UK, so not subject to any remittance claim.

Planning for Tax Status

As we have seen, UK resident non-UK domiciliaries can make a claim to be taxed on non-UK source income only to the extent that it is remitted to the UK. It can therefore be vital to maintain a non-UK domicile despite the £30,000 tax charge. However, it is inevitable that as an individual spends more and more time in the UK, the number of ties with the UK also increases, potentially weakening the non-UK domiciled status.. It is therefore important for the individual to monitor and maintain ties with their home country such that those ties can be evidenced.

Non-residents do not need a non-UK domicile status to enjoy special income tax treatment but, if an individual is going overseas permanently, they may wish to consider whether or not it is worthwhile shedding their UK domicile and taking on a domicile of choice in their new country. This may enable them to take advantage of a non-UK domiciliary status if they have to visit the UK for a short-term stay at some point in the future.

Such a step should not, however, be taken lightly, as it will have a major effect not only on the individual's tax status but also the tax status of family members. Furthermore, if they subsequently leave the country where they have acquired a domicile of choice for anything other than a temporary absence, then their UK domicile of origin will revert (even if they do not return to the UK), unless a new domicile of choice is clearly established.

Retaining Non-resident Status

Planning UK visits to obtain or retain non-resident status will mean that foreign sources of income are excluded from the scope of UK tax.

Becoming Resident in the UK

Income received before becoming resident will be treated as capital when residence is obtained.

UK Income Tax Treatment of Non-residents

Personal Allowances

Some non-residents, including all EU citizens, qualify for UK personal allowances. In addition, many others are able to claim personal allowances under a DTA between the UK and the country where they are resident. However, unless a relevant DTA states otherwise, these allowances can be clawed back if the individual has significant sources of 'excluded' UK income which is exempted from UK taxes or is only taxed at low or standard rates. 'Excluded' UK income includes interest, dividends and state pensions.

UK Government Securities

Provided the interest does not form part of a UK trade, UK tax is not chargeable on interest arising on UK Government 'FOTRA' (Free of Tax to Residents Abroad) securities if the individual is not ordinarily resident in the UK.

UK Bank and Building Society Interest

If the account holder is not resident, the UK tax liability on interest from a UK bank or building society account is limited to the tax, if any, deducted at source, unless they are carrying on a trade, profession or vocation through a UK branch or agency. Where available personal allowances and reliefs produce a lower tax liability, it is possible to claim the repayment of any tax over-deducted.

UK deposit takers normally deduct UK tax (currently at 20%) when interest is paid or credited to the account, but anyone who is not ordinarily resident in the UK can arrange to have interest paid without tax deductions by completing a declaration form. This can effectively reduce the actual tax liability to nil.

UK Tax-efficient Investments

Investment in Individual Savings Accounts (ISAs) are not available to individuals unless they are resident and ordinarily resident in the UK, are a Crown employee or married to or in a civil partnership with a Crown employee. However, existing ISAs can be retained by investors who become not resident.

UK Dividends

Dividends are 'excluded' income and are not therefore liable to additional income tax, but may affect the availability of personal allowances.

UK Rental Income

UK rents are subjected to higher rates of taxation where appropriate. Tenants and letting agents paying rents to non-resident landlords are obliged to deduct taxes at source unless HMRC have given approval for the rents to be paid gross. Approval is generally given, provided the landlord's UK tax affairs are up to date.

UK Earnings

Only remuneration physically earned in the UK for duties that are not incidental to any overseas employment is liable to UK taxation, but this liability arises irrespective of where it is paid.

PAYE is due where the employee has a UK employer or is an overseas employee answerable to a UK employer (even if they are actually paid by their overseas employer). UK employees working full-time overseas can apply for an 'NT' (no tax) PAYE code so that their remuneration can be paid without UK PAYE tax deductions. Overseas employees with some UK workdays for a UK employer can apply for a code that only subjects the proportion of their remuneration physically earned in the UK to UK PAYE tax deductions.

Separate rules apply for social security contributions. It is possible for income not assessable to UK income tax to be liable to UK National Insurance contributions and for income liable to UK income tax to be subjected to social security in another country.

UK Business Profits

Profits earned in the UK by a non-resident from a trade, profession or vocation undertaken wholly or partly in the UK or, where only partly carried on in the UK, from the part of the trade carried on in the UK, are liable to UK income tax.

Double Tax Relief

The UK has a number of DTAs with other countries which allows residents of those countries to claim reliefs and exemptions on certain types of UK source income. The terms of each individual agreement must be checked, but they normally include special rules for short-term employments and self-employments (usually up to six months) carried out in the UK, visiting teachers and researchers, pensions and annuities, royalties, dividends and interest.

UK Tax Treatment of Individuals who are Resident but not Domiciled or not Ordinarily Resident

Bringing Overseas Investment Income to the UK

Individuals who are resident but are not UK domiciled or who are not ordinarily resident can restrict UK taxation on overseas investment income to only that income that is remitted to the UK if the claim is made. This treatment is described as 'the remittance basis'.

Care must be taken with respect to the remittance of overseas income, as it not only relates to cash transfers to the UK, but also to what are called 'constructive remittances'. For example, a loan used in the UK and repaid out of overseas funds, would be caught. This includes credit card payments where the card has been used to buy services or goods in the UK, but the bill is paid out of overseas funds.

Significant planning can be done around remittances, in particular prior to an individual's arrival in the UK. This is because all cash owned on arrival, including income earned before they arrive, is treated as capital. This capital should be isolated and can then be brought into the UK at any time free of UK income tax.

Once the individual has become resident in the UK, special attention should be paid to the structure of overseas bank accounts, ensuring that different accounts are used to separate income, capital gains and pure capital. This is important so that the onerous UK tax rules on mixed funds are not triggered and so that it is easier to identify the nature of the funds being remitted.

If an individual's bank account contains multiple sources, ie income and capital, or capital gains, HMRC have introduced special rules to identify what is being remitted to the UK.

Individuals taking advantage of the remittance basis of assessment will usually have the majority of their funds invested offshore. An account containing capital can be increased by funds that have been subjected to UK income and/or CGTs, gifts and proceeds from the disposal of non-UK assets that created capital losses.

There is a lot of anti-avoidance legislation governing tax planning in this area, including significant changes in the Finance Act 2008, so care must be taken when creating structures and schemes that seek to take advantage of the remittance basis of assessment.

The UK Taxation of Earnings

Irrespective of domicile, employees who are not ordinarily resident in the UK will only be assessed on earnings for duties performed wholly or partly overseas if those earnings are remitted to the UK: there are significant tax planning opportunities for such individuals, even if paid by a UK employer. Non-UK domiciliaries who are ordinarily resident are only liable to UK tax in respect of remuneration earned from an overseas employer in respect of an employment performed wholly overseas, if that remuneration is remitted to the UK.

Non-UK domiciled employees with overseas employers may be able to claim corresponding approval in respect of their employer's pension scheme. This effectively entitles them to the same reliefs as for a UK-approved pension scheme, which means that the employer's contributions are tax-free and tax relief can be claimed for any employee's contributions.

Non-domiciled individuals may also be able to claim tax reliefs in respect of home travel costs for themselves and their families which are borne by their employers. There are special conditions to determine the period for which this can be claimed.

In certain circumstances, employees coming to the UK for a period of less than two years may be able to benefit from significant tax reliefs in relation to accommodation and related costs. Planning in this area may involve major cooperation from the employer.

Double Tax Relief

Individuals coming to the UK may find that income is liable to tax in the UK and the country where the income arises. In such cases, any DTAs between the two countries will determine which country has primary taxing rights and how the other country will give double tax relief, if appropriate. The UK normally gives such relief by allowing a tax credit for the foreign tax against the UK liability arising on the relevant income. This effectively reduces the overall liability to the higher of the two tax bills.

Even if no DTA exists, the UK will usually allow a foreign tax credit against the UK tax due on overseas income provided that tax is paid in the country where the income arises. Where foreign tax arises elsewhere, such as the individual's home country, it is necessary to check whether any DTA with that country prevents the UK from taxing the income. If not, a double tax situation could exist.

As mentioned, the new £30,000 remittance basis tax charge should qualify under the Double Tax Agreements for relief, although this is as yet untested.

The Offshore Vehicle

The essence is to invest in a vehicle situated in a low tax country such that the gross or near gross income is reinvested and the taxpayer pays tax only on the disposal of the investment, or disposes of the investment in the vehicle. The use is restricted by the Offshore Fund Legislation.

It is still possible to hold a portfolio within an offshore bond avoiding CGT and deferring income tax until the bond is surrendered, providing collectives are used. If the bonds are 'personal portfolio bonds' then an additional tax charge will arise under the regulations.

There is substantial anti-avoidance legislation to prevent the transfer of assets overseas such that the income arises to a person overseas in a low tax country, and the UK transferor seeks to obtain a benefit from those assets or income in the future. Planning on this level requires great care.

CROSS REFERENCES

Offshore Funds **3.10**
Offshore Bonds **3.16**
CGT – Overseas Aspects **4.13**
Overseas Trusts **4.24**

4.6 Income Tax – Tax Credits

Description	A mechanism to provide that persons entitled to credits receive them directly or through their wage packets to reduce their tax and National Insurance payments, or provide a cash benefit to them where the credits exceed the National Insurance and tax liability.
Suitable for	Those with children, those who are disabled or those on low income.
Advantages	1 Seamless transparent single system of income support.
	2 Direction of payments to appropriate person.
	3 Relieving of in-work poverty and enhancing work incentives.
	4 Better support for disabilities.
	5 More responsive to changes in circumstances.
Disadvantages	1 Impact on employers.
	2 Households, not individuals, assessed.
	3 Over complicated claim forms to complete.

SPECIFIC ASPECTS

Previous Credits

Children's Tax Credit

The Children's Tax Credit was designed to replace the Married Couples Allowance and was targeted at low to middle income families with children under 16 years old. It started on 6 April 2001 and was replaced by the new Child Tax Credit on 6 April 2003.

The Children's Tax Credit was a means tested income tax allowance that reduced the tax bill of individuals, or in the case of joint claimants, the higher earner's tax bill.

Working Families Tax Credit and Disabled Persons Tax Credit

The Working Families Tax Credit (WFTC) and Disabled Persons Tax Credit (DPTC) were introduced in October 1999 and replaced on 6 April 2003 by the Working Tax Credit. As for the Children's Tax Credit, the WFTC and DPTC were means tested and were paid via PAYE for the employed earner and via the self-assessment tax return for the self-employed.

Existing Tax Credits

Child Tax Credit (CTC) and Working Tax Credit (WTC)

To be eligible for the tax credits an individual must be aged over 16 and usually be UK resident. Some non-UK residents will still qualify under certain conditions.

Couples living together as man and wife, whether actually married or not, must file a claim based on joint circumstances. Single persons should claim on individual circumstances.

The tax credit paid depends on the individual's or couple's circumstances and takes into account children, hours worked, disability, income levels, etc.

The level of income is based on the income in the preceding tax year, ie for 2010/11 the gross income for 2009/10 will be used as the basis for paying tax credits. Income from Child Benefit is not taken into account when deciding the level of credits to award, and can be received on top of the credits given.

Child Tax Credit

CTC is paid to families with at least one child or young person up to the age of 16, or under 20 (19 for years up to 2005/06) if in full-time higher education, such as A-levels, NVQ level 3 or Scottish Highers. If the child lives with another family for part of the time, a decision must be made as to who has main responsibility. CTC can only be paid to one family.

CTC is paid in addition to Child Benefit and is available to families with annual incomes of up to about £58,000 (£66,000 if there is a child under one year old). The maximum entitlement is available if an individual's or couple's income is less than £16,190.

A disability element may also be available if Disability Living Allowance (DLA) is received for a child, or a child is registered blind or has been removed from the blind register in the period 28 weeks before a claim for CTC.

The CTC is paid directly to the main carer (usually the mother) of the children. Payments may be received weekly or four weekly and are usually paid direct into a bank or building society account.

Working Tax Credit

The WTC consists of several elements and is intended to top-up the earnings of low paid working individuals. The WTC is paid via PAYE unless an individual is self-employed, where it is paid directly to the individual, usually through a bank or building society account. The 'child care' element of WTC is paid directly to the main carer of the children along with CTC.

To claim for WTC, an individual must be either:

(a) working (employed or self-employed) when a claim is made; or
(b) starting work within seven days of making the claim.

The work should be expected to last for a period of not less than four weeks, and must be paid.

The elements of the WTC are:

- the WTC base element;
- child care element;
- 30-hour element;

- disability element;
- severe disability element;
- 50+ return to work element (16–29 hours per week);
- 50+ return to work element (30+ hours per week);
- child care element for child care for one child;
- child care element for child care for two or more children.

If an individual's income, or a couple's joint income, is less than £6,420 they will receive the maximum credit. If the income is above the threshold, the amount is reduced by 39p for every pound of income over the threshold.

To qualify for WTC an individual without children must be aged 25 or over *and* work for at least 30 hours a week. If an individual is aged 16 or over, and either the individual or their partner is responsible for a child or young person, they must work at least 16 hours per week to qualify. If an individual has a disability *and* satisfies either the 'qualifying benefit' rules or the special 'fast track' rules to qualify for the disability element, the individual must also work at least 16 hours per week.

The child care element of the WTC is paid to help with the cost of paying for registered or approved child care. The child care element pays up to 80% of the child care costs to a maximum of £175 per week for one child and £300 per week for two or more children.

A couple with children may qualify for the 30-hour element if at least 30 hours are worked jointly, provided that one of the couple works at least 16 hours.

An individual may be entitled to the disability element of WTC if they work at least 16 hours a week *and* have a physical or mental disability *and* they satisfy either the 'qualifying benefit' test or the special 'fast track' rules. An individual must have a disability that is likely to last at least six months. Also, an individual's gross earnings must be at least 20% less than they were before the disability; the minimum reduction is £15 per week.

If a couple are both entitled to the disability element, as above, they may receive two disability elements.

To qualify for the 50+ return to work element, one half of a couple must be over 50 years old and returning to work after claiming out of work benefits for at least the previous six months, and must be working at least 16 hours a week.

Periods of maternity, adoption or paternity leave are considered as being periods of work for WTC purposes, provided that the minimum hours were worked immediately before the leave.

Pension Credits

The new Pension Credit was introduced on 6 October 2003 and replaced the Minimum Income Guarantee.

The Pension Credit guarantees that individuals over 60 will be paid at least £132.60 per week if single, or £202.40 per week for couples. Where an individual, or their partner, is over 65, higher rates apply.

The Pension Credit is calculated by the Pension Service, who look at the level of net income and the level of savings of an individual or couple. Where savings exceed £6,000, the excess is taken into account when calculating if the Pension Credit is allowable.

Credits may also be paid for individuals over 65 who have saved for their retirement. Up to an additional £20.52 a week can be paid to individuals or £27.09 a week to couples.

CROSS REFERENCES

4.7   Capital Gains Tax Planning

Description	Finance Act 2010 has altered the CGT regime. The Emergency Budget held on 22 June 2010 made further changes. CGT from 23 June 2010 is chargeable at either 18% (gains falling within the basic rate band) or 28% (gains falling above the basic rate band) depending on level of income also received in the year. Personal representatives and trustees will be liable at 28%. From 6 April 2010 the lifetime allowance for entrepreneurs' relief was increased from £1m to £2m. In respect of gains from 23 June 2010 entrepreneurs' relief was further increased to £5m. Between 6 April 1998 and 5 April 2010 there was a general flat rate of CGT of 18% Entrepreneurs' relief was first introduced for business gains made on or after 6 April 2008 and originally reduced the CGT rate to 10% on the first £1m per person. Prior to 6 April 2008, CGT was charged after any indexation allowance, then the applicable taper relief was applied, the resulting gains being charged at the individual's marginal rates of tax, at 10%, 20% or 40% (see Section 4.8 for more details). The nature of the assets, the size of the gain, individual circumstances and cash flow position are all factors which need to be borne in mind when giving advice.
Suitable for	Individuals, trustees and personal representatives who hold assets chargeable to CGT.
Advantages	1 Each individual has a CGT annual exemption of £10,100, below which no CGT is paid. 2 CGT can be saved by using spouses' CGT annual exemptions, their lower tax bands and any CGT reliefs. 3 Substantial CGT savings can be made from using general tax planning techniques.
Disadvantages	CGT calculations can be very complex, particularly when dealing with Entrepreneurs' Relief and often needs the help of professional tax advisers.

Indexation

This was generally only available on disposals of assets made before 6 April 2008. However, any assets that were transferred between a husband and wife or civil partners before 6 April 2008 that were owned on 6 April 2008, may still qualify for indexation allowance when ultimately disposed.

In respect of disposals made before 6 April 2008, indexation gave individuals relief for inflation on their assets held between 6 April 1982 and 5 April 1998, based on the published RPI increases. Indexation allowance was frozen at April 1998, and still given on disposals between this date and 5 April 2008.

Taper Relief

This is solely available to any gains realised between 6 April 1998 and 5 April 2008 (see Section 4.12 for more details).

The Strategy

As with any planning, there is a basic strategy to follow. Substantial tax savings can be made from using general tax planning techniques. Dealing with the basics, such as using annual exemptions and spouses' tax reliefs, can reduce the tax payable by several thousands of pounds.

Basic Planning

Points to consider include the following:
1 use the annual exemptions for both spouses or civil partners (£10,100 each);
2 ensure that both spouses make gains in order to use their lower tax bands in order to pay CGT at 18%.
3 ensure that capital losses are in the right place so that the spouse or civil partner disposing of a particular asset is able to reduce his or her liability by use of these brought forward or current year losses;
4 one spouse/civil partner sells the shares and the other repurchases the shares or transfers into an ISA, thereby using one spouse's CGT annual exemption;
5 convert income gains to capital gains to use the CGT annual exemption and to potentially reduce the tax from 50% to 18%/28%;
6 hold at least 5% of the shares and be an officer or employee, after 12 months potentially qualifying them for 10% CGT on the first £5m of gains. Consider making the spouse a shareholder/business asset holder to obtain a further £5m 10% allowance;
7 the matching rules have changed on numerous occasions, especially any disposals after 5 April 2008 which are subject to the same day, or the next 30 days, and then the shares are treated as one share pool. Disposals should be planned carefully;
8 if any capital losses are made on trading shares, it may be worth making an election to convert these into an income loss so as to receive income tax relief at 50%, compared to 18%/28% relief from CGT;
9 use trusts to save CGT. Ability to appoint the assets to other family members using their CGT annual exemptions and the trusts' CGT annual exemption.

Trading Assets

There are a number of points to consider in respect of trading assets, these are as follows:

1   Entrepreneurs' relief – this offers opportunities for those entrepreneurs who have held their shares or business assets for 12 months or more. In this situation the first £5m of gains are taxed at 10%. Care should be taken of the exact assets being disposed, as entrepreneurs' relief has a number of traps.
2   Asset freezing.
3   Use of trusts – relevant reliefs, will trusts.
4   Deferral reliefs – EIS companies and rolling over into other trading assets.
5   Hold-over relief in relation to gifts.

Non-Trading Assets

Non-trading assets are not treated as favourably under the new regime and will not be eligible for entrepreneurs' relief and hence will be taxed at either 18% or 28% . CGT planning should consider:
1   hold-over relief for IHT on gifts into trusts where the settlor cannot benefit;
2   planning before an asset rises in value by putting it into trust early;
3   holding share portfolios in a collective vehicle such as an OEIC or unit trust so that the shares/units are sold subject to CGT at 18%/28% after annual exemptions, compared to investment bonds which are taxable at up to 50% income tax.

Overseas

Overseas planning through an offshore vehicle or by becoming non-resident can still be attractive, and with careful planning tax savings can be made:
1   emigration can be considered as long as the individual is prepared to remain abroad for five complete tax years, or where double taxation agreement (DTA) relief is available;
2   use of offshore trusts provides opportunities for non-domiciled individuals but are not so good for UK-domiciled individuals;
3   conversion of capital gains to income gains, as income gains are not subject to the five years requirement for non-residence.

CROSS REFERENCES

All CGT sections   (4.8–4.13)
Unit Trusts and OEICs   3.8

4.8 CGT – The Charge to Tax

Description	CGT applies to chargeable gains arising on disposals of assets. Key points to consider are:
	1 calculation of the gains;
	2 available exemptions;
	3 EIS deferral relief;
	4 hold-over relief.

FURTHER DETAILS

CGT is payable on gains realised by individuals, trustees and by personal representatives of deceased persons.

Every gain is a chargeable gain unless expressly provided otherwise in the legislation. The legislation excludes gains under this broad definition by means of a series of exemptions which exclude certain types of gains, assets and disposals (see Section 4.9, *CGT – Exemptions and Reliefs*).

An individual will be chargeable to CGT in respect of worldwide chargeable gains accruing to him in a year of assessment during any part of which he is resident in the UK or during which he is ordinarily resident. Individuals who have acquired assets in the UK and then leave for a period of less than five complete tax years will remain chargeable to CGT on gains made on those assets while abroad and will become payable in the tax year of return.

Chargeable Assets

All forms of property, wherever situated, are assets for the purposes of CGT, with the exception of sterling. Certain assets are specifically designated as non-chargeable by legislation. In addition, the legislation provides that certain gains arising on disposals of assets which are not designated as non-chargeable shall nevertheless be exempt from CGT (see Section 4.9, *CGT – Exemptions and Reliefs*).

Disposals

CGT applies on a disposal of chargeable assets. Disposals cover sales, gifts and transfers for non-monetary consideration. Disposals also include part disposals and the loss or destruction of an asset even if no compensation is received. The transfer of assets on death is not a disposal for CGT purposes.

Calculation of Gains

A chargeable gain is calculated by deducting the allowable costs and expenditure from the gross sale proceeds. In some cases, a disposal is deemed to have been made for a consideration equal to the market value of the asset disposed of. The market value rule applies to gifts, disposals otherwise than by way of a bargain at arm's length, disposals where the consideration cannot be valued, and transactions between connected persons such as family members.

Any assets disposed after 5 April 2008, but acquired before April 1982, will use an automatic market value at 31 March 1982 as the CGT cost, (disregarding any expenditure incurred prior to April 1982).

Any expenditure or additional expenditure is allowed as a deduction if it fits within the four categories only:

1   costs of acquiring or creating the asset;
2   capital expenditure which improves or enhances the value of the asset;
3   costs of preserving title to the asset;
4   defined incidental costs of acquisition and disposal (eg valuation fees, and legal costs).

Indexation allowance was designed to give some measure of relief for the inflationary element of the gain, although this was frozen from 5 April 1998. Any disposals made between 6 April 1998 and 5 April 2008 were entitled to deduct any indexation allowance that had accrued to 5 April 1998. However, indexation allowance could not convert a gain into a loss or to increase the size of a loss. Indexation allowance has now been withdrawn for any disposals made after 5 April 2008.

Matching Rules

The matching rules were changed with the introduction of taper relief in 1998 ceasing the general pool for any acquisitions made on or after 6 April 1998 treating acquisitions on a separate basis as described below:

Disposals before 6 April 2008 were identified with acquisitions as follows:

- same day acquisition;
- acquisitions of the same asset within 30 days of a disposal (FIFO basis);
- previous acquisitions after 5 April 1998 (LIFO basis);
- pool as at 5 April 1998;
- shares held at 5 April 1982;
- shares acquired pre-6 April 1965.

The 2008 Finance Act simplified the matching rules and any disposals of shares after 5 April 2008 are now identified with acquisitions as follows:

- same day acquisition;
- acquisitions of the same asset within 30 days of a disposal (FIFO basis);
- all other acquisitions treated as one pool.

Allowable Losses

Allowable losses arising in a particular year of assessment must be set against chargeable gains of the same year, even if the net gains are thereby reduced to below the annual exempt amount. Allowable losses brought forward need only be used to the extent that current year chargeable gains less current year allowable losses (in 2007/08 and prior – before taper relief was applied) exceed the annual exempt amount. A loss is an allowable loss if a gain on the disposal would have been a chargeable gain. Therefore, losses arising on exempt assets or exempt disposals are not allowable losses.

Following the introduction of self-assessment, brought forward losses have to be differentiated between those arising pre- and post-5 April 1997. Post-self-assessment losses are used first.

Following changes in the Finance Act 2002, settlors are able to elect to set off personal capital losses against attributed overseas trust gains.

Reliefs

In addition to the exemptions for particular assets, there are a number of reliefs which operate either to exempt the whole or part of the gain from CGT or to effect a hold-over or roll-over of the gain in particular circumstances. These include the annual exemption for individuals and trustees, hold-over relief on certain gifts and EIS deferral relief.

Rate of Tax

The Emergency Budget held on 22 June 2010 altered for the first time the CGT rate mid-way through a tax year. This budget re-instated the old system of taxing gains by reference to the level of income received in a tax year. Taxpayers will now suffer tax at 18% on gains that fall within their basic rate band, and 28% on gains that fall above the basic rate band.

For gains made between 6 April 2008 and 22 June 2010 a general flat rate of 18% CGT applies. No relief is given for taper relief or indexation allowance on any capital gains made on or after 6 April 2008 as these reliefs were abolished by Finance Act 2008. This 18% CGT applied to both lower and higher rate tax payers alike.

For gains made in 2007/08 and before, an individual was chargeable to CGT at the income tax rate which would apply if the chargeable gains were added to his taxable income. If an individual was a lower or basic rate taxpayer, but the addition of his chargeable gains took him into the higher rate band, his gains were taxed partly at 10%, partly at 20% and partly at 40%.

Entrepreneurs' Relief

Entrepreneurs' relief was introduced by Finance Act 2008 and is a relief for business gains made on or after 6 April 2008 which reduces the CGT rate to 10% subject to the lifetime allowance. The lifetime allowance was £1million per person between 6 April 2008 to 5 April 2010, £2million between 6 April 2010 and 22 June 2010 and thereafter was increased to £5million in the Emergency Budget.

This relief gives individuals and certain trustees of interest in possession settlements, a £1million lifetime allowance on disposals after 5 April 2008 at an effective rate of 10%, with the balance being taxed at 18%. The precise calculation actually gives a 4/9ths reduction of the gain, and then taxes the balance to 18% (18% less 4/9ths = 10% rate) so we have referred to the rate as 10% for simplicity.

In all cases a material disposal must be made of:

- Shares or securities in an individual's personal trading company who owned at least 5% of the ordinary share capital (which also have at least 5% of the votes) in which they are an officer or employee; or
- Part or whole of a trading business or trading partnership; or
- Assets that were used for trading purposes in an individual's partnership or personal trading company.

—   In all the above cases, the person must have owned the shares/ business for a continuous period of at least one year prior to the disposal. This relief does not apply to investment gains.

There are a number of restrictions to reduce the amount of entrepreneurs' relief if the assets were not used by the qualifying business for the whole period of ownership, or for any period after 5 April 2008 where rent has been received on an asset. There are difficult rules when an individual sells their company for loan notes, and an unwelcome possible surprise when accepting earn outs.

Payment of Tax

CGT is payable on 31 January following the tax year of assessment. Where the disposal consideration is payable by instalments over a period exceeding 18 months, an individual can apply to pay the tax by instalments. He no longer needs to satisfy HMRC that payment in one sum would cause undue hardship. Interest will be charged if an instalment is paid late.

An individual can elect to pay the CGT on a disposal of certain assets by way of gift in ten equal annual instalments, the first to be paid on the ordinary due date. A similar election can be made on deemed transfers of such assets when a person becomes absolutely entitled to any settled property or where a life interest comes to an end. The election can only be made where the disposal is not eligible for hold-over relief (see Section 4.11, *Hold-over Reliefs*) or where hold-over relief is available but the amount of chargeable gains exceeds the amount which can be held over. The assets are:

1   land, or an interest in land;
2   a controlling shareholding in any company;
3   shares or securities in an unquoted company whose shares are not dealt in on AIM.

Interest is charged on the unpaid tax which will be payable with each instalment.

CROSS REFERENCES

CGT – Exemptions and Reliefs   **4.9**
CGT – EIS Deferral Relief   **4.10**
CGT – Hold-over Reliefs   **4.11**

4.9   CGT – Exemptions and Reliefs

Description	Various exemptions and reliefs may be available on a given disposal which can be broadly classified as follows: 1 Annual exemption; 2 Exempt assets; 3 Exempt gains and transfers; 4 No gain/no loss transfers; 5 Principal Private Residence Relief; 6 Reliefs.
Suitable for	Disposals of any assets.

FURTHER DETAILS

Annual Exemption

For 2009/10 and 2010/11 an individual is exempt from CGT on the first £10,100 of chargeable gains made in the tax year. If the exemption is unused in the tax year it is lost, as there is no provision to carry it forward.

Both husband and wife or civil partners are entitled to their own full annual exemption which they can set against their respective gains. Children are also entitled to their own annual exemption.

Exempt Assets

All assets fall within the scope to CGT unless they are specifically designated by the legislation as non-chargeable. The assets on which any gains arising on their disposal are exempt from CGT include the following:
1   motor cars;
2   savings certificates and non-marketable securities, ie those which can only be transferred with the consent of a government minister or national debt commissioner or those which cannot be transferred.

Exempt Gains and Transfers

In addition to exempt assets, there are a number of exemptions which apply to gains arising in defined circumstances. These include disposals of the following (subject to certain conditions):
- annual payments due under a covenant;
- chattels which are wasting assets (having useful lives less than 50 years);
- chattels where the sale proceeds are less than £6,000. If the consideration exceeds £6,000 the charge is limited to the lower of five-thirds of the excess and the capital gain is calculated under the normal rules;
- debts;
- decorations for valour and gallantry, provided they are sold by the original recipient or by someone who received them as a gift;

- foreign currency acquired for personal expenditure outside the UK. This includes money spent on the purchase or maintenance of any residence outside the UK;
- gifts of certain nationally important land, buildings and works of art, etc known as gifts for the public benefit;
- Government securities;
- insurance policies and life assurance policies;
- qualifying corporate bonds;
- pension rights;
- personal equity plans (PEPs) and individual savings accounts;
- private residences which have been the owner's sole or main residence (see below);
- shares issued under the Business Expansion Scheme (issued after 18 March 1986);
- shares issued under the Enterprise Investment Scheme;
- shares in a Venture Capital Trust;
- woodlands;
- works of art, where they are taken by HMRC in satisfaction of the payment of IHT.

The following receipts are also exempt from CGT:

- compensation or damages for any wrong or injury suffered by an individual in his person or profession or vocation;
- winnings from betting including the football pools, lotteries, horse racing and bingo.

No Gain/No Loss Transfers

There are certain transactions set out in the legislation which can be referred to as no gain/no loss transactions. These include:

1   transfers between civil partners or husband and wife;
2   deemed disposals of settled property which reverts to the settlor on the death of the life tenant.

The consideration received in such a transaction is deemed to be that amount which would result in neither a gain nor a loss arising. The acquisition cost to the transferee will be the same amount as the deemed proceeds received by the transferor. This will equal the transferor's acquisition cost. If any assets were transferred between a husband and wife or civil partners before 6 April 2008, that were owned on 6 April 2008, these may still qualify for indexation allowance when ultimately disposed after 5 April 2008.

Principal Private Residence Relief

Any gain arising on the disposal of a dwelling house by an individual is exempt from CGT, provided it has been his only or main residence throughout his period of ownership or since 31 March 1982, if shorter. If the dwelling was not occupied as the owner's only or main residence throughout the relevant period, then only that part of the gain which relates to the period when it was so occupied is exempt. However, certain periods of absence are automatically deemed to be periods of occupation irrespective of the actual circumstances. These include the final 36 months of ownership and any period of absence while living abroad because of overseas employment.

Relief will not be given where the dwelling was acquired wholly or partly for the purpose of realising a gain on a subsequent disposal. This is a subjective test and will depend on the circumstances.

A dwelling house qualifying for relief includes any garden or grounds of up to half a hectare or a larger area if the Commissioners decide that it is required for the reasonable enjoyment of the residence, having regard to the size and character of the dwelling.

An individual can only have one main residence at any given time. A husband and wife or civil partners living together can have one main residence between them. If an individual has more than one residence he can elect which of these is his main residence for any period even if in practice the one he elects is not his main residence. The election should be made within two years of the acquisition of the second property. If an election is not made, the Inspector will decide which is the individual's main residence, based on the actual facts. If an election is made it can subsequently be varied and this can give rise to planning opportunities.

Relief will be restricted where any part of the dwelling is used exclusively for business purposes (eg a room used as an office of a business) or where part of the property is let as residential accommodation. In that case the part which is let ceases to be used as the owner's main residence, and can instead be eligible for what is known as lettings relief exempting up to an additional £40,000 of gains from the charge to CGT.

Other Reliefs

There are a number of reliefs available which seek to exempt, hold-over or roll-over the gain made on the disposal of assets. These include taper relief, hold-over relief and EIS deferral relief. These are discussed in more detail in the following chapters.

CROSS REFERENCES

4.10   CGT – EIS Deferral Relief

Description	Individuals and certain trustees may defer paying tax on capital gains arising on the disposal of any assets if they reinvest the gain in new ordinary shares of a qualifying EIS company within a certain time limit.
	The effect is to defer the tax liability until the EIS shares are sold, and even then the charge can be further deferred by reinvesting the gain in different qualifying shares thereby potentially deferring the gain indefinitely.
Suitable for	Individuals who wish to defer CGT on capital gains by reinvesting in qualifying unquoted trading companies.
Advantages	1 Deferral of CGT by reinvesting realised gains (rather than the entire sale proceeds) in qualifying shares.
	2 No restriction on amount of gain which can be deferred.
	3 Income tax relief may be available up to a maximum of 20% on EIS investments made after 5 April 2008 totalling £500,000 (previously £400,000).
	4 Income tax relief can be carried back to the previous year (subject to the overall maximum claim for relief of £500,000 per tax year).
Disadvantages	1 For EIS shares issued after 5 April 2000, various conditions must be met for at least three years to avoid clawback of relief.
	2 Ordinary unquoted trading companies are often commercially risky. There are, however, financial products available on the market which allow EIS investments to be purchased at much lower risks.
Investment limits	Up to the amount of the chargeable gains realised on the disposal of any assets.

FURTHER DETAILS

Enterprise Investment Scheme

If *any* (business or investment) capital gains are made on other assets within one year before and/or within three years after an EIS share subscription, any part of the gain can be elected to be deferred into the new shares.

EIS deferral relief can be claimed even when the individual owns more than 30% of the company (which disqualifies them from claiming EIS income tax relief). There are, however, major restrictions and complicated provisions to adhere to in order to qualify and maintain the deferral relief.

Time Limits

An individual must acquire a qualifying investment within a period commencing one year before and ending three years after the disposal of the original asset. This period can be extended in limited circumstances at HMRC's discretion.

A claim must be made within five years from 31 January following the fiscal year of the qualifying investment in the individual's self-assessment tax return. To enable a claim to be made the company must first state to HMRC that the conditions are satisfied in relation to the issue at all times since the issue. It is prudent to make this statement (on an EIS 1 form) as soon as possible after the issue before circumstances prevent it being made. The company must then issue completed EIS 3 forms to the individuals for them to make a valid claim in their tax returns.

Qualifying Investment

A qualifying investment is an acquisition of newly issued, fully paid up shares in a qualifying company which have been subscribed for wholly in cash. Eligible shares are defined as ordinary shares which do not carry a present or future preferential right to dividends, or assets on a winding-up, or a present or future right to be redeemed. For shares issued on or after 6 April 2000 these conditions must be satisfied from the date of issue of shares until the third anniversary, except where the company concerned had not begun to carry on the trade in question on the date shares are issued then the conditions must be satisfied from the third anniversary date on which it begins to carry on such trade.

For shares issued on or before 5 April 2000 the conditions must be satisfied throughout the period of five years.

Where the assets disposed of are shares or securities, the reinvestment cannot be in shares of the same company or another group company.

The shares must be subscribed for cash. Second-hand shares acquired by way of purchase, gift or inheritance will not qualify, nor will newly issued shares acquired by a non-cash subscription.

Qualifying Company

For the reinvestment to qualify, the company must be unquoted and either a trading company carrying on a qualifying trade, or a parent company of a trading group. The company must be unquoted at the beginning of the period, with no arrangements for it to become quoted or a subsidiary of a company which may become quoted.

From 6 April 2006, the value of the company's gross assets must not exceed £7m (previously £15m) immediately before the share issue and £8m (previously £16m) immediately afterwards. In a group situation, the £7m and £8m figures relate to the aggregate value of the group's assets which exclude shares in, and loans to any subsidiaries. From 19 July 2007 the EIS company must not have raised more than £2m from the issue of shares within 12 months prior to the current issue. The EIS company must also have less than 50 full-time equivalent employees at the date the EIS shares are issued.

Qualifying Trade

A qualifying trade is defined as any trade conducted on a commercial basis with a view to the realisation of profits, subject to it not representing a substantial amount of an excluded trade. Excluded trades include:

- dealing in land, commodities, futures, shares, or other financial instruments;
- dealing in goods (unless ordinary wholesale or retail distribution);
- leasing (for shares issued on or after 6 April 2000, licence fees and royalties which arise from an intangible asset are not excluded from the Scheme);
- providing legal or accountancy services;
- various financial activities;
- property development;
- farming;
- forestry;
- operating hotels, nursing homes and residential care homes;
- shipbuilding, coal or steel production.

The Relief

The mechanism that allows CGT to be deferred applies so that the chargeable gain which would have arisen on the disposal is effectively postponed until a 'chargeable event' occurs. The amount of the chargeable gain which can be postponed is the lower of:

1   the chargeable gain on the disposal (before any applicable taper relief if made prior to 6 April 2008);
2   the amount subscribed for the shares; and
3   the amount specified in the claim.

   This allows an individual to choose how much of the gain he wants to be covered by the relief.

Chargeable Events ie Deferral Relief Withdrawn

The deferred gain will come into charge if and when any of the following events occur:

1   the acquired shares cease to be eligible shares (eg preferential rights are assigned to them);
2   the company ceases to be a qualifying company (eg it begins a non-qualifying trade);
3   the individual becomes non-resident (except where the individual goes abroad for full-time employment and returns to the UK within three years, not having disposed of the acquired shares);
4   the shares are disposed of other than to a spouse.

Use of Funds

The money raised by the share issue (ignoring any insignificant amount) has to be used by the company wholly for the purpose of an existing trade within 24 months of the share issue. Prior to the Finance Act 2009, 80% of the cash raised had to be used within 12 months of the share issue and the balance within the following 12 months or, in the case of a new trade, within 12 months and 24 months of the start of the new trade.

Anti-avoidance

Anti-avoidance provisions provide that a subscription for shares in a qualifying company will not be treated as an acquisition of eligible shares if there are arrangements for:

1   the subsequent acquisition, exchange or disposal of the shares;
2   the cessation of the company's trade (although note that EIS relief is not affected by bona fide liquidation, and as from 6 April 2000 a company will continue to qualify but for the actions of the receiver in bankruptcy of an individual) or for the disposal of the company's chargeable business assets;
3   protection for investors (by means of insurance, indemnity or guarantee etc) against investment risks.

Relief will also be clawed back (ie the deferred gain will come into charge) if there is a return of any of the value of the investment to the individual at any time up to two years before and ending immediately before the third anniversary of the date the shares are issued, or if the company or subsidiary does not begin to trade within three years of issuing the EIS shares.

This would include situations, for example, where the investor receives a benefit from the company, rents property to the company at a rent above the market rate, or receives excessive remuneration from the company. It will also apply where the individual is lent money and the loan would not have been made if the individual had not acquired, or proposed to acquire, the shares.

Amounts of value received of less than £1,000 or amounts which are insignificant in relation to the shares against which the gain is deferred are ignored for return of value. Where value is received from the company by the investor and the investor gives value back to the company, EIS relief may not be lost provided the complex rules are met.

Taper Relief – only for Gains made before 6 April 2008

CGT taper relief applies for EIS investments where a chargeable gain arises after 6 April 1999 and the original shares were issued on or after 6 April 1998. The taper relief period is extended to include the period of ownership after 17 March 1998, but void periods may build up, as the taper clock is only active whilst the investor has the relevant EIS shares, and three years are allowed after a disposal in which an EIS investment can be made.

Planning Opportunities

EIS deferral relief can sometimes achieve a full CGT exemption rather than a mere deferral. For example, CGT on rolled-over gains can be avoided altogether if the individual sells the shares at a time when he is non-UK resident provided he does not:

1   for shares issued on or after 6 April 2000, become non-UK resident from the date of issue until the third anniversary, except where the company concerned had not begun to carry on the trade in question on the date shares are issued, then the conditions must be satisfied from the third anniversary date on which it begins to carry on such trade (for shares issued on or before 5 April 2000 the period in which he must not become non-UK resident is within five years of the share issue); and

2   return to the UK within five complete tax years of his departure.

3   tax savings can be made if investment gains are deferred from 2007/08 into EIS shares.

Alternatively, if the individual dies holding the shares, the deferred gain will fall out of charge altogether and the base cost of the shares will automatically benefit from a tax-free uplift, so that the shares will be inherited with a base cost equivalent to their market value at the date of death. Note that the activities of the company are only restricted for the three-year period allowing the company to undertake any future activities without clawback of the relief.

Venture Capital Trusts (VCT)

Investments in VCTs acquired before 6 April 2004 qualified for a special form of CGT deferral similar to EIS deferral relief. The main difference was that the relief was only available in respect of an investment which also qualified for VCT income tax relief. This means the relief was limited to total VCT investments of up to £100,000 per tax year. Moreover, the reinvestment period was shorter, commencing one year before but ending only one year after the date on which the gain arose. This two-year period could straddle three tax years so that it was possible to shelter a gain of up to £300,000. When both income tax and CGT deferral relief applied to a subscription for shares, the individual may have qualified for total tax relief of up to 60%. CGT exemption on gains made on the VCT shares themselves (excluding the deferred gain) is still available.

For investments acquired after 5 April 2004, income tax relief is available at 40% and from 6 April 2006 at 30% up to a maximum investment of £200,000.

CROSS REFERENCES

Enterprise Investment Scheme   **3.12**
Venture Capital Trusts   **3.13**
CGT – Taper Relief   **4.12**

4.11 CGT – Hold-over Reliefs

Description	A gift of an asset is deemed to take place at market value for CGT purposes. Therefore a tax charge may arise without any funds being available to pay it. However, relief is available in the following cases:
	1 A disposal of business assets otherwise than by a bargain at arm's length;
	2 A disposal of assets otherwise than by a bargain at arm's length on which there is an immediate IHT charge.
	The relief postpones the tax charge on the chargeable gain which would otherwise accrue to the transferor by shifting the liability to the transferee when he disposes of the asset.
Suitable for	Individuals who wish to defer CGT on a gift or disposal of business assets at an undervalue, or who transfer any assets into a discretionary trust.
Advantages	1 Payment of CGT deferred.
	2 Facilitates tax planning.
Disadvantages	1 Partial relief not available.
	2 Donee starts new taper relief clock.

FURTHER DETAILS

Hold-over reliefs are available in two situations:
1   gifts of business assets; and
2   gifts of any assets where an IHT charge arises.
    The two situations are set out separately below.

Gifts of Business Assets

A gain on a disposal of business assets otherwise than by way of a bargain at arm's length (eg a gift or sale at an undervalue) may be held over. To qualify for relief, the recipient of the gift (the 'donee') must be UK resident and ordinarily resident. Relief will be denied where a donee is UK resident yet treated as being resident outside the UK by virtue of a provision in a double taxation treaty, and would not be liable to UK tax on a gain arising on a disposal of the asset in question.

    Hold-over relief will only be given on a claim being made by both the person who makes the gift (the 'donor') and the donee, unless the recipients are trustees. As the election is to hold over a gain which would otherwise be chargeable, in principle it is necessary to agree the amount of that gain with HMRC so that the election should be accompanied by the necessary valuations. However, HMRC have confirmed that a computation of the gain is not required. Both parties have to request this treatment in writing and supply certain information.

Relief is given by reducing the amount of the gain and the amount of consideration deemed to have been paid by the transferee by an amount equal to the held-over gain. Relief for any IHT payable on a disposal for which hold-over relief has been claimed may be obtained by the transferee when he subsequently disposes of the asset. This would arise in the situation where a gift is made on which hold-over relief is claimed, and where no IHT had been paid as it was a potentially exempt transfer. If the transferor dies within seven years of the gift so that IHT becomes payable by the transferee, the chargeable gain on a disposal by the transferee will be reduced by the lower of the amount of IHT paid and the chargeable gain.

Business Assets

Business assets are defined as follows:
1   assets used by the transferor for his trade, profession or vocation;
2   assets used by the transferor's personal company in a trade;
3   an asset used for a trade by a subsidiary of the transferor's personal company;
4   unquoted shares in a 'trading' company or the holding company of a trading group (see restrictions below);
5   quoted shares if the 'trading' company concerned is the transferor's personal company (see restrictions below);
6   agricultural property or interests in agricultural property which qualifies for agricultural property relief under the IHT rules.

For gains made prior to 6 April 2008, it is worth noting that a landlord renting an asset to a trading company entitled him to a proportion of business asset taper relief from 6 April 2000 onwards. This was extended from 6 April 2004 to include lettings to unincorporated trading businesses.

Restriction of Relief

Relief will be restricted in the following circumstances:
- where the asset disposed of was not used for the purposes of the trade during the entire period of ownership, the gain eligible for relief will be reduced proportionately;
- where the asset disposed of is a building or structure, part of which has been used for the purposes of the trade concerned, during all or a 'substantial' part of the ownership period, the held-over gain is reduced as is 'just and reasonable';
- where the asset disposed of consists of shares and the company owned non-business assets;
- where the asset disposed of consists of shares or securities and the gift is to a company, hold-over relief is not available (this applies to transfers after 8 November 1999 and before 6 April 2003, or after 20 October 2003);
- for transfers after 9 December 2003, relief is no longer available for a transfer to a settlement where the settlor retains an interest or may attain an interest.

Clawback of Relief

There will be a clawback of CGT hold-over relief where the transferee ceases to be UK resident or ordinarily resident within six years after the end of the year of assessment in which the disposal was made. A chargeable gain will be deemed to have accrued to the donee immediately before that time. However, if an individual ceases to be UK resident or ordinarily resident because of overseas employment, no clawback will arise providing the individual returns and becomes UK resident or ordinarily resident within three years.

Planning Opportunities

Under the hold-over relief rules, either the whole chargeable gain must be held over or it will be subject to CGT with the benefit of the annual exemption. Where any gain will not exceed the annual exemption, no claim for hold-over relief should be made.

Where an individual is considering gifting shares in a company which holds investments, the investments could be turned into cash or some other exempt asset such as gilt-edged securities shortly before the disposal. This will avoid a restriction in the hold-over relief available.

Where such investments are held, care must be taken to ensure that the company or group still qualifies as a trading company or group as defined by the CGT taper relief rules. If not, no relief will be available.

GIFT OF ASSETS ATTRACTING AN IMMEDIATE IHT CHARGE

The second situation where hold-over relief is available is where there is a disposal otherwise than by a bargain at arm's length of any assets which attracts an immediate IHT charge. IHT does not actually have to be paid, for example, where the gift falls within the nil rate band (see Section 4.15, *IHT – The Charge to Tax*) or 100% business property relief or agricultural property relief is available. Relief is only available in the following cases:
1   on a gift between individuals or on the creation of a trust (in which neither the settlor nor his spouse is a beneficiary) where such gifts are not treated as potentially exempt transfers (PETs);
2   on a gift to or by trustees which are not potentially exempt transfers.

The held-over gain on the disposal is the chargeable gain otherwise accruing. Relief is given by deducting this amount from the gain otherwise accruing to the transferor and from the consideration otherwise regarded as being given by the transferee.

The relief operates in the same way as the relief for gifts of business assets and the qualifying conditions are the same.

Relief is not available for a transfer which is a PET. A PET may become a chargeable transfer if the transferor dies within seven years. However, no relief is available in such circumstances.

This form of hold-over relief takes priority over the relief given on a gift of business assets. It may be attractive when a transfer of shares in a family company which owns non-business assets is being considered. That is because there is no apportionment of the chargeable gain where non-business assets are owned by the company in contrast to the hold-over relief on gifts of business assets.

FA 2004 introduced anti-avoidance measures aimed at preventing taxpayers seeking to exempt disposals of two properties by making a disposal of the second property to a discretionary trust. Previously, gains could have been held over on the transfer of the property to the discretionary trust. Providing an eligible beneficiary then occupied the property, the entire gain would be exempt on the future disposal or transfer of the property by the trustees by virtue of principal private residence relief. With effect from 10 December 2003, if the settlor claims hold-over relief on the transfer into trust, the trustees will not be entitled to principal private residence relief. These measures also apply to transfers out of the trust. If the trustees claim hold-over relief, the beneficiary taking possession of the property will not be able to claim principal private residence relief. Transitional rules apply to gifts of property made into trust before 10 December 2003. Gains will be time apportioned between pre- and post-10 December 2003, with only the pre-10 December 2003 gains qualifying for principal private residence relief.

CROSS REFERENCES

IHT – The Charge to Tax   **4.15**
Discretionary Trusts   **4.23**

4.12   CGT – Taper Relief*

Description	Taper relief no longer applies on any capital gains made between 6 April 1998 and 5 April 2008. This chapter only therefore relates to capital gains made on or before 5 April 2008. Taper relief reduced the amount of the chargeable gain according to the period for which the asset had been held after 5 April 1998, with a greater reduction for business assets than others.
Suitable for	Individuals, trustees and personal representatives who held business assets for at least one year and non-business assets for at least three years, that previously would have been eligible for indexation on disposal.
Advantages	1 No upper limit on amount of relief. 2 Gains on business assets that had been held for two years or more were taxed at effective rates as low as 10%. 3 Much simpler in most cases to calculate than indexation allowance. 4 Non-business assets acquired pre-17 March 1998 qualified for an extra taper year in addition to the period of ownership after 5 April 1998.
Disadvantage	The taper is applied to net gains after the deduction of losses of the same year and those carried forward.

*Only applies to gains made on or before 5 April 2008

FURTHER DETAILS

The 2008 Finance Act has now introduced a flat rate of 18% CGT and abolished taper relief on any capital gains made on or after 6 April 2008. The introduction of taper relief was part of the Government's aim of encouraging long-term investments, by reducing the effective rate of CGT on longer held assets.

Taper relief was introduced to replace indexation allowance (only applied up to April 1998). An increased amount of taper relief was received the longer the asset was held after 5 April 1998. Where the asset was held on 17 March 1998, one additional 'bonus' year of taper relief was added solely in respect of non-business asset gains. The maximum reduction available on non-business assets was 40%, as shown in the table below:

Taper Relief for Non-business Assets

Complete years of ownership after 5 April 1998	% of gain chargeable	Equivalent tax rate	
		Higher rate taxpayer	20% rate taxpayer
0	100	40	20
1	100	40	20
2	100	40	20
3	95	38	19
4	90	36	18
5	85	34	17
6	80	32	16
7	75	30	15
8	70	28	14
9	65	26	13
10 or more	60	24	12

Business Assets

The Finance Act 2002 enhanced the relief for business assets considerably. Maximum relief for disposals of business assets on or after 6 April 2002 was achieved after two complete years of qualifying ownership rather than four years as per the original 1998 legislation.

The amount of taper relief received on business assets was much higher than non-business assets. Business assets were:

- shares in a qualifying company;
- assets used for the purposes of the trade of a qualifying company or its subsidiary;
- assets used for the purpose of a trade carried on by the individual or trustees, either alone or in partnership;
- assets held for the purposes of an office or employment held by that individual with a person carrying on a trade;
- from 6 April 2000, an asset which was held by an individual and used for trading purposes by a third party's trading unquoted company;
- from 6 April 2004, an asset which was held by an individual and used for trading purposes by any individual, partnership, etc.

For the Period from 6 April 1998 to 5 April 2000

The requirements were that the company was either a trading company or a holding company of a trading group in which the taxpayer held shares which either:

- carried 25% or more of the voting rights in the company; or,
- carried 5% or more of the voting rights in the company and the individual was a full- time working officer or employee of that company.

From 6 April 2000

A qualifying company was a trading company or the holding company of a trading group and one or more of the following conditions were met:

(a) The company was unlisted where none of its shares were listed on a recognised stock exchange nor was a 51% subsidiary of a listed company. The Plus-listed market became a recognised stock exchange on 19 July 2007. However, shares listed on say, the Alternative Investment Market or other such secondary markets, are 'not listed' for these purposes.

(b) Where the company was listed, the individual (or eligible beneficiary of a trust owning the shares) needed to be an officer or employee of it, or of a connected company.

(c) Where the company was listed and the individual worked as an employee or officer and owned 5% or more of the shares. Note there was a previous requirement for the person to be a full-time working officer or employee prior to 2000.

(d) A non-trading company or the holding company of a non-trading group and the following conditions were met:

  (i) The individual was an officer or employee of it, or of an associated company; and,

  (ii) the individual and his family members did not have an interest in more than 10% of the shares in the company.

To qualify as a trading company, it must have existed wholly for carrying on a trade apart from activities having no substantial effect on the company's activities. 'Substantial' was taken to mean more than 20% of one or more of: turnover, assets (which includes excess cash), profits, management time, etc.

Due to various amendments in the legislation in 2000, 2002 and 2004, these changes do not affect the status of assets held prior to that date. For example, a full-time employee of an unlisted company would need to have held at least 5% of the shares in that company prior to 6 April 2000 to qualify for business asset taper relief in the first two years, with no minimum shareholding requirement after 5 April 2000. This may therefore cause some assets to qualify for mixed business and non-business use (see below for more details). In such circumstances a technique was used to restart the taper clock by, say, settling the assets in a non-settlor interested trust, particularly if the two-year full taper period applied.

From 17 April 2002

Any company which owned 51% subsidiaries was treated as a holding company, irrespective of its other activities.

For shares in a joint venture (JV) company to qualify for business asset taper relief, 75% of the JV company has to be owned by five or fewer shareholders and the taxpayer must own at least 10% of the ordinary share capital.

The rate of taper relief for a business asset disposal is:

		Equivalent tax rate	
Years of ownership after 5 April 199	*% of gain chargeable*	*Higher rate taxpayer*	*20% rate taxpayer*
0	100	40	20
1	50	20	10
2 or more	25	10	5

Mixed Business and Non–business Use

Where an asset had been used partly as a business asset and partly as a non-business asset and the period of ownership was less than ten years, it was necessary to apportion the gain between the periods of business and non-business use.

Identification Rules for Shares

As mentioned in Section 4.8, the matching rules for identification on the disposal of shares were changed for disposals on or after 6 April 1998 but before 5 April 2008. Identification shares sold before 6 April 2008 that were acquired after 5 April 1998 were on a Last In Last Out basis. These identification rules applied to individuals but not to companies, as taper relief does not apply to companies.

Enhancement expenditure on assets accrued taper relief from the date of the original acquisition. This contrasts with the rules applying to indexation allowance.

Losses

If any capital losses were made in a tax year, these were firstly set off any capital gains (before deducting any taper relief). When there was more than one gain in a tax year, any loss could be deducted so as to give the lowest charge to tax.

Inter-spouse Transfer

Transfers between spouses are still made on a no gain/no loss basis for CGT. Where an asset was transferred from one spouse to the other after 5 April 1998, the taper relief was calculated on the subsequent disposal by reference to the aggregate of the separate periods of ownership of the two spouses. However, whether the asset was a business or non-business asset for taper relief purposes in this aggregate period was based either on the donor spouse's ownership prior to the gift then on the donee spouse's ownership, or solely on the donee's ownership, depending on whether the asset was shares or other business assets. The rules for inter-spouse transfers were very complex and consequently could have resulted in business asset taper relief being obtained or lost in respect of prior periods. Specialist advice was essential.

Roll-over and Hold-over Relief

Where a gain was rolled over or held over into a new asset, the taper relief on the old asset was lost. Therefore a new taper relief period started from the date the donee acquired the asset, sometimes increasing the effective rate of CGT.

Deferred Gains

When any gains were deferred into new assets such as depreciating assets or into Enterprise Investment Scheme shares, the taper relief earned prior to the deferral was 'frozen'. When, say, the EIS shares are sold, the original gain came into charge minus any entitlement to taper relief solely based on the old asset Note that any disposals made after 5 April 2008 will lose any previous taper relief entitlement.

Restrictions

Taper relief was suspended for the period during which the assets exposure to risk has been limited. HMRC have confirmed that the normal commercial arrangements on the sale of a company of receiving loan notes for the shares are not caught by this. This enabled full taper relief to be structured on the sale of a company. Where a company was sold and the individual accepted qualifying corporate bonds these gains were deferred, the gain calculated, and the taper relief clock 'frozen', with any consequential CGT being paid when the bonds were encashed. If the individual had instead accepted non-qualifying corporate bonds, the taper clock continued and the full gains charged when encashed. If any of these bonds are encashed after 5 April 2008, all previous taper relief will be lost.

Prior to 17 April 2002, taper relief is denied for periods prior to a change in the activity of a company or a value shifting event. The Finance Act 2002 provided that any period of time after 6 April 1998 when a close company was not 'active' would not count towards the qualifying holding period or the relevant periods of ownership for shares or securities in the company, but a change in activities will no longer stop the taper clock totally. Constant monitoring of group activities is required to protect taper relief.

4.13 CGT – Overseas Aspects

Description	CGT is charged on gains arising on the disposal of the worldwide assets of an individual who is resident or ordinarily resident in the UK. Non-UK domiciled residents are assessed on UK gains and overseas gains remitted to the UK (subject to an election below).
Suitable for	Those with substantial potential capital gains with the ability to go overseas for at least five complete tax years.
	Non-UK domiciliaries who can structure remittances to minimise gains taxable in the UK.
Advantages	1 Gain exempt from UK CGT.
Disadvantages	1 Certain gains crystallised by temporary non-residents remain chargeable upon return to the UK within five years, but with only one year's annual exemption.
	2 Leaving the UK permanently may crystallise deferred gains.
	3 Upheaval and personal arrangements of going abroad.

FURTHER DETAILS

An individual who is resident or ordinarily resident in the UK during any year of assessment is taxed on his worldwide chargeable gains if domiciled in the UK.

An individual who is neither resident nor ordinarily resident in the UK is generally not liable to CGT on gains even if they result from a disposal of assets situated in the UK.

CGT may be avoided by an individual leaving the UK, achieving non-residence and then disposing of the asset in question. However, there are stringent requirements to comply with.

Meaning of Residence, Ordinary Residence and Domicile

UK CGT is levied in accordance with an individual's tax residence, and establishing whether one is resident, ordinarily resident or domiciled in the UK is critical to determining a UK liability. The definitions for these terms are the same as for income tax purposes, which are described in detail in Section 4.5. However, in addition, special rules apply for CGT purposes only, for individuals who are 'temporarily non-resident' in the UK and for individuals who leave, or come to, the UK part way through a tax year.

Coming to and Leaving the UK

Prior to 17 March 1998, anyone who left the UK and ceased to be UK resident and ordinarily resident was not charged to CGT for gains arising on disposals made after their departure. This was by statute in years of complete non-residence and by concession for the year of departure.

This treatment is now only available to individuals if they were neither resident nor ordinarily resident in the UK for the whole of at least four of the seven tax years immediately preceding the tax year of their departure. The rule is designed to prevent temporary visitors to the UK from continuing to be liable to UK CGT following completion of their stay in the UK.

Anyone else leaving the UK will remain liable to UK CGT for the full year of their departure. Any gains crystallised after their departure up to the following 5 April must also be declared on the relevant tax return unless the proceeds and gains are below the de minimis limits for the year.

If the individual has left the UK permanently (that is, they are not 'temporarily' not resident (see below) there will be no liability to UK CGT on gains arising in the subsequent years, provided the gain has not arisen in respect of assets used in a trade carried on in the UK. It is not possible to avoid CGT on assets used in a trade by removing the assets from the UK or by ceasing to trade in the UK, as a deemed disposal at market value will be treated as having occurred.

By concession, individuals who become resident in the UK during a tax year, having been neither resident nor ordinarily resident in the UK at any time during the five tax years immediately preceding the tax year of their arrival, are not liable to UK CGT on gains arising during the period from 6 April to the date of their arrival. Those who do not qualify for the concession are liable to CGT for the full year of their arrival.

When an individual becomes UK resident, there is no uplift in base cost to exclude gains arising before arrival. Conversely, the UK does not normally levy an exit charge on assets owned when an individual becomes not resident. There are, however, certain instances where a gain that has previously been held over, deferred or rolled over may become chargeable to CGT on departure.

A gain deferred under the gift relief provisions will become liable to CGT if the recipient becomes not resident and not ordinarily resident within six years of the end of the tax year in which the gift was made. Becoming non-resident before owning EIS or VCT shares for three years will trigger CGT to become payable on the gains originally deferred. These charges will not normally apply if overseas employment causes the individual to become not resident and not ordinarily resident, provided they resume their UK resident and ordinarily resident status within three years.

Temporary Non-residence

Individuals are regarded as temporarily non-resident if they were UK resident or UK ordinarily resident for four of the seven tax years before the year of departure and then become UK resident and UK ordinarily resident within the next five complete tax years.

Any gains and losses realised on assets owned on departure, that are realised in a tax year whilst temporarily not resident, are assessable in the year of return to the UK. Only a single year's annual CGT exemption applies, so individuals who are caught by this rule can be disadvantaged when compared with their position if they had remained resident and ordinarily resident.

Gains and losses on assets bought and sold whilst not resident and not ordinarily resident in the year of departure and subsequent years (but not the year of return), do not accrue when residence resumes, therefore can be realised free of CGT during complete years of non-residence. If losses have arisen on assets bought after departure, individuals should consider delaying the disposal until after they return.

Gains and losses arising in different tax years whilst temporarily non-resident are pooled. This means that a loss in one year could be used effectively to mitigate a gain in a previous or subsequent year.

It is possible that gains caught on return will have been taxed in the country where the individual was resident. In this case it is possible to claim a deduction for the foreign tax paid against the UK CGT but only to the extent of the UK liability, which effectively means that the amount payable is the higher of the two tax bills.

Some double taxation agreements (DTAs) provide tax residents of the contracting countries exemption from CGT in the other country on certain gains, such as the disposal of moveable assets like shares.

It is advisable to check the tax position in the country of residence before realising any gains.

Unremittable Foreign Gains

Where there is a gain on an overseas asset which is assessable but cannot be remitted to the UK because of local legal restrictions or executive action by the local government or the unavailability of foreign currency, and this is not due to any want of reasonable endeavours on the part of the individual, CGT will only be charged when the restrictions lift.

Foreign Currency and Assets held in a Foreign Currency

Foreign currency is an asset for CGT purposes. The disposal of foreign currency can therefore give rise to a capital gain or a loss. Deposits and withdrawals from a foreign currency account are treated as acquisitions and disposals. When computing an individual's gain or loss on foreign currency, one has to use the exchange rate applicable on the dates of each acquisition and disposal.

No chargeable gains or allowable losses arise on the disposal of currency acquired by an individual for the personal expenditure outside the UK of themselves or their family. This includes any expenditure on the provision or the maintenance of a non-UK residence.

Care must be taken when calculating the gain or loss accruing on assets held in a foreign currency, as this will include the exchange rate gains and losses as well as the increase or decrease in the value of the asset. This is achieved by using the exchange rate applicable on the date of each transaction so that the exchange fluctuation can result in a chargeable capital gain arising on an asset that is sold at a loss (and vice versa).

CGT Liability of Non-UK Domiciliaries

Where an individual is resident or ordinarily resident but not domiciled in the UK, gains on the disposal of UK assets are chargeable at the time of disposal, irrespective of where the monies are received. Gains on the disposal of assets situated outside the UK are also chargeable at the time of disposal unless a claim for the remittance basis to apply has been made. If a claim is made, gains on the disposal of assets situated outside the UK are taxable only when remitted to the UK, ie the remittance basis. The claim (and cost) of remittance basis after 6 April 2008 need careful consideration (for instance see 4.5 earlier).

Losses on overseas assets can now be eligible for UK tax relief. However, care must be taken to ensure that future claims for such losses are enabled, by making the appropriate election in the first year that remittance under the FA 2008 provisions is claimed, regardless of the then current asset, gain and loss profile.

Gains on overseas assets are computed in the same way as gains on UK assets. However, as stated above, UK tax will not be chargeable if a claim for remittance basis has been made and the gains are not remitted to the UK. For details of what constitutes a remittance please see Section 4.5.

It has always been important to segregate funds and plan remittances, but that is even more critical since 6 April 2008, particularly where remittances are made from a mixed fund ie a bank account containing income, capital and gains. Accordingly, management and remittance of offshore capital gains needs care.

Foreign tax credit relief is available when overseas gains become assessable on remittance, but only to the extent of the lower of the UK liability or the foreign tax paid on the assessed gain (which may not be the full gain). Effectively, this means that the total payable is the higher of the two tax bills.

Planning Opportunities

The Finance Acts 1998 and 2005 have made it far more difficult for those seeking to avoid UK CGT by becoming non-resident. In particular, the requirement to be not resident and not ordinarily resident for five complete tax years will make this route impractical in most cases. There are, however, still other planning strategies including:

1   converting the capital gains to an income gain and going non-resident, as income gains are not subject to the five-year rule;
2   using CGT exempt investments, such as gilt-edged securities and qualifying corporate bonds, National Savings Certificates and Premium Bonds, SAYE contracts, investments held within ISAs and PEPs, private homes which have been treated as your only or main residence (including by election) where one's tax status allows this;
3   using the replacement of business assets relief rules on disposals of qualifying business assets.

CROSS REFERENCES

4.14　Estate Planning

Estate planning is concerned specifically with mitigating the effects of IHT, but it is vital to also consider CGT when making a gift. IHT was introduced in 1986 and is the principal tax on the transfer of assets either during lifetime or on death.

The Strategy

Estate planning can only be considered on an individual basis to suit the requirements of each individual. The size of the estate, nature of the assets, interaction with other taxes, available income, family circumstances and the willingness of the individual to make lifetime gifts are all factors to take into account.

Size of Estate

The smaller estate up to, say, £500,000 will have limited scope for substantial lifetime gifts. The value of the family house plus other investments necessary to produce spendable income will comprise the bulk of the estate. Any gifts of substance could reduce the financial security of the donor.

Every individual has a nil rate band on death, £325,000 for 2009/10 (rising to £350,000 in 2010/11). Finance Act 2008 introduced the ability to transfer this nil rate band between the estates of husband and wives or civil partners. The effect is that on the death of the surviving spouse or civil partner, any unused nil rate band from the first death can be used by them.

The simplest way to meet any inheritance tax liability on death is to use an insurance policy which will provide a tax-free sum in the beneficiaries' hands on the death of the surviving spouse.

Larger estates have much greater flexibility in making lifetime transfers. Assets can be passed to the next generation with no IHT arising provided the donor survives seven years. A generation can be skipped by passing assets on. Regular gifts by high income earners may also be exempt. Once a donation strategy has been adopted, the tax estimated to be due on the residual estate can be funded by insurance in a tax-efficient manner.

Nature of the Assets

Cash is the easiest form of asset to transfer, but many people do not have surplus cash. Assets which are expected to appreciate over the years are the most appropriate gifts. However, with the currently generous reliefs on business and agricultural property, many assets with potential for capital appreciation will be wholly exempt from IHT on death. Much estate planning is now concerned with ensuring that assets do not fall outside these privileged categories.

Care must be taken not to fall within the gift with reservation or pre-owned asset rules, but the retention of some form of control over the asset may be possible through the use of trusts.

Available Income

It is normally unwise to make gifts or transfers to such an extent that income is reduced below an acceptable level, after taking into account the effects future inflation could have on that income.

Capital can be invested to produce income as outlined in some of the Investment sections. Generally the higher the income the easier it is to make regular gifts and provide a fund to meet the eventual IHT liability on death.

The use of high income during the working years to fund an efficient pension will also build a sound framework to enable subsequent gifts to be made without jeopardising financial security.

Family Circumstances

An individual with no close family has different problems from someone who is married with a family. The single individual can, for example, use discretionary trusts to remove assets from the estate, leaving the decision as to the precise beneficiaries of the trust until some time later. If the single individual has no person in mind for receiving the estate on death, IHT can be avoided by gifting to charities and other exempt bodies.

The married person has much greater flexibility: the exemption for transfers between husband and wife, the nil rate band of both husband and wife, the use of trusts to pass on to children and the ability to skip generations. The exemptions are there waiting to be used.

The following sections start with an explanation of the main provisions of IHT. The concept and use of the five main types of trust are explained next, followed by an explanation of wills.

Interaction with Other Taxes

Stamp Duty

Subject to complications with regard to mortgaged property, there is generally no stamp duty on gifts.

Capital Gains Tax

There is generally no CGT on death, and the cost of assets will be uplifted to the probate values for future CGT purposes. Lifetime gifts will give rise to a CGT disposal of the asset, and CGT may be charged subject to the annual gains exemption. It is also possible to use EIS Deferral relief to roll over a gain on a gift. Some gifts will qualify for hold-over relief, enabling a capital gain on a gift to be passed on to the recipient. There is a possibility of CGT and/or IHT becoming chargeable on a lifetime transfer and this must be carefully reviewed.

4.15 IHT – The Charge to Tax

Description	IHT applies to chargeable transfers, whether by way of lifetime gift or a deemed transfer of an estate on death. Key points to consider are: • the calculation of the value transferred; • available exemptions; • potentially exempt transfers; • relief for business and agricultural property; • the cumulation period; • the rate of tax and the availability of tapering relief; • the funding of IHT; • the instalment option for paying tax; • the separate taxation of husband and wife; • the special provisions for trusts.

FURTHER DETAILS

The Chargeable Amount

It is the loss suffered by the donor on the transfer rather than the benefit to the donee which is taken into account[1]. This is particularly significant for shares in family companies where a gift of a small number of shares leads to the donor losing voting control. A transfer of value may arise from a failure to exercise a right, as well as from a gift of assets. The value of a person's estate on death is the aggregate market value of all his assets, net of liabilities. However, there are special rules on loans and debts, for example to restrict relief where a gift is coupled with a loan back. A person is treated as owning the underlying assets contained in a settlement the income of which he is entitled to receive as it arises.

Seven-Year Cumulation Period

IHT operates by cumulation of an individual's lifetime transfers with the value of his estate on death, plus the assets contained in a settlement in which the individual has a life interest at death (if relevant). The cumulation of lifetime gifts is restricted to a seven-year period.

Rate of Tax

There is a nil rate band of £325,000 (2010/11), and a flat rate above this of 40%. Both the 40% rate and the nil rate band will remain the same, in 2011/12 (the nil rate band will not increase now until the tax year 2015/16). The lifetime charge is at 50% of these rates for chargeable lifetime transfers (currently at 20%). However, if the donor dies within seven years, the charge may be increased by the loss of the 50% reduction, but it is tapered for transfers made more than three years before death, and the value on which the charge is applied is the value of the asset at the date of transfer rather than the date of death.

Allocation of Exemptions

HMRC allocates annual exemptions to lifetime gifts in chronological order of transfers irrespective of whether the transfer is a chargeable transfer or a potentially exempt transfer. This means that if a potentially exempt transfer precedes a chargeable transfer in the same tax year the available annual exemption will be allocated to the potentially exempt transfer, and unless the donor dies within seven years of a potentially exempt transfer any annual exemption allocated to it will be wasted.

Exemptions on Death

There are certain exemptions which are available on death. There are specific rules for dealing with these where Agricultural Property Relief or Business Property Relief is available.

Tapering Relief

On the death of an individual, the tax charge on potentially exempt transfers (see Section 4.17) and chargeable lifetime transfers within the preceding seven years is recalculated, with the first transfers using the nil rate band if appropriate. The full rate of tax (but not the chargeable amount) applicable to each transfer is reduced, providing the donor has survived at least three years. The percentage of the full rate chargeable is shown in the appendix. Transfers falling within the nil rate band will not benefit from taper relief.

Quick Succession Relief

Relief is given where two transfers of the same property occur within a five-year period and each transfer is chargeable to IHT. The IHT payable on the second transfer is reduced by a percentage of the tax charged on the first transfer. The amount of relief available reduces annually during the five-year period.

Other Taxation Aspects

Capital Gains Tax

A gift of a chargeable asset is a disposal for CGT. Any CGT borne by the donee reduces the value of the transfer for IHT purposes. Only certain gifts qualify for hold-over relief. Broadly, these are:
- gifts of business assets;
- gifts of shares in an unquoted trading company;
- gifts of shares in a personal trading company even if the shares are quoted or on the AIM;
- gifts to and from trusts.

The held-over gain reduces the donee's acquisition cost. Hold-over relief is available to individual and trustee donors and donees provided the donee is UK resident and the settlor has no interest in the settlement, either directly or indirectly via their spouse or minor child. Hold-over relief for business assets gifted to a company by way of a transfer of shares or securities no longer qualify for this relief. However, for transfer of assets other than shares or securities, relief is still available on gifts to UK resident company donees provided the company is not controlled by non-UK residents connected with the donor. Any IHT on the transfer may be set-off against the future chargeable gain on the asset.

It is advisable to consider carefully valuation for CGT purposes if there is a series of gifts.

Stamp Duty

No stamp duty is chargeable on lifetime gifts except where the property gifted is subject to a charge assumed by the donee, for example a mortgage on land.

CROSS REFERENCES

IHT – Exemptions   **4.16**
IHT – Potentially Exempt Transfers   **4.17**
IHT – Business Property Relief   **4.19**
IHT – Agricultural Property Relief   **4.20**

4.16   IHT – Exemptions

Description	Various gifts made by individuals qualify for a specific exemption and, in addition, lifetime use of the nil rate band for chargeable transfers can give rise to a further valuable 'exemption'. In a family situation, IHT planning can make use of one or more of the following to build up gradually funds outside an individual's estate: <ul><li>annual exemption;</li><li>small gifts exemption;</li><li>transfers between spouses or civil partners;</li><li>gifts in consideration of marriage or civil partnership;</li><li>normal expenditure out of income;</li><li>dispositions for family maintenance.</li></ul> A husband and wife or a civil partner can each take advantage of the exemptions.
Suitable for	Gifts made on a regular basis whether of cash or other property. Certain exemptions can be used to build up funds in trust, or for life assurance funding of later IHT liabilities.
Advantages	1 Reduces value of estate without charge to tax. 2 Trusts may enable retention of control.
Disadvantages	1 Certain exemptions are lost if not used each year. 2 Not always possible with small estates.

FURTHER DETAILS

Annual Exemption

Each individual may give up to £3,000 every tax year during his or her lifetime free of IHT. Any unused balance can be carried forward for one year only, but the current year's exemption must be used before the balance which is brought forward. Gifts covered by this exemption may be made outright or to trustees. For example, a gift to a discretionary trust of an asset within the annual exemption would be free of IHT. (It would also qualify for hold-over relief for CGT purposes.)

Small Gifts Exemption

Outright lifetime gifts of up to £250 to any one person in a tax year are exempt. The exemption is in addition to the annual exemption, and applies to any number of such gifts made to different persons. However, the exemption cannot be used to offset the first slice of a larger gift or a series of gifts which in total exceed £250.

Gifts between Spouses or Civil Partners

Transfers of any property between spouses or civil partners, either during lifetime or on death, are exempt from IHT provided the recipient spouse or civil partner is domiciled in the UK. Where the recipient spouse or civil partner is not domiciled in the UK, the exemption available is limited to property worth £55,000. There are special domicile rules for IHT.

Where one spouse or civil partner has insufficient resources to make maximum use of IHT exemptions, the other spouse or civil partner may provide funds from which gifts can be made. Provided the gift between the spouses or civil partners is not conditional on the recipient making the further gift, HMRC will not normally apply the associated operations rules.

Gifts in Consideration of Marriage or Civil Partnership

For any one marriage or civil partnership, the limits are:
- £5,000 if given by a parent of a party to the marriage or civil partnership;
- £2,500 if given by a grandparent or remoter ancestor or by a party to the marriage or civil partnership;
- £1,000 for others.

Nil Rate Band

Although not strictly an exemption, the first £325,000 of chargeable transfers for 2010/11 (remaining at £325,000 in 2011/12) are charged at nil rate. After seven years, a lifetime chargeable transfer is excluded from the cumulative total and provided the individual survives, there will be the benefit of another nil rate band.

Dispositions for Family Maintenance

Lifetime gifts for the maintenance of a spouse or civil partner, child or dependent relative of the donor are exempt in certain circumstances. This exemption could be used in a school fees scheme.

Other Exemptions

The other, perhaps less common, exemptions are:
- waivers of remuneration or dividends in certain circumstances;
- gifts to charity which become the property of the charity or are held on trust for exclusively charitable purposes;
- gifts to qualifying political parties;
- transfers of national heritage property subject to detailed conditions;
- trust property situated outside the UK if the settlor of the trust was not domiciled in the UK under the special domicile rules for IHT;
- a reversionary interest under a trust except in certain circumstances;
- transfers which are deductible for income tax purposes, eg charitable covenants and Gift Aid payments;
- transfers conferring pension benefits;
- certain foreign currency accounts of persons who died not domiciled, not resident and not ordinarily resident in the UK;

- interest-free loans which are repayable on demand – these generally have no IHT implications for the lender;
- a holding in an authorised unit trust or share in an open-ended investment company if the owner is an individual domiciled outside the UK.

CROSS REFERENCE

IHT – Gifts with Reservation **4.18**

4.17 IHT – Potentially Exempt Transfers

Description	These are gifts by an individual which are not covered by one of the exemptions. Finance Act 2006 introduced new legislation to prevent transfers onto trust from being treated as a PET from 22 March 2006. However, transfers onto a trust for the disabled still qualify.
Suitable for	Gifts of cash, assets with no in-built capital gain but with potential for growth such as shares in a new company, business assets which qualify for business property relief and CGT reliefs.
Advantages	1 Enables substantial amounts to be transferred without an immediate charge to IHT, and the possibility of complete exemption.
Disadvantages	1 Difficult for elderly or individuals in poor health to use.
	2 CGT may be payable on the gift with no relief for IHT if it becomes payable.
	3 Only excess over available exemption is potentially exempt.

FURTHER DETAILS

During Lifetime

No IHT is due on potentially exempt transfers at the time that they are made, and they are ignored for the purposes of calculating the cumulative lifetime total while the donor is still alive. However, the gift absorbs any available exemption, so chargeable gifts should be made before gifts which qualify as potentially exempt. They will become fully exempt from IHT if the donor survives seven years, providing there has been no reservation of benefit.

Death within Seven Years

If the donor does not survive seven years, the transfers will be treated as chargeable lifetime gifts in the years that they were made. This will involve calculating the cumulative total of chargeable lifetime transfers in the seven years preceding each gift in order to work out the IHT liability. Exempt transfers (including potentially exempt transfers which the donor has survived for seven years) will not be included in the cumulative total. The IHT rates applied to the cumulative total will be those current in the year the donor dies. Depending upon the period by which the donor has survived his gift, the rates may be subject to tapering relief. This may be worthless if the gift falls within the nil rate band.

Where potentially exempt transfers are subsequently brought into charge, this could have an impact on the tax rates applicable to chargeable lifetime transfers or distributions from trusts which were made at a later date.

Liability to Pay

The donee has responsibility for reporting that a potentially exempt transfer has become chargeable, and is also primarily liable for payment of the tax. If he does not pay, the personal representatives will become liable instead. For deaths after 8 March 1999, the personal representatives to the best of their knowledge and belief must give details of all chargeable transfers made by the deceased within seven years of death.

Capital Gains

The donor might be liable to CGT on the gift of a chargeable asset. The donee might then become liable to IHT if the donor does not survive seven years. The donee can only add the IHT as a 'cost' for CGT purposes on a future sale if the original gift attracted hold-over relief.

Not Qualifying

Gifts to companies where the shareholders benefit indirectly from an increase in the value of their shares, will not qualify as potentially exempt transfers. Neither will gifts by companies qualify, despite the rule which provides that where a close company makes a transfer of value, it is treated as having been made by the company's participators.

4.18   IHT – Gifts with Reservation

Description	Where an individual makes a disposal by a gift (including a sale at undervalue), the property will be treated as subject to a reservation if:
	1 the donee has not assumed full possession and enjoyment of the gift by the beginning of the relevant period; or
	2 the property is not enjoyed to the complete or almost complete exclusion of the donor throughout the relevant period; or
	3 the property is not enjoyed to the complete or almost complete exclusion of any benefit to the donor by contract or otherwise, throughout the relevant period.
	The relevant period is the period ending on the date of the donor's death and beginning seven years prior to the death, or the date of the gift if later.
Disadvantages	1 Possible double charge to tax.
	2 Careful planning required.

FURTHER DETAILS

The Tax Impact

At the date of death, if the individual has gifted any property subject to a reservation, that property will be brought into the deceased's estate and charged to IHT. Despite this, there will be no equivalent CGT-free uplift to the base cost which would be available if the deceased had actually owned the asset at death. The donee will primarily be liable for the tax, and a gift with reservation deemed to be part of the donor's estate on death cannot be the subject of a deed of variation. Agricultural and business property relief may be available on the deemed gift. Where the donor has made a gift with reservation but ceases to reserve a benefit, he is deemed to have made a potentially exempt transfer at that time. The donor will then have to survive the seven-year period before the gift falls out of a potential charge to tax on his death.

Double Charges

If the lifetime gift was a chargeable transfer to a trust, there could be IHT on the original gift, within the trust itself (see Section 4.23) and on the settlor's death. Generally, trusts of which the settlor is a beneficiary should be avoided. Where the individual dies within seven years of the lifetime gift, the potential double charge on the lifetime transfer and at death may be mitigated.

Exemptions

Except in the case of annual exemptions and gifts out of income, gifts within the exemptions outlined in Section 4.16 will not fall within the gifts with reservation rules.

Tracing Rules

There are special provisions where other property has been substituted for the property gifted, for example share exchanges. Where a gift is of cash to an individual (but not a trust), so that the donee takes possession of the gift, any property subsequently acquired with the cash should not be affected by the rule concerning the exclusion of the donor from benefit, but care is needed with associated operations.

Market Rent

Where the gift consists of property, such as an interest in land or a chattel, continued occupation or enjoyment of the gift by the donor is ignored where a full market value rent is paid by the donor to donee for the use of the property. The parties to the transactions should be separately advised over the 'market rent', and there should be regular reviews to ensure that the position is maintained.

Avoiding Future Reservation

There are provisions to cover the position where the donor's circumstances have changed since making the original gift so that he is unable to maintain himself through old age, infirmity or otherwise, and the donee is a relative and makes reasonable provision for the care and maintenance of the donor by providing him with property in which to reside.

Even if a gift is not originally subject to a reservation, care is needed by the donor subsequent to making a gift to ensure that no future action on the part of himself or the donee creates a gift with reservation.

HMRC Press Release

HMRC have indicated that the following need not be gifts with reservation although the facts of each case will need to be examined at the relevant time:

- Gifts involving a benefit for the spouse, although care is needed with associated operations.
- Gifts of part of an asset.
- Gifts involving excluded property.
- Gifts into a settlement of which the settlor is a trustee.
- Gifts of business property (eg partnership assets) where the shares of profits and losses subsequently are in line with the donor's and donee's continuing relevant interest in the property.
- Gifts of family company shares where the donor remains as a director of the company on continuing commercial arrangements involving reasonable remuneration, etc.

Interest in Land

The *Ingram* case held that the creation of a lease to be retained by the donor and the gift of the freehold reversion, was not a reservation of benefit. The lease was normally for just in excess of the donor's life expectancy, and on death leasehold and freehold interests merged into one valuable asset in the hands of the beneficiaries of the estate. For gifts of interest in land after 8 March 1999, the gifts with reservation rule is considerably extended to cover situations where the donor or his spouse has a significant right or interest, or is party to a significant arrangement in relation to the land. 'Significant' has quite an extended meaning, and covers situations which would not normally be significant, eg the receipt of rent.

The gift with reservation rules also apply to gifts of an undivided share in land after 8 March 1999, unless certain exemptions apply. The provisions do not apply to assets which are not land.

Pre-owned Assets

FA 2004 Sch 15 introduced new legislation regarding the taxation of pre-owned assets. The legislation has been brought in to counter various schemes which were designed to avoid IHT by avoiding the gifts with reservation rules.

From 6 April 2005, an income tax charge will be imposed on the annual benefit of using, or enjoying, an asset that was once owned by the user (and has not been sold by him at an arm's length price for cash), where such use is enjoyed free of charge or at below market value. The charge will also be extended to apply to assets which the user did not formerly own, but which were purchased with funds provided by him. Both tangible and intangible assets will be within the charge.

The charge will not apply where:
- the asset ceased to be owned before 18 March 1986; or
- the asset is now owned by the taxpayer's spouse; or
- the asset in question still counts as part of the taxpayer's estate for IHT purposes under the existing gifts with reservation rules; or
- the taxpayer was formerly the owner of the asset only by virtue of a will or intestacy subsequently varied; or
- the use or enjoyment is merely incidental, including cases where an out and out gift to a family member comes to benefit the donor following a change in their circumstances.

There is a de minimis limit. No charge will be levied where the aggregate of the chargeable amounts under any of the provisions in respect of a particular tax year does not exceed £5,000.

The benefit will be calculated by reference to the rental value in the case of land, and by reference to an annual benefit charge which will be calculated by imputing a percentage of capital value in the case of chattels and intangible assets (modelled on the existing rules for taxing benefits in kind for employees). Legislation prescribes a valuation date of 6 April, and there is only a need to carry out valuations every five years once an initial valuation has been done. In respect of land, the charge will be on the appropriate rental value. This also applies to chattels, but intangibles are revalued accordingly. In calculating the chargeable amount, payments made under any legal obligation in relation to occupation/use may be deducted.

The chargeable amount is also adjusted to take into account any cash consideration given for the initial disposal.

Pre-existing arrangements will escape the new charge if they are dismantled, or the donor begins to pay full market rent, before the start date of 6 April 2005. Alternatively, a taxpayer may elect to remain outside the income tax charge (in relation to the assets specified in the election), but in that case the asset in question will be treated as part of their estate for IHT purposes while they continue to enjoy it. The time limit for this election was initially by 31 January 2007, but has been extended by Finance Act 2007 to the 31 January following the year of assessment, or such later time as HMRC allow.

CROSS REFERENCES

IHT – Business Property Relief   **4.19**
IHT – Agricultural Property Relief   **4.20**

4.19 IHT – Business Property Relief

Description	The relief takes the form of a discount in the value which becomes chargeable to IHT either on a lifetime transfer or on death. To determine whether the relief is due it is necessary to review whether:
	1 the business is a qualifying business;
	2 the asset is 'relevant business property';
	3 the asset has been owned for the minimum period required.
	The nature of the asset will determine the rate of the relief: either 100% or 50%.
	The asset may have to qualify for the relief on more than one occasion if it is part of a lifetime transfer.
Suitable for	Sole traders and partners in partnerships who are able to pass on the business in the family; shareholders of unquoted trading companies/ substantial shareholders in quoted trading companies.

FURTHER DETAILS

Qualifying Business

Any business carried on for gain, including a business carried on in the exercise of a profession or vocation, can qualify. Excluded is a business dealing in shares or securities, land or buildings, or holding or making investments, unless the business is that of a market maker or the company is a holding company of an otherwise qualifying group. The value of the interest of a Lloyd's underwriter will be included. The asset need not be in the UK.

Rate of Relief and Relevant Business Property

100% Relief

- A sole proprietor's business or an interest in a business (eg that of a partner).
- Unquoted securities of a company which by themselves or in conjunction with any other securities and any unquoted shares owned by the transferor give voting control of the company.
- Any unquoted shares.

50% Relief

1 Land, buildings, machinery or plant owned by the transferor (or a trust – see (c) below) and used wholly or mainly for the purposes of a business carried on by:

(a)   a company of which the transferor had control; or

(b)   a partnership in which the transferor was a partner; or

(c)   the transferor, provided the property is settled property and the transferor was entitled to an interest in possession under the terms of the relevant trust. Relief may be available at 100% rather than 50% where the property owned by the trust is being transferred at the same time as the transferor is disposing of his business or his interest in a business (eg on death).

2   Shares or securities of a company which are quoted, and which by themselves or in conjunction with other holdings owned by the transferor give voting control of the company.

In determining whether or not the transferor has voting control of a company, any shares or securities in the company owned by his spouse or civil partner are aggregated with his own. Voting rights attaching to shares held in trust are attributed to any beneficiary who is for the time being entitled to receive the income from the shares.

Minimum Period of Ownership

In order to qualify for relief:

(a)   the transferor must have owned the business property for two years immediately before the transfer; or

(b)   the property must have replaced other relevant business property, and both properties together must have been held for a combined period of at least two years out of the five years immediately prior to the transfer.

The following should be noted for the purposes of (a) and (b) above:

1   If the transferor inherits the property on the death of his spouse or civil partner, the deceased spouse's/partner's period of ownership is added to that of the transferor.

2   Where unquoted shareholdings have been acquired within the two-year period in (a) above in exchange for other shares in a capital reorganisation or company amalgamation or reconstruction, the transferor's ownership of the previous shares will count towards the two-year period.

3   Where the transferor acquires the property on a death other than that of his spouse or civil partner, he is treated as having owned the property as from the date of death.

4   The two-year ownership period may be set aside where the transferor or his spouse/civil partner acquired the business property as a result of a transfer of value if the earlier transfer was itself eligible for business property relief and one or both of the relevant transfers took place on death.

Lifetime Transfer

Tax on lifetime transfers which are not potentially exempt will be calculated subject to business property relief.

Where lifetime transfers take place within seven years of the death of the transferor, the relief will be available to reduce the tax or additional tax chargeable, although the following points should be noted:

1   The transferee must continue to own the property transferred, or a suitable replacement, throughout the relevant period beginning with

the transfer and ending with the death of the transferor (or transferee if earlier). If only part of the property is retained, a proportionate charge will arise on the death of the transferor.

2   A reorganisation of share capital which has not been treated as a disposal for CGT purposes will not be considered a disposal of the original property for business relief purposes. The incorporation of a business is also deemed not to be a disposal.

3   Where the original property or part of it is sold, business property relief may still be available if all of the proceeds are reinvested in other qualifying property on arm's- length terms. Reinvestment must take place within a qualifying period and the relief will be available even if the donor dies during the period. The qualifying period is three years (or longer if the Board allows).

4   Immediately before the end of the relevant period the property must qualify for business property relief, assuming a notional transfer by the transferee (although in cases where the original property was sold and the proceeds had not yet been reinvested in other qualifying property before the donor's death, the notional transfer is assumed to occur when the replacement property is acquired).

5   Relief dependent upon the donor having control of the company does not require the donee to have control when considering the notional transfer mentioned at 4 above.

Alternative Investment Market

Shares on the Alternative Investment Market (AIM) are treated as unquoted.

Agricultural Property Relief

Agricultural property relief and not-business property relief is given where the conditions for both are met. Where the value of relevant business property is partly attributable to an asset qualifying for agricultural property relief, the remainder will obtain business property relief if the qualifying conditions are met.

Valuation

The valuation of relevant business property is determined in accordance with normal valuation principles. In the case of an unincorporated business, or an interest in an unincorporated business, the value is its net value – the value of the business assets (including goodwill) less the liabilities of the business.

Mortgages

If the business property has been charged as security for a loan, the charge must be deducted from the value of the property before relief is given. Unsecured loans will be apportioned between the various assets making up an individual's estate in proportion to values. Therefore, wherever possible, loans should be secured on assets not qualifying for IHT relief.

Excepted Assets

Any value attributed to excepted assets will not qualify for relief. These are assets which are:

1   not used wholly or mainly for the purposes of the business throughout the two years prior to transfer (or since acquisition if more recent); and

2   not required at the time of transfer for future use in the business.

Assets which have been used, at any time, wholly or mainly for the personal benefit of the transferor or a connected person cannot be said to have been used at that time for the purposes of the business.

Instalments

IHT arising on business property can be paid by annual instalments over a period of ten years. (For further details see Section 4.29, *IHT – Payment and Funding the Tax.*)

Exceptions

Property subject to a contract for sale (see Section 1.11, *Partnership Assurance*) does not qualify for relief. However, sales in the course of the incorporation of a business which is to continue, and where the consideration is wholly or mainly in the form of shares or securities of the acquiring company, are ignored. Likewise a contract for a sale of shares or securities in a company as part of a reconstruction or amalgamation will not prevent relief from being available.

Shares in a company which is being wound up (otherwise than for the purpose of a reconstruction or amalgamation where the business of the company is to continue thereafter) will not qualify for relief.

Gifts with Reservation

Business property caught by the gifts with reservation rules can still attract business property relief on the release of a reservation, and/or on the death of the donor or donee. The qualification rules are applied to a deemed transfer by the donee. However, in determining whether 100% relief is due on shares or securities, they are treated as still owned by the donor (ie aggregated with any shares, etc still held by the donor).

Capital Gains Tax

Assets which qualify for business property relief would generally attract CGT hold-over relief in respect of capital gains on lifetime transfers.

CROSS REFERENCES

Partnership Assurance   **1.11**
Farming   **3.29**
Lloyd's   **3.30**
Woodlands   **3.31**
IHT – Agricultural Property Relief   **4.20**
IHT – Payment and Funding the Tax   **4.29**

4.20 IHT – Agricultural Property Relief

Description	The relief takes the form of a discount in the value which becomes chargeable to IHT either on a lifetime transfer or on death. The relief is only given on the 'agricultural value' of property and not on any development or other value. It is necessary to consider whether the asset is 'agricultural property' and the donor's interest in it. There are two rates of relief: 100% and 50%. The asset may have to qualify for the relief on more than one occasion if it is part of a lifetime transfer.
Suitable for	Agricultural land which the donor occupies personally, or as a partner in a partnership, or through a company which the individual controls. Let land can also qualify, as can shares in a farming company.

FURTHER DETAILS

Agricultural Property

This means agricultural land or pasture situated in the UK, Channel Islands, Isle of Man or any state within the European Economic Area, and includes woodland and any building used for the intensive rearing of livestock or fish if they are occupied with agricultural land or pasture and the occupation is ancillary to that of the agricultural land or pasture. It also includes cottages, farm buildings, and farmhouses, together with land occupied with them, which are of a character appropriate to the property. Buildings used in the breeding and rearing of horses on a stud farm qualify as farm buildings. Sporting and fishing rights do not qualify.

Amount and Nature of Relief

100% Relief

This applies where:
- the donor's interest in the property immediately before the transfer carries the right to vacant possession, or the right to obtain vacant possession within the next 12 months; or
- in relation to transfers of value, and other events occurring on or after 1 September 1995, the property has been let on a tenancy beginning on or after that date.

Under transitional provisions, tenanted land let before 10 March 1981 will also qualify for relief at 100% if:

(a) the land would have qualified for 50% relief under the earlier rules had it been transferred before 10 March 1981; and
(b) the donor's interest has not at any time between 10 March 1981 and the date of the gift carried the right to vacant possession, or the right to obtain vacant possession within the next 12 months, and has not failed to do so as the result of any act or deliberate omission of the donor.

50% Relief

This applies in any other case, including that part of any tenanted land let before 10 March 1981 which would not have qualified for 50% relief under the earlier rules as a result only of the restriction of relief under the earlier rules to the greater of 1,000 acres or land worth £250,000.

Minimum Period of Ownership or Occupation

In order to qualify for relief, the agricultural property must have been either:
(a) occupied by the donor for the purposes of agriculture throughout the period of two years prior to the date of the transfer; or
(b) owned by the donor and occupied by him or someone else for the purposes of agriculture throughout the period of seven years prior to the date of the transfer.

The following should be noted for the purposes of (a) and (b) above.
- If the donor inherits the property on the death of his spouse or civil partner, he is also regarded as having inherited the occupation and ownership periods of the deceased spouse/partner.
- Occupation by a company controlled by the donor or by a Scottish partnership in which the donor is a partner, is treated as occupation by the donor personally.
- Where the property occupied by the donor at the date of the transfer replaced other agricultural property, the two-year occupation period will be satisfied if the respective periods of occupation by the donor for agricultural purposes together totalled at least two years out of the five years preceding the transfer. A similar rule applies in respect of the seven-year ownership period, and the periods of ownership of the donor must comprise at least seven years out of the ten years preceding the transfer.

Shares and Securities

Agricultural property relief is also available for shares and securities in a company which holds agricultural property where part of their value can be attributed to the agricultural value of the property, and the donor had control of the company immediately before the transfer. The general time limits of two years' occupation or seven years' ownership apply to the company as regards the agricultural property and to the donor as regards the shares.

Agricultural Value and Business Property Relief

Relief applies only to the agricultural value of the property. This is determined as if the property were subject to a perpetual covenant prohibiting use other than for agricultural purposes. In some circumstances, business property relief may be available in respect of any excess value. The assets of a farming business other than the land and buildings will normally be eligible for business property relief. For further details see Section 4.19, *IHT – Business Property Relief.*

Mortgages

If the agricultural property has been charged as security for a loan, the charge must be deducted from the value of the property before relief is given. Unsecured loans will be apportioned between the various assets making up an individual's estate in proportion to values. Therefore, wherever possible, loans should be secured on assets not qualifying for IHT relief.

Lifetime Transfers

Tax on lifetime transfers which are not potentially exempt will be calculated subject to agricultural relief.

Where a lifetime transfer has been made within seven years of the death of the transferor, agricultural relief will be available to reduce the tax or additional tax chargeable, although the following points should be noted:

- The transferee must continue to own the property transferred or a suitable replacement throughout the relevant period beginning with the transfer and ending with the death of the transferor (or transferee if earlier). There must be no binding contract for sale at the relevant date.
- The transferee or another must occupy the property for agricultural purposes during the relevant period, and it must be agricultural property immediately before the death. If only part of the property is retained, a proportionate charge will arise on the death of the transferor.
- In the case of shares or securities, the company must continue to own the property during the relevant period, with occupation by the company or another for agricultural purposes.
- A reorganisation of share capital which has not been treated as a disposal for CGT purposes will not be considered a disposal for agricultural relief purposes. The incorporation of a business is also deemed not to be a disposal.
- Where the original property or part of it is sold by the donee, agricultural relief may still be available if all of the proceeds are reinvested in other agricultural property on arm's-length terms. Reinvestment must take place within a qualifying period and the relief will be available even if the donor dies during the period. The provisions above must apply to the original and replacement property. The qualifying period is three years (or longer if the Board allows).

Instalments

IHT on agricultural property may be paid by annual interest-free instalments over ten years.

Sale Contracts

No relief is available if at the time of transfer the donor has entered into a binding contract for the sale of the agricultural property, or the shares and securities in a company which holds agricultural property.

Gifts with Reservation

Property caught by the gifts with reservation rules can still attract agricultural relief on the release of a reservation, and/or on the death of the donor or donee. The qualification rules are applied to a deemed transfer by the donee, but the donor's period of ownership and occupation (before and after the transfer) can be taken into account.

Capital Gains Tax

Agricultural land and buildings (but not shares in a company owning agricultural land) which qualify for agricultural relief, would attract CGT hold-over relief on a lifetime gift.

CROSS REFERENCES

4.21 Life Interest Trusts

Description	A means of providing funds managed and controlled by trustees to provide an income benefit for named beneficiaries.
Suitable for	Individuals where the donor wishes them to have an income benefit from assets but not to have control of the capital. Such trusts could be used for family company shares or agricultural property.
Advantages	1 To pass the benefit of personal wealth to others but to retain flexibility over the ultimate beneficiary of the capital.
	2 The gift into trust will qualify for CGT hold-over relief.
	3 Income tax may be suffered on the trust income at a lower rate than income in the hands of the donor.
	4 The trustees retain control of the capital.
Disadvantages	1 Generally irreversible.
	2 Some administration required.
	3 There may be IHT payable if the value of the gift exceeds the nil rate band. If the trust is created after 21 March 2006 there may be charges to IHT every ten years, and when trust capital is appointed to a beneficiary.
	4 Income tax and CGT consequences if settlor, spouse or a minor child of the settlor is a beneficiary.

FURTHER DETAILS

The deed establishing the trust will define the interest of the beneficiaries (eg adult children) in the income of the trust at the outset. The deed will also define the beneficiaries of the capital in due course (eg the children's offspring). However, the deed can be drawn up to give flexibility so that the trustees will have powers to distribute some or all of the capital to the income beneficiaries in due course, or to revoke an income beneficiary's interest in the trust in favour of another potential beneficiary (eg to benefit that person's children).

The settlor may be one of the trustees and retain the power to remove and appoint trustees. Trustees should be chosen with care and be persons the settlor trusts implicitly to carry out his wishes on any matter on which they have discretionary powers, provided these do not conflict with their duties as trustees. Caution is needed with any transactions between the settlor and the trustees.

Life interest trusts are particularly useful where an individual wishes to reduce his estate for IHT and adult beneficiaries are involved (eg children and other family members) but the individual does not wish control of the capital to pass to the beneficiaries. A life interest trust can also be considered in will planning to give flexibility for future IHT gifts.

If non-resident trustees are appointed, special rules apply for CGT and income tax purposes but not for IHT (see Section 4.24, *Overseas Trusts*).

Taxation Aspects

Inheritance Tax

A gift into trust is, subject to the normal exemptions and reliefs, a transfer of value by the settlor for IHT purposes. A transfer after 21 March 2006 into a life interest trust will be a chargeable transfer with tax at the lifetime (20%) rate being charged on amounts in excess of the nil rate band. The only exception is if the trust is created for the benefit of a disabled person, when the gift will be a potentially exempt transfer.

Trusts Created before 22 March 2006

The beneficiaries entitled to a share of the income of trust property are treated for IHT purposes as being the owners of a proportionate part of the trust property. Therefore, if a beneficiary is entitled to one-quarter of the trust income, his estate for IHT will be deemed to include one-quarter of the trust capital regardless of whether or not it remains in trust after his death. It follows that distributions of capital to beneficiaries which proportionately reduce their income entitlement will not give rise to any IHT, as the capital will already be deemed to comprise part of their estates.

The trustees may wish to exercise powers to revoke the entitlement of an income beneficiary, or the beneficiary himself may wish to surrender his interest in the trust, eg to accelerate the contingent interest of his children. However, if this is done, the income beneficiary will make a chargeable transfer for IHT, and a tax charge at 20% on the value above the nil rate band will arise, unless the trust assets attract business or agricultural property relief. If, as a result of the revocation or surrender, the donee becomes absolutely entitled to the trust assets, the donor beneficiary will make a potentially exempt transfer for IHT.

Any capital remaining in trust and from which the beneficiary is entitled to the income at his death will be aggregated with the beneficiary's other estate – his personal capital and any other pre-22 March 2006 trust funds from which he is entitled to the income. The overall IHT liability on the beneficiary's aggregate estate will be attributed to the component parts of the estate, eg if the beneficiary's share of the trust fund represents 40% of the total estate, the trustees will bear 40% of the total tax liability out of the beneficiary's share. If the beneficiary prefers a higher proportion of the total tax to be borne by his share of the trust fund rather than his personal estate, he can make lifetime gifts of his personal assets which, if they prove to be chargeable transfers (because he dies within seven years of making the gift), will possibly utilise the nil rate band.

Trusts Created after 21 March 2006

The beneficiaries of trusts created during the life of the settlor after 21 March 2006 are not treated as being owners of the trust assets for IHT purposes unless the trust is for the benefit of a disabled beneficiary. Instead, the IHT regime which applies to Discretionary trusts (see Section 4.23) will apply, with the trust funds being subject to IHT charges every ten years and when capital is distributed from the trust.

If the post-21 March 2006 trust is created by a Will and meets certain requirements (known as an immediate post-death interest), the trust funds will be part of the beneficiary's estate for IHT.

Capital Gains Tax

A gift of chargeable assets into trust may involve the realisation of chargeable gains by the settlor. Where the trustees are UK residents, the gains may be held over until realised by the trustees. Hold-over relief cannot be claimed if the settlor, his spouse/civil partner or minor child, can benefit from the trust funds. UK resident trustees are liable to CGT, subject to an annual exemption of half that available to individuals. Currently, the annual CGT exemption for trustees is £5,050. If the same person has, on or after 6 June 1978, made more than one trust, the annual exemption will be divided between those trusts. The full individual's annual exemption is available for trusts benefiting mentally disabled persons or persons in receipt of an attendance allowance or of a disability living allowance, by virtue of entitlement to the care component at the highest or middle rate. Capital distributions by the trustees to beneficiaries may attract CGT, although hold-over relief should apply to trusts created after 21 March 2006.

Chargeable gains realised by UK resident trustees will suffer tax at 28% from 23 June 2010.

Income Tax

The trustees must account for income tax on the income of the trust property and must file tax returns for this purpose. The tax is at the basic rate of 20%, but where the credit attaching to dividends and other income from investments/savings is less than 20%, the trustees will not have to pay the difference. The beneficiaries entitled to the income may be subject to a higher rate of tax with a credit for the tax paid by the trustees, or a beneficiary may be able to reclaim part or all of the tax suffered by the trustees, but no repayment is available in respect of the 10% notional tax credit arising on dividends. Where the beneficiary is the settlor's spouse or civil partner, the settlor will be liable to any higher rate tax. Care must be taken if there is a possibility of the capital reverting to the settlor.

Reversionary Interest

A reversionary interest in a life interest settlement lies with the individuals who have the right to the capital after the death of the life tenant. A gift of a reversionary interest is exempt from IHT. However, the interest must not have been acquired for any consideration in money or money's worth, it must not be one held by the settlor or his spouse, nor must it be a reversionary interest in excluded property.

A gift of property into a trust will generally not involve any charge to stamp duty.

CROSS REFERENCES

4.22 Accumulation Trusts

Description	A means of transferring assets to trustees for the benefit of young beneficiaries.
Suitable for	Individuals wishing to benefit young children of the family.
Advantages	1 A method of transferring assets for the benefit of young beneficiaries. Beneficiaries of the same class yet to be born can be included, provided there is at least one living beneficiary of that class.
	2 Income is not required to be paid out to the beneficiaries until an age selected by the settlor at the outset (subject to the accumulation period) although it can be tax effective to do so. Capital can remain under the control of trustees for very long periods.
	3 Trustees have powers to control the entitlement of a beneficiary.
	4 Capital gains on transfers into the trust can be held over.
Disadvantages	1 Administration costs.
	2 Irreversible.
	3 There may be IHT payable if the value of the gift exceeds the IHT nil rate band. There may be charges to IHT every ten years and when trust capital is appointed to a beneficiary.

FURTHER DETAILS

Property is held by trustees for the benefit of one or more infant children contingently upon attaining a certain age. The beneficiaries need not be named individually but may be identified by class, eg 'the grandchildren of the settlor'. There must be at least one living beneficiary of that class when the trust is made.

When the beneficiaries reach the specified age, the current income must be paid to them. However, they need not have any right to capital, which may continue to be held by the trustees and may ultimately pass to other beneficiaries, eg their own children.

Until the beneficiaries reach the specified age, the trustees may pay out income and/or capital for their maintenance or education or other benefit, which can be tax effective. Undistributed income must be accumulated in the trust, and regular distributions of capital (eg for school fees) should be avoided.

The settlor may be one of the trustees and retain the power to remove and appoint trustees, but careful consideration will be needed to establish whether the settlor, in exercising his powers as trustee, has reserved a benefit in the assets. The trustees will usually pay careful attention to the wishes of the settlor in all matters on which they have discretionary powers, provided those wishes do not conflict with their duties as trustees. The settlor will usually provide a letter of wishes for the trustees to guide them in carrying out their responsibilities. The letter should be updated as family circumstances change. This is particularly important if the settlor is not one of the trustees.

Accumulation trusts are particularly useful where the parent or grandparent wishes to reduce his estate for IHT, but because of the age or circumstances of the beneficiaries straightforward gifts are not practical or desirable.

However, Finance Act 2006 took away most of the previous IHT advantages of Accumulation Trusts. They are now taxed in a similar way to Discretionary Trusts (see Section 4.23) and the latter usually offer greater flexibility. For this reason it is now very rare for Accumulation Trusts to be created.

Taxation Aspects

Inheritance Tax

The transfer of assets into trust will be a transfer of value by the settlor for the purposes of IHT. The transfer will be a chargeable lifetime transfer, and unless the assets qualify for Business Property relief or Agricultural Property relief, tax at 20% will be payable on the excess over the nil rate band, taking account of any other chargeable transfers the settlor has made in the previous seven years.

For lifetime trusts created after 21 March 2006, the trust funds will be liable to IHT every ten years and when capital is distributed from the trust. The system of periodic charges is similar to that which applies to Discretionary Trusts (see Section 4.23).

Trusts in existence at 21 March 2006 will only escape the periodic charges if the terms are such that the beneficiaries will become absolutely entitled to the trust funds at an age no greater than 18.

There is a limited exemption from the periodic charges for trusts coming into effect after 21 March 2006 under the will or intestacy of a parent for the benefit of his bereaved child. If the child becomes absolutely entitled to the trust funds on attaining age 18 there will be no further IHT charge other than that which may have been paid on the parent's death. If the child becomes absolutely entitled at age 25, there will be a charge at that time not exceeding a maximum of 4.2% of the trust funds. In both cases there will be no ten-year charge even if the trust lasts for ten years or more.

However, if the child does not become absolutely entitled until after age 25, the IHT ten-year and distribution charges will apply. They will also apply to will trusts created by grandparents regardless of the specified age.

Capital Gains Tax

A gift of chargeable assets into trust may involve the realisation of a chargeable gain by the settlor. By use of a hold-over election, CGT may be deferred until the assets are realised by the trustees. A similar hold-over election can be made when those assets are distributed to beneficiaries by the trustees.

Trustees are chargeable to CGT on their disposals of assets, subject to an annual CGT exemption (£5,050). Where the same person has, on or after 6 June 1978, made more than one trust, the annual exemption will be divided between the relevant trusts.

The trustees will be liable to tax on chargeable gains at 28% from 23 June 2010.

Income Tax

Income received by the trustees before a beneficiary is entitled to it is chargeable at the rate applicable to trusts (now 50% on all income excluding UK dividend income or 42.5% on gross UK dividend income). However, an income tax basic rate band of £1,000 is available for all trusts paying tax at the rate applicable to trusts. Trust income of £1,000 or less, received net of tax, will not attract further income tax liability. Where the settlor has made more than one trust (at any time) the basic rate band will be divided between the relevant trusts.

Where the beneficiaries are 'vulnerable' they will be treated as if the trust does not exist, and all trust income and gains relevant to them will be taxed on them.

If the income is distributed to the beneficiaries, they may be able to recover all or part of that tax depending on their personal circumstances. If the beneficiaries are infant unmarried children of the settlor, income in excess of £100 distributed will be assessed on the settlor until the children reach 18. These trusts operate at maximum tax efficiency where grandparents are the settlors, as any income distributed is treated as that of the child.

Income distributions need to be carefully monitored, particularly where it has been the trustees' policy to fully distribute income in the past. Excess income distributions may result in an additional tax charge on the trustees in order to frank the tax credit on the distributions in the beneficiaries' hands. Consideration should be given to changing the investment base (at least in part) but there can be CGT consequences of taking this action which would need to be quantified.

All trusts are subject to anti-avoidance legislation. In particular, the settlor should reserve no right to benefit personally from the fund and any dealings between the settlor and the trustees must be treated with extreme caution.

CROSS REFERENCES

IHT – Potentially Exempt Transfers   **4.17**
Life Interest Trusts   **4.21**
The Young   **5.2**

4.23　Discretionary Trusts

Description	Trusts which provide that the capital and income are to be distributed at the trustees' discretion.
Suitable for	Individuals wishing to set aside assets for the future benefit of a number of potential beneficiaries and who wish to retain the maximum flexibility as to the manner in which the income and capital are to be distributed ultimately. Ideal if set up within the settlor's nil rate band for IHT (currently £325,000) with assets which would not otherwise qualify for CGT hold-over relief.
Advantages	1　Distributions of income or capital can be made according to the needs and circumstances of beneficiaries as they occur over the life of the trust.
	2　A wide range of beneficiaries can be included (eg settlor's widow or widower) therefore giving maximum flexibility.
	3　Income can be accumulated for the whole of the trust period which can be up to 125 years.
	4　All assets transferred to such a trust could attract CGT hold-over relief.
Disadvantages	1　Administration required.
	2　A transfer into the trust could attract lifetime IHT.

FURTHER DETAILS

A discretionary trust is usually set up for the maximum period permitted by trust law (125 years), subject to discretionary powers of the trustees to terminate it at some earlier time. A wide range of potential beneficiaries is included to allow for all possibilities – often by class identification rather than by name, eg 'the children and remoter issue of the settlor'.

The trustees are given extensive discretion as to the time and manner in which to deal with the trust assets, although in some cases they may have to obtain first the consent of a designated individual. They will have power to accumulate income for the whole of the period allowed by trust law (125 years) unless a shorter period is included in the Trust Deed; they may distribute income or capital to all or any of the potential beneficiaries; they may create sub-trusts for particular beneficiaries or classes of beneficiary.

The settlor may be one of the trustees and retain the power to remove and appoint trustees. The trustees will usually pay careful attention to the wishes of the settlor in all matters on which they have discretionary powers, provided that those wishes do not conflict with their duties as trustees. The settlor will usually provide a letter of wishes for the trustees to guide them in carrying out their responsibilities. The letter should be updated as family circumstances change. This is particularly important if the settlor is not one of the trustees.

Taxation Aspects

Inheritance Tax

The transfer of assets into trust will be a transfer of value by the settlor for the purposes of IHT. Such a transfer will not be a potentially exempt transfer and will thus immediately be a chargeable transfer subject to the normal exemptions and reliefs. The amount chargeable may fall within the nil rate band (currently £325,000) below which no IHT is chargeable and will be left out of account in the cumulative transfers after seven years. Any amount in excess of the nil rate band will suffer tax at 20%.

Discretionary trusts are subject to a system of periodic charges to IHT at ten year intervals and whenever capital is distributed, appointed or transferred onto other trusts or to any one or more beneficiaries of the trust. The periodic charge is at 30% of the lifetime rate, and thus the maximum charge on the ten year anniversary will be at an effective rate of 6% (ie 30% of 20%). This level of charge may prove to be a small price to pay for the maximum flexibility offered by this type of trust in planning a family's IHT position.

An individual who has made little by way of transfers of value, so that the nil rate band of tax is available, may suffer no IHT disadvantage if he now wishes to make a settlement of no more in value than the nil rate band or the nil rate band plus available reliefs (eg business or agricultural property relief). It may be beneficial to make two or more such settlements amounting to the nil rate band in aggregate. A husband and wife or civil partner should make separate trusts, as they each have their own nil rate band. Unless the value of the settled property increases substantially, the trust property may escape IHT for many years. An IHT review of the trust should in all cases be carried out prior to the first ten year anniversary of its creation.

The settlor should take care not to be included in the class of potential beneficiaries, otherwise he will have reserved a benefit in the trust assets. They could therefore attract a further IHT charge on his death, or when he was removed from the class of beneficiaries.

Capital Gains Tax

By use of the election for hold-over, any capital gains on the transfer of chargeable assets into trust may be held over until realised by the trustees. This election can be made even if IHT is not payable on the transfer because it is within the nil rate band. A hold-over election will be available on the transfer into trust only if the trustees are UK residents and on the transfer out of trust only if the beneficiary is UK resident. Hold-over elections cannot be made if the settlor, his spouse/civil partner or minor child can benefit from the trust funds.

These hold-over elections apply on all types of assets. On a transfer into trust, the election is made solely by the transferor. On a transfer out of trust, the election is made by the trustees and the beneficiary jointly.

There are provisions whereby the trustees may become liable to CGT if, having made a hold-over election on the distribution of an asset to a UK-resident beneficiary, the beneficiary becomes neither resident nor ordinarily resident in the UK before disposal of the asset and within six years of the end of the year of assessment in which the distribution out of the trust occurs. In view of this potential CGT liability, the trustees will normally seek an indemnity from the beneficiary or reserve sufficient assets of the beneficiary's share of the trust fund to meet any potential liability.

Subject to an annual exemption (currently £5,050), trustees are chargeable to CGT on disposals made by them within the trust. Where the same person has, on or after 6 June 1978, made more than one trust, the annual exemption will be divided between the relevant trusts. The trustees' chargeable gains will suffer tax at 28% from 23 June 2010.

Income Tax

The income of the trust will bear income tax in the trust at the rate applicable to trusts (50% on all income except UK dividends or 42.5% on gross UK dividend income). However, an income tax basic rate band of £1,000 is available for all trusts paying tax at the rate applicable to trusts. Trust income of £1,000 or less, received net of tax, will not attract further income tax liability. Where the settlor has made more than one trust (at any time), the basic rate band will be divided between the relevant trusts. Any payments of income to beneficiaries will be net of income tax of 50% and, depending on the personal circumstances of the relevant beneficiaries, they may be able to reclaim some or all of the tax.

If unmarried children of the settlor are paid income or capital from the trust during minority, the settlor will be assessed on the payments as if they are his *income* (see Section 4.22, *Accumulation Trusts*). Income distributions need to be carefully monitored. Excess income distributions may result in an additional tax charge on the trustees in order to frank the tax credit on the distributions in the beneficiaries hands.

Any transactions proposed between the settlor and the trustees, even on an arm's-length basis, must be treated with *caution*. Unless the settlor excludes himself and his spouse/civil partner (but not widow or widower) from any benefit from the trust funds, he will be assessed to tax on the income of the trust. However, the liability will be paid by the trustees and the settlor will receive credit in his self-assessment for the tax paid by them.

Trusts for the Vulnerable

With effect from 6 April 2004 a new tax regime was introduced in respect of vulnerable beneficiaries, whereby the trustees pay the same amount of tax as the beneficiary would have paid had the trust income been his. The trustees are therefore able to take into account the vulnerable beneficiary's personal allowances and starting and basic rate bands. For this special treatment to apply, it is necessary for a joint election to be made by the trustee and the vulnerable beneficiary.

CROSS REFERENCES

4.24 Overseas Trusts

Description	Trusts, the trustees of which are resident outside the UK.
Suitable for	Since 19 March 1991 the advantages of new overseas trusts have been restricted, and the rules were further tightened from 17 March 1998. Further changes were introduced by FA 2006 and take effect from 6 April 2007.
Advantages	1 Non-domiciled settlor and non-domiciled beneficiary – exemption from IHT and possible exemption from CGT (but beneficiary may be subject to payment of £30,000 tax charge to take advantage of remittance basis rules). Possible deferral of income tax liability.
	2 Non-domiciled settlor and domiciled beneficiary – exemption from IHT. There could be a deferral of income tax which would otherwise be chargeable on an arising basis.
	3 Domiciled settlor – pre-17 March 1998 settlements for grandchildren. Deferral of CGT whilst capital profits retained by trustees and possible deferral of income tax.
Disadvantages	1 Costs of administration.
	2 Selection of reliable trustees outside the UK.
	3 Loss of control over the trust property.
	4 Complex anti-avoidance tax law involved. Subject to provisions applying to all trusts – wherever the trustees reside – plus special legislation concerned with overseas assets and trusts which could mean that the settlor will be liable to UK tax even though not personally a beneficiary of the trust.
	5 UK beneficiaries receiving capital payments from overseas trusts after 5 April 1992 may be liable to a surcharge on their CGT liability

FURTHER DETAILS

The essential feature of these arrangements is that a significant amount of wealth is put in the hands of trustees outside the UK who may have wide discretion as to the manner in which it is to be used for beneficiaries. The settlor must be satisfied that the trustees will prove to be reliable and competent. He will have to take account of any political risks which might affect the mobility and security of the trust fund, his exposure to personal UK tax liability on the trustees' income and gains and the potential diminution in the trust fund if the trustees incur a non-UK tax liability. The trust can be of the three types previously described – life interest, accumulation or discretionary.

Taxation Aspects

Since 17 March 1998, the taxation treatment has depended on the following:
- when the trust became non-UK resident;
- the domicile and residence status of the settlor when the trust assets were settled and in the relevant tax year;
- the relationship of the beneficiaries to the settlor;
- any changes or additions to the trust's beneficiaries or assets;
- the status of the beneficiary when payments are received from trustees.

From 6 April 2007, on a transfer between settlements, the residence and domicile status of the settlor will be tested at the time of the transfer as well as at the time when the property first became settled.

Trustees

Income Tax

If none of the trustees is resident in the UK, prima facie the income of the trust is chargeable to UK tax only to the extent that it derives from the UK. Income tax will be chargeable at the basic rate (20%) on trust income deriving from the UK (10% on UK dividends and 20% on savings income) or, if the trustees have discretion as to its payment to the beneficiaries or are able to accumulate income, at the rate applicable to trusts (50% or 42.5% for UK dividend income).

Capital Gains Tax

Foreign trustees are not liable to CGT on UK assets except on certain assets where the overseas trust carries on a trade in the UK through a branch or agency. Where UK trusts are exported after 18 March 1991 the retiring UK trustees will be liable to an exit charge on trust gains accrued to the date of export based on the market value of trust assets at that time. Foreign trustees will also be liable to UK CGT on gains realised during the period from the date of export to the following 5 April.

From 6 April 2007, if at least one trustee is resident in the UK and at least one is not resident, the trust is treated as resident in the UK for CGT and income tax purposes unless the settlor was not resident, not ordinarily resident or domiciled in the UK at the relevant time (ie the time when the settlement was created or the time of any transfers between settlements).

Inheritance Tax

The liability of the trustees to IHT depends upon the tax status of the settlor when the trust was established. If the trust property is located overseas and the settlor was not UK domiciled, the assets will be exempt from IHT as excluded property (this exemption is not limited to non-resident trustees). Otherwise, the trust assets will remain liable to IHT. A trust settled whilst the settlor is still non-UK domiciled and in which the settlor retains an interest in possession or is in the class of discretionary beneficiaries could therefore be a useful tool in protecting an individual's foreign assets from an IHT charge arising after he has acquired a UK domicile. See Section 4.5, *Income Tax – Overseas Aspects* for further information on the acquisition of a UK domicile and Section 4.31, *Inheritance Tax – Overseas Aspects* for further information on becoming deemed domiciled in the UK.

The Settlor

Income Tax

The settlor will gain no income tax advantage if he or his wife/civil partner retains any interest in the property unless not resident and not ordinarily resident in the tax year in which income arises. All transactions between the settlor and the trustees need careful consideration in view of the anti-avoidance legislation.

Capital Gains Tax

A transfer of assets into the settlement will be liable to CGT, subject to the tax status of the settlor and the nature and location of the assets.

The position after 17 March 1998 is that UK resident and domiciled settlors will be liable to tax on gains as they arise on or after 17 March 1998, irrespective of when the trust was created. The only exceptions to this are trusts where the beneficiaries are:

- grandchildren of the settlor where the trust was created before 17 March 1998;
- beneficiaries of a trust created before 19 March 1991 who are:
    - children of the settlor under the age of 18,
    - unborn children of the settlor,
    - future spouses of the settlor or his children,
    - persons other than the settlor, his adult children, their spouses or companies which they control.

Prior to Finance Act 2002, a UK settlor who was assessable on gains accruing to an offshore trust could not set any personal capital losses against those gains. A settlor may now elect for such a set-off.

Inheritance Tax

A UK domiciled settlor can be liable to a lifetime IHT charge on transferring assets into an overseas trust unless the transfer qualifies as potentially exempt, or available exemptions and the nil rate band covers the transfer. The transfer will only qualify as potentially exempt if the trust is for the benefit of a disabled beneficiary. If the settlor is included as one of a class of discretionary beneficiaries when the trust is established, the property transferred will be caught under the reservation of benefit rules unless it falls within the definition of excluded property. A settlor who is neither domiciled nor deemed domiciled in the UK for the purposes of IHT is able to make an IHT-free transfer of foreign assets to trustees.

The Beneficiaries

Income Tax

The amount of trust income taxable in the UK in any year will depend upon the beneficiary's interest in the trust (eg discretionary or interest in possession) and his tax status.

If a beneficiary is resident or ordinarily resident, and domiciled in the UK he will be taxable on his income from the trust. Where the trustees have power to accumulate income, the beneficiary's income tax liability will be deferred until such time as he receives a benefit (whether of income or capital) from the trust. Where the beneficiary has available personal allowances and is a lower rate taxpayer, a regular distribution of trust income may be more tax efficient than allowing income to accumulate and perhaps be taxed in full in a later year, for instance on a beneficiary becoming absolutely entitled to trust assets. However, if there is any possibility of a beneficiary being not resident and not ordinarily resident at the time of receiving a benefit from the trust, any UK income tax liability on accumulated income may be avoided altogether.

A UK income tax liability for a beneficiary may also be avoided where the settlor has been taxed on the income by virtue of anti-avoidance legislation.

The tax treatment of overseas trust income arising to a non-domiciled individual will depend upon the extent of his interest in the trust, his residence status and whether or not the trust income or any benefit provided out of this income is remitted to the UK. In accordance with provisions included in the 2008 Finance Act, in general a UK resident, non-domiciled beneficiary will only be able to claim the remittance basis on non-UK income if he pays the £30,000 tax charge.

A distribution made out of capital in anticipation of subsequent income of the trustees being accumulated will not escape an income tax charge in the later years over which income is accumulated.

Capital Gains Tax

On or after 17 March 1998, the status of the settlor when the trust was created becomes irrelevant. All gains arising on or after this date are potentially chargeable on a beneficiary who receives a capital payment or benefit from the trust. However, the beneficiary will not be liable unless he is resident in the UK As a result of provisions included in the 2008 Finance Act a resident, non-domiciled beneficiary will not avoid tax on capital payments or benefits, although the remittance basis can be claimed on payment of the £30,000 tax charge.

Where the settlor is neither resident nor ordinarily resident, the gains of the trustees will need to be computed each year without the benefit of an annual exemption (the trust gains) and these are carried forward year by year. When a beneficiary receives a capital distribution from the trust (ie one which is not deemed to be income) he will be liable to CGT to the extent that there are accrued trust gains or such gains arise in a subsequent year.

Where a capital distribution is made after 5 April 1992, the beneficiary's CGT liability may be increased by a surcharge. The level of the surcharge will depend on the number of years which have elapsed between the trustees making the gain and the beneficiary being liable for CGT on a distribution.

The surcharge is on the CGT liability at a rate of 10% per annum for a maximum period of six years (ie maximum surcharge is 60% of the CGT payable). There are special identification rules to determine the rate of the surcharge with gains of a later year being deemed to be distributed before gains of an earlier year (last in, first out or LIFO).

Inheritance Tax

A charge to IHT on a beneficiary's interest in an overseas trust will depend upon the type of interest held and whether or not the settlor was non-domiciled at the date the settlement was made.

CROSS REFERENCES

Income Tax – Overseas Aspects　**4.5**
CGT – Overseas Aspects　**4.13**
Life Interest Trusts　**4.21**
Accumulation Trusts　**4.22**
Discretionary Trusts　**4.23**
IHT – Non-UK Domiciliaries and Other Overseas Aspects　**4.31**

4.25 Private Charitable Trusts

Description	A means of providing funds for charitable purposes with tax advantages.
Suitable for	Individuals wishing to set aside funds to provide financial support for charitable work through a private charity, rather than making donations to a public charity.
Advantages	1 The satisfaction of personally administering a fund for the benefit of charitable activities.
	2 Freedom of choice subject to tax requirements as to allocation of income or capital to charity generally.
	3 Tax exemption providing certain requirements met.
Disadvantages	1 Irreversible.
	2 Administrative costs.
	3 Compliance with Charities Commission requirements.

FURTHER DETAILS

Setting up the Trust

A private charitable trust is usually set up by an individual transferring property to trustees to hold the capital and income on trust to benefit charities, not necessarily restricted to UK charities.

The donor may be one of the trustees and thus be directly concerned with the administration of the trust fund, including the exercise by the trustees of their discretion regarding the charities which are to benefit.

The charitable trust should be registered with the Charity Commission and will receive a registered charity number. The procedure is set out by the Charity Commission. They require an application form (CC5a) and a declaration form (CC5c), a certified copy of the dated trust deed showing the names of the first named trustees and witnesses to their signatures. Model governing documents are available. The name of the charity is entered on the Charity database when the charity is registered.

All charities must comply with the accounts requirement of the Charities Act 1993 (as amended).

Taxation Aspects

Gift of Capital

An outright gift to a charitable trust is exempt from CGT and IHT. The value of any property held in a charitable trust as a result of a transfer by an individual or his spouse/civil partner is related property for the purposes of valuing property in the individual's estate, eg unquoted company *shares*. Gifts made after 5 April 2000 of qualifying investments, typically shares and securities, will also benefit from income tax relief under the Gift Aid Scheme. From 6 April 2002, gifts of land and buildings may benefit from income tax relief under the Gift Aid Scheme.

Taxpayers completing self-assessment tax returns from 2003/04 onwards, are able to nominate a charity to receive any tax repayment that is due. This can be done by completing form SA100 Charity. A list of the charities registered for this purpose can be found on the HMRC website. Each charity on the list has been given a unique code which should be used on the form to identify the charity to receive the donation. The list will be updated on a quarterly basis. Gift Aid will apply to the donation, and HMRC will pay the tax on Gift Aid donations to charities without the charity making a claim.

Gift out of Income

The Gift Aid Scheme governs all donations after 5 April 2000, and relief for higher rate tax is available for any size of donation and the declaration for relief may be made before, at the time of, or after the donation. Payments made from 6 April 2003 until the date an individual's tax return for the previous year is submitted, can be treated as though paid in that previous year.

Tax Status of Charity

Property held on charitable trusts is normally exempt from CGT and IHT. Exemption from income tax is normally available in respect of dividends and interest, so that tax deducted at source and tax credits will be repaid on making a claim to HMRC. Since 5 April 1999, the notional tax credit attaching to UK dividends is no longer repayable.

A charity will be subject to a restriction of its tax relief if it:

1   applies funds for non-charitable purposes;
2   passes funds to an overseas body without taking reasonable steps to satisfy itself that the funds will be applied for charitable purposes; or
3   loans or invests funds in certain limited ways which it cannot show to be:
    (a)   for the benefit of the charity; and
    (b)   not for tax avoidance purposes.

Trading profits are exempt where the trading is in the course of actually carrying out the charity's primary purpose.

Where a charity normally distributes its funds to other charities, the tax exemptions may still be given provided the funds are distributed to qualifying charities, for direct charitable activities and for qualifying administrative expenses. Where the funds are not distributed, the charity's tax reliefs will be restricted.

CROSS REFERENCES

IHT – Exemptions   **4.16**
Married with Older Children   **5.6**

4.26 IHT – Wills

Description	A document containing the legal declarations of an individual concerning the distribution of his possessions on death.
Suitable for	Everyone over the minimum age with testamentary capacity.
Ages	Minimum age in England and Wales 18; in Scotland minimum ages 12 and 14 for girls and boys respectively.
Advantages	1 The individual decides how his possessions should be distributed after his death and who his beneficiaries will be.
	2 Avoids complications after death under intestacy.
	3 Makes clear who is to obtain a grant of representation and administer the estate.
	4 The individual appoints executors of his choice to administer the estate
	5 Guardians for minor children can be appointed.
	6 To minimise Inheritance Tax.
Disadvantage	1 A number of formalities are required if the will is to be valid, thereby making professional help advisable.

FURTHER DETAILS

Everyone should make a will, no matter how small the prospective estate. The will should be kept under regular review and take account of changes in the individual's life, eg marriage, the birth of children, divorce and changes in assets.

If no will is made, or a will disposes of only part of the individual's assets, the estate will be distributed according to the intestacy rules, which may produce unwanted results.

It is also important to note that assets held on joint tenancies, say, by husband and wife, pass to the survivor on the first death, regardless of any provisions in the will. This is in contrast to the position applying if property is held as tenants in common, where the deceased's share of the asset passes under the terms of the will, which may therefore be the preferred planning route in many cases.

It is important that wills are reviewed regularly to ensure that the disposition of an estate reflects the testator's current wishes and family changes, and is also tax-efficient. The will, where possible, should ensure that advantage is taken of any available nil rate band, and also that reliefs for agricultural and business property are used. If there is a surviving spouse, advantage can be taken of the surviving spouse exemption to defer IHT on the estate in excess of the reliefs and the nil rate band.

Assets could be left to the surviving spouse by way of a trust under which the spouse receives a life interest in the income, but the trustees have powers to advance capital and/or to appoint capital in favour of other beneficiaries (eg children). The trust could:

(a) protect the assets for the deceased's family in the event of a remarriage;

(b) give flexibility allowing assets to be redirected to other beneficiaries;

(c) enable the spouse/trustees to arrange lifetime transfers which may be outside the gift with reservation rules;

(d) protect assets against nursing home fees.

However, Finance Act 2006 changes to trust taxation with effect from 22 March 2006 must be taken into account.

Intestacy Rules – English Law

- If the deceased was married and there are no issue, the surviving spouse will take absolutely the deceased's personal chattels and the first £450,000, plus a half share of any residue. The other half share of any residue will pass to the parents of the deceased, or if neither is alive, to the deceased's brothers and sisters of the whole blood or their issue if they have predeceased. If there are no living parents or brothers and sisters of the whole blood or their issue, the surviving spouse will take the whole estate.

- If the deceased was married and there are issue alive at the date of death, the surviving spouse takes absolutely the deceased's personal chattels and the first £250,000. The remainder is held on statutory trusts and is divided equally between the surviving spouse, who takes only a life interest in one half, and the remaining half is held on trust for the deceased's issue. On the death of the surviving spouse, the first half-share will also pass to the issue. The surviving spouse may redeem the life interest in the estate in return for a capital sum calculated in accordance with statute. This may be appropriate when the beneficiaries are all adults, as the whole estate may then be distributed.

  In respect of the previous two paragraphs, the surviving spouse will only be entitled to the estate if they survive the intestate by 28 days, where the intestate died after 31 December 1995.

- If the deceased leaves no spouse but leaves issue, the estate is divided between the issue equally per stirpes.

- If the deceased leaves no spouse or issue, the estate will pass to the deceased's parents. If neither parent is alive, the deceased's nearest relatives will inherit. The order of priority is as follows:

  (a) Brothers and sisters, of the whole blood and the issue of any who have predeceased.

  (b) Half-brothers and half-sisters and the issue of any who have predeceased.

  (c) Grandparents.

  (d) Aunts and uncles (being brothers and sisters of the whole blood of a parent of the intestate) and the issue of any who have predeceased.

  (e) Half-brothers and half-sisters of the deceased's parents and the issue of any deceased half-uncle or half-aunt.

If there is no living beneficiary, the deceased's estate will pass to the Crown, the Duchy of Lancaster or the Duchy of Cornwall.

Common Law Spouses

They obtain no benefit under the intestacy rules, although anyone financially dependent on the deceased can make a claim for financial provision out of the estate under the Inheritance (Provision for Family and Dependants) Act 1975.

Formalities for a Valid Will – English Law

- The will must be signed by the testator or by some other person in his presence and by his direction. The testator must either sign his will or acknowledge his signature in the presence of at least two witnesses present at the same time. Each witness must sign the will or acknowledge his signature in the testator's presence, and in the presence of each other. In order to avoid complications, it is generally desirable that the testator and the witnesses should remain together throughout the signing of the will[1]. The witnesses are there to witness the testator's signature, that it is not made under duress and that the testator has the mental capacity to make the will. It is not necessary that they should be aware of the contents of the will.
- Bequests made to a witness or spouse of a witness are generally invalid, and such bequests will fall into the residue of the estate. However, the validity of the remainder of the will is not affected. No beneficiary or executor (or anyone married to a beneficiary or executor) should be a witness.
- A blind or mentally ill person should not witness a will[1]. Otherwise, anyone over the age of 18 can be a witness.
- Where there is any doubt as to the mental capacity of the testator, it is advisable to have the will witnessed by at least one registered medical practitioner.
- All manuscript amendments or additions to the will should be initialled by the testator and by both witnesses before the will is signed.
- Nothing should be attached to the will with a paper clip or anything similar and, to avoid any subsequent enquiries, the pages of the will should be numbered and signed by the testator so that it is clear no pages have been detached or inserted.

CROSS REFERENCES

IHT – Wills Written on a Discretionary Basis **4.27**
IHT – Post-Death Deeds of Disclaimer and Variation **4.28**

REFERENCE

[1] *Re Gibson's Estate* (1949)

4.27 IHT – Wills Written on a Discretionary Basis

Description	A document containing the legal declarations of an individual concerning the distribution of his estate on death and conferring on his executors discretionary powers to vary the terms of distribution within two years of his death (for certain tax benefits) or within the discretionary period (usually 80 years).
Suitable for	Anybody who requires the maximum flexibility in determining the eventual beneficiaries of the estate.
Advantages	1 Allows the surviving spouse to pass assets to children and grandchildren and so obtain IHT, CGT and income tax advantages in the long term for the benefit of the family.
	2 Allows the decision to be made according to tax law, the assets in the estate and the financial and health circumstances of the surviving spouse and family requirements following death.
	3 The surviving spouse – as one of the personal representatives – can be given an absolute power of veto on any distributions.
Disadvantages	1 The will may appear complicated to a layman.
	2 The testator gives up to his executors the right to determine how his estate is to pass.
	3 It may be necessary to pay IHT on the estate before probate is obtained, and in some rare circumstances there may be CGT problems.

FURTHER DETAILS

General Explanation

The will is written in two parts.

The first part is written on conventional lines and disposes of the whole of the estate of the testator by specific legacies and gifts of the residue. The conventional part of the will may provide for greater financial security for the surviving spouse than is required. Those provisions will apply *unless* the executors decide otherwise following death.

The second part of the will deals with the circumstances in which the executors have discretionary powers to override the conventional part of the will and to distribute part of the estate within a class of beneficiaries named or identified in the will. The testator will normally set out in a memorandum of wishes how he would prefer the estate to be distributed.

When the time for decision is reached, the surviving spouse and any other executors are able to consider whether part of the estate should pass directly to other members of the family. If not already used, advantage can be taken of the IHT nil rate band to which the deceased spouse was entitled and the potential beneficiaries may express the wish that, for instance, their own children should benefit – thus creating income taxable only at the rate appropriate to that generation or possibly income to be accumulated during the minority of those children.

Assets which pass to the surviving spouse will – unless the subject of further lifetime gifts – pass on the death of the survivor and so attract IHT at the rate relevant to his or her total estate.

It is often preferable to establish a discretionary trust for the maximum period permitted by trust law (usually 80 years), subject to discretionary powers of the trustees to terminate it at some earlier time. If the trust is broken within two years of death, the benefits set out in this section will be available. If the trust is not so broken within the two years it will continue, with the trustees able to pay income or capital or both on the terms set out in the will.

Taxation Aspects

Any exercise by the executors of their discretionary powers within two years of the death is backdated to the date of death and treated as if effected by the deceased for IHT purposes. Therefore, no IHT consequences arise for those beneficiaries who lost any interest in the estate as a result of the exercise of the executors' discretion. If the executors do not exercise their discretion before applying for probate, then IHT will be payable on the whole estate. Tax can be reclaimed at a later date if an appointment is made in favour of a surviving spouse. No appointment should be made to the surviving spouse within three months of the testator's death. Transfers might be effected to use business property relief which might not be available on the surviving spouse's death. However, if the spouse is likely to survive for a period of seven years, the executors could consider leaving part of the estate to pass to the surviving spouse, IHT-free, with the spouse making potentially exempt transfers at a later date.

The selective use of the discretionary powers will enable the executors to deal specifically with assets which attract special relief, eg business and agricultural property, Lloyd's assets and unquoted shares.

The creation of interests in trust – allowing the accumulation of income – may provide the opportunity for IHT on certain assets which qualify for the instalment payment basis to be financed from the income generated by those assets. This may be very useful in the case of shares in a family company.

The distribution of the estate by the executors may involve disposals for CGT purposes if the assets increase in value between death and exercise of the trustees' discretion. For example, if the administration of the estate is complete and the trust property vests in the trustees before appointment then the trustees acquire as legatees and CGT may arise on the appointment to the beneficiaries.

No ad valorem charge to stamp duty will arise on any exercise by the executors of their discretionary powers.

Other Alternatives

The same general effect as a will written on these lines may be achieved by the surviving spouse disclaiming or varying part of his or her inheritance within two years of the death. (See Section 4.28, *Post-Death Deeds of Disclaimer and Variation.*)

The discretionary will – with the surviving spouse as one of the executors – can be considerably more flexible and easier to administer in practice than either of these alternatives. It also has significant income tax advantages where a discretionary trust is established of which a surviving spouse is a beneficiary, or where a parent would otherwise be deemed to be the settlor of a fund for the benefit of his infant unmarried children.

CROSS REFERENCES

IHT – Wills   **4.26**
IHT – Post-Death Deeds of Disclaimer and Variation   **4.28**

4.28 IHT – Post-Death Deeds of Disclaimer and Variation

Description	Document under which a beneficiary disclaims a benefit under the will after the testator has died, or which alters the disposition of an estate under a will or which alters the devolution of an estate under intestacy.
Suitable for	Individuals who inherit assets surplus to their needs.
Advantages	1 Enables an individual to transfer assets inherited within two years of the relevant death with no personal IHT or CGT implications.
	2 Allows post-death tax planning in respect of an estate.
	3 In some circumstances leads to a reduction in the IHT on an estate.
Disadvantages	1 IHT payable on estate of deceased may be increased.
	2 Person making disclaimer or variation may be regarded as settlor for income tax purposes.
	3 Time limit for variation.

FURTHER DETAILS

Within two years of an individual's death, those who benefit under the will or under the intestacy rules may disclaim or vary the provisions under the will without IHT or CGT implications for themselves. Normally, a disclaimer will be relevant only where successive interests in the property are set out in the will or under the intestacy rules, so that it is clear to whom the property is to pass following the disclaimer. Otherwise, the assets may not pass in the way the original beneficiary intended. In some cases a variation will be required.

A disclaimer or variation may be made in respect of any property comprised in the estate of the deceased immediately prior to death, except settled property in which the deceased had any interest, or property deemed to be part of his estate because the deceased had reserved a benefit over it. No consideration in money or money's worth must be given for the disclaimer or variation, but an exchange of inheritances is allowed.

The disclaimer or variation may be made whether or not the administration of the estate is complete and the assets distributed. It may be made either before or after probate is granted. However, only one variation may be made in respect of the same property.

The disclaimer or variation must be made in writing by the beneficiary under the will or intestacy and any other relevant parties.

The individual disclaiming an asset or giving it away under a deed of variation must be over 18. If they are under 18 then court permission must be obtained.

Where a disclaimer is made within two years of the relevant death, the benefit disclaimed is treated as never having been conferred for IHT and CGT purposes. Therefore, there are no IHT or CGT consequences for the person making the disclaimer. However, there may be an IHT impact on the estate in respect of which the disclaimer is made, for example where the surviving spouse disclaims a legacy and thereby loses the IHT spouse exemption in respect of the property disclaimed.

In order to avoid IHT and CGT consequences for a person making a variation (as opposed to a disclaimer), it was necessary to make an election to HMRC. From 1 August 2002 an election is no longer necessary, however, the variation must be made within two years of the relevant death and the variation itself must state that it is to apply in respect of either IHT or CGT or both. This is, hence, a specific statement within the deed. The alteration, which is the subject of the deed of variation, is then treated as if it had been made by the deceased at probate value. A specific statement in respect of IHT will be made in most circumstances, but it may not always be beneficial to also make a specific statement in respect of CGT, so the pros and cons should be considered before deciding to make such a statement. The specific statement should be contained within the written instrument, and the personal representatives of the deceased must join in where the variation increases the liability of the estate.

Taxation Aspects

Inheritance Tax

A disclaimer or variation can be useful in IHT planning. Where a beneficiary already has a large estate which will attract a charge to IHT on death, the opportunity to dispose of inherited property which will only add to the future IHT liability can be attractive. Where the IHT nil rate band has not been used in respect of the deceased's estate, it is possible to make use of it by a variation within two years of the death. Property which is subject to the gifts with reservation rules cannot be the subject of a variation or disclaimer. Unless other reliefs (eg business property relief) are to be utilised, transfers in excess of the nil rate band may create an IHT charge unnecessarily. Interest will accrue on any IHT arising as a result of a variation or disclaimer if the tax is not paid by the due date based on the date of death under the normal rules (see Section 4.29, *IHT – Payment and Funding the Tax*). Alternatively, a variation may be made to reduce or eliminate the IHT liability on the estate of the deceased, eg where the disposal by will gives rise to a charge to IHT and a variation is then effected disposing of the property to the spouse of the deceased. The surviving spouse might later be in a position to make lifetime transfers.

Capital Gains Tax

For CGT purposes, a disclaimer made within the two-year period will automatically be treated as effective from the date of death, so that there is no disposal by the person making the disclaimer. The beneficiaries acquiring the disclaimed property will acquire it at its probate value. No election to HMRC is required.

In order to avoid a disposal for CGT purposes by the person making a variation within two years of death, it was necessary to make an election to HMRC. See the changes from 1 August 2002 described above in respect of IHT and CGT. If a specific statement is made within the deed of variation in respect of CGT, there will be no disposal for CGT by the person making the variation. The beneficiaries, following the variation, will acquire the relevant property at its probate value for CGT purposes. In some cases, it may be beneficial not to make a specific statement in respect of CGT, eg where the deemed gain on the disposal by the person making the variation will be within his CGT annual exemption. In these circumstances, the beneficiaries following the variation will acquire a higher CGT base cost in respect of the property. The deemed gain arising on a variation will generally be the excess of the value of the relevant property at the date of the variation over its probate value. HMRC regard the person who effects the variation as a settlor for CGT purposes. This view was upheld by Harman J in the case of *Marshall v Kerr* (see [1991] STC 686), rejected by the Court of Appeal (see [1993] STC 360), but finally upheld by the House of Lords (see [1994] STC 638).

Income Tax

For income tax purposes, a variation or disclaimer is not retrospective and thus income enjoyed by the transferor cannot be assessed upon the person to whom the disposal is made. The person who effects the variation will normally be regarded as the settlor for the purposes of income tax, with the consequence that any income arising to his children as a result of the variation while they are under 18 and unmarried will be assessed on him if income in excess of £100 is actually paid out to or for their benefit.

CROSS REFERENCES

IHT – Wills   **4.26**
IHT – Wills Written on a Discretionary Basis   **4.27**

4.29 IHT – Payment and Funding the Tax

IHT ACCOUNTS

The donor of a lifetime gift is generally required to deliver an account to HMRC Capital Taxes Office if the gift is not exempt or potentially exempt from IHT. However, no account is required if the gift consists of cash or quoted shares or securities and the value transferred by the donor after any exemptions, together with the value of any transfers in the previous seven years, does not exceed the current Nil Rate Band. For transfers of any other assets, the value transferred, together with the value transferred in the previous seven years, must be less than 80% of the current Nil Rate Band, and the value of the current transfer before taking account of any Business or Agricultural Property Relief together with the value of any transfers in the previous seven years, must not exceed the current Nil Rate Band. Nevertheless, even in these circumstances, HMRC reserve the right to call for an account.

The trustees of a settlement are required to deliver an account to the Capital Taxes Office on form IHT 100 whenever an event occurs in relation to the settlement which is not exempt from IHT. For chargeable events occurring on or after 6 April 2007, for settlements which meet all the conditions below, there is no need to file an account as they will be an excepted settlement if:

Either

- the trustees are resident in the UK throughout the existence of the settlement ;and
- no interest in possession exists in the trust property (ie no one has an immediate right to income or capital) at the time of the chargeable event; and
- the trust assets are held in cash throughout; and
- no additions of capital are made by the settlor; and
- no other trusts were created by the settlor on the same day; and
- the total value of the trust assets throughout the existence of the settlement does not exceed £1,000.

Or

- the settlor is domiciled in the UK at the time when the settlement was created and throughout its existence until the earlier of the chargeable event or the death of the settlor; and
- the trustees are resident in the UK throughout the existence of the settlement; and
- no other trusts were created by the settlor on the same day; and
- no interest in possession exists in the trust property (ie no one has an immediate right to income or capital) at the time of the chargeable event;
- on the occasion of the chargeable event the value transferred by the chargeable transfer does not exceed 80% of the current Nil Rate Band.

The personal representatives of a deceased who died domiciled or died deemed domiciled for IHT purposes in the UK, are required to deliver an account to the Capital Taxes Office in respect of the deceased's estate. For all estates which do not qualify as excepted estates form IHT 400 is required (which replaced form IHT 200 in November 2008). Smaller estates (known as 'excepted estates') should complete form IHT 205. To qualify as an excepted estate there must be no tax to pay, and the following conditions are required in respect of deaths on or after 1 September 2006:
Either
- the gross value of the estate, which includes property passing by will or intestacy, by survivorship, by nomination, or under a trust, is less than the Nil Rate Band;
- any trust assets in which the deceased had an interest in possession were held in a single trust and do not exceed £150,000 in value;
- the value of the estate outside the UK totals not more than £100,000;
- any chargeable lifetime gifts made within seven years of death were only of cash, quoted shares or securities, or land and buildings (and contents given at the same time) and do not exceed £150,000 in total value;
- the deceased had not at any time made a gift with reservation of benefit;
- there is no IHT charge on an alternatively secured pension fund;
Or
- the gross estate does not exceed £1,000,000 and any estate which is above the Nil Rate Band passes to the deceased's spouse or civil partner or to a charity/qualifying body;
- where the deceased died domiciled outside the UK (and had never been domiciled or treated as domiciled here) and their UK estate comprises cash or quoted shares/securities where the value does not exceed £100,000.

In practice, where the deceased has left a will and no IHT is payable on the estate, the account will be delivered in the first instance to the Probate Registry with the application for probate.

The recipient of a lifetime potentially exempt transfer is liable to make a return if the gift proves to be chargeable as a result of the transferor's death. The recipient of a gift subject to a reservation is liable to make a return where the transferor retained the reservation until death.

If the Capital Taxes Office (CTO) considers that an IHT liability arises, an appropriate assessment will be issued.

Accounts in respect of lifetime gifts and by trustees of settlements must be delivered within 12 months of the end of the month in which the gift is made or, if later, within three months of the due date for payment of the IHT. Accounts in respect of deaths must be delivered within 12 months of the end of the month in which the death occurs or, for personal representatives, if later, within three months of the date on which the personal representatives first act.

DUE DATE FOR PAYMENT

The due date for the payment of IHT is normally six months after the end of the month in which the chargeable transfer is made. However, on a chargeable lifetime transfer made between 6 April and 30 September inclusive in any year, the due date for payment is not until 30 April of the following year.

On a death, the IHT on the deceased's personal estate (property other than land, buildings, and trust property from which the deceased was entitled to the income during his lifetime) must be paid to the CTO before delivery of the account in respect of the estate to the Probate Registry. No grant will be made unless any IHT which is due has been paid.

Personal representatives may draw on funds held in the deceased's bank, building society or national savings account solely for the purpose of paying any IHT that is due before the grant of representation can be issued. An agreement between participating banks and building societies and the Treasury enables the participating institutions to transfer funds, direct to HMRC to pay the IHT due. Arrangements for payment are made via form D20. Tax or additional tax arising as a result of the transferor's or settlor's death is due six months after the end of the month in which the death occurs.

If the tax is not paid on the due date, interest is chargeable.

INTEREST RELIEF

Relief against income tax is available to the personal representatives of a deceased person who take out a loan which is used to pay IHT on the deceased's personal property. The tax must be paid before the grant of representation or confirmation. The tax must arise on property to which the deceased was beneficially entitled immediately before his death, and which passes to the personal representatives – or would pass to them if it were situated in the UK. The interest on the loan will qualify for relief only for the period of 12 months after the loan is made.

TRANSFERS OF PROPERTY IN LIEU OF IHT

Applications may be made to HMRC for certain categories of national heritage property to be accepted in whole or part satisfaction of an IHT liability. The agreement of the relevant Secretary of State has to be obtained. The categories of property are as follows:

- and and buildings with a particular amenity value, eg an outstanding historic building;
- objects associated with a building which has itself been accepted in lieu of tax or which is owned by the Crown, a government department or a national heritage body;
- pictures, prints, books, manuscripts, works of art, scientific objects, or other items of pre-eminent national, historic, scientific or artistic interest.

The application has to be made before payment of the tax has been made. In cases where payment has to be made to obtain probate, then the intention to transfer property to the state must be notified to HMRC at the time of payment.

PAYMENT BY INSTALMENTS

The following property qualifies for instalment payments:
1   Land and buildings wherever situated.

2   Shares or securities which gave the donor, deceased or trustees control of the company at the time of the transfer.

3   Unquoted shares or securities where HMRC is satisfied that the tax attributable to their value could not be paid in one sum without undue hardship.

4   On a transfer on death, unquoted shares or securities where the tax on those shares, securities and any other instalment option property is at least 20% of the total tax due.

5   Unquoted shares where the value transferred attributable to them exceeds £20,000 and they represent at least 10% of the nominal value of the company's share capital or, if they are ordinary shares, at least 10% of the nominal value of the company's ordinary share capital.

6   The net value of a business or of an interest in a business.

7   Woodlands.

Interest is normally payable on instalments from the date on which the first instalment is due. The first instalment is due on the date the whole tax would be due, if it were not being paid by instalments. The interest accrues on the whole unpaid tax and is added to each instalment and paid accordingly.

However, in some cases, interest is charged only whilst the instalments are in arrears, and, therefore, each instalment is interest-free if paid on time. Tax attributable to the following property is payable by interest-free instalments:

- Shares or securities falling within 2 to 5 above.
- A business or an interest in a business.
- Property qualifying for agricultural relief

The remaining tax due may be paid in one sum at any time with interest due to the date of payment. The unpaid balance becomes payable immediately if the relevant property is sold or, in the case of a lifetime transfer, there is a further chargeable transfer otherwise than on death or, in the case of settled property, it ceases to be held in trust.

There are special rules for the payment of tax by instalments on woodlands.

CROSS REFERENCES

Lloyd's **3.30**
Woodlands **3.31**
IHT – Agricultural Property Relief **4.20**
IHT – Insurance **4.30**

4.30　IHT – Insurance

Description	A means of gradually passing funds to the next generation in a tax-efficient manner to build up a fund to settle IHT liabilities on death.
Suitable for	Individuals who may have a liability to IHT on their death and who wish to provide their beneficiaries with funds to settle the liability (or to protect the potential IHT liability during the seven year PET period).
Advantages	1　Policy proceeds fall outside the deceased's estate for IHT purposes.
	2　Policy proceeds are normally free of all taxes in the hands of beneficiaries.
	3　The policy is an asset which can normally be encashed immediately upon production of a copy of the death certificate (rather than having to wait for probate).
	4　Sophisticated schemes allow income and capital effectively to be split.
Disadvantages	1　Premiums for trust policies are regarded as gifts for IHT purposes, although the annual or normal expenditure out of income exemptions should prevent any actual charge arising, unless the premiums are particularly high.
	2　Existing policies assigned into trust will be treated as a gift for IHT purposes (deemed as a PET).
	3　The age of the individual and state of health will affect the premiums payable.

FURTHER DETAILS

Commercial Aspects

Life assurance has an important role to play in planning for IHT purposes. By using policies written under trust, large IHT-free funds can be left to heirs on death and the funds can be used to pay the liability to IHT arising on the deceased's other assets without any actual charges to tax arising during the settlor's lifetime.

Where a liability to IHT arises on a deceased's estate, the tax due must normally be paid before the estate can be distributed to beneficiaries. The benefit of providing funds from a life policy written under trust is that, provided the settlor has appointed additional trustees and they are living at the date of death, a claim on death will be paid out by the life company without waiting for the usual production of probate or grant of representation (although see Section 4.29 – *Payment and Funding the Tax – Due date for payment*, regarding new arrangements with some banks and building societies). This makes the policy an asset which can be encashed immediately on production of a copy of the death certificate.

The provision of an IHT-free fund with which to pay any such liability is therefore of advantage, since not only is the beneficiary's share of the estate increased, but also there need be no enforced sale of interests in the properties comprising the estate, or other personal and family inheritances, with the inherent difficulties in disposing of or mortgaging property. A policy owned by an unquoted trading company which pays out on the death of a shareholder may provide a cash sum to enable the company to purchase that individual's shares in a tax-efficient manner. Alternatively, a policy owned by a surviving shareholder or business partner may provide a cash sum for them to buy the deceased's share of the business from their beneficiaries (subject to the shareholder or partnership agreements).

Wills

When considering the best ways to effect an 'IHT policy', it should always be established how the individuals' wills are written.

For example, if Mr and Mrs Smith both have mutual wills leaving their estates to each other and, on the second death, to their children, only one policy is required and it should be written on their joint lives, on a last survivor basis, in trust for the children. In this way, the IHT-free fund will be paid to the children on the second death of Mr and Mrs Smith, when the IHT on the estate may arise. No charge to IHT would arise on the first death due to the surviving spouse exemption.

Should the wills be written to leave part of the estate to the children on each death, whole life policies on the lives of both Mr and Mrs Smith in trust for the children should be effected, so that a separate fund is available to meet the IHT which may arise on each death.

Existing Policies not Under Trust

For those individuals with existing policies not written under trust, the position can easily be remedied by assigning the policy to trustees, who will then hold the policy proceeds for the beneficiaries chosen by the policyholder. Most insurance companies provide draft deeds of assignment free of charge.

A charge to IHT may, however, arise on an assignment value of the policy, which might take future bonuses (if applicable) into account. The potential charge should, however, be mitigated by the annual exemption or the Nil Rate Band below which IHT is not payable. Clearly the sooner the policy is assigned, the lower the potential charge to IHT.

Types of Trust

'Flexible' Trust A 'flexible' or 'power of appointment' trust, permits the settlor, if named as a trustee, to vary the ultimate beneficiaries under the trust.

The trust itself effectively consists of two parts. In the first part the settlor appoints the class of beneficiaries whom he may wish the trustees to benefit. This class should be as wide as possible and could include the settlor's spouse, although it should not include the settlor as he would be making a gift with reservation. In the second part of the trust deed the settlor appoints those to whom the trustees must pass the policy proceeds if no appointment is made. These are known as the default beneficiaries who have the 'interest in possession', which stops the trust being treated as discretionary. The trustees usually have the power to appoint the trust assets to anyone named in the trust, up to two years after the settlor's death.

A potential charge to IHT arises when an appointment is made away from those named as default beneficiaries, based on the value of the share appointed. If, however, the appointee is the settlor's spouse, domiciled in the UK, no charge to IHT will arise.

Married Women's Property Act Trust The other common form of trust, although of diminishing importance, is the Married Women's Property Act Trust.

The Married Women's Property Act 1882 (MWPA) provides that a policy effected by a man or woman on his or her own life and expressed to be for the benefit of his or her spouse and/or children will create a trust, and the policy proceeds will not form part of the estate of the life assured or be subject to his or her debts. The advantage of effecting a policy under the MWPA is that the beneficiary's interest in the policy is protected against the life assured's creditors, unless it can be shown that the policy was effected and the premiums were intentionally paid to defraud the policyholder's creditors.

It should be noted, however, that the Act cannot be used where:
- the beneficiary of the trust is to be someone other than the spouse or child (including an illegitimate or adopted child) of the life assured;
- the policy is to be written on joint lives or life of another basis.

Taxation Aspects

The premiums paid on life policies written under trust will be chargeable transfers for IHT purposes, but are likely to be covered by the annual or normal expenditure out of income exemption. The policy proceeds on the death of the life assured will be free of all tax in the beneficiaries' hands.

If chargeable gains arise following a chargeable event under the policy, the person liable for the tax due will be the beneficial owner of the policy. Such a charge to tax can, however, be reclaimed from the trustees of the settlement.

Types of Policy and Uses

If an individual is seeking to leave an IHT-free fund for heirs, then a regular premium whole life policy will be appropriate. The cover could be provided by a with- or without-profits policy (although without-profits policies are now not often used), by a policy (low cost, whole life) combining a decreasing term element and a with-profits element or by a unit-linked policy (see Part 1, *Insurance* for further details). Depending upon the age of the individual, the premium costs rather than the amount of IHT involved could be the limiting factor on the cover acquired. Generally, the younger an individual taking out such cover, the cheaper the annual cost. An elderly person may wish to consider purchasing an annuity to fund the annual premium.

As an alternative, a single premium whole life policy may be used. Most of these policies are unit-linked and are similar to single premium investment bonds but with greater life assurance cover. As these are not qualifying policies, there could be a higher rate tax charge on death. Some insurance companies seek to negate this charge by restricting the surrender value of the policy to the original single premium purchase price.

Again, the elderly may replace the income lost from the capital invested in the single premium policy by purchasing an annuity, although annuity rates may not be attractive.

Where an individual has made a lifetime transfer, the donees could be exposed to an IHT charge or additional charge for a seven-year period. Term assurance, either giving a level or decreasing cover, should be considered in these circumstances. Again, the amount of the premium cost could determine the cover available. However, in looking at the cover requirement, a number of factors would need to be considered. The possibility of tapering relief and the possibility that tax bands will be indexed would affect the position. Any lifetime transfers in the previous seven years, whether potentially exempt or not, could affect whether or not a particular gift is chargeable.

Decreasing term cover would normally only be used where the lifetime transfer would give rise to an actual liability to IHT on death within seven years. Such gifts become chargeable at the time they were originally made and may be covered by the nil rate band, and taper relief would not apply as no IHT would be chargeable to which taper could apply.

Inheritance Trust and PETA Plans

These plans were insurance arrangements designed to reduce the estate by gifts into policies for beneficiaries with the donor able to receive an 'income' from the policies. New schemes were stopped on 18 March and 16 July 1986. Plans taken out before those dates remain effective as follows.

The loan plans and PETA plans remain effective. The reverse loan plans are caught, and loans to the donor after 17 March 1986 will not qualify as a deduction on the donor's death. Any repayment of a post-17 March 1986 loan could qualify as a potentially exempt transfer.

Loan Trusts

This is a simple method of saving IHT while retaining income and flexibility for the future. This involves setting up a trust for selected beneficiaries with a nominal gift. Then an interest-free loan is made to the trust and these monies are invested by the trustees into a single premium insurance bond. The benefits of the plans are:
- the value of the asset (the loan to the trust) is frozen for IHT purposes;
- the investment growth of the bond is outside the estate for IHT purposes;
- if there is a requirement to retain 'income' then the trustees simply operate a regular withdrawal plan in the individual's favour. These payments are then treated as repayments of the original loan.

An example:

Loan trust set up for	£100,000
Trustees repay 5% pa tax free 'income'	£5,000

Assuming investment bond increases in value by 6% pa

IHT position after	**5 years**	**10 years**	**15 years**
Trust value	£105,637	£113,180	£123,276
Remaining loan	**£75,000**	**£50,000**	**£25,000**
Balance free of IHT	£30,637	£63,180	£98,276
(Trust value less loan)			
Tax saved at 40%	£12,255	£25,272	£39,310

Back-to-Back Plans

A more established approach to making gifts whilst still receiving an income is the traditional back-to-back plan. This plan is a combination of two products: a whole-of-life policy and a purchased life annuity.

The bulk of the lump sum is invested in the annuity and this provides a guaranteed income. Part of the guaranteed income then goes to meet the regular premiums for the whole-of-life policy. The policy is written under trust, so the benefits payable on death pass to the beneficiaries free of any liability for IHT. The key advantage of this plan is that it will bring about an immediate IHT saving. This is because the capital used to purchase the annuity will not form part of the individual's estate on death. Moreover, the proceeds from the insurance policy will be held in trust and therefore also outside the estate.

More Complex Schemes

A number of insurance companies provide schemes which seemingly solve the classic IHT problem – how to gift capital but retain income.

The loan trusts outlined above are a form of this, but other schemes provide for an initial gift with the retention of rights to a number of prearranged bond maturities for the next 20 years. As HMRC accept that the individual concerned is likely to receive some of the original gift back during his life by the way of maturing bonds, they will agree a discount on the initial gift/PET. This can often be 50% or more of the PET leading to a substantial IHT reduction if the client dies within a few years of making the PET.

Homeowner's Loan/Reversion Scheme

This is a method of achieving an immediate IHT saving using capital locked up in a house. Occupation of the house can continue for life without affecting the reservation of benefit rules, as the only gift involved is the payment of life policy premiums. It is only suitable for those aged over 70 (or 75 for married couples).

A loan is raised under the special concession for older homeowners, typically up to a maximum of £30,000, at a fixed rate of interest with the loan repayable on death. The capital is then used to purchase a lifetime annuity and the income from this funds premiums on a whole-of-life policy, issued in trust for nominated beneficiaries. On this basis, only the premiums are gifts, which fall within the annual exemptions and the policy proceeds are free of IHT. Up to £12,000 of IHT is saved at little or no cost.

More sophisticated schemes now allow for higher level loans at fixed or nil interest rates in return for a share in the capital appreciation of the property. These schemes are often in connection with long-term nursing care planning and offer effective IHT solutions.

CROSS REFERENCES

4.31 IHT – Non-UK Domiciliaries and other Overseas Aspects

Description		Consideration of the influence domicile has on the potential charge to IHT, and other associated overseas aspects.
Advantages	1	Possibility of removing assets from a potential charge to IHT.
	2	Exempt transfers between spouses can be used to optimise the split of their joint wealth.
Disadvantages	1	Deemed domicile rules may bring previously excluded property into IHT charge.
	2	Possible restriction of exemption of transfers between spouses.

FURTHER DETAILS

Domicile

The concept of domicile is fundamental to Inheritance Tax (IHT), and whilst 'domicile' is not statutorily defined, the term must be construed in accordance with general law. Further guidance on domicile is given in Section 4.5.

The territorial limits of IHT are set by the excluded property rules. With some minor exceptions, all property situated in the UK is potentially chargeable to IHT irrespective of whether it is in UK or foreign ownership, and the charge is also imposed on foreign property in UK ownership. What IHT does not seek to charge is property situated outside the UK which is owned beneficially by a person who does not have a UK domicile, or settled property situated outside the UK where the settlor was domiciled outside the UK when the settlement was made.

Determining domicile is therefore of crucial importance, and in addition to the normal legal understanding of domicile, there is specific legislation which gives it an extended meaning for the purposes of IHT. This legislation rules that an individual who is domiciled abroad under general law is still deemed to be domiciled in the UK in the following two situations:

- if he has been domiciled in the UK within the three immediately preceding years from the time at which the question of domicile arises;
- if he was resident in the UK in not less than 17 of the 20 years of assessment ending with the year of assessment in which the question of domicile falls.

Once domicile for IHT purposes has been established, the general rule is that UK domiciled individuals are chargeable to IHT in respect of property anywhere in the world, and non-UK domiciled individuals in respect of property in the UK.

Domicile and Excluded Property

Property situated outside the UK is excluded property if the person beneficially entitled to it is an individual domiciled outside the UK. That is, any transfer of such property will not give rise to an IHT liability. The individual must also not be deemed to be UK domiciled by virtue of either of the rules mentioned above.

Therefore, a non-domiciled individual holding excluded property should consider gifting some or all of this property before achieving 17 out of 20 years of UK residence. Similarly, a non-UK domicillary who has recently shed their UK domicile should consider delaying any transfers of potentially excluded property until three tax years have elapsed since acquiring their new domicile, so as not to be caught by the deemed domicile rules.

Domicile and Transfers between Spouses

Transfers between spouses who are either both UK domiciled or neither UK domiciled are exempt from IHT for both lifetime and death transfers, and since husband and wife are each entitled to the IHT nil rate band (currently £325,000) before transfers become taxable, it is clearly sensible for the joint wealth to be arranged in such a way that each takes full advantage of their joint entitlements.

For IHT purposes, a couple of mixed domicile (where one is domiciled in the UK and the other is not) have to take extra care in their tax planning. Transfers from a UK domiciled spouse to a non-UK domiciled spouse do not qualify for the unlimited inter-spouse exemption and, instead, are eligible for a £55,000 exemption which can only be used once. But significant value can still be transferred, because in addition to the £55,000 exemption, the UK domiciled spouse will have an additional amount of £325,000 that can be transferred within the nil rate band. Furthermore, lifetime transfers are Potentially Exempt Transfers (PET) and after seven years a PET will fall out of account.

Planning Opportunities

One situation where the deemed domicile rule need not be looked at negatively, is where you have one UK domiciled spouse and one non-UK domiciled spouse who has been resident here for a long time. Normally this would mean that transfers from the UK domiciled spouse to the non-UK domiciled spouse would only be exempt up to a total transfer of £55,000, as mentioned above. However, if the non-UK domiciled spouse is close to being deemed domiciled under the '17 out of 20 year' rule, then consideration should be given to deferring the transfer until the non-domiciled spouse has become deemed domiciled, with the result that full exemption would then be available.

Dealing with Potential Double Taxation

It is quite possible that the situation could arise whereby foreign capital taxes could also be chargeable in addition to IHT in the UK, particularly where the property concerned is held outside the UK and the beneficial owner is UK domiciled.

As with taxes on income and capital gains, UK law provides for double taxation relief in relation to IHT both by a comprehensive system of unilateral relief applicable to taxes of a specified character imposed by all countries, and also by a system of bilateral double taxation agreements. The agreements may also give guidance in cases of doubt on determining the place where any property is to be treated as situated for the purposes of IHT.

The number of double taxation agreements granting relief for taxes on estates, inheritances and gifts is far smaller than the number affording relief in respect of income and capital gains. There are currently ten UK double taxation agreements relating to IHT, and these are as follows:

- France
- India
- Republic of Ireland
- Italy
- Netherlands
- Pakistan
- South Africa
- Sweden
- Switzerland
- United States

These agreements fall into two categories:

1   Agreements negotiated in relation to estate duty, which continue in force with respect to IHT chargeable on death. It should be noted that these agreements apply only to IHT chargeable on death and do not affect the IHT chargeable on lifetime transfers; and

2   Double tax agreements negotiated since the introduction of capital transfer tax (CTT) in 1975, and which therefore apply to lifetime transfers as well as those upon death.

Of the ten current agreements, those relating to France, India, Italy and Pakistan are originally estate duty agreements which now extend to IHT. The remaining six countries have double taxation agreements specifically relating to CTT/IHT.

CROSS REFERENCES

Income Tax – Overseas Aspects   **4.5**
Overseas Trusts   **4.24**

Part 5   The Life Cycle

5.1 Introduction

As an individual progresses through life, circumstances will change. In analysing the main planning concepts which might be most appropriate as the individual gets older, various ages have been identified along with the relevant planning points.

The first stage is *the young*. Planning here is likely to focus upon gifts from parents and grandparents who often use trusts to provide for school fees. On the tax side, it will be important to utilise all available reliefs and to avoid HMRC regulations relating to parental settlement.

The second age encompasses that of the *single years*. This age may well include further education, typically university, and there is still likely to be a fair amount of financial input from parents.

The third age is *married with no children*. Property purchase is likely to be a feature here. Younger couples are also likely to be saving for the first time, possibly with a view to accumulating capital ahead of the arrival of children.

Married with young children is the fourth age. Protection for the family in the event of illness or death of the breadwinner(s) will be important with term assurance, critical illness and evidence of income protection being a feature of this type of planning. Also, when parents decide to have their children privately educated, a school fees planning scheme may well be started.

This is followed by the fifth age – *married with older children*. Various protection insurances may need to be renewed or remain in place as the educational intentions of the children become clear, ie whether or not they intend to go on to university and, if so, what length of course they intend to pursue. Also, due to increased incomes, parents will now begin to think seriously about accumulating wealth for their own retirement.

The sixth age is *pre-retirement*. This is likely to be the age of maximum capital accumulation – with the children off their hands and possibly mortgages repaid, parents should be in a strong position to add to pensions or to establish equity-based portfolios whether directly or through investment in unit trusts.

Retirement is the seventh age. The difficulty here will be adjusting to a new and probably lower level of income and a completely different set of circumstances. Increased leisure time can be expensive!

5.2 The Young

Advantages		
	1	Treated as separate persons for taxation purposes.
	2	Child benefit is not taxable.
	3	Each child is entitled to a personal allowance.
Disadvantages	1	Some income may be taxed as the parents' income.
	2	Unable to enter certain contractual arrangements.
	3	It is generally easy to invest a child's money on their behalf but the ability to withdraw may be restricted for very young children.
Planning	1	Gifts from parents should be invested in tax exempt investments, eg certain National Savings products or in non-income producing assets, such as single premium bonds, some offshore funds, premium bonds, stamps, etc.
	2	Many families wish to educate their children privately and this will require a substantial outlay in school fees. Gifts from grandparents for this would reduce their estates for IHT purposes and avoid the income derived being aggregated with the parents' income. Parents wishing to make provision should start as soon as possible.
	3	Accumulation settlements can be tax efficient in enabling the older generation to pass on assets to minor children.
	4	16 and 17 year olds can invest cash in ISAs.
	5	Minors can invest in stakeholder pensions.

FURTHER DETAILS

Little planning can be achieved by a child on its own, but there is considerable scope for planning carried out by parents, grandparents and other relatives/family friends.

Income Tax

A child is a taxable person quite separate from his parents. Each child is entitled to a personal allowance to be set against any income received. Parents have a responsibility in submitting repayment claims and tax returns when the child receives taxable income. A repayment claim cannot be made more than five years after 31 January next following the year of assessment to which it relates after the end of the relevant year of assessment. It is no longer necessary to produce documentary evidence to enable repayment to be made but such documentation should be retained to satisfy any query by HMRC.

If income in excess of £100 per annum arises on capital gifted by a parent and the child is unmarried and under 18, then the income will be treated as the parent's income and taxed at the parent's marginal rate. It is preferable for such gifts to be made by the spouse who pays no tax or tax at the lower rate.

The source of the funds at the disposal of the child determines the tax treatment and in turn the most suitable type of investment.

If the gift is from either parent (including investment of child benefit for the child) and will produce income in excess of £100 per year, consider investment in assets producing a tax-free return, a return not subject to income tax or where taxable income can be deferred until the child is 18 or over. Thus consideration should be given to National Savings children's bonds, National Savings Certificates, insurance based investments such as endowment policies, and single or regular premium investment bonds.

Income from gifts from grandparents or other family members is not deemed to be the parents' and is not taxed until the child's income exceeds his own personal allowance. Preferred investments would include Government Fixed Interest Stock, bank or building society accounts, National Savings investments (and especially children's bonds), unit trust saving schemes and offshore investments.

Child Trust Fund

In the 2003 Budget the Chancellor announced the Child Trust Fund (CTF), providing children born from 1 September 2002 with an endowment at birth provided by the Government.

The main components are:

- an initial endowment at birth for every child of £250, rising to £500 for children from low income families who also qualify for full Child Tax Credit. Around a third of all children will qualify for the higher amount;
- allowing additional contributions to be made by parents, family members and friends, up to an annual limit of £1,200;
- being accessible when children reach 18 years of age, whereupon there will be no restriction on the use of assets; and
- being delivered through open market competition, accounts being available from April 2005, enabling a wide range of authorised providers to offer the CTF.

However, the Government has now stated that it will be phasing out the Child Trust Fund. From August 2010 CTF payments will be reduced from £250 to £50, with children from lower income households receiving £100, down from £500. Children will no longer receive an additional payment when they are seven and from January 2011 the payments will be abandoned altogether.

Tax Credits

From 6 April 2003 the children's tax credit was replaced by the child tax credit. See Section 4.6, *Tax Credits* for further details.

ISAs

Since 6 April 2001, 16 and 17 year olds are able to invest in a mini cash ISA or the cash component of a maxi ISA.

Stakeholder Pensions

Minors are also entitled to invest £3,600 each year into a stakeholder pension without the need for earnings.

Capital Gains Tax

A gift can be made to a child to utilise the CGT annual exemption (currently £10,100). Each parent could transfer assets to their children up to the amount of the annual exemption without any CGT becoming payable. The child will be treated as owning the asset and will have his own annual exemption to use.

Trusts

Where a parent wishes to gift assets to his child he can do this using the mechanism of a trust. The possibilities are as detailed below.

Bare Trust

A bare trust can be created for the benefit of a child by transferring the assets to trustees who will hold the property for the child's benefit. On reaching 18, the child will have the right to call for the property. The child will be treated as owning the property and will be able to use his annual exemption against gains realised by the trust.

As explained above, if the settlor is the child's parent, any income paid to or for the benefit of the child will be deemed to be that of the parent. Where, however, the income is not distributed to the child until he is 18, the income will be treated as the child's income and any personal allowance can be used.

Bare trusts set up after 8 March 1999 are no longer of such benefit as the income arising, in excess of £100, is assessed on the parent settlor whether it is retained or paid out. Pre-9 March 1999 trusts will continue as before but funds added to such settlements will be caught by the new rules.

Accumulation and Maintenance Trust

An accumulation and maintenance trust can be a tax efficient means of transferring assets to trustees for the benefit of children, (see Section 4.22). An advantage of such a trust as compared with a bare trust is that provision can be made for beneficiaries as yet unborn. Under a bare trust, the amount held for each child must be fixed at that date and cannot be varied. In contrast, with an accumulation and maintenance trust, it is possible to defer the time when the child can receive capital by the trustees using their discretion. It is also possible to vary the size of each child's share, thus indicating the flexibility of such trusts.

With effect from 22 March 2006, there was a change in the IHT treatment of gifts into Accumulation and maintenance trusts and during the life of the trust (see Section 4.22).

Life Interest Trust

A life interest trust provides that one or more beneficiaries are entitled to the income from the trust fund whilst allowing the capital to vest in someone else. A beneficiary entitled to the income will be subject to income tax. Where the settlor is the parent of the beneficiary, then the income and capital gains will be treated as the parents' whilst the beneficiary is under 18.

With effect from 22 March 2006, there was a change to the IHT treatment of gifts into life interest trusts and during the life of the trust (see Section 4.21).

Discretionary Trust

A discretionary trust can provide for several existing beneficiaries drawn from different generations and is perhaps the most flexible type of trust. The trustees have complete discretion over the payment or retention of income and capital and can favour one or more beneficiaries in preference to others.

Prior to 22 March 2006, discretionary trusts were treated more harshly than other types of trust for IHT. Gifts into the trust are chargeable transfers rather than potentially exempt and the trust is liable to periodic IHT charges (see Section 4.23). However, since 22 March 2006, new accumulation and maintenance and life interest trusts are subject to the same IHT regime as discretionary trusts which may now become more popular due to their greater flexibility.

With regards to the underlying investment within the discretionary trust, unit-linked policies cannot provide any guarantee of the maturity monies, although they do provide the potential for greater investment growth. Some companies offer low start endowment plans, the premiums increasing in later years as the parent's income increases. In addition 'high start' schemes are available, the premiums reducing in later years. Policies should be reviewed regularly to check that the ultimate value will be as originally planned.

Deferred Temporary Annuity

Using a deferred temporary annuity may be more advantageous where school fees are required within seven and a half years, due to the contrasting ways different types of policies are taxed.

Monthly premiums can be paid to a deferred annuity, which guarantees a fixed level of fees when required. Premiums are paid throughout the period of deferral and if necessary the fee paying term of the policy. Life assurance can be added to guarantee the fees should death occur.

Some companies market unit-linked annuities specifically for the payment of school fees. Some annuity providers build a guaranteed minimum return (albeit low) in order to safeguard against poor performance, as the value of the units can fall.

The income paid from the annuity will be treated as part income (which will be subject to tax) and part return of capital (and therefore not taxable).

This type of funding may not be as suitable as some other methods for parents paying income tax at the higher rate.

Should the annuity be surrendered at any stage a charge to both basic and the higher rates of tax may arise on the profit or gain from the policy.

Current annuity rates do not make this an attractive route.

Unit or Investment Trusts

Regular monthly payments may be made by way of a unit trust or investment trust savings plan into a growth based unit or investment trust. For basic rate taxpayers this route should, over the longer term, produce a better return than life assurance, although unit and investment trusts as an investment medium may be regarded as more volatile.

Individual Savings Accounts (ISAs)

The tax benefits attaching to ISAs make them attractive for such plans, as were PEPs and TESSAs before ISAs replaced them.

Provision of Fees out of Capital

Compounding

A number of schools offer schemes whereby a lump sum can be paid in advance of the child commencing his education, in return for which a guaranteed level of fees will be paid by the school. Considerable savings can be made and it is certainly worth enquiring whether or not the school chosen has its own scheme before considering alternative methods of capital funding. Care should be taken to check what happens if the child does not go to the designated school.

School Fees Educational Trust

Worthwhile savings can be made on the provision of school fees if a capital sum is invested in an educational trust in advance of the fees being required. The longer the period of deferral, the greater the saving.

The educational trust schemes can start virtually immediately or be deferred for as long as necessary. Provision of fees may be made on a level or escalating basis.

The capital payment is made to trustees of a charitable educational trust who, in turn, after a deduction for administration charges, invest in a fixed or unit-linked annuity provided by one of the established life companies. As the termly fees are required, the insurance company pays the annuity instalment to the trustees, who in turn forward a cheque (payable to the school concerned) to the parent.

The payments should not be subject to income tax in the hands of the child or the individual investor. Should the plan be affected by trustees of an existing settlement, HMRC reserve the right to treat the payments of fees as income in the hands of the child.

School fees educational trusts are flexible and deal with most contingencies. Should there be an under-provision of fees the parent will be liable for the additional sums required. An over-provision can be paid to the investor as and when it arises, although it will be taxed in his hands as investment income. It is possible, however, to come to an arrangement with the school that the 'excess' can be used as a credit for the next term's fees or extra-curricular activities, such as school holidays.

If a parent is the investor and retains the right to recover the funds the value of the trust will form part of their estate for IHT purposes on his death. Any other investor retaining the right of recovery will be treated as having made a lifetime transfer each time fees are paid and any residual value of the trust will form part of his estate on their death. If the right is waived the transfer into trust will be treated as a lifetime gift but subsequently the funds will be regarded as outside their estate for IHT purposes. However, a waiver of the right to surrender may reduce future flexibility.

If the scheme is surrendered by a parent exercising the right to terminate the plan or by the trustees exercising their discretion under the trust deed to pay the value of the plan to the parent, a potential liability to CGT may arise on any gain.

The criticism of these schemes apart from possible IHT liabilities is that in many instances the capital is tied up for a long time and that at least comparable results can be obtained by capital investment outside such an arrangement.

Trusts in existence on 20 June 1996 will continue to be tax free on a concessionary basis, whilst all trusts made after that date will not.

The certainty of payment will remain the main attraction of such schemes.

Single and Regular Premium Bonds

A single premium bond could be affected on the life of the parent. Alternatively, the parent could take advantage of relatively new products that allow regular premiums to be made into a policy, and have similar features to a single premium bond.

The availability of a tax deferred 'income' for up to 20 years if no more than 5% per annum of the original investment is withdrawn from the bond can provide an attractive source of funds for school fees especially for higher rate taxpayers.

The unused 5% can be rolled up and used in the years when fees are required. Should the 5% limit be exceeded, however, a potential charge to higher rate income tax may arise. In some circumstances it may be possible to mitigate the charge. If the policy is taken out in the name of and on the life of a child most tax consequences are avoided if the funds were not provided by the parents but few companies are able to write such policies.

If trustees (eg of an accumulation and maintenance trust) intend to take out such policies they should ensure that the trust deed gives them sufficient investment powers, and also powers to distribute capital to beneficiaries in due course. If the 5% level is exceeded there will be a potential charge to higher rate tax on the settlor(s) which can be recovered from the trustees. If amounts from regular withdrawals are paid to 'income' beneficiaries a liability may arise despite the decision in *Stevenson v Wishart*.

Unit and Investment Trusts and OEICs

Capital could be invested into a unit or investment trust or a portfolio of unit trusts as a means of obtaining tax efficient growth by way of various equity markets. Long-term returns should be higher than those available, for example, from guaranteed annuity schemes, but the investment risk is also correspondingly higher. Low-yielding capital growth trusts would enable the investor to take advantage of personal CGT exemptions and reliefs on the sale of units to provide fees.

Individual Savings Accounts (ISAs)

Capital sums invested into ISAs may provide for tax efficient investment for growth over the medium and longer term, as all income and gains generated within an ISA are exempt from tax, as they were for PEPs.

Gilt-edged Securities

A guaranteed lump sum each year to pay fees can be provided by investment in gilt-edged securities. There is no CGT on the sale of such stocks but tax at 20% on accrued interest may be payable.

Stripped gilts structured to tie in with the required payments should be considered. Whilst it is possible to sell stock when fees are due to be paid, if interest rates at the time are high the return from the stock may not be as much as anticipated.

It is also possible to combine the purchase of a series of suitable (ideally, low-coupon) gilts with one or more endowment policies, with the earlier-maturing gilts funding any early fees required and the endowment(s) funding fees from seven and a half years onwards.

National Savings Children's Bonus Bonds

While the maximum investment is limited to £1,000 per issue they represent a further method of funding fees if neither the child's parents nor other relatives or friends have utilised this type of investment (see Section 3.28, National Savings).

Immediate Loans

Where no advance provision is made insurance schemes are of little use. There are, however, 'instant fees schemes' available which operate by way of secured loans. The lending source takes a first or second charge on a residential property, in the best instances at rates of interest similar to those of a conventional mortgage. In most other respects the loan is also similar to a standard mortgage, except that interest is only charged on the amounts actually drawn down at any given time to pay the fees up to that point.

However, the parent usually has to continue repaying the loan long after the fees have ceased to be required and the overall cost is high (as is the case with conventional mortgages).

Repayment of the total amount borrowed is normally by way of an endowment policy or the cash commutation of an acceptable pension scheme, but could also be from the proceeds of a unit or investment trust savings scheme or ISA.

University Costs

Now fees are an everyday part of University life parents will need to give consideration to funding for these costs. All the above methods can be used, together with the fact that income arising on gifts from parents is taxed on the child rather than the parent once the child reaches 18.

CROSS REFERENCES

5.3 Single

Advantages	1	Lack of dependants may mean that there is no need to provide for dependants.
	2	Possibly more flexible in location and employment and therefore portable arrangements are preferred.
	3	Able to contribute to stakeholder pension even if there are no earnings.
Disadvantages	1	Need to consider provision for protection should incapacity arise and there are no others to provide assistance.
	2	Those who are co-habiting but not married need to consider matters which are automatically dealt with if married, eg IHT.
	3	Increasingly have a debt burden following Higher Education.
Planning	1	Ensure plans entered into have sufficient flexibility to change with circumstances, eg be able to encash without penalties if say buying a home or moving abroad.
	2	If taking out term assurance, consider convertible options which may not require later medical checks.
	3	Write a will particularly if co-habiting.
	4	When buying property and sharing it with others, take specific legal advice on the arrangements.

FURTHER DETAILS

Home Alone

This period will often commence with continuing education at a college or university followed by the starting of a career. The main planning objectives would include the following.

- Before embarking upon a career, the individual may wish to go overseas. If non-UK residence is established then overseas trusts set up earlier by parents or grandparents may be distributed to the individual overseas with minimum UK tax. The recipient should be able to return to the UK in due course, but the five-year non-residence rule for CGT exemption needs to be considered carefully.
- The individual may well have little capital but without dependants will have few outgoings. The main objective would be to channel earnings into a savings plan. This may not be a settled period and any such plans should be as flexible as possible. Thus ISAs, high interest bank and building society accounts and National Savings products may be attractive. Once a level of stability is reached then an investment or unit trust savings plan might be appropriate.

- Life insurance-related investments may not be appropriate, however, as they may need to be cashed in as circumstances change. For a basic rate taxpayer the taxation structure of life funds is not attractive, although, whilst as an alternative the short-term nature of guaranteed income bonds makes them attractive for basic rate taxpayers (as there should be no higher rate charge on withdrawals), the underlying investment performance may sometimes be questionable. Policies with maximum flexibility or convertability may enable relatively cheap insurance to be taken out and changed later without the need for medical tests at the time of change.
- Any pension arrangement should be transferable or portable. Equity linked funds within the personal pension schemes have historically provided a better long-term return than non-equity funds. Stakeholder pensions should be considered as £3,600 net of tax, may be invested without the need to pay these out of income. These could form part of a lifetime plan in that they could be 'retired' after age 50 (age 55 from 2010) and the tax-free lump sum be used to fund one's own children's education or other needs.
- If the individual has no close family, then consideration should be given to protection should they fall ill or be out of work through ill health.
- Consider the employer's share scheme arrangements and the potential for capital growth and implications of moving to other employment.
- Repayment of student loans may take some time to repay and the ones with the highest interest should be repaid first. There may be a temptation to run up interest and credit cards at this time and control needs to be exercised to keep spending within sensible limits. Tax credits may be available for those with low income.

CROSS REFERENCES

5.4 Married with No Children

Advantages	1	Gifts made by close relatives in consideration of marriage will be IHT-free up to certain limits.
	2	Transfer of assets between husband and wife will be free from CGT and IHT.
Planning	1	Equalisation of assets to utilise any CGT annual exemption. A transfer of assets can ensure that both husband and wife utilise their personal allowances and lower and basic rate bands.

FURTHER DETAILS

This is likely to be a period of two incomes to boost savings and then high expenditure when a suitable residence is acquired.

Savings

Savings plans may still need to remain flexible to facilitate purchase of a house and prepare for the loss of one income as the family expands. Investments producing capital growth with income should be considered together with high interest bearing savings accounts. Unit trusts and investment trusts should provide a spread of risk. ISAs could also be considered.

Gifts on Marriage

Parents and grandparents to both parties to the marriage are able to make IHT-free gifts on marriage and have the opportunity therefore to make substantial outright gifts free of IHT (see Section 4.16, *IHT – Exemptions*).

Purchase of Property

The purchase of a property will be one of the major decisions and burdens, and the type of mortgage will have to be considered.

With a *repayment mortgage* each monthly payment comprises part capital and part interest structured to pay off the capital by the end of the term of the loan. There are two types:
- level repayment where monthly payments are constant;
- increasing repayment where repayments start lower than level repayment but the monthly payments increase over the term.

An *endowment mortgage* monthly loan repayment consists of interest only. A further monthly payment funds an endowment policy designed to repay the capital at the end of the term. There are four types:
- with-profits: very expensive as it should provide a substantial surplus over the funds actually required to repay the loan;

- low-cost endowment: a small surplus is normally anticipated though not guaranteed;
- low-cost, low-start: cost increases over first few years;
- unit-linked: investments in unit-linked funds subject to more volatility than traditional with-profits policies.

Borrowers using endowment policies to repay the capital sum borrowed should realise that projections as to growth are only projections and they should review their policies on a regular basis.

A *pension mortgage* is an interest-only mortgage with the lender looking to the commutation monies receivable on retirement for repayment of the capital. Principally available to the self-employed and employees in personal or 'executive' pension schemes but some lenders will also consider group pension schemes.

A *flexible mortgage* offers daily interest calculation and allows accelerated payment, underpayment and usually payment holidays to be taken.

A *current account mortgage* contains in one account the borrower's current account and a large overdraft facility for the mortgage. Monies credited to the account are effective overpayments of the mortgage.

An offset mortgage account links all the borrowers' accounts as though it was a current account mortgage but keeps all the various accounts, eg current, deposit, mortgage separate.

Property and Capital Tax

Couples each owning a residence on marriage benefit from the CGT exemption, which will apply for three years from the date the original property ceased to be occupied. A married couple should also consider whether they will hold the property as joint tenants or tenants in common. If the property is held as joint tenants, it will automatically pass on death to the surviving spouse. If it is held as tenants in common then each half share is a distinct and separate share and will pass under the individual's will.

If the life assurance from a death-in-service policy is not sufficient, further insurance should be considered to enable the surviving spouse to pay off the capital borrowed and continue to live in the property.

Employee Share Schemes

If either party to the marriage works for a company, any opportunity to acquire shares in the company should be considered. The various ways are set out in Section 3.11, *Employee Share Schemes*. Participating at an early stage in a growing company can produce substantial capital in due course.

Equalisation of Assets

A transfer of assets after marriage could enable both parties to save CGT. A couple may consider transferring assets to each other where one party has already utilised their annual exemption but wishes to realise further capital gains. No CGT will be payable on transfers between spouses.

Consideration should be given to ensuring that both a husband and a wife fully utilise the personal allowances, basic rate tax band, lower rate tax band (for dividends and savings income only from 2009) and CGT annual exemption to which each is entitled. This may well necessitate a reorganisation of some of their investment holdings. When, for example, a husband is a higher rate taxpayer and his wife does not have an income, he can transfer income-producing assets to her without any CGT liability. In addition, any income arising will be taxed at the basic rate of tax rather than the higher rate.

Insurance

For young lives, term insurance would provide funds for the survivor of an untimely death of one of them. Level term insurance could be taken out to cover the next few years and at that time could be renewed. It is advisable that the policy be written into trust for the spouse. Decreasing term insurance may be taken out in conjunction with the mortgage on the home. A convertible term policy could be taken which later could be converted to an endowment or whole life policy. Critical illness cover may also be worth considering.

Pensions

Pensions should be of increasing importance particularly if they can be used in conjunction with house purchase arrangements. Personal pension schemes give considerable flexibility and need to be weighed up carefully and compared to membership of a company-sponsored scheme if this is an option. The likely period of employment and the costs and charges associated with a personal pension scheme are also important points to consider. The selection of the fund into which the pension scheme monies are invested is very important. Equity-linked funds have historically provided a better long-term return than non-equity funds.

At the very least each party should contribute to the stakeholder pension scheme at a cost of £3,600 gross.

Making a Will

Both parties should make a simple will to avoid the problems that can arise on an intestacy and to ensure certainty at a time of distress. Any will made prior to marriage will have been automatically revoked on any marriage. Under the intestacy rules a spouse will receive personal chattels, statutory legacy of £450,000 together with half of the residuary estate if there are no children. The other half would pass to the parents or siblings of the deceased. If there are children the spouse receives a statutory legacy of £250,000 plus a life interest in half the remainder, the children take the other half absolutely. If the deceased has no family the spouse receives the whole of the estate..

Civil Partnerships

HMRC were given the power in Budget 2005 to make regulations ensuring that civil partnerships of same-sex couples receive the same treatment for married couples for all tax purposes. Tax changes have taken effect from 5 December 2005 – the date the Civil Partnership Act 2004 came into effect. The tax affairs of same-sex couples considering entering into a civil partnership should be considered carefully. Whilst treatment as a married couple is in the main advantageous, there could be disadvantages: for example the limitation to only one principal private residence, the rules on association for company control and connected parties for CGT purposes.

CROSS REFERENCES

5.5   Married with Young Children

Advantages	1	Allowed to contribute to stakeholder pension even if no income.
	2	Children's tax credits may be available.
Disadvantages	1	One of the two incomes may be lost and expenditure may increase.
	2	Possible school fees provisions.
Planning	1	Equalisation of assets to utilise any annual exemption for CGT purposes. A transfer of assets can ensure that both husband and wife utilise their personal allowances and lower and basic rate bands.
	2	Transfer of income-producing assets to non-working spouse to utilise their personal allowance.
	3	Timing of disposals of chargeable business assets to maximise CGT annual exemption.
	4	Revise wills.

FURTHER DETAILS

Capital Gains Tax

In the event of savings being realised disposals of chargeable assets should be timed to maximise the annual CGT exemption. Any surplus funds available for short periods of say less than one year should be placed on high interest cheque accounts or Internet accounts to maximise the return. Long-term capital growth investments should be considered in view of the recent fall in interest rates where there is unlikely to be any call on the funds for at least five years.

Income Tax

If a spouse has ceased working or their earnings have decreased substantially, transfers of income producing assets should be made so the personal allowance is utilised. Full use should be made of all individual allowances.

Where it is possible, the spouse should continue to be employed in the family business.

Tax credits have replaced the married couples' tax allowance for those on low to middle incomes with children under 16. There is an additional allowance for the first year of a child's life.

Gifts to Children

Where gifts are made to the child, either directly or to a trust of which they are beneficiaries, by a parent, then any income in excess of £100 per annum arising to a child who is unmarried and under 18 will be treated as the parent's income and taxed at the parent's marginal rate of tax. It is therefore preferable for such gifts to be made by the spouse who pays no tax or tax at the lower rate or by grandparents or others. The use of a bare trust may be considered – see Section 5.2, *The Young*.

Inheritance Tax

In the event of one party having more assets than the other, to make use of the nil rate band on death, there could be an inter-spouse transfer to equalise both parties' estates.

The term equalisation does not mean splitting the joint estate in half but rather ensuring that both spouses have sufficient assets to use up their nil-rate IHT band £325,000 after taking into account assets such as the house which may pass to their spouse by survivorship. Where the recipient spouse is non-domiciled careful planning will be required.

Any such transfer will be exempt from CGT.

School Fees

School fees planning should continue using one or a combination of the various suggestions in Section 5.2. The existence of external funding (eg from grandparents) or a lump sum will reduce the need to invest in a regular savings plan.

Life Assurance

As there is a need to protect the family from untimely events life insurance will play an ever-increasing role. Term assurance is a necessity and those with net relevant earnings for a personal pension scheme will qualify for full tax relief on the allowable proportion of premiums which may be allocated to such assurance for plans implemented prior to 1 August 2007 in an occupational pension, or 6 April 2007 if any other type of pension. Those in pensionable employment may be entitled to death-in-service benefits of up to four times their salary. A family income benefits life insurance policy may be worth considering. Endowment assurance may be taken out in conjunction with school fees planning.

Health Insurance

Income Protection would provide income in the event that the policyholder is unable to work for a prolonged period due to illness or disability (as opposed to death) and should be particularly considered by the self-employed. Critical illness cover may also be an attractive option – it is designed to pay a lump sum on the diagnosis of certain life-threatening or debilitating (but not necessarily fatal) conditions such as a heart attack, stroke and cancer.

Pensions

Pension provision assumes much greater importance whether the individual is self-employed or employed; this is discussed in the retirement planning sections. The non-working partner should consider making contributions of up to £3,600 gross into the stakeholder pensions. Children are also able to contribute to stakeholder pensions and this could form part of some very long-term planning.

Wills

Both parties' wills need revision to cover any addition to the family. Assuming roughly equal estates then each party might leave their estate to the survivor unless they do not survive jointly, in which case the estate passes to the child in trust. It may be prudent to insert a guardianship clause to provide care for the child in the event of both parents dying.

Grandparents may be reminded about the benefits of passing part of their assets to their grandchildren in the form of trusts. They might also wish to rewrite their wills onto a discretionary basis to maximise the flexibility of estate planning on death.

CROSS REFERENCES

5.6 Married with Older Children

Advantages	1	Possible restarting or increasing the non-working spouse's earnings.
	2	Time to replenish savings and top up pensions.
Disadvantages	1	School fees commitment.
	2	Generally higher outgoings.
	3	Possible break up of relationship.
Planning	1	Ensure pension arrangements are adequate.
	2	Write any life assurance in trust for other family members.
	3	Consider gifting premiums of life assurance within the annual IHT exemption.

FURTHER DETAILS

Savings

This time presents the opportunity to save and invest. High interest cheque accounts and Internet accounts will maximise the income return. Capital protection may be provided by index-linked gilts with capital growth from unit trusts and investment trusts spreading the risk. A balance will need to be achieved to provide liquidity in the event of children's unexpected costs. The ISA allowance each year should be used where possible. 16 and 17 year olds are entitled to subscribe for mini-cash ISAs and the cash component of maxi-ISAs.

Employee Share Schemes

The opportunity to invest in one's employing company under one of the employee share routes should be taken – subject to normal commercial evaluation. The possibility of substantial growth, particularly if the company is going to the market or is already listed, is attractive. This should supplement and complement other investments.

School Fees

Where provision for school fees has not been made, and in the absence of a lump sum gift from grandparents, a loan against pensions or a second mortgage on the main residence may be one route to follow.

Marriage Breakdown

There is always a possibility that the marriage may break down. The taxation aspects are as follows.

Income Tax

- Separation is not treated as a cessation or commencement for those sources of income, which have special rules regarding the basis of assessment in opening and closing years. The income from these sources is treated as continuing.

Capital Gains Tax

- Transfers of assets between spouses at any time during the year of separation are not chargeable, provided both are resident in the UK.
- Transfers of assets after the year of separation are generally chargeable, although the spouses continue to be connected parties until the decree absolute.
- If the matrimonial home is sold the principal private residence rules apply. If the matrimonial home is transferred to the separated wife or ex-wife the transfer is exempted from CGT by concession, provided she has continued to live there and the husband has not elected for another property to be his principal private residence (if he has elected, part of any gain may be chargeable). If a new property is to be purchased for the wife by the husband and immediately transferred to the wife, the capital gain is likely to be nil. It will probably be cheaper, however, to gift the funds to the ex-wife and allow her to purchase the house in her own name.

Inheritance Tax

- The exemptions applying to transfers between spouses apply up to the date of the decree absolute.
- Limited relief is available for transfers made for maintenance of former spouses.
- The related property rules cease to apply from the date of decree absolute. This would be relevant where, for example, the separating spouses each hold shares in a family company which between them give control.
- Transfers pursuant to court orders are normally deemed not to have gratuitous intent and therefore are not chargeable transfers. Additionally, relief may also be available if capital is transferred pursuant to a court order, such capital being used to maintain a child or children of a party to the marriage.

Stamp Duty

Transfers between spouses are dutiable in the same way as on transfers between third parties. Transfers of property pursuant to court orders are specifically exempted from ad valorem duty.

Taxation Planning on Marriage Breakdown

Maintenance Payments

It is no longer attractive from a tax viewpoint to arrange for maintenance payments to be paid to a child of the marriage although the parent may wish to make payments to the child for other reasons.

As there will be no tax advantage in providing school fees by way of a court order the parent may prefer to receive the invoices from and make payment to the school direct. Since 6 April 2000 no tax relief has been available for pre- or post-1998 maintenance payments and recipients of maintenance payments are exempt from tax on them. Where one of the parties was over 65 on 5 April 2000 the payer can continue to obtain relief at 10% up to a maximum payment of £2,670.

Generally

Where possible, any rearrangement of assets should take place within the tax year of separation.

If a charge to CGT is likely to arise as a result of complying with the terms of the financial settlement and the decree absolute is due early in a tax year, tax may be saved if the parties agree that part of the transfer is made by agreement before the end of the previous tax year, thereby using two years' exemptions available to the transferor.

There is no limit to the IHT exemption applying to transfers between UK domiciled spouses but this exemption is lost when the decree becomes absolute. The possibility of transfer by agreement prior to the decree absolute should be considered. Failing this, reliance must be placed on the provision which allows transfers for the maintenance of an ex-wife to be exempt.

The wills of each party should be reconsidered and rewritten.

Pensions on Divorce

The Pensions Act 1995 requires courts to take account of the value of private pension benefits in all divorce cases coming before them after 1 July 1996. The key aspects of the Welfare Reform and Pensions Act 1999 include:

- the option of pension sharing on divorce or nullity of marriage;
- the financial settlement on divorce will allow pension rights to be transferred in whole or in part between spouses;
- retaining the offset of pension rights against other assets;
- continuing with earmarking and attachment arrangements if preferred;

These aspects will only apply to divorce or nullity proceedings commenced after the legislation has been brought into force on 1 December 2000, thereby extending the options available to divorcing couples to the following ways of dealing with pension assets:

Offsetting This is a clean break option that provides the ex-spouse with cash compensation for a 'lost' pension entitlement.

Earmarking This means waiting for a share of the ex-spouse's pension on retirement. However, if the spouse dies before retiring there may be no pension to pay over.

Sharing This is the most radical option as it allows the ex-spouse to take a share of the pension pot and either set up a personal pension plan, or use the funds to become a shadow member of the spouse's pension fund. The spouse who gives up a proportion of the pension fund, post-April 2006 will now be able to make good the 'lost' contributions, however the pension credit will count towards to recipient's standard lifetime allowance. The divorcing couple will also face charges estimated to be up to £1,200 to carve up the pension scheme.

The Government envisages that most pensions will be split equally, but the court will decide, taking into consideration other assets. Once the division has been decided, the scheme must implement the carve-up within four months. The basic state pension is not affected by these rules.

The level of the ex-wife's state pension will depend upon her own contribution record and a part of her former husband's record. The ex-wife may use the contributions of her former husband for all tax years falling within the period of marriage, or the period beginning with the start of the wife's working life, and ending with the divorce, whichever is most favourable. Enquiries should be made to the DSS as to the wife's prospective pension and consideration should be given to its possible increase by paying Class 3 voluntary contributions.

Other Tax Planning

Charitable Giving

Gifts may be made in favour of the Charities Aid Foundation which will distribute the annual amount (including the repayable tax) to charities nominated by the donor. Through the use of vouchers the donor is able to vary the charities to benefit each year.

A donor may make a gift in favour of a private charitable trust of which he is the settlor and perhaps also a trustee. Such trusts must now satisfy charitable expenditure guidelines if the covenantor is to obtain higher rate tax relief. For further details see Section 4.25, *Private Charitable Trusts*.

There are no stamp duty, CGT or IHT consequences in respect of Gift Aid. Gift Aid has replaced Deeds of Covenant with effect from 6 April 2000. Existing Deeds will continue so long as they remain unchanged. Where payments are made to charities a Gift Aid declaration prior to, at the time of, or after the payment, will enable the donor to obtain higher rate tax relief (if applicable) on the gross payment. There is no minimum limit for Gift Aid, lower rate taxpayers can use Gift Aid provided that overall they pay sufficient income tax to cover the tax reclaimed. Non-taxpayers should not make Gift Aid declarations.

Payroll giving

There is a payroll deduction scheme whereby an individual employee may, with the agreement of their employer, request that a sum they specify be deducted from their earnings each pay day and handed over to an agent to pass to a charity of their choice.

The specified sums are treated as a deduction from income in computing income tax liability. PAYE is operated on the sum received by the employee net of their charitable contribution thus giving tax relief at source.

Life Insurance

Life insurance plays an important role for savings and IHT planning. By effecting whole life policies in trust for others and gifting premiums within the annual IHT exemption a tax-free fund is placed in the beneficiaries' hands on the death of the settlor. This enables IHT to be paid and if the tax is likely to arise on the death of the surviving spouse the policies should be written on a joint life last survivor basis.

Income Protection Plan

Income Protection should be established to provide for the loss of income and increased associated costs from permanent sickness if not already in place.

Pension Schemes

Assuming that an occupational pension scheme is in existence then the related planning opportunities should be considered. These include additional voluntary contributions, salary exchange, increased benefits and funding for past years as well as the use of pension-linked loans. The employer may be able to pay special contributions in times of high profitability. Employees not in pensionable employment and the self-employed should invest in personal pension schemes.

Children are able to make their own £3,600 contributions to stakeholder pensions and this could form part of some very long-term planning.

Inheritance Tax Planning

The time may not yet have arrived when parents can pass on substantial amounts to their children by way of trust, although grandparents should be encouraged to do so before it becomes too late to save any meaningful amounts of IHT using the seven-year survivorship with potentially exempt transfers. Consideration should be given to funding for the IHT on the second death.

CROSS REFERENCES

5.7 Pre-Retirement

Advantages	1	Reduction of expenditure on children.
	2	Higher incomes creating more spendable income.
	3	Possible gains from realisation of share options and other assets.
Disadvantages	1	Pension top up now very important.
	2	Possible health complications.
	3	May need to help grandchildren.
	4	Need to plan for IHT.
Planning	1	Consider using zero coupon bonds and offshore funds to defer income until retirement and realise in low income year.
	2	Consider pension arrangements.
	3	Top up pension schemes by maximising annual premiums to schemes.
	4	Consider making lifetime gifts to children to minimise IHT.

FURTHER DETAILS

Investments

The ability to invest in a wide range of investments now emerges. Those investments producing capital growth with or without income are of particular importance. A properly structured unit trust or share portfolio would probably top the list. A second property or holiday letting arrangements could be attractive. The opportunity to invest in sophisticated and in some cases slightly more risky investments is covered by the investments detailed in Part 3, *Investments*.

With a view to tax mitigation, zero coupon stocks and offshore funds could defer income until retirement and be realised in a year of low income.

Employed in the Business

The planning associated with a spouse employed in the family business remains relevant. Planning would include:

- bringing a spouse into partnership to enable profit sharing to maximise the spouse's reliefs, allowances and lower rates of taxation;
- passing shares to the spouse to enable dividend income to utilise their allowances, lower tax rates;
- setting up separate pension arrangements for the spouse either as part of the business pension or as a specific executive pension plan.

Life Insurance

Savings and investment using life insurance would encompass maximum investment plans for regular savings and single premium bonds and capital conversion schemes for lump sum investment.

Income Protection Plan

Income Protection would provide much needed peace of mind where one party is working particularly hard. For some, this may lead onto considerations as to the attractions of Critical Illness cover too. Part of the planning should be to maximise financial security in retirement and consideration to be given to funding future long-term care requirements.

Pensions

At this stage every opportunity for pension planning should be explored, particularly those outlined in the sections on *Retirement Planning* in Part 2. The greater flexibility of pension schemes provides the incentive to maximise benefits. Consider stakeholder pensions for the non-working spouse.

Tax Planning

The IHT and CGT strategies and opportunities presented need to be considered and implemented (see Section 4.14, *Estate Planning*). Where absolute lifetime gifts are not desirable, the discretionary trust route should be considered, particularly for the first major gift. Great care is needed with existing trusts and new trusts may only be advantageous in a few situations. Decreasing term insurance left in trust for the heirs can be used to cover any contingent liability to IHT in the seven years after a gift.

Any residual balance of IHT should be provided by way of a whole life assurance policy. Wills should be reviewed.

CROSS REFERENCES

5.8 Retirement

Advantages		
	1	Increased personal allowances.
	2	State pension available.
	3	May continue to contribute to stakeholder pensions until age 75.
Disadvantages	1	Increased health risk and costs.
	2	Normally reduction in income.
	3	Reliance on capital built up to date to provide for the future.
Planning	1	To ensure financial security, particularly should help be required due to failing health in later life.
	2	To pass any excess assets over to the next generation, balancing current CGT against future IHT.
	3	To protect the rump of the estate with appropriate insurance.

FURTHER DETAILS

Income

The investment strategy will require a balance between high return investments and capital growth. The balance between these categories of investment and index-linked investments will depend on the assets, commitments and life expectancy of the individuals.

The Non-Taxpayer

Here the emphasis will be on investments producing a high return combined with protection against inflation. A comparatively high return but with no inflation protection is provided by National Savings investment account, capital bond and pensioners bond. High coupon gilts may (depending on the inflationary and interest rate outlook) be attractive. Building society and bank deposit accounts can be used as the interest can be received gross. In suitable circumstances, offshore building society accounts and offshore money funds may also be worth considering. A hedge against inflation could be provided by index-linked gilts and National Savings index-linked certificates although the income from these would be low.

Depending on available interest rates, purchased life annuities may be attractive for males over 70 and females over 75. The lump sum investment produces a fixed annuity for life. Care should be taken to anticipate increases in the inflation rate as high inflation would erode the value. Particular caution should be exercised when considering annuities because of the loss of control over the capital.

Equity release plans are a means of creating income or capital using the equity in the investor's home. There are now a number of schemes on the market with a variety of different options. Some allow the home owner to release equity from their home, which is then invested in an investment or an annuity in order to generate an income. Some plans require the homeowner to pay the monthly interest on the resultant mortgage, whereas some allow for the interest not to be paid but instead 'roll-up', increasing the amount of outstanding debt. Equity release plans are often the most suitable solution to a homeowner's income or capital need but they can be expensive, particularly if paid off early, and the question of ultimate ownership of the underlying property on death should be fully investigated before such a scheme is signed up.

The Basic Rate Taxpayer

The basic rate taxpayer would find all the above investments useful. The after-tax return of building society term shares may be very competitive with the National Savings accounts.

Despite the relatively low yield offered by most equities, investment and unit trusts many investors will do better in the long run to seek capital gains (tax free up to £10,100 per person per annum). Such investments are best viewed over a long term and one's life expectancy must be considered together with liquidity availability.

The Higher Rate Taxpayer

The picture is much the same as for the basic rate taxpayer with CGT-free £10,100 and the 5% tax-free withdrawal from bonds particularly important.

ISAs may be encashed in to give tax-free income and capital gains and EIS investments held for over three years (five years for investment pre-6 April 2000) realised free of CGT. Endowment insurance policies may well be cashed in tax free if the qualifying periods have passed.

Otherwise the above remarks in respect of the need to preserve capital rather than seeking high yields need to be borne in mind and the attractions of index-linked gilts examined carefully if inflation is a fear.

Taxation

Higher levels of personal allowance are available for individuals aged between 65 and 74, and 75 and over, at any time during the tax year subject to their income levels.

For a married couple the husband will be entitled to a higher rate of married couple's allowance if either he or his wife falls into the over 75 age bracket by reference to the older life.

For 2010/11 the maximum allowance is £9,490 for a single person aged 65–74. The age allowance is reduced if the taxable income exceeds £22,900; the reduction is one-half of each pound of age allowance for every one pound of excess.

Total income is gross and therefore includes tax deducted from income before receipt. Withdrawals from single premium bonds up to the 5% limit would not be included in total income. Care should be taken in arranging investment income to avoid the age allowance reduction if possible.

For those aged over 75 the senior age allowance is £9,640 for a single person plus a further allowance of £6,965 (relieved at 10%) for a married couple. These allowances are reduced in a similar way where taxable income exceeds £22,900. The minimum married couples allowance is £2,670.

A wife will be able to set her allowances against all sources of her income including any National Insurance Retirement Pension that she receives by virtue of her husband's contributions.

Planning

Reference should be made to Part 4, *Tax Planning* as many people like to review their IHT as part of the pre-retirement planning exercise and again around the age of 70–75 at the same time as updating their wills and calculating the level of resources they wish to retain both to provide income for living expenses and cash to pay possible future nursing home costs in the longer run. At this or an earlier stage it may be desirable to move to a smaller house to provide spare capital or to sell a family business and maximise taper relief.

IHT planning needs to be considered. Such planning comes in three stages:
- firstly, to ensure financial security in retirement;
- secondly, to give away, alienate or freeze assets not required to provide that security; and
- thirdly, to ensure IHT can be funded out of the rump assets providing the financial security either by their own realisability value or an appropriate insurance arrangement.

Financial security in retirement is the key, where there is an insufficiency of income an individual may need to unlock income from capital assets, for example by using a Equity Release Plan as set out in Part 1. Income may be needed to fund nursing care, which could cost of the order of £25,000 per annum, or more, in a nursing home. In the absence of a growth plan taken out earlier, capital again may have to be unlocked.

The further message is to give away assets whilst there is a fair chance that the donor will survive seven years. But if planning is left too late a 'Catch 22' problem can develop as some IHT will be payable whether gifting during life or on death. CGT may loom much larger than IHT as there will be a CGT-free uplift if assets form part of the estate on death. This aspect will need to be weighed against the potential for 'freezing' the value of a growth asset by making a lifetime gift but the possibility that in so doing one accelerates a CGT charge in some circumstances. From 2009/10 CGT is charged at a flat rate of 18%.

Funding for IHT by way of whole life assurance policies may be very expensive, although a purchased life annuity to fund the premiums can be satisfactory (depending on age and rates) whilst term insurance can be used to cover any contingent IHT liability in the seven years after the gift. Again the writing of such policies in trust should be considered so as to fall outside the estate on death.

Control of Assets

Consideration should be given to implementing a lasting power of attorney which enables one's assets to be controlled by, say, a family member in the event of the individual being unable to do this personally for physical or mental reasons.

Wills should be reviewed so as to maintain flexibility, particularly to use up the deceased's nil rate band and accommodate changes in the next generation.

CROSS REFERENCES

Index